Moving Toward a Just Peace

Clinical Sociology: Research and Practice

Series Editor:

JOHN G. BRUHN
New Mexico State University, Las Cruces,
New Mexico

This series explores key research and practice in this rapidly expanding field. Topics include ethical and legal aspects; the nature of client relationships; methods of intervention and evaluation; and the role of clinical sociology in specific settings. This open-ended series appeals to students and teachers in sociology, social work, community psychology, public health, health education, and counseling.

For further volumes:
http://www.springer.com/series/5805

Jan Marie Fritz
Editor

Moving Toward a Just Peace

The Mediation Continuum

Springer

Editor
Jan Marie Fritz
University of Cincinnati
Cincinnati, Ohio
USA

ISSN 1566-7847
ISBN 978-94-007-2884-4 ISBN 978-94-007-2885-1 (eBook)
DOI 10.1007/978-94-007-2885-1
Springer Dordrecht Heidelberg New York London

Library of Congress Control Number: 2013953580

Printed on acid-free paper

Springer is part of Springer Science+Business Media (www.springer.com)

Peace and Justice

THE JOINT HIGH COMMISSION.

PEACE TO JUSTICE.—"AFTER YOU, MADAME."

Thomas Nast (1840–1902) is "often spoken of as the first great American cartoonist" (Murrell and Chipman 1936, p. 472). United States (U.S.) President Abraham Lincoln reportedly said that Nast was "our best recruiting sergeant" for the Union in the U.S. Civil War (Paine 1904, p. 69; Murrell and Chipman 1936, p. 472; Reaves 1987, p. 61) and U.S. President Ulysses S. Grant declared that Nast, as a political cartoonist, "did as much as any one man to preserve the Union and bring the (U.S. Civil) War to an end" (Paine 1904, p. 106; Reaves 1987, p. 61). While Nast particularly is known for his wood engravings depicting the corruption of elected officials in New York City, popularizing the symbols – a donkey and an elephant – of the two main political parties in the U.S. and creating a modern drawing of Santa Claus, he also drew two goddesses who represented Peace and Justice.

The drawing included here is Nast's "The Joint High Commission;" it appeared in *Harper's Weekly* on March 11, 1871. This picture shows Peace saying to Justice, "After you, Madame." Nast, on a number of occasions, drew Peace and Justice together – e.g., "Justice and Peace – United We Stand, Divided We Fall" (1876) and "Justice brings Peace" (1877). Like Nast, mediators believe that to have real peace, there also must be justice.

References

Murrell, W., & Chipman, N. P. (1936). Nast, gladiator of the political pencil. *The American Scholar, 5*(1), 472–485.

Paine, A. B. (1904). *Th. Nast: His period and his pictures*. New York: Harper & Brothers.

Reaves, W. W. (1987). Thomas Nast and the president. *The American Art Journal, 19*(1), 60–71.

Foreword

Mediation is a process built upon dialogue, an essential ingredient in advancing the Culture of Peace. The mediator helps the parties think "outside of the box" for possible solutions to the dispute, broadening the range of possible solutions. We know that every conflict is unique and the one-size-fits-all approach would not be advisable. Confidence-building, sincere impartiality, and candid informality are key to credible mediation efforts.

Many of today's conflicts involve a complex web of objectives and actors, local and regional dimensions that pose difficult challenges for any mediation initiatives. While disputes of the 1970s and 1980s were mostly ideological, the present situation is dominated by unconstitutional changes in governments, disputed elections, incomplete political transitions, social tensions, and intercommunal violence. We must not overlook the fact that "violence is often perpetuated by authorities that do not respect the rights of their people." As a result, today's mediators need to have varied expertise to address a more complex web of substantive issues like constitutions, justice, governance, human rights, concerns of the vulnerable population, and security issues.

The Charter of the United Nations identifies mediation as an important means for the peaceful settlement of disputes and conflicts. As early as 1992, its publication *The United Nations Handbook on the Peaceful Settlement of Disputes Between States* articulated the understanding of mediation of disputes between States and continues to serve as a useful resource. The recent *Guidance of Effective Mediation* prepared by the UN deserves our recognition. Another critical response tool was the establishment of UN's Standby Team of Mediation Experts, who are deployable within 72 hours.

The United Nations believes that the recent increase in the number of conflicts after nearly two decades of decline as well as in the nature and types of these conflicts has brought in added interest in the role of mediation in peaceful settlements of disputes. There have been significant efforts during recent years to raise awareness and highlight the increasing importance of mediation in conflict prevention and resolution.

Importantly, both the President of the 66th session of the UN General Assembly in his forward-looking framework of four priorities advancing the theme of "Mediation for Peace," which was a much-needed value addition to the work of the UN in the area of peaceful settlement of disputes, and the Secretary-General in his five-year action agenda for his second term in office have prioritized the promotion of mediation to enhance coordination and cooperation. All the three successive Secretaries-General – Boutros Boutros-Ghali, Kofi Annan, and Ban Ki-moon – have underscored the need for increased and creative use of mediation efforts to address the challenges to peace and security.

A matter of important relevance has been the growing recognition that local mediators having in-depth knowledge of the society as well as acceptability and credibility to the parties in dispute can usefully lead local mediation efforts or complement regional or international initiatives. In this context and to ensure more inclusiveness, civil society actors, in particular women and the youth, are demanding their due and rightfully greater voice in mediation processes at all levels, albeit with varying degrees of success.

With the adoption of the Security Council Resolution 1325 in 2000 for which the conceptual breakthrough was achieved during my Presidency of the Council, the role and contribution of women's participation at all decision-making levels of peace processes received the much-needed formal recognition. Greater attention, however, is required in this area at national, regional, and international levels for real implementation.

Likewise, repeated calls for the protection of civilians have been made, in particular to prevent violence against women and to protect children. In this context, I would especially recall the pioneering role played by the Nonviolent Peaceforce in various conflict areas.

Increased and imaginative use of mediation is needed in the future in order to prevent conflicts more effectively and to resolve existing and future conflicts more expeditiously. Violence, strife, and conflicts and their economic and social costs continue to challenge the international community and take a heavy toll on nations and people around the world. Amidst evolving international realities, it is crucial that the UN does its best to continue to craft its peace and security capacities and strategies to live up to the expectations of the global community. Especially, steady progress is to be made to achieve the four concrete targets on women and mediation set by the UN Secretary-General for 2016, namely, the appointment of a woman as a United Nations chief mediator, increased representation of women in mediation and negotiation teams, provision of gender expertise, and systematic consultation of women's civil society organizations.

If we cannot engage and prepare ourselves to resolve our conflicts without war, violence, vengeance, retaliation, coercion, and injustice, we will find ourselves unable to survive, both as a human race and as a sustainable planet. Belonging to one humanity, we need to end our disputes and face our challenges through mediation, through peaceful, nonviolent, nonaggressive ways, thereby abolishing war of all kinds forever from the face of the earth.

This book by Professor Jan Marie Fritz is aimed to generate better understanding of the mediation approaches and their effective use in the prevention and resolution of conflicts. It is a wonderful contribution in advancing the objective of a more peaceful world. I am confident that the book will receive a warm welcome from all who believe in dialogue and reconciliation, in peaceful resolution of disputes, and, above all, in ensuring that the Culture of Peace takes deep roots in all of us individually and collectively.

Ambassador Anwarul K. Chowdhury
Former Under-Secretary General and
High Representative of the United Nations

Contents

About the Contributors

Lauren Abramson Ph.D., a psychologist, is the founding director of the Community Conferencing Center, as well as an assistant professor in child psychiatry at Johns Hopkins School of Medicine. She has been involved with the study of emotion for 25 years. Bringing conferencing to inner-city Baltimore in 1995, she has helped elucidate the theoretical underpinnings of the community conferencing process and continues to grow a conferencing program in Baltimore where police, courts, juvenile justice, schools, and communities are using the process as a nonauthoritarian alternative to dealing with serious crimes and conflicts. Her email address is labramso@jhmi.edu.

Diana Chigas J.D., M.A.L.D., is a professor of the practice of international negotiation and conflict resolution at the Fletcher School of Law and Diplomacy, Tufts University. She is also codirector of the Reflecting on Peace Practice Program at CDA Collaborative Learning Projects in Cambridge, Massachusetts, USA. At CDA, she has worked with nongovernmental organizations (NGOs), donor agencies, and intergovernmental agencies to improve the effectiveness of peace programming and the impacts of development and humanitarian assistance on peace and conflict. Prior to joining CDA, she worked as a facilitator, trainer, and consultant in negotiation, dialogue, and conflict resolution at Conflict Management Group. Her work included development of strategies, training and advice on preventive diplomacy in the Organization for Security and Cooperation in Europe (OSCE) "track two" discussions in El Salvador, South Africa, Ecuador, and Peru and in the Georgia/South Ossetia peace process, as well as facilitation of interethnic dialogue in Cyprus. She is the author of *What Difference Has Peacebuilding Made? A Study of Peacebuilding and the March'04 Riots in Kosovo*. She also has written numerous chapters and articles on contributions of NGOs and unofficial intermediaries to conflict transformation and on evaluation of peacebuilding activities. Her email addresses are dchigas@cdacollective.org and diana.chigas@tufts.edu.

Anwarul K. Chowdhury served as Ambassador and Permanent Representative of Bangladesh to the United Nations in New York from 1996 to 2001 and as the Under-Secretary-General and High Representative of the United Nations, responsible for the most vulnerable countries of the world, from 2002 to 2007. He was the Senior Special Advisor to the UN General Assembly President (September 2011 – September 2012). Ambassador Chowdhury was President of the UN Security Council in 2000 and 2001 and President of the UNICEF Board in 1986 and 2000. He is an inspirational champion for sustainable peace and development and has ardently advanced the global movement for the culture of peace. He pioneered a number of initiatives. Among them are: the UN General Assembly's adoption of the landmark Declaration and Programme of Action on Culture of Peace and the proclamation of the International Decade for Culture of Peace and Nonviolence for the Children of the World (2001–2010). Equally significant was his crucial leadership that led to the UN Security Council's adoption of Resolution 1325 (Women and Peace and Security). Ambassador Chowdhury has received many awards including the U Thant Peace Award, UNESCO Gandhi Gold Medal for Culture of Peace, Spirit of the UN Award, and the University of Massachusetts Boston Chancellor's Medal for Global Leadership for Peace. He also has been given an Honorary Doctorate from Soka University of Tokyo and a Doctor of Humane Letters degree from Saint Peters University (US). His email address is anwarulc@hotmail.com.

Cheryl Cutrona Esq., is the executive director of the Good Shepherd Mediation Program (GSMP) and an adjunct professor of mediation advocacy and practice as well as alternative dispute resolution (ADR) at the Temple University Beasley School of Law. Over the last 25 years, she has trained thousands of community volunteers, lawyers, and law students to be mediators, conflict managers, and conflict coaches in Pennsylvania, South Africa, Guam, and Israel. She mediates for the Pennsylvania Department of Education Office of Dispute Resolution, the Philadelphia Bar Association Lawyer Fee Disputes program, the Landlord-Tenant Appeals Mediation Program, and the United States Postal Service REDRESS. She arbitrates for the Better Business Bureau, DeMars & Associates, and the Philadelphia Court of Common Pleas Arbitration Center. She sits on the board of directors of the Pennsylvania Council of Mediators, and the editorial board of *Conflict Resolution Quarterly*. In 2008, she received the Pennsylvania Bar Association ADR Committee's Sir Francis Bacon Dispute Resolution Award. In 2010, the Pennsylvania Council of Mediators named her "Peacemaker of the Year." Her email address is ccmed8r@aol.com.

Jan Marie Fritz Ph.D., C.C.S., a certified clinical sociologist, is a professor at the University of Cincinnati (USA) and, a senior research fellow with the Centre for Sociological Research at the University of Johannesburg (SA). She was a Fellow (2012–2013) at the Woodrow Wilson International Center for Scholars in Washington, DC (USA) and, in 2011, the Fulbright Distinguished Chair in Human Rights and International Studies at the Danish Institute for Human Rights (DK). She is the president of the clinical sociology division of the International Sociological Association (ISA), a former president of the Clinical Sociology Association (now the Association for Applied and Clinical Sociology), and a former chair of the sociological practice section of the American Sociological Association. She is a former vice president of the ISA, serves on the ISA's executive committee and is the senior ISA representative to the United Nations. She has written extensively about clinical sociology, mediation, and the national action plans that are based on the UN Security Council Resolution 1325 Women and Peace and Security. Her publications have appeared in Portuguese, Spanish, French, English, Italian, and Ukrainian. She is a commissioner with the Commission on the Accreditation of Programs in Applied and Clinical Sociology, a consultant for academic departments for the American Sociological Association's Department Resources Group, and a special education mediator for the state of Kentucky. In 2008, she received the faculty award for Outstanding Research and Creative Work from the College of Design, Architecture, Art and Planning at the University of Cincinnati. In 2010, she received the American Sociological Association's award for a Distinguished Career in Sociological Practice, and, in 2011, she received the annual award, the Better World Award, from the Ohio Mediation Association. Her email address is jan.fritz@uc.edu.

Jenny Theron Kervarrec M.A. (International relations), is Director of Shades of Green, a sustainable event management and exhibition management company based in Durban, South Africa. She was Coordinator of the Peacemaking Unit at the African Centre for the Constructive Resolution of Disputes (ACCORD). In this capacity, her responsibilities included planning and implementing her Unit's programmes, and overseeing the budgets. Previously, she managed ACCORD's Burundi intervention and was based in Bujumbura, Burundi for almost four years. Her email address is jenny@sgevents.co.za

David Moore Ph.D., is a communication consultant based in Melbourne, Australia, and a principal with Sydney-based Primed Change Consulting. David has taught politics and history, as well as peace and conflict studies at Melbourne, Charles Sturt, La Trobe, and Queensland Universities. Through the first half of the 1990s, he was involved in international reforms that brought the conferencing process to justice and education systems. He worked in the Queensland Premier's Department before cofounding Transformative Justice Australia (TJA). From 1996 through 2002, he trained facilitators in Australia, Canada, the USA, Scandinavia, and the UK and provided conflict management services to Australian organizations. This work inspired playwright David Williamson's Jack Manning Trilogy – *Face to Face, A Conversation, and Charitable Intent* (1999–2001) – and Michael Rymer's *Face to Face* (2011), an award-winning film. David's more recent work includes adaptive change workshops using professional actors and dramatized scenes, and organization-wide, constructive communication projects. His email address is david@primed.net.au.

Eleanor Ann Nwadinobi M.B.B.S. (Medicinae Baccalaureus, Baccalaureus Chirurgiae – Bachelor of Medicine, Bachelor of Surgery), M.A. (human rights), is a medical doctor and human rights activist. A pioneer in the widow's rights movement in Nigeria, Nwadinobi is the president of the Widows Development Organization (WiDO). She has worked for over 15 years protecting widows whose rights have been violated in Enugu State, Nigeria. She is the author of *Widowhood:*

Facts, Feelings and the Law and a contributor to several publications including "Women's Global Health and Human Rights." Nwadinobi has served on several boards including the UN NGO DPI Executive Committee, where she is the immediate past sub-Saharan Africa regional representative. She is the founding zonal coordinator of the Centre for the Eradication of Violence Against Women (CEVAW), a coalition of NGOs in the South East of Nigeria. Nwadinobi is also an international speaker and recipient of a number of awards. These include the Irene Ighodaro Prize for Outstanding Contribution to the Medical Women's Association of Nigeria and the Ambassador of Widows Award from Umuada Igbo Nigeria. In 2009, Nwadinobi was given the honorific title of "Ada Eji Eje Mba" by the Abia State Government (Nigeria). This title sometimes is translated as "the daughter whose name opens doors in foreign lands" and sometimes as "the daughter who represents us far and wide; our ambassador." Her email address is elenwad@yahoo.co.uk.

Michael Ribant M.A., a doctoral student in the Department of Geography at Northern Illinois University, has taught world geography, GIS, remote sensing and mapmaking. He also has done analysis for the Geospatial Lab at the University. His research interests are in the areas of urban geography, GIS, spatial analysis, geovisualization, and human rights. Prior to entering the doctoral program, he was a business person on Wall Street (New York) and in California. An avid fisher, he is the editor of two books about fishing: *The U.S. Bass Atlas* and *The U.S. Trout Atlas.* He created almost all of the figures for this volume. His email address is mikeribant@hotmail.com.

Jerome Sachane As Deputy Director of the African Centre for the Constructive Resolution of Disputes (ACCORD), He has extensive experience in administration and fundraising. He is a trainer, facilitator and mediator in the field of conflict resolution. He holds professional membership positions with the Public Relations Institute of South Africa, South African Institute of Management and Black Management Forum. He joined ACCORD in February 1993 as the Head of the Regional Office at the University of the Western Cape. His email address is jeromes@accord.org.za

Maria R. Volpe Ph.D., is professor of sociology and director of the Dispute Resolution Program at John Jay College of Criminal Justice, City University of New York (CUNY). She also is the director of the CUNY Dispute Resolution Center. Dr. Volpe has lectured, researched, and written extensively about dispute resolution processes. In addition to teaching and research, she mediates conflicts in educational settings, conducts dispute resolution skills training, administers grant-funded projects, and facilitates for a wide range of groups. At John Jay College, she has created and facilitated town meetings, cops and kids dialogues, Muslim/non-Muslim student dialogues, Black/Jewish dialogues, intergenerational dialogues, and Asian American student discussions. Since 9/11, she initiated the NYC-DR listserv, the monthly NYC-DR Roundtable Breakfast, and other dispute resolution public awareness projects. She is an editorial board member of *Conflict Resolution Quarterly* and *Negotiation Journal* and past president of the Society of Professionals in Dispute Resolution (now the Association for Conflict Resolution) and serves on many advisory boards. She has received a number of awards for her distinguished career in the field of dispute resolution, including the 2008 Lawrence Cooke Peace Innovator Award, 2010 Association for Conflict Resolution of Greater New York Achievement Award, and 2011 Frontline Champion Award. Her current research focuses on police use of mediation, conflict resolution in higher education, dispute resolution responses to disasters since 9/11, informal responses to conflict used by immigrants, roots of diversity in the dispute resolution field, and barriers to minority participation in dispute resolution. Her email address is mvolpe@jjay.cuny.edu.

Ariella Vraneski Ph.D., M.Sc., B.Arch., is a senior researcher and lecturer at the Technion – Israel Institute of Technology and also an ADR practitioner. For two decades, she has had a private planning office. Vraneski is the initiator and chairperson of the Conflict Resolution Research Group (CRRG) at Technion's Center for Urban and Regional Studies. She also serves as the chairperson of CRRG and of QPD (the Qualitative Planning and Development NGO). In 2008, she joined the Israeli Shared Society Program. Since 2000, Vraneski has been affiliated with the Institute of Conflict Analysis and Resolution (ICAR) at George Mason University in the USA, and with several academic institutes in Europe and Asia.
Since the 1980s, Vraneski has been involved in research, curriculum development, and practice regarding urban, environmental, and regional dispute resolution. Among her latest projects are "Promoting and Implementing Integrated Coastal Zone Policies, Plans and Management: Challenges, Practices and Tools," "Sustainable Development, Strategic Planning and Green Architecture Programs for Minority Communities in Israel," and "Dialog among Industry, Community and Government on Environmental Issues." Her email addresses are ariellav@tx.technion.ac.il and avraneski@yahoo.com.

List of Figures

List of Tables

Chapter 1
Introduction

Jan Marie Fritz

Mediation, the facilitated discussion of disputes and conflicts, is a flexible approach that can be used to help us achieve global peace. This volume, *Moving Toward a Just Peace: The Mediation Continuum,*[1] brings together mediators, scholar-practitioners, and a veteran diplomat to discuss the life and times of mediation in very different settings. The continuum of mediation is about the expanding roles (from prevention through societal transformation) assumed by mediators. It also is about the urgent need for mediators working at different intervention levels (for instance, those mediating in the local community and those representing governments that are addressing large and complicated problems of crisis management/peacebuilding) to learn from each other in joint training exercises, forums, practice arenas and publications. In this way, mediators, and others interested in effective outcomes, will learn more about the similarities and differences of their practices and new ways of collaboration.

This introductory chapter begins with discussions of peace and justice; mediation; mediation as intervention; the mediation continuum; and conflict, mediation and peace. The chapter concludes with an introduction to the contents of the volume.

[1]This book would not have been completed without the support of organizations. I held the Fulbright Distinguished Chair in Human Rights and International Studies at the Danish Institute of Human Rights (2011) in Copenhagen and was a Fellow at the Woodrow Wilson International Center for Scholars (2012–2013) in Washington, D.C. I am very grateful to the Fulbright program, Danish Institute for Human Rights and Woodrow Wilson Center for giving me the time to complete this book. I also would like to thank urban geographer Mike Ribant for his excellent work in developing figures and maps for this volume and Carlos Jean-Baptiste and Mike Ribant for their fine work as editors.

J.M. Fritz (✉)
Professor, University of Cincinnati, USA and Senior Research Fellow, Centre for Sociological Research, University of Johannesburg, South Africa
e-mail: jan.fritz@uc.edu

J.M. Fritz (ed.), *Moving Toward a Just Peace: The Mediation Continuum*,
Clinical Sociology: Research and Practice, DOI 10.1007/978-94-007-2885-1_1,

Peace and Justice

On October 28, 1931, Mahatma Gandhi (1869–1945)[2] spoke at the Montessori Training College in London, England (Gandhi 2010; Gandhi and Montessori 2010). Maria Montessori (1870–1952), an Italian physician and innovative educator of children, was in the audience. Gandhi talked about her and to her when he said:

> You have very truly remarked that if we are to reach real peace in this world and if we are to carry on a real war against war, we shall have to begin with children, and if they will grow up in their natural innocence, we won't have the struggle, we won't have to pass fruitless idle resolutions, but we shall go from love to love and peace to peace, until at last all the corners of the world are covered with that peace and love for which, consciously or unconsciously, the whole world is hungering.[3]

Seven years later, in 1938, Eleanor Roosevelt (1884–1962), a renowned activist and wife of United States President Franklin Roosevelt,[4] published *This Troubled World.* She ended her slim volume (47 pages) in the following way:

> We will have to want peace, want it enough to pay for it, pay for it in our own behavior and in material ways. We will have to want it enough to overcome our lethargy and go out and find all those in other countries who want it as much as we do.
>
> Some time we must begin, for where there is no beginning there is no end, and if we hope to see the preservation of our civilization, if we believe that there is anything worthy of perpetuation in what we have built thus far, then our people must turn to brotherly love, not as a doctrine but as a way of living. If this becomes our accepted way of life, this life may be so well worth living that we will look into the future with a desire to perpetuate a peaceful world for our children. With this desire will come a realization that only if others feel as we do, can we obtain the objectives of peace on earth, good will to men.

---

[2]Mohandas Karamchand Gandhi is known as Mahatma (great soul) Gandhi. Gandhi "is often spoken of as the 'father' of the new nation-state of India" (Brown 2011, p. 1) and he influenced "to a greater or lesser degree . . . many of the freedom struggles of the mid-to late-twentieth century (Prabhu 2001, p. 2). Gandhi thought that "harmony comes with neither passivity nor blindness . . . " (Terchek 2011, p. 117). His "embodiment of nonviolent resistance to injustice in many different forms continues to stir the moral imagination of the world more than 50 years after his death" (Prabhu 2001, p. 2).

[3]There are thousands of certified Montessori schools (and others that are not certified) in many countries. Thayer-Bacon (2011, p. 4) said teaching in one of the Montessori schools "gave me a way to experience a pedagogical approach that recognizes the importance of cultural diversity, while helping children learn how to be active, engaged, critically aware, self-assured, self-directed, and self-disciplined citizens of democracies-always-in-the-making." For Maria Montessori, "violence and war are not natural occurrences but aberrant outcomes of aberrant educational and child-rearing practices. Education and child-rearing that did not interfere with normal development would allow the nature of humanity to reveal itself as peaceful and motivated by work for the improvement of all of society; not just for personal gain" (Roos 2012, p. 89).

[4]In 1932, Eleanor Roosevelt's husband, Franklin, was elected the 32nd President of the United States; he held that office from 1933 until 1945. In 1939, Eleanor Roosevelt appeared on the cover of *Time*, a news magazine. The publication called her "an oracle to millions of housewives" as well as the "world's foremost female political force" (Beasley 2000, p. 518). Eleanor Roosevelt was known for strongly supporting civil rights, helping found the United Nations, heading the United Nations Human Rights Commission and serving as US Ambassador to the United Nations under both Presidents Truman and Kennedy.

And more than 40 years later, in 1985, the Bahá'í[5] central body, The Universal House of Justice, issued a statement – "The Promise of World Peace" – that said peace was "inevitable." The document was written "To the Peoples of the World" and began as follows:

> The Great Peace towards which people of good will throughout the centuries have inclined their hearts, of which seers and poets for countless generations have expressed their vision, and for which from age to age the sacred scriptures of mankind have constantly held the promise, is now at long last within the reach of the nations. For the first time in history, it is possible for everyone to view the entire planet, with all its myriad diversified peoples, in one perspective. World peace is not only possible but inevitable. It is the next stage in the evolution of this planet... Whether peace is to be reached only after unimaginable horrors precipitated by humanity's stubborn clinging to old patterns of behavior, or is to be embraced now by an act of consultative will, is the choice before all who inhabit the earth... Failure to stem the tide of conflict and disorder would be unconscionably irresponsible.

Parts of the world do want peace, but the movement toward that goal is often slow and uneven. And if that peace is to last, it must be a *just peace*,[6] one that is both inclusive and fair. Mediation and the varied work of mediators and mediating bodies are important elements of the movement toward peace. This book discusses selected roles of mediators and mediating organizations in preventing, reducing and resolving disputes and conflicts at different intervention levels.

Mediation Defined

According to United Nations Secretary-General Ban Ki-moon (2012b), "mediation is one of the most effective methods of preventing, managing and resolving conflicts." Mediation is a rights-based, humanistic and creative process in which one or more impartial individuals help parties (disputants), with their consent, discuss an issue or issues that concern one or more of them. This process is sometimes referred to as facilitated negotiation. *Rights-based* mediation takes into account everyone's human rights. A rights-based approach means that a mediation is concerned with achieving at least a minimum standard of well-being for parties, and those they represent, as a right of all people. Mediations should not undermine the interests of the vulnerable. A broad definition of *humanism* is used in regard to mediation. This definition of humanism goes beyond being anthropocentric (human centered) and biocentric (moral consideration given to all living things) as

---

[5]The Bahá'í Faith is a monotheistic religion founded in nineteenth century Persia; it emphasizes the spiritual unity of all people.

[6]According to Albin (2009, p. 592), "In many situations, particularly in a longer term perspective, the issue is not whether peace or justice is to be chosen or prioritized for both are clearly needed in some sense." Albin, goes on to say that there are core questions to be answered including "What kind of justice and what kind of peace should be promoted?... (and) How are the pursuits of these two values... best timed, sequenced and combined over time?"

it also includes respect for the natural environment.[7] Mediation that is *creative* can generate new concepts, ideas, or associations. Creative thinking, according to Debra Gerardi (2001), requires openness, listening, risk-taking, trust, and collaboration. Mediations should allow and encourage these characteristics in order to foster new analysis and decisions.

The mediator (or mediation team)[8] establishes an open, trusting setting in which parties are encouraged to discuss facts as well as their personal feelings about the issue or issues that brought them to the discussion. After all parties have been identified and included,[9] mediation is usually conducted as a flexibly-structured process and can be free-flowing or more controlled. If the outcome of this process is an agreement, it would be shaped by the parties and satisfactory to them.

Mediation is used to try to settle a wide variety of disputes between and among individuals, organizations, communities, protesters and governments as well as combinations of these disputants. Mediation can be an excellent method for resolving some kinds of disputes in part because it can be faster and less expensive than the alternatives. Most importantly, the parties can create their own resolution to a dispute rather than have a decision imposed upon them. There are times, however, when mediation may not be a good choice for disputants. For instance, if one of the parties does not agree to participate; serious violations of the law have occurred; or the prevailing power of a party is not allowed, by one or more parties, to be a subject of discussion.

It is useful to outline the principles, attitudes, and tools needed by a mediator in conducting interventions. While these may differ somewhat depending on the level of intervention (e.g., individual, community, nation), they include: having an ethical framework,[10] practicing inclusiveness, working with the people's interests and opportunities, encouraging recognition of other viewpoints, demonstrating interdependence as a factor in the change process, encouraging capacity building, having relevant knowledge and knowing how to access more of it, and having a long-term perspective. Mediators need to be open-minded, courageous (at times), and able to work well with others.

---

[7] This broad definition covers, for instance, mediations dealing with the environment, land use and land ownership.

[8] Mediation is interdisciplinary with mediators coming from many disciplinary backgrounds including peace and conflict studies; counseling; law; environment; labor studies; and clinical sociology. It is useful to think about how the disciplinary background of a mediator or a mediation team may affect the design and approach to mediation. See, for instance, "Clinical Sociological Contributions to the Field of Mediation" (Fritz 2008).

[9] Some countries have legislation or official guidance that makes it difficult to talk with certain parties (e.g., people or organizations identified as terrorists). Mediators and mediating organizations need to know that it is not illegal for them to talk with all parties.

[10] James Laue and Gerald Cormick discussed the approach of interveners in their 1978 article, "The Ethics of Intervention in Community Disputes." For Laue and Cormick, the basic values for a mediator were freedom, justice, and empowerment. It is worth discussing if the assumptions, values, and principles will be the same for mediators in different kinds of mediation, particularly when the outside influences (e.g., funders, participants, and mediator's employers) may have different assumptions, values, and principles.

Mediation as Intervention

Intervention is about involving one's self as a "third party" in an existing situation. There are, of course, many kinds of interventions such as having an advisor, coach, consultant, or judge. In the case of mediation, the intervenor enters a situation that has been defined as problematic (by one, some or all parties) in order to help the participants understand, deal with, alter or leave the situation.

The role of the mediator can involve one or more levels of focus from the individual to the global.[11] Even though the mediator or mediation team may specialize in one or two levels of intervention (e.g., divorce mediation, crisis mediation at a national level), the practitioner may move among a number of levels (e.g., individual, organization, national) in order to analyze or develop intervention strategies.

The intervention levels (from individual through global) are represented in Fig. 1.1 as circles (without a hierarchy) to indicate that no intervention level is assumed to be inevitably more important than another. The lines among the levels help show that a mediator may focus on one level (which could be shaded for emphasis) but also that a mediator (or a mediation team member) can have an additional level of focus or at least a background in other levels. This additional knowledge can be quite useful in mediation.

It can be helpful to distinguish between the terms *conflict* and *dispute* (See Fig. 1.2). Conflicts are large (perhaps very large) and their boundaries cannot easily be established. In a conflict, it sometimes is not easy to identify all the stakeholders

Fig. 1.1 The levels of intervention

[11] The global level refers to work done on a worldwide basis as well as to a time when other worlds may be involved with this world.

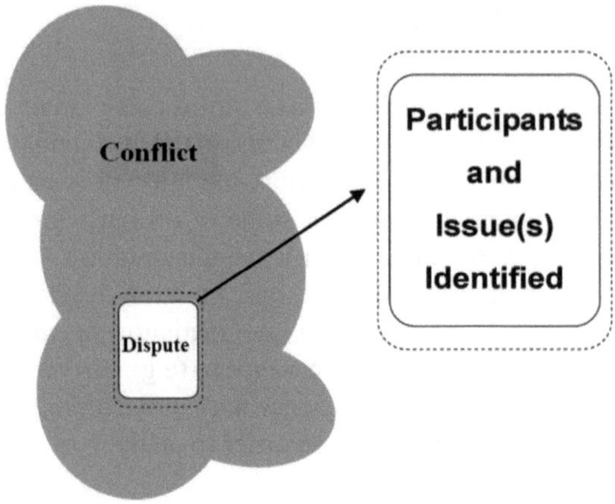

Fig. 1.2 Relationship between conflict and dispute

(parties) or all the relevant issues. A dispute can be part of a larger conflict (e.g., a disagreement between a manager and an employee in a company located in a war zone), but it also may be a disagreement that is much less likely to be part of anything larger (e.g., a disagreement between male acquaintances at a bus stop about who should get on the bus first). A dispute is a disagreement between identified stakeholders who can rather easily define their issues. It is much easier to mediate a dispute than it is a conflict.

Mediations and disputes/conflicts go through stages or phases. Two figures can help explain this process. The first one (Fig. 1.3 The Life History of a Dispute or Conflict) can be used to deal with all disputes and conflicts.

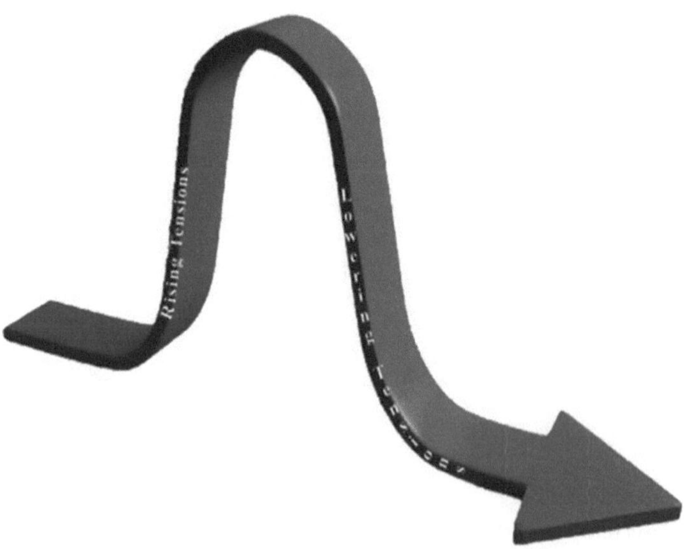

Fig. 1.3 The life history of a dispute or conflict

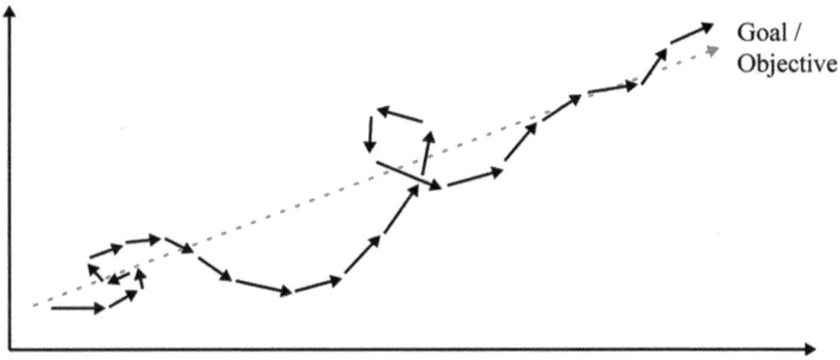

Fig. 1.4 Progress toward a goal or objective

The model provided here (about increasing tensions – decreasing tensions)[12] is only one model of a dispute or conflict. For instance, if the situation only continues to get worse, there will be no downswing at the end; if the escalation period takes a very long time, but things are settled quickly, the line on the left hand side will be much longer than the one on the right. Using this general model, a mediator/facilitator/interventionist can make decisions about the intervention strategies that might be used at different phases of a dispute or conflict. For example, intervention might come at early point to try to avoid the need for mediation at a later date.

The second model (Fig. 1.4) shows trajectory for a mediation. Again, this is only one possible scenario. Two general points can be made about the phases in this model. First, it is possible not only to progress through the phases but also to cycle back through them as necessary. Figure 1.4 shows that progress toward a goal should not be depicted by a straight line. One might expect that if the mediation generally stays on track, more of the cycling back will be at the beginning or middle of the process. If there are unusual problems (e.g., change of leadership, change of direction of the organization, plateau in terms of effort), the trajectory and cycling back might be seen differently. The second point is that the length of time required for each stage will depend on a number of factors, including the number and intensity of issues that need to be discussed.

Mediators differ in their approach to mediation (e.g., control or influence). The ends of the line in Fig. 1.5 indicate that a mediator's approach might be directive (advising parities about what to do) or facilitative (a party-centered approach). The mediator's approach could be between facilitative and directive and it also could change during the course of a mediation. The decision about whether a mediation will be more or less facilitative or directive will be made because of one

[12]This model is based on one developed by the United States Institute for Peace (n.d., p. 11). The USIP model is a fully-developed one for analyzing conflicts.

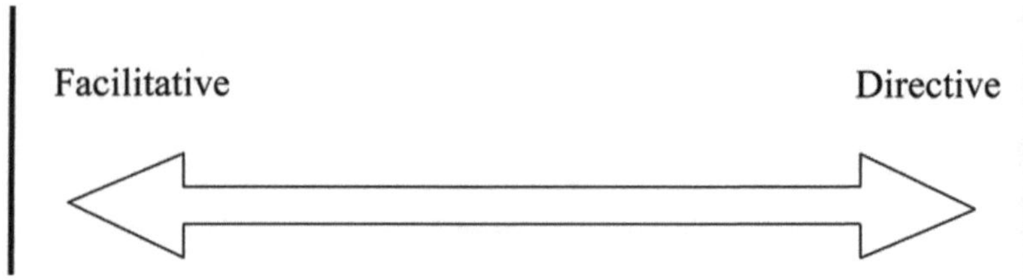

Fig. 1.5 Approach to mediation

or a number of factors (e.g., party preference, mediator preference, preference of the sponsoring organization, training received by mediator, the particular setting in which mediation takes place).

A mediator, like other change agents, looks at the context in which changes will take place. The mediator and parties need to identify and review the internal and external forces that may foster or resist change at the onset of or during the change process. This is a particularly creative part of the mediator's work and is basic in the selection of intervention tools and techniques for effective, sustainable change.

The Mediation Continuum: The Roles of Mediators and Mediating Organizations

In 1978, Laue and Cormick identified five roles that intervenors may play in community disputes. These were: activist, advocate, mediator, researcher and enforcer. They noted that these roles could be differentiated in three ways: "the intervenor's organizational and fiscal base; the intervenor's relationship to the parties – the degree of identification with one party and range of empathy for, and access to, the other parties; and the skills the intervenor brings to bear on a conflict situation." In discussing the role of mediator, they gave a rather typical definition for a mediator[13] not unlike the one in this chapter.

As the field of mediation has grown and developed, so have the roles assumed by mediators (including mediating organizations). Mediators work at all the intervention levels and, in part because they have different disciplinary backgrounds and the organizations they work for have expanded needs, they are not only doing mediations but are involved in other kinds of intervention work. It is not unusual to find a mediator involved, for instance, in coaching those involved in negotiations or using the Appreciative Inquiry approach (Stratton-Berkessel 2010) to help a community group or formal organization develop a conscious and cooperative awareness of its strengths and possibilities. Mediators also are involved in prevention efforts that

[13]They also noted, however, that "a fiscal and organizational base acceptable to the disputing parties (and ideally, in most situations, independent of them) is crucial."

strengthen an organizational process for a system in order to possibly enhance a "culture of peace" and avoid mediations. For example, mediators have been trained to help school systems by facilitating group meeting processes as models for parents, teachers and school administrators who will decide on plans for students with special education needs. Mediators from certain disciplines have research backgrounds and they conduct research, for instance, about various aspects of the conflict intervention process or they write about mediation systems. Some mediators have the skills to put dispute and conflict intervention programs in place. And still others have served as negotiators,[14] analysts, peacemakers and peacebuilders.

There is a range of skills and experience at different intervention levels as well as many mediation approaches, theories and models available from which to choose. It is important that mediators with different backgrounds and experiences have the opportunity to train, process experiences and work together. It also is important that those putting mediation programs in place are informed about the variety of work undertaken by mediators and the reasons that mediators need to be able to choose among the different models, theories and approaches in order to effectively address problematic situations.

Conflict, Mediation and Peace

On September 13, 2011, Nassir Abdulaziz Al-Nasser, the president of the 66th session of the United Nations (UN) General Assembly, gave his opening remarks to the UN Secretary-General and the General Assembly. He said there would be four main areas of focus that would frame the work of the General Assembly during this session and that the first focal area would be "the peaceful settlement of disputes."

> History has shown that peaceful settlements, including those brokered through mediation efforts, provide the most cost-effective and long-lasting solution for disputes. And in today's world, the need to find peaceful resolution to disputes has become more relevant and urgent than ever. For this reason, I have suggested the theme "The role of mediation in the settlement of disputes" for the General Debate this year. Of course, this theme has a broad and multi-faceted nature. I expect Member States to touch upon different aspects of this matter through their own experience and perspective. In the last few years, we have witnessed a momentum within the United Nations and in many regions regarding the efforts of mediation and other tools of peaceful means. It is my intention to actively pursue this issue in the 66th session with a view not to only sustaining the work that has come before, but also to increasing this momentum. It is my view that the General Assembly should, through its revitalization, become more engaged and empowered on issues of mediation, so that it can fulfill its role as the world's preeminent peacemaker at this major juncture in international relations.

[14]According to Zartman (2009, p. 322), "Negotiation, the process of combining conflicting positions into a joint agreement is synonymous with conflict resolution, and is the most common (although not the only) way of preventing, managing, resolving and transforming conflicts."

And on June 25, 2012a, Ban Ki-moon, the UN Secretary-General, issued a report on the role of mediation in preventing and resolving conflicts. The report was provided in response to the UN General Assembly's first resolution on mediation (65/283, adopted by consensus in 2011). In the report, the Secretary-General highlighted eight trends in the area of conflict and mediation:

- One, research shows that after nearly two decades of decline, the numbers of conflicts have begun to increase once again ... Even though the majority of these conflicts are intra-State, a quarter of them are internationalized, that is external parties and troops are involved in supporting one or more of the parties.
- Two, there remains a considerable number of intractable low-intensity conflicts that could escalate into violence... While a few of those disputes have been referred to the International Court of Justice, and some continue to be managed through good offices and mediation, others risk becoming major flashpoints with regional and international ramifications...
- Three, many of today's conflicts involve a complex web of objectives and actors, local and regional dimensions that pose difficult challenges for mediators. These conflicts often transcend the borders of one country, spreading instability and humanitarian challenges and augmenting the number of potential conflict parties... Contemporary conflicts require mediators to balance a political mandate with urgent humanitarian considerations, establish a coherent but inclusive mediation process, and build incentives for engagement in the process while upholding international legal frameworks and norms... The range of complex issues to be addressed means mediation requires greater and more varied expertise...
- Four, the field of mediation has become more diverse and crowded. Regional, subregional and other international organizations as well as non-government organizations and private individuals are increasingly involved in mediation activities. At their best, mediating actors have coalesced behind a lead mediator... At worst, competition and disagreement over strategy and funding have permitted parties to forum shop, therefore hampering peace efforts...
- Five, there is growing recognition that mediation is not the exclusive purview of external mediation actors. Local mediators who come from the conflict country can usefully lead local mediation efforts or complement regional or international initiatives....
- Six, civil society actors, such as the youth and women groups [sic], are rightfully demanding a greater voice in political transitions and mediation processes... The need to make mediation processes more inclusive of the broader society has focused new attention on the process management aspects of mediation...
- Seven, over the past decade, greater efforts to implement legal and normative frameworks have required mediators to adjust their approaches... The United Nations cannot condone amnesties for war crimes, genocide, crimes against humanity and gross violations of human rights... Responsibility to Protect has in itself become a point of reference in country discussions by the Security Council. Mediation has been considered as one important tool to live up to this

responsibility... With the adoption of Security Council Resolution 1325 (2000), the promotion of women's representation in peacemaking became an expectation for conflicting parties and mediators...

- Eight, supporting mediation efforts has become an important task of our special political missions, peacekeeping missions and other United Nations presences in the field. Mediation is not the exclusive occupation of envoys and does not end with the signing of a peace agreement. My special representatives in field missions mediate on a daily basis to support compliance with and implementation of signed agreements, and routinely work with the parties to manage new sources of conflict... Mediation capacity and support is essential in the fragile political environments even in the absence of an ongoing formal peace process.

This June report had an annex that provided guidance for mediators to help develop an effective mediation process and outcome. In September, the annex was released as a separate document, the *United Nations Guidance for Effective Mediation.*[15] The eight "key fundamentals" (p. 3) were identified as:

> good preparation; consent of the parties; impartiality on the part of the mediator (runs a fair process); inclusivity (all viewpoints heard); national ownership (parties as well as the broader society are committed to the mediation process); respect for international law and normative frameworks, coherence, coordination and complementarity (when there are a number of actors) among mediation efforts, and the development of quality peace agreements.

While this list particularly speaks to the experiences of those mediating large, multi-party and, perhaps, violent disputes and conflicts,[16] each of the fundamentals can stand as is or be adapted by those mediating other kinds of disputes.

This section has focused on three recent UN statements about conflict and mediation. It would be easy to think, if one just read these excerpts, that peace can be obtained by addressing only the large, violent conflicts. As Maria Montessori, Mahatma Gandhi, Eleanor Roosevelt, Bahá'í Faith representatives and many others have reminded us, for there to be lasting peace, we also will have to educate our children in a new way, change our behavior to make brotherly/sisterly love a way of living and personally embrace peace and justice.

[15]The Policy and Mediation Division of the United Nations Department of Political Affairs published its *Guidance for Mediators addressing Conflict-related Sexual Violence in Ceasefire and Peace Agreements* in 2012. The Department notes that the guidance benefited from material generated for a United Nations Inter-Agency High-Level Colloquium held in 2009. In March 2013, the UN Secretary-General provided a guidance note on racial discrimination and protection of minorities and cited the UN Guidance for Effective Mediation in discussing "conflict prevention, peace-making, conflict-resolution and preventive diplomacy initiatives."

[16]The foreword by UN Secretary-General Ban Ki-moon indicates that the document supports "professional and credible mediation efforts around the world." It also says it "encompasses the wealth of experience of mediators working at the international, national and local levels." The document appears to deal more with experiences at the national and international level rather than with the range of activities that take place at the local level.

The UN documents provide useful guidance for mediation efforts. The documents, do, however, leave us with some important questions to be discussed. For instance, if a number of mediation efforts are in place in a conflict or post-conflict area, under what circumstances should these efforts be coordinated? Which type of organization or organizations should take the lead in coordinating mediation efforts and how is this to be decided? How do we obtain the necessary resources to support effective mediation as well as implementation and compliance? Do these documents give enough emphasis to mediating disputes and conflicts that are small, non-violent or do not involve regional or national factions? Is there clear guidance regarding impunity and amnesty for all kinds of mediations? Is there enough guidance about identifying and dealing with harmful cultural practices? Does the use of diplomatic language (what one should consider rather than what one must do) result in inclusion? It is hoped that this volume will, in many ways, invite this discussion.

Contents of the Volume

The chapters that follow this introduction are divided into two parts. The first section contains several short essays about some of the basics of mediation. The second section is a discussion of selected areas of application.[17]

Basics. There are a number of basics in the field of mediation, but only three topics were selected to be covered in some depth: cultural considerations; creativity; and models, theories and approaches. *Culture* is an important, often perplexing, topic for mediators. As Cathleen Kuhl (personal communication, September 12, 2011), a court mediator, noted "the issue of cultural competency has flummoxed me for years.. and I will risk you concluding that I'm a cultural coward." The chapter defines culture, mentions harmful traditional practices and looks at cultural competency/cultural diplomacy in relation to mediation. *Creativity* is the subject of the second essay. In some mediation arenas, creativity is something of an endangered species because the employers of mediators give the mediators very little room to be creative. This chapter discusses the conditions that foster creativity and the extent to which creativity should be part of mediation. *Mediation models, theories and approaches* are covered in the final essay. Some mediators and some organizations that employ mediators do not have much information about the range of models, approaches and theories. The more mediators understand the models, approaches and theories, the more they will be able to explain and assess what they do. This also will help disputants, mediators and those who run mediation programs make informed choices about mediation possibilities.

---

[17] The articles in both sections are meant to be stand-alone pieces and so there may be some overlap in the handling of topics.

Selected areas of application. Ten chapters are included in this section. From the United States, there are chapters on the history and future of community mediation; the use of mediation by police; and developments in special education mediation. From Nigeria, a physician discusses a project that intervened on behalf of widows. Representatives from South Africa's African Centre for the Constructive Resolution of Disputes (ACCORD) write about their capacity-building work in Burundi. From Israel, there is a discussion about the effects of having a high number of people trained as mediators and introduced to peer mediation in schools. There also is a chapter on the creative facilitation of meetings and one about innovative community conferencing programs.

The section concludes with two chapters dealing with international issues. The first is about UN Security Council Resolution 1325 (Women and Peace and Security) and gender justice. It includes information about the extent to which women are involved in peacebuilding efforts including mediation. The last chapter is about the role of non-governmental organizations (NGOs) in peacebuilding efforts. It provides a framework for looking at the contributions and limitations of the mediating organizations that are involved in peace initiatives.

Governments, non-governmental organizations, community-based organizations, businesses, unions and individuals must all work together to effectively deal with issues of security, full employment, inclusion, as well as access to education, health care, housing and food. Mediators work with people who face challenges in all these areas. Mediation that is based on human rights rules, regulations and commitments is one of the flexible tools that can be used at all levels of intervention to move us toward a just peace.

References

Albin, C. (2009). Peace vs. justice – and beyond. In J. Bercovitch, V. Kremenyuk, & I. Zartman (Eds.), *The SAGE handbook of conflict resolution (580–594)*. London: Sage.

Al-Nasser, N. A. (2011). Opening remarks of the President of the 66th session of the United Nations General Assembly, New York. 13 Sept 2011. http://www.un.org/en/ga/president/66/statements/index.shtml

Beasley, M. H. (2000). Eleanor Roosevelt's press conferences: Case study in class, gender, and race. *The Social Science Journal, 37*(4), 517–528.

Brown, J. (2011). Introduction. In J. Brown & A. Parel (Eds.), *The Cambridge companion to Gandhi* (pp. 1–8). Cambridge: Cambridge University Press.

Fritz, J. M. (2008). Clinical sociological contributions to the field of mediation. In J. Fritz (Ed.), *International clinical sociology* (pp. 85–96). New York: Springer.

Gandhi, M. (2010). Gandhi and Montessori: A speech in London. Montessori life. 2: 42–43. First published in Young India, November 19, 1931.

Gandhi and Montessori: A Speech in London. (2010) *Montessori life 22*(2), 42–43.

Gerardi, D. (2001). Developing creativity and intuition for resolving conflicts: The magic of improvisation. Retrieved from http://www.mediate.com/articles/geradi.cfm. Accessed 15 Apr 2013.

Ki-moon, B. (2012a). Strengthening the role of mediation in the peaceful settlement of disputes, conflict prevention and resolution, Report of the United Nations Secretary-General. 25 June 2012. (A/66/811,25).

Ki-moon, B. (2012b). Foreword. *United Nations guidance for effective mediation*. New York: United Nations. Retrieved from www.peacemaker.un.org. Accessed 15 Apr 2013.

Laue, J., & Cormick, G. (1978). The ethics of intervention in community disputes. In G. Bermant, H. Kelman, & D. Warwick (Eds.), *The ethics of social intervention* (pp. 205–232). Washington: Hemisphere Publishing Corporation.

Prabhu, J. (2001). Gandhi, visionary for a globalized world. *ReVision, 24*(1), 2–8.

Roos, S. (2012). The Montessori method: The development of a healthy pattern of desire in early childhood. *Contagion: Journal of Violence, Mimesis and Culture, 19*, 87–122.

Roosevelt, E. (1938). *This troubled world*. New York: Kinsey & Company Inc.

Stratton-Berkessel, R. (2010). *Appreciative inquiry for collaborative solutions: 21 strength-based workshops*. San Francisco: Pfeiffer, A Wiley Imprint.

Terchek, R. J. (2011). Conflict and nonviolence. In J. Brown & A. Parel (Eds.), *The Cambridge companion to Gandhi* (pp. 117–134). Cambridge: Cambridge University Press.

Thayer-Bacon, B. (2011). Maria Montessori: Education for peace. *Factis Pax, 5*(3), 307–319.

United Nations. (2012). *Guidance for mediators addressing conflict-related sexual violence in ceasefire and peace agreements*. New York: Department of Political Affairs, Policy and Mediation Division. January. www.un.org/peacemaker

United Nations General Assembly. (2011). Opening Remarks of the President of the 66th Session of the United Nations General Assembly. Retrieved from http://www.un.org/en/ga/president/66/statements/openingremarks-13092011.shtml. Accessed 15 Apr 2013.

United Nations Secretary-General. (2012a). *Report of the Secretary-General on strengthening the role of mediation in the peaceful settlement of disputes, conflict prevention and resolution*. 25 June 2012. http://daccess-dds-ny.un.org/doc/UNDOC/GEN/N12/346/41/PDF/N1234641.pdf?OpenElement. Accessed 15 Apr 2013.

United Nations Secretary-General. (2012b). *Guidance for effective mediation*. Retrieved from www.peacemaker.un.org. Accessed 15 Apr 2013.

United Nations Secretary-General. (2013). *Guidance note of the Secretary-General on racial discrimination and protection of minorities*. March. Retrieved from http://www.ohchr.org/Documents/Issues/Minorities/GuidanceNoteRacialDiscriminationMinorities.pdf. Accessed 15 Apr 2013.

United States Institute for Peace (n.d.) *Module 3. Conflict Management*. U.S. Online Training Course for OSCE, including REACT. http://react.usip.org

Universal House of Justice, The, Bahá'í Faith. (1985). The promise of world peace" Retrieved from http://info.bahai.org/article-1-7-2-1.html

Zartman, I. W. (2009). Conflict resolution and negotiation. In J. Bercovitch, V. Kremenyuk, & I. W. Zartman (Eds.), *The sage handbook of conflict resolution* (pp. 322–339). London: Sage.

Part I
Basics

Chapter 2
Cultural Considerations

Jan Marie Fritz

Culture is a central focus in anthropology and a topic of interest in a number of the other social sciences and humanities (e.g., Goldstein 1957; Swidler 1986; Throsby 2001) And, as one might expect, it is either an important topic or a growing concern in many practice fields such as clinical sociology, education, medicine, business, school psychology, counseling, public administration,[1] forensic evaluations and mediation (e.g., Busch et al. 2010; Moule 2012; Fritz 2008; Frisby 2009; Starr et al. 2011; Philip and McKeown 2004; Rice 2007; Baumgartner 2009; Perlin and McClain 2009). This chapter defines and discusses culture, provides some examples of cultural differences, discusses cultural competency, and, finally, looks at cultural competency/cultural diplomacy in relation to mediation.

Culture

Over the last 500 years, culture has been defined in a number of ways (e.g., see Throsby 2001, p. 3; Monk et al. 2008, pp. 6–14; Elgström 1994, pp. 293–4). It first meant the process of tilling the soil (agricultural improvement) but, by the sixteenth century, it still meant cultivation, but now it was cultivation of the mind or intellect

[1]According to Rice (2007), "the focus on culture and cultural competency in public administration and public service delivery in the USA is evolving very slowly" because, in part, the field "has supported culture blind services and programs (and) a focus on cultural differences/cultural variations does not fit the traditional neutrality/equality principles."

J.M. Fritz (✉)
Professor, University of Cincinnati, USA and Senior Research Fellow, Centre for Sociological Research, University of Johannesburg, South Africa
e-mail: jan.fritz@uc.edu

J.M. Fritz (ed.), *Moving Toward a Just Peace: The Mediation Continuum*, Clinical Sociology: Research and Practice, DOI 10.1007/978-94-007-2885-1_2,

(the cultured or refined person). By the early nineteenth century, culture had a broad context and it referred to the "intellectual and spiritual development of civilization *as a whole*" (Throsby 2001, p. 3).

Culture is now defined, in the literature of scientists and practitioners, as something more than intellectual development. It refers to a group or society's way of life in a given setting and its social heritage. Culture is about shared values, attitudes, goals, traditions as well as norms and actual behavior that characterize a group and are passed down by the group to following generations. Culture is "the means through which people understand the world" (Pearson 2011, p. 179) and becomes a standard from which to evaluate the actions of others (Ross 1993, p. 21).

Within a society, there are collectivities of people that share many of the aspects of the broader culture but also share some additional characteristics with those who they think are most similar. These groups (e.g., young people, people with disabilities) have *subcultures* that may be defined by one or more characteristics including the following (USDHHS 2003, p. 9):

> national origin; customs and traditions; length of residency . . . ; language; age; generation; gender; religious beliefs; political beliefs; sexual orientation; perceptions of family and community; perceptions of health, well-being and disability; physical ability or limitations; socioeconomic status; education level; geographic location; and family and household composition

Culture is, to some (e.g., Elgström 1994; Bercovitch and Elgström 2001, pp. 5–6; Trefon 2011, p. 109), a fuzzy, vague, intricate, imprecise, elusive and/or difficult term as it seems to encompass so much and its edges are not very clear. Because of this, it can be difficult to know if something is due to culture or should be more appropriately seen as subcultural or individual. Also, in many instances, individuals and even some experts only use the term culture in a limited way exclusively for or emphasizing race and ethnicity or majority and minority status based on race and ethnicity.

Even if the term is imprecise and intricate, it is usually seen as an important consideration. Jenny Pearson (2011, p. 179), the director of a Cambodian capacity-building NGO (non-governmental organization), wrote that "the essential starting point for effective capacity development is culture, culture, culture!" That does not mean, however, that enough attention is paid to cultural similarities and differences within a society and between societies. For instance, Theodore Trefon (2011, p. 108), in his discussion of culture in the Democratic Republic of the Congo, said the following about those offering development aid:

> While culture may be omnipresent, often as vacuous stereotypes . . . , drawing on cultural reality to accompany and facilitate reform is woefully absent from the reform agenda. This absence results from Western experts viewing Congo as they think it should be, based on imported paradigms and world views, instead of accepting it as it is. The expectations of ordinary people are rarely taken into account because they are disassociated from debates about institutional reform. They are political outsiders. This disassociation results from the breach between foreign experts who interact with the local elites – the political insiders . . .

Trefon thinks that if the cultural facilitators and barriers of people in the communities were taken into account, "communities (would) achieve independence and engage in assertive citizenship . . . "

And Kappler and Richmond (2011), in their discussion of peacebuilding and culture in Bosnia and Herzegovina, note that the European Union "has a tendency to treat culture as an instrument that can only be taken into consideration when doing so is conducive to the Union's political projects in the region." As an example they mention that "most museums, choirs, galleries and musicians . . . are usually denied funding and support" while "a cultural approach linked to the goals of an official peacebuilding project (e.g., human rights training for teachers) would be funded provided it is a project of a larger, well-established organization rather than one proposed by a smaller group."

Some find it useful to compare cultures in terms of some broad characteristics (opposites). For instance, cultures can be seen as individualistic or collectivist[2] (Hofstede 1980), having differences in terms of power distance,[3] or as having high or low-context communication styles[4] (Hall 1976). Others (see Davidheiser 2010, pp.128–129) prefer more complex and/or descriptive approaches when comparing cultures.

There also are terms to describe different kinds of cultural situations. It might be useful here to use the concepts *cross-cultural*, *intercultural* and *transcultural*. Based on the work of Avruch and Black as featured in discussions by Busch et al. (2010), *cross-cultural* will refer here to situations based within a larger culture. This looks at collectivities that share a larger culture (in many aspects) but have subcultural differences (frequently in terms of power). *Intercultural* will be used to look at situations involving individuals and/or groups that have two or more cultures. *Transcultural* would be looking for universal rules in dealing with individuals and groups in cross-cultural and intercultural settings. This chapter and the book focus on multicultural activities including ones that are cross-cultural and intercultural.

Understanding Cultural Differences

Writers usually make a strong case for paying attention to culture by giving striking examples. I will be no different and begin with a case presented by Norine Dresser (1996, pp. 38–39) that has been used (see Moule 2012) to encourage educators to

---

[2]This individualism/collectivism approach describes the degree to which a society focuses on individuals (independent, self-realization, loose ties to groups, contractual relationships, emphasizing competition) or groups (no one is an individual, uniqueness is a secondary interest, harmony and cooperation within the group is emphasized, people are seen as interdependent).

[3]This refers to how much emphasis is placed on hierarchy.

[4]Low-context cultures (e.g., United States, northern Europe) have communication patterns that are direct/explicit/linear while high-context cultures (e.g., Latin America, Japan) have indirect/circular communication patterns.

be more effective teachers in the United States by recognizing the importance of cultural differences:

> (Ms.) Gussman is one of the best English teachers in the school. She spends every weekend reading her immigrant students' compositions and making careful comments in red ink. To soften her criticisms, she says something positive before writing suggestions for improvement, using the students' names to make the comments more personable. "Jae Lee, these are fine ideas, but . . . " These red-inked notes send shock waves through the families of her Korean students, but (Ms.) Gussman is unaware of this until the principal calls her into the office.

Koreans, particularly those who are Buddhists, only write a person's name in red at the time of death or at the anniversary of a death. Therefore, to see the names of their children written in red terrified the Korean parents.

Fisher et al. (2000, p. 42) recount what happened between two participants during a training course:

> A . . . man (from an African country) was having a dialogue with a woman from Eastern Europe. He, in his natural cultural style, was standing very close to her and looking directly into her eyes while speaking. She, having a very different cultural expectation about normal conversation, perceived his manner as aggressive and intimidating. In her own cultural style, she was continually backing (away), trying to put more distance between them, and also averting her eyes from looking directly at his. He perceived her behaviour to indicate that she was not interested, or at least not understanding, the point he was trying to make, and this caused him to continue moving closer to her and to make his point even more forcefully.

And, finally, Monk et al. (2008, p. 47), in their book about multicultural counseling, said the following about non-Native Americans working with Native Americans:

> Native American populations (in the United States) are extraordinarily diverse in their languages and identities. It is impossible to make general recommendations regarding counseling interventions for those who identify as Native Americans . . . Different customs and languages among Native Americans, in addition to the individual differences within tribes, produce huge variation in the lives people live. Perhaps even more significant than these intertribal and within-tribal variations are the differences that most ethnic minorities in the United States experience because of the degree of acculturation to mainstream American culture . . . There is a significant continuum extending from those Native Americans born and reared on a reservation, perhaps even speaking their mother tongue, to persons identifying as Native American who live in a city and have completely lost touch with any tribal ancestry.

These examples are important because they allow us to understand there can be dramatic differences in the ways people from different cultural backgrounds see and do things. And the last example reminds us that culture is a very complex[5] phenomenon and while we need to be sensitive to the real possibility of cultural

---

[5]Complexity can be something quite interesting, rather than a problem. As Monk et al. (2008, p. 2) noted: ". . . an appreciation of complexity enriches us with more possibilities for making a difference in the world . . . (We should not) seek to eliminate complexity by tying the concept (of culture) down too tightly . . . to do so risks discounting someone's real experience."

differences, at the same time we must understand there is huge variation in the degree to which someone's individual[6] and group identity can be understood in relation to her or his own culture.[7]

Cultural Competency

Cultural competency is about working more effectively with individuals and groups from a variety of backgrounds. It is an ongoing process as well as a goal toward which systems, agencies and/or individuals "must continually aspire" (Rorie et al. 1996). For those who are practitioners and working with people who are diverse, culture has become a central concern. If it isn't a concern, there are consequences, as Jean Moule (2012, pp. 5–6) has noted, in her "primer for educators:"

> Research consistently shows that schools (in the United States) are not welcoming places for culturally different students. On average, these students drop out earlier and achieve at lower educational levels than their mainstream counterparts ... Only when culturally competent teaching is routinely available will culturally different students have a chance to reach their full potentials.

Cultural competency has been defined in different ways (see Vasquez 2010, pp. 128–129).[8] As the concept is used here, it refers to a set of attitudes, behaviors, policies and procedures that enable a system, agency and/or individual to function effectively with culturally diverse individuals and communities (Chung 1992; Randall-David 1994; Rorie et al. 1996; Lecca et al. 1998). The diversity can be in terms of ethnicity, race, religion, socioeconomic class, age, education, type of work, gender and/or many other factors.

Just as there are differences in the definitions of cultural competency, there also are different conceptual approaches. Sue, Ivey and Pederson (Sue 2006, p. 238), for instance, developed a "widely recognized conceptual scheme" that included three general areas: cultural awareness and beliefs, cultural knowledge, and cultural

---

[6]Identity development is a dynamic – shifting and evolving – process that responds to multiple and changing cultural contexts. The idea of individual identities includes those people with "border identities" (Rosaldo 1993) who, for various reasons, do not quite fit (by their own thinking or that of a group) the definition of a group. An example might be a person with a multiracial background who is not accepted or does not feel accepted by one or both groups.

[7]According to Monk et al. (2008, p. 31): "There is wide agreement among multicultural researchers that within-group differences of an identifiable group are as great if not greater than between-group differences."

[8]Joutsenvirta and Uusitalo (2010, p. 380), writing in the *Journal of Business Ethics*, define cultural competence as "the sensitivity of the firm toward the surrounding societal and cultural changes in customer values and behavior, and the ability to transfer this knowledge into meaningful business practices."

skills. Vasquez (2010) offered an approach, based on a definition of cultural competency developed by Steng and Stelzer, that emphasized cultural sensitivity, cultural knowledge and cultural empathy.

I prefer an approach that identifies seven components. These are *cultural assessment* (a periodic appraisal of one's own individual or agency cultural background and how it may affect practice); *cultural knowledge* (information about different cultures); *cultural sensitivity* (appreciation of other cultures and subcultures); *cultural skills* (methods that are appropriate to use with people from other cultures and subcultures); *cultural encounters* (having direct interaction with people from other cultures and subcultures); *cultural empathy* (the ability to connect on an emotional level) and *initiative* (taking action in some way, if warranted, to deal with a discovered problem/oppression). Some discussions of cultural competency do not include the assessment or initiative components,[9] but I think it is important that both be included as the first raises awareness and the second encourages involvement which might be just a small step in dealing with a potential or actual problem.

A focus on cultural competency could lead to improved communication and, perhaps, changes in attitudes and behaviors. The idea has been seen as so important that a government agency or professional association might mandate that it be taken into consideration or that practitioners in a particular field should all go through some kind of training in cultural competency.

A great deal has been written, particularly in the field of medicine (e.g., Lie 2009; Sue 2006; Wachtler and Troein 2003; USDHHS 2003; Sloand et al. 2004), about cultural competency in terms of steps for improvement, guiding principles and training. Good ideas (e.g., see USDHHS 2003) for programs and other activities often involve respecting diversity, profiling the cultural composition of a community, recruiting workers who are representative of the community, providing ongoing cultural competence training, ensuring that services are accessible, appropriate and equitable, and involving culture brokers (e.g., community leaders and organizations) representing diverse groups. Ægisdóttir and Gerstein (2010, pp. 177–182) think that to be competent in multicultural and international counseling, a program needs to enhance awareness, knowledge, skills and motivation for international learning and experiences.

There are a number of approaches to teaching cultural competency. Sloand, Groves, and Brager (2004, pp. 3–6) identified many of the "traditional (as well as) creative" approaches that have been used by nursing schools. These included coverage in all courses and clinical experiences; on-site experts from several cultures; technology-based curriculum; cultural immersion in national and international settings; student placements in clinical sites with diverse populations; relevant fiction and non-fiction literature is assigned; annual workshops; an annual cultural

[9]Hart et al. (2009, p. 20), for example, present a framework that distinguishes between cultural competence (person actively seeks advice and consultation) and cultural proficiency (person is respectful of cultural differences and proactively promotes improved cultural relations). The framework provided in this chapter includes initiation/being proactive as part of cultural competency.

diversity celebration and a permanent committee on cultural competency to monitor and evaluate all cultural competency efforts.

There are also a number of exercises that have been developed to call attention to and encourage the development of cultural competence in trainings and courses. Some of these are part of mediation materials (e.g., Fisher et al. 2000, p. 44; LeBaron and Alexander 2010) and others (e.g., Ring et al. 2008) come from a number of fields but can be adapted for mediator training and education.

In addition, there are some approaches to assessing or evaluating what has gone on in cultural competency workshops and courses. Lie (2009) discussed the Tool for Assessing Cultural Competency Training (TACCT) that was developed by the Association of American Medical Colleges. The tool has six domains of learning (e.g., health disparities, community strategies, bias/stereotyping, self-reflection) and 42 learning objectives (e.g., define race, ethnicity and culture; identify and collaborate with an interpreter; nonjudgmental listening to health beliefs). Lie (2009, p. 487) thinks the tool can "identify a variety of feasible and appropriate outcome measures to demonstrate curricular effectiveness." And Thom and Tirado (2006, p. 646) developed and validated a 13-statement "Patient-Reported Provider Cultural Competency Scale" that included the following:

- My doctor asks me why I think I got sick.
- My doctor talks with me about traditional healing remedies I may use.
- When discussing diagnosis and treatment, my doctor asks if I would like to include family members in the discussion.
- My doctor asks if I understand his or her instructions, and if I do not, repeats them when necessary.

While cultural competency sounds like an idea that could be very useful,[10] some think the term "competency" is problematic. They have noted that individuals may never become competent in dealing with those from a few, much less all, cultural backgrounds and/or they don't see the need to use the term competency. (Alternative titles for this area within the field of mediation could be, for instance, cross-cultural or intercultural mediation or culturally responsive mediation.[11])

Some have objected to the way cultural competency training is implemented. The critics say this training makes it appear that if you learn certain things you are competent and, the critics continue, there is the danger of reinforcing stereotyping. Anthropologists Kleinman and Benson (2006) think it is better to use an ethnographic approach (one that emphasizes the native's point of view) and ask people (e.g., clients, parties, patients) what they think about a topic (and understand that those answers may or may not be connected to their culture).

---

[10]One trainer (Chun 2010, p. 616), working only in a medical setting in the United States, noted that she "opted for and continues to use 'cultural competence' because it is a term recognized by government agencies, accrediting bodies and other institutions."

[11]The characterization "culturally responsive" comes from a 1996 report by Steven Weller and John Martin that is cited by John Samiento (2000).

Others have objected to the kinds of questions that have been asked after completing cultural competency sessions. As Monk et al. (2008, p. 46) have noted:

> Stereotypical generalizations can still persist, and these perspectives are granted authoritative status in the multicultural literature. For example, in multiple choice licensing exam questions, examinees might still be asked to identify how you would counsel a newly emigrated Egyptian client or a gay client recently infected with AIDS or choose the best approach for counseling African American clients. The simplistic and naive nature of these questions can be deeply offensive. It is as though candidates were being asked how to treat a particular character disorder or psychological problem rather than a person.

Maria Chun (2010, pp. 615–618) described, in detail, problems she had implementing a cultural competency training module as part of a postgraduate training curriculum in a department of surgery. The postgraduate surgery trainees strongly disliked the evaluation component which they thought was "judgmental and hierarchical." There was resistance to self-reflection and many felt the training about cultural competency was a waste of time. The students wanted fewer role plays and less "political correctness." Many trainees and faculty members "had difficulty viewing culture beyond race and ethnicity." The trainees "wanted to simplify culture into concrete "dos and don'ts" for use with patients. The trainees thought if they had "good interpersonal and communication skills, there was no need to learn specific cultural skills." Chun concluded that medical students need to be introduced to culture by discussing their own culture in medical settings, you need institutional and trainee "buy-in" to have effective cultural training, the training initiative has to have a long time frame (not just be a module) and it is helpful to use a validated and standardized assessment tool.

Even though some assessment is taking place, the lack of assessment and evaluation of cultural competency initiatives has been noted. For instance, Frisby (2009, p. 855) wrote:

> that an overwhelming majority of cultural competence articles (across a variety of disciplines) reflect little more than print advertisements for why cultural competence is important..., how it is defined..., how it should be measured..., what professional organizations are doing to make sure you get it..., how to address barriers to getting it..., how to know if you have it..., and problems that are likely to occur if you don't have it... There is a virtual absence in the literature of critical analyses that evaluates evidence for the construct validity of the cultural competence concept.

And, according to Maria Chun (2010, p. 613)," The glow of cultural competency training initiatives is fading in the light of higher expectations for an evidence base prior to acknowledgement that their introduction has had a positive impact."

Cultural Competency and Mediation

Many experts in the field of counseling have suggested that all of counseling is, "to some extent, multicultural" (Monk et al. 2008, p. 30) and professor Allen Ivey (2008, p. 51) has even said that "all counseling and therapy is ultimately multicultural and that failing to be aware of and being unwilling to deal with culture is literally unethical." These authors are using the "more inclusive definition of culture (that) considers lifestyle, gender, and socioeconomic factors in addition to ethnic and racial differences" (Monk et al. 2008, p. 30).

All of mediation can also be said to usually be multi-cultural. As Kaushal and Kwantes (2006, p. 9) have noted, "a person's cultural background will influence every aspect of the conflict process ranging from the goals that are considered incompatible, why they are seen as so, what one chooses to do about it" and the outcome. LeBaron and Zumeta (2003, p. 464) also said that "naming disputes is a cultural act (and) deciding how to frame and respond to them is also completely bound up with culture." And Chia et al. (2004) described mediation practices in the Chinese and Malay communities in Singapore and found that culture affects the design and emphasis of those mediations.[12] For the field of mediation, then, a broad definition of culture is appropriate (including factors such as age, work type, and training), cultures are seen as complex,[13] mediators think culture is a very important consideration[14] and mediation, whether one is dealing with two parties or many groups of people, almost always involves cultural differences.

Research findings have underlined the importance of culture in relation to mediation outcomes in international conflicts. Bercovitch and Elgström (2001, p. 16), for instance, indicated that there is "a very strong relationship between cultural differences and mediation outcomes." The researchers noted that cultural differences led to fewer successful conflict management outcomes in international conflicts and that "cultural differences present some of the most formidable challenges to mediators" (Bercovitch and Elgström 2001, p. 17). And Leng and Regan (2003) analyzed 725 mediation attempts in militarized interstate[15] disputes that occurred between 1945 and 1995. They found mediations were more likely to succeed when parties had similar social (religious) cultures and if parties shared similar democratic political cultures.

Irini Stamatoudi (2009), an attorney who has been a legal advisor about issues related to the illegal trafficking of antiquities, sees culture as a possible "bargaining chip" in negotiations and mediations when countries have culture as an important value. In an article about mediation and cultural diplomacy, Stamatoudi noted that the majority of cases that return artifacts to their place of origin are not

---

[12]In working with Chinese parties, for instance, Chia et al. (2004, p. 461) noted that mediators "use proverbs and ancient idioms to remind parties of the code Zuo Ren, which tends to defuse hostility and pave the way to an amicable resolution."

[13]According to Monk et al. (2008, pp. 49–50), "there are always competing axes of cultural membership and... we cannot reduce these to singular dimensions without creating distortions."

[14]Sociologist Margaret Herrman et al. (2001) identified "cultural and diversity competency" as one of 13 skill areas and "cultural issues" as one of 18 knowledge areas that are important for mediators who intervene in "interpersonal disputes (e.g., community, employment, family or smaller commercial disputes)."

[15]According to Wiegard (2011, p. 6), "interstate... disputes occur when there is a disagreement between government officials (in) two or more sovereign states...."

settled through judicial decisions, but, instead, are resolved through negotiation and mediation. Stamatoudi noted that mediation, by institutional or non-institutional agents, is not a rigid process and so even if a state does not want to return an artifact, agreements may be made, for instance, about "exhibition exchanges, cooperation in research and excavations (or the) creation of museum annexes" (Stamatoudi 2009, p. 116).[16] Stamatoudi (2009, p. 117) also said that "one could argue that mediation and cultural diplomacy (the exchange of ideas and other aspects of culture to foster mutual understanding) are the most promising tools in the area of return of cultural treasures to their countries of origin."

For many mediators, culture is a central concern but they also indicate this can be a very problematic area. A very serious problem, noted by physician/mediator Eleanor Nwadinobi in her discussion of the treatment of widows in Enugu State, Nigeria (Chap. 10), is harmful traditional/cultural practices. According to Kouyaté (2009), there are "thousands" of harmful traditional practices and these include "early/forced marriages; female genital mutilation[17]; massage of the clitoris; lip plates; food taboos; force-feeding; breast ironing; kidnapping/abduction; domestic violence against women; sexual exclusion of wives; sororate and levirate; dry sexual intercourse; trokosi[18]; and widowhood rites." Mediators need to be aware of harmful traditional practices and have approaches to deal with them. Many have noted the importance of seeing these harmful practices as human rights issues. Nwadinobi also notes the "crucial" importance of having traditional rulers, "the custodians of culture," involved in helping "change the status quo."

Cathleen Kuhl (personal communication, September 12, 2011), a court mediator in the United States, mediates different kinds of situations than Nwadinobi, but she also is concerned about cultural matters:

> The issue . . . (of) cultural competency is an important one, and one that has flummoxed me for years. In the past, I have asked others to attend . . . training(s that I give) and address this topic, as I do not feel I am qualified to (be a trainer) in this area . . . . Warning: I am now about to ramble on with many thoughts I have about this topic – (with) precious few conclusions, and I will risk you concluding that I'm a cultural coward. This topic has soooo many angles, and there is so much that could be said, I frankly get overwhelmed just thinking about it . . .
>
> For example, if the two disputants (have) different cultures, that, in and of itself, may contribute to the conflict; that's fairly obvious. If the mediator (has) a different culture

[16]According to Stamatoudi (2009, p. 118), mediation is preferred by parties (rather than going to court) for a number of reasons including the diversity of legal traditions in different countries, high cost of a court case, difficulty of enforcing court decisions, difficulty of providing proof and belief that cases may not be heard because of time limitations.

[17]According to a 2004 (p. 5) World Bank report, "Every year, two million girls are subject to mutilation, which traditional communities call 'female circumcision' and the international community terms 'female genital mutilation' (FGM) or 'female genital cutting' (FGC) . . . It is estimated that 98 % of Somali women and girls have undergone some form of genital mutilation."

[18]Girls "are surrendered to fetish temples to live there and be used as domestic servants or sexual slaves. They are being made to pay for crimes which are said to have been perpetrated by a member of the girl's family or for some social wrongdoing generations before the birth of the girl" (Kouyaté 2009, pp. 4–5).

than the disputants, that could give rise to difficulties in the resolution - mediator just doesn't get it, party/ies distrust of mediator; that's understandable, but how does a mediator know when that is happening as this can be subtle and hard to identify, parties may be reluctant to identify this, etc.? How (can we) create a non-adversarial mediation process in an adversarial legal culture– this one is something I think about and strive to do with various degrees of success. How (do we) respect each disputant's cultural needs when those needs may conflict with a basic tenet of mediation? For example, how (should we) deal with the mediation principle of empowerment when a disputant holds cultural beliefs that appear to run counter to that principle? Then there is the daunting task of learning the multitude of cultural "earmarks." In which culture is it considered improper to make eye contact? In which culture does nodding mean "I'm listening," not "I agree." In which culture is hand shaking not acceptable?

Kuhl is not a "cultural coward," but one who knows this is an important and complex issue and is concerned that cultural matters are being addressed appropriately. This mediator isn't asking for a list of do's and don'ts, like the post-graduate surgery trainees who went through the cultural competency training; this mediator is asking for guidance.

After all, mediators can deal with cultural differences at all points of the mediation process. This includes their trainings, their preliminary conversations with the participants in a mediation and any conflict analysis that might be developed before beginning a mediation. Cultural differences are found in the mediation itself,[19] seen in specific phases of mediations (Brigg 2003, p. 304), need to be considered in drawing up of an agreement, and can even be a factor in the moments after the signing of an agreement.[20] Culture also can be very important in the follow-up (if any) to an agreement[21] and in the mediator's thinking about every action. After a mediation is completed, mediators frequently go over (and over) the specifics of the completed mediation process and its outcome. Culture is frequently a big factor in their thinking. They are concerned, for instance, about whether the process

[19]Some mediation settings may be inappropriate or inhospitable to some parties for a variety of reasons including cultural ones. Weller et al. (2001, p. 195), for instance, noted that few Spanish-speaking litigants entered family mediation in one particular US city and the authors thought that one reason might be that the mediations were held in an "imposing" downtown courthouse rather than in a community setting. Settings also may be comfortable but may be used to influence behavior during a mediation. In the Malay community in Singapore, for instance, a mediation would be held in the home of a wealthier member of the extended family. According to Chia et al. (2004, p. 455), the host "acts as an observer or authority figure" for the mediation and "any misbehavior (violence or verbal abuse) is considered impolite and disrespectful to the host."

[20]For instance, depending on the cultural background and/or emotional state of mediation participants after a mediation agreement has been signed, there are some who may want to hug the mediator. There also may be some people in the room who think, based on their cultural background, that this is a business arrangement and it is not appropriate for the mediator to accept hugs from anyone.

[21]Weller et al. (2001, p. 197) studied Latino families and mediation in one particular city in the US. The researchers noted that Spanish-speaking participants in mediation might want the mediator to help them for a period of time after a mediation agreement is written: "The mediator may serve as an institutional connection for the parties, helping them tie into other social agencies in the community."

was respectful of everyone, whether power issues were addressed[22] and whether the process could have been handled in a better way.

I will use one of these areas – training – as an example of the challenges of dealing with culture. Training can take place in a workshop, course or program. Sometimes trainers have introduced culture as a separate module while others have integrated it throughout the training. The training also might be prescriptive (frequently the case in shorter trainings based on expertise), elicitive (approaches are developed that "respect and build from the cultural context" of those involved in the mediation training) or some combination of the two (Lederach 1995, p. 68, 120). I teach a course in mediation that discusses culture throughout the course. Prescriptive and elicitive approaches are covered and the students are exposed to different mediation models as well as encouraged to combine models and develop new ones.

The 10-week mediation course begins with a discussion of cultural competency and it is a thread that runs through the whole course. Here is a brief description of the cultural competency experience:

> Students each write a short autobiography (including a focus on their experiences with people from different cultural backgrounds) and are introduced to the idea of cultural competency and its seven components. Students are then asked to choose an organization or event that will, based on what they had written in their autobiographies, put them with those who have a culture or subculture that is unfamiliar to them. Some students choose, for instance, religious experiences, union or political meetings, programs for young children, high-level ballet classes, visits to assisted living facilities, or attending self-help (e.g., Alcoholics Anonymous) or advocacy groups. All students write reflective essays about their experiences. At the end of the 10 weeks, those who would like to discuss their experiences do so with the others in the course listening and participating to the extent that they would like to do so.
>
> Some students agonize over which new experience to try. Some pick something very personal (e.g., a drug recovery program) and appreciate that they won't have to discuss their selection with the others in class. Others pick something very personal and absolutely want to discuss this with the class.[23] I was surprised (at first) to find that some students describe this experience as the best learning experience they have had during their university career. Several students have said that this should be a requirement for all college students. I think why this may work (for many students) is that the experience takes place over a fairly long

---

[22]As Monk et al. (2008, pp. 49–50) have noted, "cultural identifications always exist in the context of cultural power relations that are constantly shifting and changing."

[23]One student, for instance, thought her mother was a recovering alcoholic but this had never been mentioned or discussed in the family while she was growing up or after she had moved away from home. She told her mother that she was going to go to a recovery meeting for alcoholics in the city where her university was located. Her mother told her (for the first time) that she was a recovering alcoholic and invited her to come home and attend the regular meetings with her. She met people her mother had known for years and the mother discussed everything with her daughter. I thought for sure that the daughter would not want to discuss this experience with the class. On the day of the discussion, this student was the first to speak about her experience and was actually leaping out of her chair to get the chance to tell the others. The daughter wanted to tell everyone in the class that the exercise not only helped her learn about culture, but how grateful she was for the open discussion that had taken place in her family.

> period of time, culture is a thread that runs through the whole course, no one is forced to talk or share experiences and there are no tests to see if they had, in fact, understood more about a group or changed their attitudes or behavior.

The difference between this course and some of the cultural competency approaches used in the medical school training is basically that the students/trainees in this course are not tested for their growth in competency. They are encouraged to try new cultural experiences over a 10-week period, write about them and then, near the end of the course, there is a discussion of their activities. Courses in a medical setting could be similar in terms of having a longer time frame and encouraging new cultural activities, but medical courses also may include testing for competency.

Training frequently involves the use of role plays. Sometimes cultural differences can make the role plays problematic and ineffective. Here is an example based on a real situation that has been provided by Michelle LeBaron and Nadja Alexander (2010, p. 151):

> Laura and Marie, two newly-minted PhDs in conflict resolution, are engaged by a major international development agency to design training for a court-connected mediation project in Michadja, a fictitious country somewhere outside the west... They want to be sure to deliver a training course that is engaging, clear and so compelling that their Michadjan hosts clamour for their return.
>
> At the outset of the training, they invite a participant, Moses, to participate with them in a role play to demonstrate the dynamics of mediation. Moses had been identified by the hosts of the training as a 'natural mediator' – someone people trust to solve problems. Several of his community members are participants in the training, all from a local indigenous group, along with other non-indigenous participants. Laura asks Moses to play her husband while Marie mediates a dispute about where the two will go on summer vacation. Moses is willing, and both trainers are pleased with his obstinate portrayal. They are elated at this animated start to the training, and ready to keep up the momentum after a break.
>
> But during the break, it becomes clear that all is not well in Michadja. Several of Moses' community members cluster around him, demanding to know whether things are off balance between him and his wife in real life. Faced with his denials, they express disappointed surprise that he chose to take on the identity – even make believe – of another's spouse. It was both disrespectful and inappropriate, they opine, and he realizes he had not thought carefully enough about community norms.

LeBaron and Alexander (2010, pp. 156–157) cite research that indicates that role playing may encourage student interest, increase motivation and result in favorable attitudes, but that it does not result in a significant difference in learning when compared to a more traditional lecture approach. Given the cultural problems that also may be involved in prescribed role playing, LeBaron and Alexander (2010, pp. 158–159) suggest other activities such as real experiences (e.g., taking a field trip for lunch and having the group choose a menu) rather than fictitious ones. Role plays also can be adapted for culturally diverse settings. This approach might involve having the participants identify an appropriate dispute for discussion, asking participants to modify a prescribed role play or designing a role play as close to real life as possible. The bottom line for LeBaron and Alexander (2010, p. 166) is that trainers from the West who are working in other regions of the world should be very cautious in using role plays and supplement any role plays "with a wide variety of experiential activities."

We have only discussed training, one of many possible areas of interest for mediators regarding cultural differences. It still is possible to make a few general points. Culture is a very important topic for mediators, but a difficult one. Mediators understand that culture is a part of our consciousness and does not come in neat boxes.[24] Mediators do not expect to understand everyone's culture, but seek to improve their understanding of cultures and subcultures and the possible (but not inevitable) influence of culture on attitudes and behavior.

Beyond Cultural Competency: Cultural Diplomacy

The field of mediation covers the full range of disputes – from individuals with differences of opinion to international conflicts. For the field of mediation, it may be that "cultural competency" is not the best choice of words as we want to focus on the benefits of enhanced understanding of the complexity and richness of culture. The word "competency" may set the bar too high[25] and without a necessary reason. And as John Paul Lederach (1995, p. 129) reminded us more than 15 years ago, "culture should not be understood by conflict resolvers and trainers primarily as a challenge to be mastered and overcome through technical recipes." Training about culture doesn't lend itself easily to testing to see if one has increased competency and the testing does not seem to be something that has been well-received by at least some trainees.

One concept that we might consider is *cultural diplomacy*. Cultural diplomacy[26] is a broad term that can be defined as the exchange of ideas, information and other aspects of culture between and among individuals and groups in order to foster mutual understanding.[27] And culture is a "vast resource . . . for producing a multitude of approaches and models in dealing with conflict" (Lederach 1995, p. 120) Cultural diplomacy can help create trust, encourage the development of relationships which can last beyond changes in governments or heads of organizations, and is a vehicle for discussion when formal relationships between

[24] As LeBaron and Zumeta (2003, p. 471) have noted: "Cultural competence in process design and practice helps make mediation a welcoming process marked by flexibility, inquiry, sensitivity, and the awareness that in contemporary multicultural society one size does not fit all."

[25] Sue (2006, p. 244) noted, for instance, that "it is difficult to be fully culturally proficient in working with the clients from many diverse groups."

[26] Cultural diplomacy has been considered by some to be "the linchpin of public diplomacy" (US Department of State 2005).

[27] This definition is a variation of the one provided by Cummings (2003, p. 1): "the exchange of ideas, information, art and other aspects of culture among nations and their peoples in order to foster mutual understanding."

groups don't exist or are strained.[28] Because mediators work at all levels (individual through international) and mediation tries to facilitate improved cross-cultural and intercultural understanding and communication, mediation should be considered an important effort in cultural diplomacy.[29]

References

Ægisdóttir, S., & Gerstein, L. H. (2010). International counseling competencies: A new frontier in multicultural training. In J. G. Ponterotto, J. M. Casas, L. A. Suzuki, & C. M. Alexander (Eds.), *Handbook of multicultural counseling* (3rd ed., pp. 175–188). Los Angeles/London/New Delhi/Singapore/Washington, DC: Sage.

Baumgartner, R. J. (2009). Organizational culture and leadership: Preconditions for the development of a sustainable corporation. *Sustainable Development, 17*(2), 102–113.

Bercovitch, J., & Elgström, O. (2001). Culture and international mediation: Exploring theoretical and empirical linkages. *International Negotiation, 6*(1), 3–23.

Brigg, M. (2003). Mediation, power, and cultural difference. *Conflict Resolution Quarterly, 20*(3), 287–306.

Busch, D., Mayer, C., & Boness, C. M. (Eds.). (2010). *Intercultural and regional perspectives on cross-cultural mediation*. Frankfurt am Main: Peter Lang.

Chia, H., Lee-Partridge, J. E., & Chong, C. (2004). Traditional mediation practices: Are we throwing the baby out with the bath water? *Conflict Resolution Quarterly, 21*(4), 451–462.

Chun, M. B. J. (2010). Pitfalls to avoid when introducing a cultural competency training initiative. *Medical Education, 44*(6), 613–620.

Chung, D. (1992). Asian cultural communities. In S. Furuto (Ed.), *Social work practice with Asian Americans* (pp. 274–275). Newbury: Sage.

Cummings, M. C. (2003). *Cultural diplomacy and the United States government: A survey*. Washington, DC: Center for Arts and Culture.

Davidheiser, M. (2010). Human social behavior, cultural perspectives and conflict mediation: A multi-variate analysis of Gambian dispute processing. In D. Busch, C. Mayer, & C. Boness (Eds.), *International and regional perspectives on cross-cultural mediation* (pp. 127–150)). Frankfurt am Main: Peter Lang.

Dresser, N. (1996). *Multicultural manners: New rules of etiquette for a changing society*. New York/Chichester/Brisbane/Toronto/Singapore: Wiley.

Elgström, O. (1994). National culture and international negotiations. *Cooperation and Conflict, 29*(3), 289–301.

Fisher, S., Abdi, D., Ludin, J., Smith, R., Williams, S., & Williams, S. (2000). *Working with conflict: Skills and strategies for action*. London/New York: Zed.

Frisby, C. L. (2009). Cultural competence in school psychology: Established or elusive construct? In T. B. Gutkin & C. R. Reynolds (Eds.), *The handbook of school psychology* (pp. 855–885). Hoboken: Wiley.

Fritz, J. M. (2008). Clinical sociology contributions to the field of mediation. In J. M. Fritz (Ed.), *International clinical sociology* (pp. 85–114). New York: Springer.

[28]These points are based on ones made by the US Department of State's (2005, p. 16) Advisory Committee on Cultural Diplomacy.

[29]However, as LeBaron and Zumeta (2003, p. 471) have noted, mediation is not a "substitute for efforts to address the systemic inequities and injustices that must be ameliorated if fairness and justice are to be part of our multicultural mosaics."

Goldstein, L. J. (1957). On defining culture. *American Anthropologist, 59*(6), 1075–1081.
Hall, E. T. (1976). *Beyond culture*. New York: Random House.
Hart, J., Silva, S., Tein, N., Brown, A., & Stevens, K. (2009). *Assessment of strategies for providing culturally competent care in title x family planning clinics: Final report*. Prepared for the Office of Family Planning, Office of Population Affairs, U.S. Department of Health and Human Services. Altarium Institute.
Herrman, M., Hollett, N., Gale, J., & Foster, M. (2001). Defining mediator knowledge and skills. *Negotiation Journal, 17*(2), 138–152.
Hofstede, G. (1980). *Culture's consequences: International differences in work-related values*. Beverly Hills: Sage.
Ivey, A. E. (2008). Response to chapter 2: Complexity and culture. In G. Monk, J. Winslade, & S. Sinclair (Eds.), *New horizons in multicultural counseling* (pp. 50–54). Los Angeles/London/New Delhi/Singapore: Sage.
Joutsenvirta, M., & Uusitalo, L. (2010). Cultural competencies: An important resource in the industry-NGO dialog. *Journal of Business Ethics, 91*, 379–390.
Kappler, S., & Richmond, O. (2011). Peacebuilding and culture in Bosnia and Herzegovina: Resistance or emancipation? *Security Dialogue, 42*(3), 261–278.
Kaushal, R., & Kwantes, C. T. (2006). The role of culture and personality in choice of conflict management strategy. *International Journal of Intercultural Relations, 30*, 579–603.
Kleinman, A., & Benson, P. (2006). Anthropology in the clinic: The problem of cultural competency and how to fix it. *PLoS Medicine, 3*(10), 1673–1676.
Kouyaté, M. (2009). Harmful traditional practices against women and legislation. Expert paper prepared for a United Nations Expert Group Meeting on good practices in legislation to address harmful practices against women. EGM/GPLHJP/2009/EP.07. May 11.
LeBaron, M., & Alexander, N. (2010). Exporting mediation through role plays: Intercultural considerations in knowledge transfer. In D. Busch, C. Mayer, & C. M. Boness (Eds.), *International and regional perspectives on cross-cultural mediation* (pp. 151–168). Frankfurt am Main: Peter Lang.
LeBaron, M., & Zumeta, Z. D. (2003). Windows on diversity: Lawyers, culture, and mediation practice. *Conflict Resolution Quarterly, 20*(4), 463–472. doi:10.1002/crq.39.
Lecca, P. J., Quervalu, I., Nunes, J. V., & Gonzales, H. F. (1998). *Cultural competency in health, social, and human services: Directions for the twenty-first century*. New York: Garland.
Lederach, J. P. (1995). *Preparing for peace: Conflict transformation across cultures*. Syracuse: Syracuse University Press.
Leng, R. J., & Regan, P. M. (2003). Social and political cultural effects on the outcomes of mediation in militarized interstate disputes. *International Studies Quarterly, 47*(3), 431–452.
Lie, D. (2009). A framework for enhancing and assessing cultural competency training. *Kaohsiung Journal of Medical Science, 25*(9), 486–492.
Monk, G., Winslade, J., & Sinclair, S. (Eds.). (2008). *New horizons in multicultural counseling*. Los Angeles/London/New Delhi/Singapore: Sage.
Moule, J. (2012). *Cultural competence: A primer for educators* (2nd ed.). Beverly: Wadsworth Publishing.
Pearson, J. (2011). *Creative capacity development*. Sterling: Kumarian Press.
Perlin, M. L., & McClain, V. (2009). Where souls are forgotten. *Psychology, Public Policy, and Law, 15*(4), 257–277.
Philip, G., & McKeown, I. (2004). Business transformation and organizational culture. *European Management Journal, 22*(6), 624–636.
Randall-David, E. (1994). *Culturally competent HIV counseling and education*. Rockville: Maternal and Child Health Bureau, U.S. Department of Health and Human Services.
Rice, M. F. (2007). A post-modern cultural competency framework for public administration and public service delivery. *International Journal of Public Sector Management, 20*(7), 622–637.
Ring, J. M., Nyquist, J. G., Mitchell, S., Flores, H., & Samaniego, L. (2008). *Curriculum for culturally responsive health care: The step-by-step guide for cultural competence training*. Oxford/New York: Radcliffe.

Rorie, J. L., Paine, L. L., & Barger, M. K. (1996). Primary care for women: cultural competence in primary care services. *Journal of Nurse-Midwifery, 41*(2), 92–100.
Rosaldo, R. (1993). *Culture and truth: The remaking of social analysis*. Boston: Beacon.
Ross, M. H. (1993). *The culture of conflict*. New Haven: Yale University Press.
Samiento, J. (2000). Culturally responsive alternative dispute resolution for Latinos. Retrieved from http://www.mediate.com/articles/samiento.cfm.
Sloand, E., Groves, S., & Brager, R. (2004). Cultural competency education in American nursing programs and the approach of one school of nursing. *International Journal of Nursing Education Scholarship, 1*(1), 1–8. Retrieved from http://www.bepress.com/ijnes/vol1/iss1/.
Stamatoudi, I. (2009). Mediation and cultural diplomacy. *Museum International, 61*(1–2), 116–120.
Starr, S., Shattell, M., & Gonzales, C. (2011). Do nurse educators feel competent to teach cultural competency concepts? *Teaching and Learning in Nursing, 6*(2), 84–88.
Sue, S. (2006). Cultural competency: From philosophy to research and practice. *Journal of Community Psychology, 34*(2), 237–245.
Swidler, A. (1986). Culture in action: Symbols and strategies. *American Sociological Review, 51*(April), 273–286.
Thom, D. H., & Tirado, M. D. (2006). Development and validation of a patient-reported measure of physician cultural competency. *Medical Care Research and Review, 63*(5), 636–655.
Throsby, D. (2001). *Economics and culture*. Cambridge: Cambridge University Press.
Trefon, T. (2011). *Congo masquerade: The political culture of aid inefficiency and reform failure*. London/New York: Zed.
U.S. Department of Health and Human Services. (2003). *Developing cultural competence in disaster mental health programs: Guiding principles and recommendations.* DHHS Pub. No. SMA 3828. Rockville: Center for Mental Health Services, Substance Abuse and Mental Health Services Administration.
U.S. Department of State. (2005). *Cultural diplomacy, the linchpin of public diplomacy*. Report of the Advisory Committee on Cultural Diplomacy. September. Washington, DC.: U.S. Department of State
Vasquez, M. J. T. (2010). Ethics in multicultural counseling practice. In J. G. Ponterotto, J. M. Casas, L. A. Suzuki, & C. M. Alexander (Eds.), *Handbook of multicultural counseling* (3rd ed., pp. 127–145). Los Angeles/London/New Delhi/Singapore/Washington, DC: Sage.
Wachtler, C., & Troein, M. (2003). A hidden curriculum: Mapping cultural competency in a medical program. *Medical Education, 37*(10), 861–868.
Weller, S., Martin, J. A., & Lederach, J. P. (2001). Fostering culturally responsive courts: The case of family dispute resolution for latinos. *Family Court Review, 39*(2), 185–202.
Wiegard, K. E. (2011). *Enduring territorial disputes*. Athens: University of Georgia.
World Bank (2004). *Female Genital Mutilation/Cutting in Somalia.* Report of the World Bank and the United Nations Population Fund. November 2004. http://www.siteresources.worldbank.org/INTSOMALIA.

Chapter 3
Creativity

Jan Marie Fritz

A few years ago I gave a presentation in the United States to a large group of mediators. At the end, a woman, whom I will call Barbara, stood up to ask a question. Barbara said she was a mediator in a court and that she was required to complete a mediation session in no more than 25 minutes. Some in the audience gasped or laughed when they heard that she was expected to mediate in such a small amount of time. Barbara wanted to know if what she was doing, in that short period of time, could still be called mediation. She had been taught that mediation should meet the needs of the parties and discuss possible solutions. To do this appropriately, she thought it would take more than 25 minutes.

When mediation enters institutional settings such as the work place and court, restrictions are often set for mediators about the approach they must use, the time allowed for mediation and which topics can – or cannot – be included in a final agreement. This brings us to the topic of a mediator having options and what it means when a mediator's creativity is lost or restricted. This chapter discusses creativity, the conditions that foster creativity and the extent to which creativity is part of mediation. Finally, Barbara's question – about mediating in a very short period of time – will be discussed.

J.M. Fritz (✉)
Professor, University of Cincinnati, USA and Senior Research Fellow, Centre for Sociological Research, University of Johannesburg, South Africa
e-mail: jan.fritz@uc.edu

J.M. Fritz (ed.), *Moving Toward a Just Peace: The Mediation Continuum*,
Clinical Sociology: Research and Practice, DOI 10.1007/978-94-007-2885-1_3,

What Is Creativity?

Creativity, essential for innovation,[1] attempts to generate new and useful concepts, ideas, processes, objects, associations or other outcomes. The process entails tolerance or even acceptance of contradiction and, if more than one person is involved in developing ideas, it is useful to include those with a variety of thinking styles. Creativity has been the subject of a great deal of research over the last 50 years (e.g., Treffinger 1986) focusing, for instance, on how individuals can be creative at work, in the arts and sciences, in solving tasks and in marketing; children's creativity; creativity of important scholars, and how people can be encouraged to think creatively (e.g., Taylor 1964; Runco 1986; Runco and Okuda 1988; Runco and Chand 1995; Richards and Wilson 2007; Cropley and Cropley 2009; Unsworth and Clegg 2010; Bilton and Cummings 2010; Hon 2011).

Creativity, like cultural competency, is both a process and an outcome. As Shalley and Zhou (2008, p. 4) have noted, "it is an iterative process, involving reflection and action, seeking feedback, experimenting, and discussing new ways to do things in contrast to just relying on habit or automatic behavior." Shalley and Zhou (2008, pp. 5–6) also found that creativity is an outcome defined as something that is seen as "novel" and "useful" and Gilson (2008, p. 305) has expanded this in saying that creativity "as an outcome … refers to the production of novel and useful products or services by an individual, group or organization."

Jeff Dyer et al. (2011, p. 2, 235) interviewed almost 100 inventors, talked with "founders and CEOs of game-changing companies… (and) studied CEOs who ignited innovation in existing companies" over an 8-year period. They concluded (2011, p. 3):

> Most of us think creativity is an entirely cognitive skill; it all happens in the brain. A critical insight from our research is that *one's ability to generate innovative ideas is not merely a function of the mind, but also a function of behaviors.* This is good news for us because it means that *if we change our behaviors, we can improve our creative impact.*[2]

There has been a lot of discussion about the creative process by itself or as "the steps taken or creative acts that result in (a creative) outcome" (Gilson 2008, p. 305). There are a number of models of this process, generally having three to five stages. Because the models are rather similar, only the one developed by Parnes et al. (1977) is mentioned here. It was chosen because the language is similar, in some ways, to some approaches to mediation. The stages of the creative process in the Parnes et al. model are fact finding; problem finding and defining; idea finding; solution finding and acceptance finding.

---

[1] According to West and Richter (2008, p. 215), "Creativity can be seen as the development of new ideas, while innovation implementation is the application of those new ideas in practice." Using this distinction, it follows that creativity is a necessary prerequisite for innovation. Mann (2011, p. 255) notes that "creativity and innovation are central to thinking and planning for national change and transformation, productivity and performance and social and economic success."

[2] According to Dyer et al. (2011, p. 21), "creative ideas spring from behavioral skills (that individuals) can acquire to catalyze innovative ideas in (themselves) and in others."

What Fosters Creativity?

Charles Prather (2010, p. 30), a management consultant, begins the discussion of creativity in his book by saying that only 20 % of his workshop participants say they are creative. Yet, when he asks how many of them dream at night, almost all indicate they do. Prather says dreams show we are creative and cites Chic Thompson (2007), author of *What a Great Idea!: 2.0*. According to Prather (2010, p. 30), Thompson says, based on informal surveys of his clients, that these are the top 10 places (beginning with the tenth place) *where* we are creative:

10. While performing manual labor
9. While listening to a sermon
8. On waking up in the middle of the night
7. While exercising
6. During leisure reading
5. During a boring meeting
4. While falling asleep or waking up
3. While sitting on the toilet
2. While commuting to work
1. While showering or taking a bath

Prather (2010, p. 30) underlines that "while at work" was not on the list for creative moments, but it should be noted, that at least several of the activities – such as taking part in boring meetings or listening to sermons – could happen in work settings.

Ariella Vraneski (2006), a mediator in Israel, goes further than Prather in assessing the number of people who can be creative. She says all human beings have the ability to be creative. Even if all people have the capacity to be creative, that does not mean this happens or happens easily. Fostering creativity is particularly important in an intervention process and situations have to be examined to see what fosters or hinders creativity or imaginative thinking.

As creativity has been studied for at least 50 years, experts have clear ideas about what is needed. John Adair (2007, p. 36), an expert in leadership development, noted that "chaos, confusion and informality are the seedbeds of creativity." Creativity, according to Debra Gerardi (2001), requires openness, listening, risk-taking, trust, and collaboration. Shalley and Zhou (2008, p. 4) indicated that for an individual to be creative, she or he needed to "engage in certain processes . . . for example, . . . examine unknown areas . . . , seek out novel ways of performing a task, and link ideas from multiple sources." Dyer et al. (2011, p. 3) think that a creative person has to "think different . . . (and) act different." They found that innovators frequently questioned, observed intensely, networked with diverse individuals and constantly were trying things out (experimenting).

Göran Ekvall (1996), based on work he did in the 1980s, identified 10 factors that are associated with creativity: *Challenge* (to what degree are people challenged and emotionally involved in the work), *Freedom, Idea Support, Trust/Openness, Dynamism/Liveliness* of the organization, *Playfulness/Humour, Debates* (different viewpoints/ideas are discussed), *Conflicts* (if personal and emotional tension interfere with work), *Risk taking* (tolerate uncertainty) *and Idea Time*. Prather (2010, p. 112, 128) also added one characteristic to Ekvall's list: *Value diversity of problem-solving style.* The results of problem-solving exercises are improved by including people with different approaches, "backgrounds, abilities and interests."

Based on all of this, it seems a combination of individual characteristics and situations or structures allows/encourages/promotes creative analysis and intervention. This assessment points to the componential theory of creativity. It is similar to some other theories of creativity in psychology and organizational studies,[3] but "with different emphases and somewhat different proposed mechanisms (Amabile and Mueller 2008, p. 35). In this theory, influences on creativity include three within the individual – "*domain-relevant skills* (including knowledge, expertise, technical skills, intelligence and talent in the area of the problem), *creativity-relevant processes* (connected to personality and valuing independence, risk-taking, taking new perspectives on problems, a disciplined work style) and *intrinsic task motivation* (something is of interest to the problem solver rather than undertaken because of extrinsic reward)" – and one factor outside the individual – *the work environment* (Amabile and Mueller 2008, p. 35).

Prather (2010, pp. 32–44) discusses techniques that teams can use to encourage creativity and innovation. These include brainstorming,[4] the ladder of abstraction,[5] and pattern-breaking (or out-of-the-box) thinking.[6] The techniques chosen don't have to be "outside of the box." Perhaps being "on the edge of the box" (particularly if only one person is involved) may be a better place to foster that creative spark combined, of course, with enough room/time/space in the setting for idea development.

Prather (2010, p. 38) also mentioned some possible problems in facilitating creativity. He noted, for instance, that giving a reward for creativity could be problematic if a person who is expected to be creative thinks the reward is for something that the judging panel will find to be acceptable. Prather thinks that when a reward is involved for a creative outcome, that outcome could be "more mainstream and therefore less creative and less innovative."

---

[3] According to Bilton (2007, p. 23), "creativity theory has demonstrated a growing skepticism towards individual trait-based models of creativity of the type propounded in the 1960s. Behaviourist models are criticized for ignoring external conditions."

[4] Brainstorming is a group technique "in which group members freely and spontaneously present ideas, in a positive environment in which critical or negative thinking is suspended" (Prather 2010, p. 33).

[5] A ladder is drawn and an abstract/general concept is written at the top of the ladder and, by asking how something will be done, the group can move down the ladder to specific actions (Prather 2010, pp. 35–36).

[6] Mann (2011, p. 257) says, however, "that attempts to 'teach' creativity as a set of generic rules and principles ('think outside the box') and techniques (e.g., 'do some brainstorming) is irrelevant for genuine creativity but may be useful as a tool for 'everyday creativity', i.e. routine problem-solving."

Does Creativity Need to Be Part of Mediation?

Mediators certainly talk about the creativity of their work.[7] Maria Volpe, a past president of the national mediation association in the United States, in her chapter on police and mediation, cites the work of others (Mayer 2004; McGillis 1997) in noting that mediation's "diverse applications have become increasingly creative" and that "over the years, community-based mediation programs began to creatively and energetically reach out to local organizations and groups." Volpe also thinks mediation is a stimulus that has shown police officers ways to be creative in making talk work. Like Volpe, Steve Mehta (2011) thinks mediation has an effect on participants. Metha said "one of the key things that a mediator can provide for clients is the ability to think creatively." Cheryl Cutrona, a director of a community mediation center, discusses, in her chapter about the mediation centers, her peace theater project. She has told me that this was one of the most creative projects she has put in place. Ron Kelly (Hedeen and Kelly 2009, p. 119), a San Francisco-based mediator, said that he "treated the development of (his) entire mediation practice as an art project, with creativity at the heart of it" and that there is "enormous room for creativity in (the) field (of mediation)." Eleanor Nwadinobi, in her chapter about her mediation work on behalf of widows, reminds us that "creative and innovative approaches that are employed in the process of mediation should be recorded for dissemination."

Public policy mediators – including those who work on environmental matters – think there is a big "opportunity for creativity in their work" (Goldberg and Shaw 2010, p. 247). According to Susan Carpenter (Goldberg and Shaw 2010, p. 247), "the range of creativity can be much greater in the public policy area (than other areas of mediation)... Many (government) agencies (in the United States) are shifting toward a more collaborative practice... and they want a mediator to come in and help them design a conversation so that issues and perhaps potential outcomes can be outlined up front – it's more conflict prevention that intervening." And Lawrence Susskind (Goldberg and Shaw 2010, p. 247) has written:

> the opportunities to be more creative as a public policy dispute mediator arise partly from the fact that there are more issues involved in such conflicts, in comparison to typical commercial disputes, which creates greater opportunity for creative trade-offs, and that mediation is also less a matter of routine in public policy matters.

Howard Bellman (Goldberg and Shaw 2010, p. 248) also thought there "was a greater likelihood of creative problem solving in public policy matters than in business/commercial matters." But he also noted that even if a business case involves a court or administrative agency, there is still a lot of "room for creativity (in the) remedies."

Mediators frequently have stories about the creative outcomes of their mediations. It is not unusual for the parties to agree on points that no one (e.g.,

[7] Abramson and Moore, who run community conferences but are not mediators, write about the creative outcomes in the conferencing process they use with schools in their chapter in this volume. They also indicate that they do not think of mediation as a creative process.

parties, representatives, mediators) had thought of before the mediation. The creative ideas for resolution come out of the exchanges and the process that has been put in place to look for solutions. As examples of creative outcomes, please see the two boxed examples in this chapter. One example comes from Mary McLain (personal communication. April 27, 2011), a former federal mediator in the United States who dealt with employment disputes, and the other from Cathleen Kuhl (personal communication. May 19, 2011), a mediator who works in a court setting.

Example One *I worked for the U.S. government mediating complaints of employment discrimination. Had these complaints been litigated and a finding made for the complaining party, the remedy would be defined by law and precedent. In mediation that precedent is the standard in the minds of the attorneys, but in the eyes of the parties there are more possibilities.*

Once, in an age-discrimination complaint, a 70-year-old, long-term employee was laid off, indisputably because he was of retirement age. While he had talked about retirement, he wasn't quite ready yet. He thought his longevity, expertise and loyalty protected him. And, as he and the owner had a long personal history, his feelings were hurt when he was abruptly let go. The employer thought the selection of this man was a practical solution as it would cause the least harm to the business and the other workers.

The retail business catered to collectors, hobbyists and children interested in the hobby. The employee, like the others in the rather small company, was passionate about this hobby and, as much as anything, very sad about no longer being in the company of like-minded fellows. When the employer began to understand the other man's perspective he proposed, and they settled on, his helping the employee secure an especially coveted and rare piece that, without the employer's assistance, would have been very difficult to obtain.

No precedent recommended this remedy.

Mary McLain

Creativity is not only found in outcomes, however. It also is found in preparatory or preventive work, the design of the process, the approach that is used in mediation, the place the mediation is held, the way in which participants are brought into the mediation, the way in which new information is introduced and the follow-up period after a mediation. While there can be standard ways to handle all of these matters, mediators need to use expertise[8] and intuition to try what they think will be productive. If there is a sponsoring organization of some kind, it's approach needs to be open enough to allow the time and space for the mediator and the mediation to be creative.

[8]According to Mann (2011, p. 257), "Creativity is fundamentally domain specific: creative people are very rarely creative across a range of fields and domains. They are bright, motivated people who are creative through immersion and deep knowledge in a particular domain. This highlights the importance of in-depth knowledge in a domain to be creative."

Example Two *When I think about the value of creativity in the mediation work that I do for the Court, what comes to mind is what I always tell parties about mediation. In mediation, parties do not have to keep the focus of their conflict solely on the "legal" issues and their solutions can often be remedies that the Court would be very unlikely to provide or order. Giving parties the freedom to explore all aspects of the conflict, not just the legal aspects, allows them to be creative in how they frame the conflict and the issues, as well as how they choose to resolve it.*

Let me share with you one story that illustrates this. Many years ago, I mediated a case which involved a violation of a municipal noise ordinance. The parties were neighbors, one lived in an apartment on the first floor and the other lived in the apartment above on the second floor. The First Floor Neighbor (FFN, for short) initiated the complaint, stating that he was a student and could not study because of the noise from the apartment above him; he said it sounded like someone was dropping bowling balls on the neighbor's floor (his ceiling). When this would happen, FFN would bang on the ceiling with a broom handle and sometimes the noise would stop. FFN complained to his landlord about it to no avail and, finally, he called the police several times. Sometimes the noise problem would abate for a while, but start up again later. The Second Floor Neighbor (SFN, for short) was a single parent who worked two part-time jobs and had a 3-year-old son.

In mediation, both neighbors began to talk with each other. Both shared that neither had spoken to each other about the FFN's complaint; FFN and SFN did not know each other. FFN asked SFN what she was doing up above to cause the noise. SFN explained that she had a very active 3-year-old who ran around the apartment a lot, falling down, playing games, bouncing balls . . . ; she wasn't sure what she could do about the noise because she simply couldn't keep her son still all the time.

They realized that their apartments were the same layout, i.e., her living room was above his, her bedroom above his, and so on. They began working on options: SFN making sure her son played in a room not above FFN's study area, a time schedule when SFN would try to keep her son quiet so FFN could study, and SFN suggested she'd try to save up enough money to buy area rugs to put over her hardwood floors to deaden the noise. When SFN made that suggestion, FFN mentioned how much he loved hardwood floors and that his apartment had wall-to-wall carpet. SFN replied that she wished her apartment had carpet, because she worried about her son hurting himself when he fell down on the hard wood. At that point, the FFN suggested to SFN the idea of switching apartments. Since the apartments were exactly the same layout and the same rent, that is what they agreed to do. FFN got the hardwood floors and the quiet he wanted; SFN got the carpet she wanted so her son could play safely and not disturb FFN.

Cathleen Kuhl

The research literature and experience show that creativity is not just in the hands of the mediator, but also in the context in which the mediation takes place. In sponsored mediation settings, for instance, I have been able to talk with participants in advance, design different processes, arrange group site visits for the participants, hold mediations that took more than the expected time (e.g., 2 days rather than 1 day), and introduce expertise (e.g., from an invited guest, through a conference call or through the distribution and discussion of a research paper). All of these were not regular or expected practices in particular mediation settings. None would have been possible without the trust and support of the sponsoring organization, which did not have to be informed about these decisions before or during the mediation.

I believe that mediators think creativity is important at all levels of practice and so I have included the concept in my definition of mediation.[9] I think that something that is centrally important has the possibility of being lost or overlooked if you don't explicitly note its importance.

And What About Barbara's Question?

Barbara had asked if she would still be considered a mediator if she had no more than 25 minutes to do a mediation in a court setting. She, and the audience, obviously had never heard of Ron Kelly (Hedeen and Kelly 2009) and his 30-minute mediations.

Kelly (telephone interview. September 9, 2011) has been a mediator more than 25 years. He teaches periodically with the University of California Berkeley's Continuing Legal Education Program and conducts mediation trainings. He has had a lot of experience mediating cases involving business professionals. He said his reputation drew clients interested in his assistance and that he never was a mediator for an organization that strictly dictated how a case was to be handled or indicated that it should be done in a very short period of time (e.g., a few hours). For the last 11 summers, he has offered mediation at Burning Man, a week-long event in the Black Rock Desert in Nevada that attracts "tens of thousands of participants" and is dedicated to "community, art, self-expression and self-reliance" (http://burningman.com).[10] According to Kelly (Hedeen and Kelly 2009, p.108):

---

[9]If a mediator is working with an organization that is going to put a mediation program in place or redesign a program, it is easier for the company representative to see that creativity needs to be part of the program design when it is part of the definition of the field.

[10]In 2011, the Burning Man event was a featured part of an exhibit about the living frontiers of architecture at Louisiana, the Danish museum of modern art. The exhibit curator, Kjeld Kjeldsen (telephone interview. November 22, 2011) had never been to Burning Man, but an artist, in 2006, had told him about his contribution to the event. Burning Man was described in the exhibit catalog (Louisiana 2011, p. 24) as a place "of alternative dwellings and vehicles that reflect all sorts of utopian ideas of a different world."

> The festival operates with a "gift economy," where participants come (to) give away something they've created or collected. I was so moved. I felt that if I were a salmon fisherman, I would have brought a hundred pounds of salmon to give away as sushi.
>
> I'm a mediator, so I set up a booth to provide mediation services.

Kelly (Hedeen and Kelly 2009, p. 108) said the festival's "emphasis on creativity" led him to design a booth[11] and a process "that would be rapid and focused." Kelly (telephone interview. September 9, 2011) tells all his participants that he facilitates 30-minute mediations for couples and gives coaching to individuals in 15 minutes. (He uses a kitchen timer to keep track of the time.) Kelly said people came to discuss "pretty normal relationship issues with couples and between family members." He described his process in the following way (Hedeen and Kelly 2009, pp. 109–110)[12]:

> When a couple comes in, I explain that first I'll listen to each one for five minutes. I say to one of them, "I'm not going to say anything, I'm just going to listen. I want you to tell me, as open-heartedly as possible, what's going on for you." I do my very best to be fully present with them and to listen with complete attention. I don't say a word. (*He says he might make a hand motion … for instance, to continue talking because there is still more time.*)
>
> Then I turn to the other person: "I don't want you to respond to what the other person said. I want you to tell me as open-heartedly as possible what's going on from your perspective, and I'm just going to listen to you."
>
> Then I explain to the first person, "The next five minutes is very structured. *("It is directive regarding the process, but not the content.")* I'd like you to answer these four questions:
>
> 1. Do you want to solve the problem?
> 2. If you had to put it in one sentence, just for now, what's the problem you want to solve?
> 3. With any problem there are a number of ways you could try to solve it. Some of them will work better than others, some you don't even want to try. I just want you to list some of the ways you could solve this problem." *("I often have to move them through their list without discussion: Suppose you're on a game show and they'll give you $100,000 for each way you can list.")*
> 4. Then in the final minute, I ask, "If you had to pick one just for now—you could pick a different one in five minutes—which one seems best to you
>
> I ask the same questions of the other person. To start the last ten minutes, I usually depersonalize or normalize the conflict. I might say, for example, "This is a very common situation I see here. The extreme conditions can easily ruin anyone's food in an hour," or "Yes, there's a great deal of easily available sex here. It puts a severe strain on many relationships." Then we work to blend together and flesh out the solutions they've

[11]The booth was a tent (enclosed on three sides to provide some shade and protection from blowing sand) with three folding chairs. Over the entrance was a large sign that said "Fighting With Anyone? Help & advice here." Kelly (telephone interview. September 9, 2011) said he really doesn't give advice, "but that is OK on the sign." At the side of the tent entrance was a smaller sign: "The Mediator is in." (Sheppard 2010).

[12]In this quote, there are quotes and comments that appear in parenthesis and italics. These points either appear elsewhere in the Hedeen and Kelly (2009) article or were mentioned by Kelly in the telephone interview on September 9, 2011.

> identified." ("*The point is not to have them come up with the right answer in five minutes; it's to encourage them to brainstorm and select a possible resolution in five minutes.*")
>
> In the last five minutes, if I'm working with only one person, one side of the conflict, I might help them think through how they will approach the other person. I often role-play how they will actually talk with the person they're fighting with.

In describing the work of a mediator, Kelly (Hedeen and Kelly 2009, p. 116), said the following:

> Immediacy speaks to how you need to be flexible and intuitive as a mediator, and the process needs to be fluid. You can have steps, a model, a game plan you think you'll be working from, but after the first ten minutes, the bull's going to leave the chute and you just need to hang on. Being present with parties, observing them to know whether they're sad or angry, or needing more information, or about to walk out—this speaks to the principle that skillful mediation is knowing where the mediation needs to go. And it's the opposite of following a game plan or a recipe.

Kelly (Hedeen and Kelly 2009, p. 118) said he used this 30-minute approach in a number of trainings and that it is a very good training tool for mediators in terms of "listening (and) actively facilitating problem solving." He also thought it "would work well in small claims court with severe time constraints." Although Kelly (telephone interview. September 9, 2011) never mediated in a small-claims court, he said he initially started thinking about developing a short approach to mediation because small-claims mediators enrolled in his training classes and told him that they were under a lot of pressure to mediate quickly.

Both Ron Kelly and Barbara were mediating and conducting the mediations in a short time. There were differences: (1) Kelly chose the 30-minute rule for himself, while Barbara was dealing with a 25-minute system imposed by the court. (2) Kelly told the participants that this mediation will take place in only 30 minutes and they can agree to that or not. A court-imposed time line can make court participants think they have few options because they must agree, or go before a judge or hearing officer. (3) Kelly could make suggestions at the end of a mediation (e.g., for continued mediation, couples counseling) although he says that he never does this (Kelly, telephone interview. September 9, 2011). The court might – or might not – allow Barbara to make suggestions for continued discussion. (4) If the parties in Barbara's case would come to an agreement, Barbara would have to write that agreement and might have to have the agreement approved by a court representative. Kelly (telephone interview. September 9, 2011) never included a written agreement in his 30-minute mediations. (5) Kelly's mediation already requires five additional minutes and, writing an agreement, would add additional time. (6) Kelly's mediations did not end with written agreements, while Barbara's cases could end with a settlement that would be considered final and binding.

Courts, for a variety of reasons, may want mediation done in a short period of time, cases handled in a specific way and no contact with disputants prior to a mediation. Courts may have decided that mediation is less expensive than standard court processes; cases sent to mediation are not complex and so they do not require a lot of exploration; and mediation should not be viewed – by either the mediators or the parties – as a creative process.

The short mediation process that Barbara described might be improved in a number of ways. First, while it can be understandable that the court has a standard approach (as this is easier to explain to mediation participants and meets the court's needs), the process would be improved if the mediator could decide when a situation warrants exceptional handling (e.g., a longer time period). This modification might allow for the creative handling of some cases and better meet the needs of some parties or kinds of cases. Second, participants would be making an informed choice if they understand that the court-backed approach must take place in 25 or 45 minutes but also are told (probably when mediation is first suggested or required) that (a) there are different approaches to mediation and (b) there are other mediation options in the community that would be acceptable (using different approaches and lengths of time). Third, it would support the integrity of the mediation process if the court did assessments periodically about how its process worked for different kinds of parties and cases and implemented changes based on what it found. Fourth, it might be useful to look at Kelly's approach and see if it could be adapted for use in some situations in court or work settings.[13]

Conclusion

The process and the outcome in a mediation, whether it involves two parties or a number of large groups, can be quite creative. Research on creativity shows that time and space are particularly important for the mediator as well as the participants. If a sponsoring organization puts restrictions in place – for instance, limiting time or insisting that only one approach be used with all cases – that can affect the quality of the mediation process and the outcomes. It also means that all participants in a mediation may think this is the only way it can be done.

Göran Ekvall (1996) identified 10 factors associated with creativity in a team or work environment. A number of those factors should be taken into account in assessing the creativity of a mediation process. These are challenge (where mediators are experiencing "joy and meaningfulness" in their work; freedom (independence); time for ideas; support (in this case of any sponsoring organization for the mediation and the mediator) and trust (of the mediator and the process). Charles Prather added diversity of problem-solving styles or, in this case, allowing or encouraging different approaches to mediation and discussions of these approaches by the mediators.

Sponsoring organizations may need to be reminded that mediation is an art and that it is creative in terms of process and outcomes. They also may need to be given some examples of how different mediation processes/circumstances can result in different outcomes. Sponsoring organizations may need to be told about the advantages of a creative mediation process (encouraging listening, empowerment,

[13]There is the possibility that the more mediation organizations or groups of mediators call attention to all these issues, that courts might simply decide to rename the process they use as something other than mediation.

problem-solving, good citizenship, commitment to fulfilling settlement terms and, possibly, caring). They also may need assistance in identifying the variety of designs that foster creative mediation.

References

Adair, J. (2007). *Leadership for innovation* (3rd ed.). London/Philadelphia: Kogan Page.

Amabile, T. M., & Mueller, J. S. (2008). Studying creativity, its processes, and its antecedents: An exploration of the componential theory of creativity. In J. Zhou & C. E. Shalley (Eds.), *Handbook of organizational creativity* (pp. 33–64). New York/London: Taylor & Francis.

Bilton, C. (2007). *Management and creativity: From creative industries to creative management.* Oxford: Blackwell.

Bilton, C., & Cummings, S. (2010). *Creative strategy: Reconnecting business and innovation.* Chichester: Wiley.

Cropley, A., & Cropley, D. (2009). *Fostering creativity: A diagnostic approach for higher education and organisations.* Cresskill: Hampton Press.

Dyer, J., Gregersen, H., & Christensen, C. M. (2011). *The innovator's DNA: Mastering the five skills of disruptive innovators.* Boston: Harvard Business Review Press.

Ekvall, G. (1996). Organizational climate for creativity and innovation. *European Journal of Work and Organizational Psychology, 5*(1), 105–123.

Gerardi, D. (2001). *Developing creativity and intuition for resolving conflicts: The magic of improvisation.* Retrieved from http://www.mediate.com//articles/geradi.cfm

Gilson, L. L. (2008). Why be creative: A review of the practical outcomes associated with creativity at the individual, group and organizational levels. In J. Zhou & C. E. Shalley (Eds.), *Handbook of organizational creativity* (pp. 303–322). New York/London: Taylor & Francis.

Goldberg, S. B., & Shaw, M. L. (2010). The past, present, and future of mediation as seen through the eyes of some of its founders. *Negotiation Journal, 26*(2), 237–253.

Hedeen, T., & Kelly, R. (2009). Practice note: Challenging conventions in challenging conditions: Thirty-minute mediations at Burning Man. *Conflict Resolution Quarterly, 27*(1), 107–119. doi:10.1002/crq.250.

Hon, A. (2011). When competency-based pay relates to creative performance: The moderating role of employee psychological need. *International Journal of Hospitality Management, 31*(1), 130–138.

Louisiana Museum of Modern Art. (2011). *Living: Exhibit (June 1 – October 2, 2011) catalog.* Humlebæk: Louisiana

Mann, L. (2011). Creativity and innovation: Principles and policy implications. In L. Mann & J. Chan (Eds.), *Creativity and innovation in business and beyond: Social science perspectives and policy implications* (pp. 254–269). New York/London: Routledge.

Mayer, B. (2004). *Beyond neutrality: Confronting the crisis in conflict resolution.* San Francisco: Jossey-Bass.

McGillis, D. (1997). *Community mediation programs: Developments and challenges.* Washington, DC: US Department of Justice, Office of Justice Programs.

Mehta, S. (2011, May). *Obstacles to creativity in mediation.* Retrieved from http://stevemehta.wordpress.com/2011/05/18/obstacles-to-creativity-in-mediation/

Parnes, S. J., Noller, R. B., & Biondi, A. M. (1977). *Guide to creative action.* New York: Charles Scribner's Sons.

Prather, C. (2010). *Manager's guide to fostering innovation and creativity in teams.* New York: McGraw-Hill.

Richards, G., & Wilson, J. (Eds.). (2007). *Tourism, creativity and development.* London/New York: Routledge.

Runco, M. A. (1986). Divergent thinking and creative performance in gifted and nongifted children. *Educational and Psychological Measurement, 46*(2), 375–384.
Runco, M. A., & Chand, I. (1995). Cognition and creativity. *Educational Psychology Review, 7*(3), 243–267.
Runco, M. A., & Okuda, S. M. (1988). Problem discovery, divergent thinking, and the creative process. *Journal of Youth and Adolescence, 17*(3), 211–220.
Shalley, C. E., & Zhou, J. (2008). Organizational creativity research: A historical overview. In J. Zhou & C. E. Shalley (Eds.), *Handbook of organizational creativity* (pp. 3–31). New York/London: Taylor & Francis.
Sheppard, Bob (2010). *Mediating at Burning Man, 2010: Getting to the authentic core and finding freedom.* Retrieved from http://sheppardlaw.com/rjs_m.htm
Taylor, C. W. (1964). *Widening horizons in creativity.* New York: Wiley.
Thompson, C. (2007). *What a great idea! 2.0: Unlocking your creativity in business and in life.* New York: Sterling.
Treffinger, D. J. (1986). Research on creativity. *Gifted Child Quarterly, 30*, 15–19.
Unsworth, K. L., & Clegg, C. W. (2010). Why do employees undertake creative action? *Journal of Occupational and Organizational Psychology, 83*(1), 77–99.
Vraneski, A. (2006). Al di là dell'arte e della scienza: Cultra e creativita nella mediazione. (Beyond art or science: Creativity and culture in interactive mediation). In L. Luison (ed), *La Mediazione come strumento di intervento sociale* (pp. 58–80). Milano: FrancoAngeli.
West, M. A., & Richter, A. W. (2008). Climates and cultures for innovation and creativity at work. In J. Zhou & C. E. Shalley (Eds.), *Handbook of organizational creativity* (pp. 211–261). New York/London: Taylor & Francis.

Chapter 4
Mediation Models, Theories and Approaches

Jan Marie Fritz

Mediation, a non-adversarial, flexibly-structured, creative process in which one or more individuals help disputants (Fritz 2004), is tied to many disciplines and available in many different kinds of settings. The mediator can be, for example, a labor negotiations specialist, a clinical sociologist working in a court, an elder in a tribe, a diplomat, a minister or a lawyer and can work, for instance, with individuals, families, neighborhoods, warring factions in a country and/or countries.

As mediators have very different areas of practice and different disciplinary backgrounds, it should be no surprise to find that they also have different models, approaches and theoretical views. Some of the models, approaches and theories have been adopted as a result of the emphasis in mediation training while others come from disciplinary education, work experiences, personal values, culture, affiliations, mediation program requirements or are the result of a combination of influences.

Sometimes the mediator's model, approach to mediation and/or theoretical view – like politics, religion or national identity – may be more "the hand that was dealt" rather than something that was chosen. For instance, a consulting group offers mediation training in a country that has no tradition of formal mediation and the mediators trained in the host country think that the consulting group's approach to mediation is the only approach or the best approach. Another example might be a case in which an employee of an organization or a volunteer is trained as a mediator

---

This chapter is based on two earlier publications: "L'approccio al conflitto: il ruolo della teoria nella mediazione" (Approaches to Conflict: Social Theory and Mediation) (Fritz 2006, pp. 24–36) and "Derriere la magie: Models, approaches et theories de mediation" (Behind the Magic: Mediation Models, Approaches and Theories) (Fritz 2004).

J.M. Fritz (✉)
Professor, University of Cincinnati, USA and Senior Research Fellow, Centre for Sociological Research, University of Johannesburg, South Africa
e-mail: jan.fritz@uc.edu

J.M. Fritz (ed.), *Moving Toward a Just Peace: The Mediation Continuum*, Clinical Sociology: Research and Practice, DOI 10.1007/978-94-007-2885-1_4,

but only is shown one approach to mediation. In these cases, it might be very difficult for the new mediator to evaluate different models, approaches or theories.

This chapter identifies some of the major approaches used by professional mediators – working independently or in teams – in the United States. It also identifies some of the theoretical underpinnings of those approaches, identifies models that can be used by those with different approaches, provides a rationale for understanding the approaches and includes some information about mediation in other countries.

Mediation Models

Models explain how practitioners should function. According to Lang and Taylor (2000, p. 101):

> Models represent appropriate, aspirational, or best practices; they include guidelines for implementing them. Most novice mediators learn a particular model and approach to mediation that encompasses guidelines, rules, procedures, and ways of understanding mediation practice . . .

Stage models are frequently used by mediators particularly for workplace and community disputes. One such model, according to Jennifer Beer (1997), author of *The Mediator's Handbook*, has seven stages: opening statement; uninterrupted time for each person to speak; exchange (arguing and discussion); setting the agenda (for discussion/resolution); building the agreement; writing the agreement and closing. Beer mentioned that separate meetings (small caucuses of some participants and/or the mediator and one or more participants) can be held at any time during the mediation. Another model, developed by Jacqueline Morineau (1998, pp. 83–88) has three stages: theory, crisis and catharsis. Lascoux (2001, pp. 161–167) discussed a six-stage model with the first stage ("création de context") being "la plus delicate et la plus longue" (the most delicate and longest). And Haynes (1994) described a five-stage family mediation model in which the mediator continues to cycle through the stages as often as necessary. During the first stage of this model the mediator gathers, verifies and shares the data.

It should be noted that the stages in stage models are frequently not distinct and that stages will differ depending on factors such as culture, mediator choice, party or sponsor preference, type of mediation and complexity of case. Some models may be ones in which no or few stages are specified or expected while other models have many stages. A complicated environmental dispute in a community, for instance, might begin with a period in which possible participants are identified and discuss the likelihood that all will participate in some kind of conflict analysis gathering. This group might then hold a series of facilitated sessions in which procedures are developed and approved that would be used in a mediation. All this preliminary work would take place before an actual mediation. Christopher Moore (2003, pp. 67–69), in his 12-stage model of mediation, devotes the first five stages to the period *before* the formal mediation actually takes place.

It is beyond the scope of this short chapter to identify all of the models used by mediators. It would be a useful exercise to do so, however, and particularly to examine the models in terms of cultural differences. Even if there was one model that could be used in all or most situations, it should be expected that there will be differences in the length of time devoted to certain stages given the wide range of cultures (within as well as between groups) and there may be differences in the stages in terms of order as well as importance. There also could be differences in the way a stage is defined, introduced or developed. And the way mediators and organizations that hire mediators rely on the models will not be the same. The models each provide a general flow for cases but there will be a range in their use – from those who rigidly follow a prescribed model to those who would not think of doing so.

Some Basic Considerations About Theory

Theory, in its broadest sense and as it is used here, refers to attempts to understand the causes and nature of a topic. Theory can attempt to address questions of a "small scope" (e.g., why an individual acts in a certain way) as well as can be seen as a world view – one's lens on how the world is functioning. Theory gives a scientist or practitioner a focus; it defines what is interesting and relevant. In doing so, it also excludes elements that are not seen as central. Theory allows us to understand and move forward in our understanding, but the cost of moving forward may be that certain considerations are diminished or left out completely. We are concerned here with not only with the focus but what has been diminished or disregarded.

Disciplines and areas of practice may view "theory" as more or less important. Some disciplines or practice fields anoint those who focus on theory so much so that it seems that members of the fold do not critically examine whether what the theorists ("high priests") have to say is true, relevant, insightful, meaningful or even helpful. Other disciplines may give lip service to the importance of theory while some disciplines or practice areas may spend little, if any, time discussing theory. We are looking here to understand the field of mediation's interest in theory and the relation of theory to practice.

A few additional points should be mentioned about theory in relation to social conflict and, particularly, mediation of disputes. First, in any discipline or area of practice, there may be one or primarily one theoretical approach (or paradigm) and it may be held implicitly or explicitly. Other disciplines and practice areas that are multidisciplinary or interdisciplinary, like mediation, may be multi-paradigm or multi-theoretical, with a range of theories to draw on and with at least some of them offering competing theoretical explanations. Second, models or frameworks (which explain how practitioners should function) may be explicitly connected to certain theoretical approaches, but they also may be presented as if they were almost without theoretical connections. The latter generally has been the case in mediation. Third, theories have different levels (micro, meso, macro) of explanation.

In disciplines and practice fields like mediation that cover more than one level, there is a need to integrate theoretical approaches. Fourth, it is particularly important to critically examine the use of both implicit and explicit theories by practitioners to assess the affects on the practice as well as the participants.

Theoretical Explanations of Social Conflict

Social conflict is opposition based on real or perceived competing interests (e.g., power), dissimilar identities and/or other differences (e.g., resources, values). Social conflict has been more or less important from the standpoint of different social science theories. Some social science theories, such as structural-functional systems approaches or interactionism (including symbolic interaction, dramaturgy and phenomenology), may not focus on conflict and, in fact, may give it little consideration. Other theories, such as Marxian conflict theory, feminist disability theory or liberationist theory, see conflict as centrally important.

It should be noted that theoreticians from different disciplines may define conflict and aggression in different ways and may differ in assessing and prioritizing relevant factors. For instance, "psychologists tend to explain aggression within a scheme of psychological causes, whereas ethologists will advocate a more biological foundation" (Brennan 1998, pp. 36–38).

The focus in this section of the chapter is on some of the more important theoretical perspectives that explicitly are connected to understanding social conflict and also on some theories which might pay less attention to conflict but are connected to the approaches used by mediators. I briefly will describe selected perspectives under the categories of biological, individual, ecological and social theories.

Biological Theories

Six theories, identified as far back as the mid-1800s, are mentioned here. They are included in this category because they emphasize, or consider as basic, biological factors in conflict.

Darwinism

Charles Darwin (1809–1882), now known as the parent of evolutionary biology, explained biological change by the idea of natural selection. Darwin thought that only those who adapted to the environment would be able to survive and live to reproduce (Van Wyhe 2002).

Social Darwinism/Evolutionary Theory

Herbert Spencer (1820–1903) was thinking about evolution and progress before Darwin published *The Origin of Species* in 1859. A sociologist-philosopher, Spencer was as well known as Darwin during the Victorian era. Spencer used the idea of "survival of the fittest" in social as well as biological analyses (Sweet 2004). Social Darwinists, those who applied Darwin's principles to human societies, focused on the roles that conflict and competition played in all levels of human interaction. Humans were thought to have "an inborn tendency toward aggression" so that they could survive (Schellenberg 1996).

Psychoanalytic Theory

Sigmund Freud (1856–1939), the parent of psychoanalysis, thought that the id (instincts) and the superego (conscience) were in conflict within the individual. The ego, the rational decision-making part of the individual, could be expected to keep the id and superego in check. Freud thought that sexual and destructive instincts were a part of each individual's id, and it would not be possible to eliminate all aggressive impulses in humans (Schellenberg 1996). Psychoanalysis is both theory and practice.

Ethology

Ethology is the scientific study of animal behaviour in natural settings. Ethologists have conducted studies that provide information about inherited predispositions to social behaviour. Many ethologists see "aggression within any species" as strongly rooted in genetic inheritance (Schellenberg 1996) and Konrad Lorenz (1996) noted that humans, because of intra-species aggression (killing of one's own species), are more aggressive than any other animal.

Sociobiology

The term sociobiology was first used by Edward Wilson in 1975. Sociobiologists see aggression as genetically based but that there is variability among the species. Human aggression is more likely to be found where there is population concentration. Aggression is not described as instinctual but rather as a natural response to specific kinds of situations.

Cognitive Neuroscience

Cognitive neuroscience, a term coined in the late 1970s, refers to the scientific study of biological layers (the nervous system, particularly neural layers of mental processes) that underlie cognition (e.g., mental processes such as perception, memory, judgment and reasoning) (Society for Neuroscience 2011). Cognitive neuroscience is "an interdisciplinary approach to understanding the nature of thought" (Cognitive Neuroscience Society 2011). Scientists in this area have begun to look at neural processing of information in relation to the resolution "of conflicts between competing social cues" (Zaki et al. 2010, p. 8481).

Individual Theories

The five perspectives discussed here primarily are connected to psychology; the fourth, social exchange, is also connected to economics and sociology. The first perspective involves both theory and practice

Psychotherapy

Psychoanalysis (mentioned above under Biological Theories) developed from a medical model but "now has yielded to large degree to numerous other forms of psychotherapy... (which may focus on reducing or resolving) negative feelings and actual or potential conflicts" (Gabel 2003, pp. 326 & 310). While the group forms of psychotherapy (e.g., brief, supportive, psychoeducational, family, marital, couples therapy) "frequently rely on techniques that were developed from work with patients in individual psychotherapy" (Gabel 2003, p. 320), new techniques have been added and the group itself is used to help reduce or resolve conflict and foster psychological change. Psychotherapists use different psychological theories (e.g., psychoanalysis, gestalt, client-centered) in their work.

Frustration and Aggression

In 1939, John Dollard and his colleagues wrote about the relationship between frustration and aggression. These researchers were trying to translate some of Freud's psychoanalytic concepts into learning theory. Researchers have found that aggression doesn't always develop when a goal is blocked (frustration) but it does increase the possibility. Cognitive aspects (such as interpreting an event as frustrating and identifying targets) are considered critical by those who continue to examine the links between frustration and aggression.

Cognitive Frame Theory

Cognitive frame theory, developed by Minsky (1975) in the field of artificial intelligence, has "roots in Bartlett's (1932) schema theory of memory" (Dewulf et al. 2009, p. 158). This theory "focuses on cognitive frames as mental structures that facilitate organizing and interpreting incoming perceptual information by fitting it into already learned schemas or frames about reality (Dewulf et al. 2009, p. 158). The "cognitive-representational" theory focuses on the way people "experience, interpret, process or represent issues, relationships and interactions in conflict settings" and notes that frames "shape and limit our understanding." The dynamics of conflicts are "frequently distorted because of biases and breakdowns in accurate information processing" (Dewulf et al. 2009, p. 160).

Social Learning

Social learning theorists believe that observational learning or modeling is what introduces us to aggression and violence (Bandura 1973). Of particular interest here are the conditioning patterns that reinforce aggressive and violent behavior.

Social Exchange

Social exchange is the analysis of the behavior with a focus on individual efforts to maximize profit and avoid costs. Variations of this theoretical approach include behaviorism, utilitarianism, and rational choice as well as an effort to examine the power dimension of exchange relationships at both micro and macro levels of social organization. Exchange theorists often see individuals in terms of conflict. However, only a few see conflict theory (discussed below under Social Theories) as a kind of exchange theory in which there is an unequal exchange of resources (Turner 2001).

Ecological Theory

Land Ethic Theory

This theory begins with the thinking of all those cultural groups (e.g., Native Americans) that saw holistic relationships among the land, water, air and all forms of life. The theory is most beautifully and memorably put on paper by Aldo Leopold (1887–1948). Leopold thought the "land ethic" was that each individual is a member of a community of interdependent parts in which the individual both competes but also has reasons to cooperate. Leopold (1949, p. 204) wrote that "the land ethic simply enlarges the boundaries of the community to include soils, waters, plants, and animals, or collectively: the land." Leopold (1949, p. 204) indicated that "a land ethic changes the role of Homo sapiens from conqueror of the land-community to plain member and citizen of it. It implies respect for (one's) fellow members and also respect for the community as such." This theory is about plain competition/selection/respectful cooperation while at the same time it is liberationist and political.

Social Theories

The first of the eight perspectives discussed here connects a number of social theories to practice. The other seven theories each have strong ties to at least a couple of fields such as psychology, sociology, literary criticism, women's studies, and/or business management.

Sociotherapy

Sociotherapists, like psychotherapists, may work with individuals and groups. According to Straus (2002, p. 381), sociotherapy includes "counseling and other change activities (that focus) on individuals as group members or in small groups." Sociotherapists have different theoretical approaches (e.g., humanist, symbolic interaction, systems, conflict, liberation) but usually the central approaches have a group or role-relationship focus rather than on what is wrong with the individuals. Sociotherapists treat "personal and interpersonal problems (based) on the principle that the problem of an individual cannot be understood outside of its social context" (Straus 2002, p. 107). Sociotherapists usually combine social and individual approaches to increase clients' understanding of conflicts and explore possibilities for change.

Framing as Interactional Co-construction

Framing "as interactional alignments or co-constructions" is connected to Bateson's (1954) work on meta-communication "in which framing is about exchanging cues that indicate how ongoing interaction should be understood" (Dewulf et al. 2009, pp. 160, 158). Frames are developed and may "shift within even short stretches of interactions." Conflict is seen as "neither a state of the world nor a state of mind, but a phenomenon that resides in the social interaction among disputants" and resolving conflicts "consists primarily in finding new alignments in the interaction among those involved" (Dewulf et al. 2009, p. 161).

Structural-Functionalism

Structural-functionalism, frequently identified as a systems approach, sees phenomena in terms of systems of relationships. Systems analysts focus on the integration within a unit (e.g., family, organization, society). Systems are seen as rather stable and change relatively slowly, only when it's necessary or adaptive (Straus 2002, pp. 26–29). Conflict might be seen as contributing energy within an organization or society but, at base, conflict is viewed as disruptive to integration and order.

Marxian Conflict Theory

Marxian conflict theory, notably connected to the work of Karl Marx (1818–1883), begins with the assumption that societies are characterized by inequality and that inequality gives rise to conflict. Conflict theorists see conflict as the central feature of a system. According to Marx, the source of conflict in modern times was the growth of capitalism and the heart of that conflict was the class struggle between owners and workers.

Multicultural Liberationist Social Theory

Multicultural liberationist social theory (e.g., African American, Latino/Latina, feminist, Native American, queer theory) rejects "universalistic theories that tend to support those in power" (Ritzer 2000). Multicultural/liberationist social theorists are inclusive and want to make systems more diverse and open. Theory is offered on behalf of those without power and these theorists try to wake up the social and intellectual world. According to Harding (2004, p. 3), "race, ethnicity-based, anti-imperial and queer social justice movements routinely produce standpoint theories." A standpoint theory views social reality from a socioeconomic position from which action can be taken.

Disability Theory

Definitions of normal are socially constructed. Disability theory recognizes the marginalization and the stigma of those who do not fit within the definition of normal.[1] Feminist disability theory (e.g., Wendell 1989; Mays 2006; Ali et al. 2011) notes there are intersecting sources of oppression and disempowerment for someone who is both female in a male- dominated society and also has a disability in a society that is "dominated by the able-bodied" (Wendell 1989, p. 105).

Humanism

Humanism is an "ethical, scientific and philosophical outlook" that is said to have "changed the world" (Kurtz 2000). The emphasis in humanism is on individual choice of "values and meaning . . . within a social and cultural context" (Glass 1972), and it has provided a framework for universal human rights (Kurtz 2000). According to John Glass (1972):

> The main task of humanistic sociology . . . would be to ask which institutions and social arrangements, supported by which values and norms, promote the capacity and ability of

---

[1]Disability studies is a "field . . . within the critical genre of identity studies" (Garland-Thomson 2003, p. 7).

> groups and individuals to make free and responsible choices in light of their needs to grow, to explore new possibilities and to do more than simply survive.

Glass and Staude (1972) noted that humanistic sociology should not be seen as just another theoretical framework but rather it can be basic to and employed with all of the theoretical frameworks. Humanism involves creating conditions to increase the "capacity and ability" (Glass 1972) of all people to make responsible choices including choices about the living and nonliving in our environment (Fritz 2002).

Postmodern Theory

Postmodern theory, emerging at some point in the 1980s (Klages 2003), is sometimes defined by what it opposes – characteristics of the modern way of thinking. Postmodernism celebrates fragmentation and replaces big "stories" that explain everything with stories that explain that which is small (e.g., local events, the situational, the temporary). No claim is made for universality, reason or stability. Postmodern theory is not only important in itself but also because of the reactions to it. The debate between those who have developed and advocated postmodern theory and those who strongly criticize it revived interest in social theory in general (Ritzer 2000).

Mediation Approaches and Theories

Individual mediators, teams of mediators as well as mediation programs (whether independent or housed in organizations) all have their own approaches to the art of mediation.[2] Sometimes there is a very good fit (e.g., an independent mediator in private practice has independent clients who are very satisfied with the approach used by the mediator), but sometimes there is a rather poor fit. For example, a company may insist that its own mediator, as an employee of the company, only use the one approach to mediation that has been approved by the company while the mediator thinks the approach needs to be modified for different situations (e.g., two colleagues who are old friends are involved in a work dispute; an employee has been fired; the company wants a written agreement but those involved in a dispute do not; or a judge has sent a court case that originated within the company back to the company for mediation).

In addition to the different approaches, there are important differences in the context and conditions in which mediations take place. Among the many issues and

[2]Alexander (2008) discussed six approaches: expert advisory mediation, settlement mediation, facilitative mediation, wise counsel mediation, tradition-based mediation and transformative mediation.

conditions: mediation when an authoritarian ideology is involved with strong views on politics, democratic processes, religion, age and/or gender; the maximum time allotted for mediation is very short; the job security of the mediator is in question; one or more parties may feel forced to take part in the mediation and community elders/leaders (insiders) are the mediators.

One of the most important considerations in the appointment of a mediator, is whether the mediator is to be an outsider (an approach most frequently used in the United States) or is, in some way, connected to the conflict or dispute. Moore and Woodrow (2010, p. 414), for instance, identified five kinds of mediators: *social network mediators* who are "trusted individuals" who are part of the "parties' social network" who "may or may not be totally impartial" but thought to be helpful; *benevolent mediators* " who are respected high-status . . . individuals whom disputants go to for advice and help in developing acceptable agreements;" *administrative or managerial mediators* who are individuals who have "formal positions in organizations" and the authority to make "decisions about contested issues," but prefer to "assist disputants to negotiate their own agreements within parameters prescribed by the organization;" *vested interest mediators* who are "powerful . . . and not neutral toward disputants or impartial regarding issues . . . , have a strong interest in the outcome of a dispute, and encourage, cajole, or coerce parties to agree;" and *independent mediators* who are "neutral regarding their relations with parties and impartial regarding issues in dispute, who provide process assistance and, on occasion," provide relevant information "and independent substantive advice" (p. 414). In discussing the outsider or insider approach to mediation, it also can be useful, particularly for certain kinds of national or international disputes, to use additional terminology to describe the mediation. Wan and Wan (2008), for instance, discuss *Mediators* (mediators with a capital "M" are official mediators) and *mediators* (community members who pave the way for official mediation).

Wan and Wan (2008), and many others, have discussed mediation *tracks*. For instance, in addition to track one (official) mediation, Diana Chigas, in her chapter in this book, identifies three non-governmental, third-party intervention levels: track one-and-a-half (unofficial interventions with decision makers), track two (unofficial interventions with unofficial actors) and track three (interventions at the grassroots level).

The following list of approaches to mediation – including the identification of some theoretical underpinnings – is intended to serve as a starting point for the discussion of mediation approaches in different countries. It is assumed that mediation is relatively voluntary (e.g., even if managers are required to take part in mediation, they can decide whether they wish to settle a matter) and conducted under rather democratic circumstances (e.g., constraints of the program should still allow a range of issues to be discussed and resolved). It also is assumed that a mediation approach might be used as a sole or only choice or that approaches could be combined in different ways.

Participant-Centered. This approach generally uses a stage model and focuses on what the parties would like to achieve through the mediation process. This may mean, for instance, that the parties want to understand each other better and/or want to reduce or resolve the issue or issues that brought them to mediation. The mediator generally acts as a facilitator. The approach is connected to humanism and, at times, may be connected to psychotherapy or sociotherapy. The latter is true particularly with therapeutic models of family mediation (Taylor 2002, p. 120).

Group/Tradition-Centered. This collectivist approach focuses on what the group has traditionally expected and/or wants now. The group's traditions/concerns are seen as more important than individual desires. Confidentiality is often less important or not a concern with this approach, the mediation may take place in a public setting and achieving a resolution for the dispute probably is very important. The mediator is likely to be a prominent or leading figure in the group and may have some connections to one or all parties. The group/tradition-centered approach is sometimes seen as a marked contrast to what has been called "modern mediation or independent mediation" (Black 2001, p. 13). This approach can be connected to systems theory.

Solution-Oriented. This approach uses a stage model and the mediator may be (basically or solely) facilitative or directive. The mediator may take part in the problem solving and, if acting in a directive way, even "push" toward a solution. The solution has the agreement of the parties, but the mediator may have had a strong hand in reaching the solution. The solution-oriented approach is strongly connected to utilitarianism, behaviorism, social exchange and rational choice but also to structural-functionalism, a systems approach in which conflict can be viewed as a disruption.

Change-Oriented. This approach focuses on change and incorporates a number of initiatives that might be separate or combined. The first initiative is one that emphasizes prevention. The mediation approach would focus on how a problematic situation could be avoided in the future. The second initiative would emphasize therapy or transformation. The approach not only would help participants understand what has happened but would focus on changing individuals' attitudes and/or behavior. Transformative approaches focus on changing participants by encouraging empowerment and recognition. In the transformative approach proposed by Bush and Folger (2004), the dispute (and its resolution) is less important than parties changing their attitudes. The parties have the responsibility for outcomes and the mediator is a facilitator who has faith in the parties to develop their mediation process. This approach can be characterized as humanistic, focused on improving communication and change-oriented. Della Noce et al. (2002, p. 50) have indicated that this approach is related to a social/communicative view of human conflict in the discipline of communicative science. If an organization insists that a transformative approach be used in mediations, the approach may also be connected to structural functionalism.

Narrative. The mediator works with the parties to develop a story about their conflict (Winslade and Monk 2000, 2002). The parties' original stories are then taken apart and replaced with a new co-constructed story. Winslade et al. (1998, pp. 38–39) summarized the key points of narrative mediation as follows:

> (1) Listening to the stories; (2) Deconstructive inquiry; (3) Searching for unique outcomes; (4) Building a counterplot; (5) Generating options; (6) Documenting change (The new story is documented in an agreement and/or in letters to the participants.); and (7) Reviewing a new history (Later, a review is held of how the understandings and agreements reached in the mediation have evolved in practice.)

The narrative approach is related to post-modern thought[3] (in which there is no objective reality but multiple realities) and humanism. The stories that result from using this approach should be based on understanding, respect and collaboration rather than on individual interests. This approach could be used on its own or with other mediation approaches including a change-oriented process.

Humanist Integrated Process (HIP). The HIP mediator generally is participant-centered but flexible about the approach used in mediation. The mediator is reflective and is expected to continually assess the interaction between/among the parties and among the parties and the mediator. Depending on the circumstances of the mediation, the mediator will integrate aspects of any of the mediation approaches listed here. This approach is similar to what Vraneski (2004) has identified as an interactive approach except HIP has an explicit connection to humanism.

The HIP approach is frequently based on a particular view of humanist theory. This humanism, focusing on free and responsible individual choices, is neither anthropocentric (human centered) or biocentered (moral consideration given to all living things). This form of humanism includes respectful consideration of the natural environment and fits very well with Aldo Leopold's (1949) land ethic theory.

Attention is given to the context or structure in which the parties' actions have been taken. If the parties are interested, there may be discussion of actions that can be initiated – by the represented individuals, departments, organizations and/or communities – to prevent, reduce and/or resolve certain conflicts. This fits well with what has been called social mediation.[4]

The HIP tradition, like several of the other approaches, is based on humanism. Humanism is mentioned in the title of this approach so that humanism is neither diminished nor overlooked. The mediators using the HIP approach also may have strong connections to multicultural/liberationist theory and they can have something in common with certain practices of sociotherapists.

---

[3]According to John Winslade (2006, p. 502), "The social constructionist perspective (used here)... is one of the most thoroughgoing articulations of postmodern ideas in psychology."

[4]According to Sweden's Erik Wennerstrom (2000, p. 18), "social mediation is a way of solving conflicts at an early stage, perhaps before they reach the level of overt conflict... France (has)... made us all rethink the different levels and stages of intervention, by launching the concept of social mediation. It covers a series of events starting at root causes, through conflict reduction to conflict management, which in fact is something more comprehensive than the concepts of mediation and prevention mostly being used today."

Conclusion

Disputants sometimes are very surprised at the outcome of a mediation and, if they like the outcome, have even gone so far as to describe the process as "magic." The magic involves a number of elements including the approach to the process. The mediation field, at this point, is only beginning to identify and distinguish among its basic approaches. And while there has been some discussion of models, there has been little discussion of the relationships linking models and approaches with theories.

Some mediators and some organizations that employ mediators have little understanding of the variety of theories or the differences in application in various settings. This may be the result of one or more situations. For instance, mediators trained in only one approach may not be exposed to an overview of the field. Also, some mediation organizations may think it is in their business interest to "sell" only the approach of their agency and minimize other approaches. And organizations that employ mediators may insist on a narrow approach because they don't want to worry about mediators "deviating" from a set approach. While "keeping it simple" may make teaching, learning and practice less confusing in some ways, it does not encourage mediators and organizations to grow and change by incorporating new ideas and refining programs. A restricted training or practice may mean that mediators are less apt to approach something creatively taking into account the unique circumstances of each mediation.

Mediators need to know about the range of models, theories and approaches in the field. The field is interdisciplinary and so professional contributions are going to come from individuals with very different disciplinary backgrounds. Also, each time a mediation begins the parties and their representatives bring their perspectives to the table. Considering and moving between models, theories and approaches encourages a mediator to remember and recognize that all those in the room are bringing their different views to the table and, given those differences, an approach that may have been effective in a previous mediation may not be the approach that will be most effective this time.

Mediators need to remember that theories allow us to focus, but that they also can give less attention to some things or leave them out entirely. While we want the strength that theory gives us, we also need to check whether a particular theory is sufficient for understanding an act or process or if it needs to be combined, enhanced or discarded in relation to a particular dispute resolution process.

The mediator also needs to seek opportunities to practice moving between and among models, theories and approaches. By doing so, the mediator strengthens her or his ability to pick and choose among them and increase the effectiveness of the work.

Does it make a difference whether we know which models and approaches are being used and which theory or theories are basic to the models and approaches? I think so. The more mediators understand the models and theories in the field, the better they will be able to explain and assess what they do. Identification and discussion of the similarities/differences and the strengths/weaknesses (in various settings) of the models, approaches and theories, will foster improvements in mediation teaching, research and practice. It also will help disputants and organizations that hire mediators or run mediation programs make informed choices about mediation possibilities.

References

Alexander, N. (2008). The mediation metamodel: Understanding practice. *Conflict Resolution Quarterly, 26*(1), 97–123.

Ali, A., Mowry, R., & Ho, K. (2011). Collective action and emancipatory aims: Applying principles of feminist practice in a shelter for domestic violence survivors with disabilities. In B. F. Waxman Fiduccia (Ed.), *Papers on women and girls with disabilities 2011.* Retrieved from http://www.centerwomenpolicy.org/programs/wammanfiduccia/documents/BFWFP_CollectiveActionandEmancipatoryAims-ApplyingPrinciplesofFeministPracticeinaShelter_000.pdf

Bandura, A. (1973). *Aggression: A social learning analysis.* Oxford: Prentice-Hall.

Bartlett, F. C. (1932). *Remembering.* Cambridge: Cambridge University Press.

Bateson, G. (1954). A theory of play and fantasy. *Psychiatric Research Reports, 2*, 39–51.

Beer, J. E. (1997). *The mediator's handbook.* Gabriola Island: New Society Publishers.

Black, A. (2001). Alternative dispute resolution in Brunei-Darussalam: The blending of imported and traditional processes. *Bond Law Review, 13*(2), 1–29. Retrieved from http://epublications.bond.edu.au/blr/vol13/iss2/4/

Brennan, W. (1998). Aggression and violence: Examining the theories. *Nursing Standard, 12*(27), 36–38.

Bush, R., & Folger, J. (2004). *The promise of mediation.* San Francisco: Jossey-Bass.

Cognitive Neuroscience Society. (2011). *Welcome page.* Retrieved from http://cogneurosociety.org

Della Noce, D. J., Bush, R. A., & Folger, J. P. (2002). Clarifying the theoretical underpinnings of mediation: Implications for practice and policy. *Pepperdine Dispute Resolution Law Journal, 3*(1), 39–65.

Dewulf, A., Gray, B., Putnam, L., Lewicki, R., Arts, N., Bouwen, R., & van Woerkum, C. (2009). Disentangling approaches to framing in conflict and negotiation research: A met-paradigmatic perspective. *Human Relations, 62*(2), 155–193.

Dollard, J. (1939). *Frustration and aggression.* New Haven: Yale University Press for the Institute of Human Relations.

Fritz, J. M. (2002). Teaching sociological practice: Starting with something special. *Sociological Practice, 4*(2), 103–111.

Fritz, J. M. (2004). Derriere la magie: Models, approaches et theories de mediation (Behind the magic: Mediation models, approaches and theories). *Esprit Critique, 6*(3). Retrieved from http://www.espritcritique.org

Fritz, J. M. (2006). L'approccio al conflitto: il ruolo della teoria nella mediazione (Approaches to conflict: The role of theory in mediation). In L. Luison (Ed.), *La mediazone come strumento di intervento sociale (Mediation as an instrument of social intervention)* (pp. 24–36). Milano: FrancoAngeli.

Gabel, S. (2003). Mediation and psychotherapy: Two sides of the same coin? *Negotiation Journal, 19*(4), 315–328.

Garland-Thomson, R. (2003). Integrating disability, transforming feminist theory. *National Women's Studies Association Journal, 14*(3), 1–32.

Glass, J. F. (Ed.). (1972). *Humanistic society: Today's challenge to sociology.* Pacific Palisades: Goodyear.

Glass, J., & Staude, J. R. (1972). The humanistic challenge to sociology. In J. F. Glass (Ed.), *Humanistic society: Today's challenge to sociology* (pp. 1–12). Pacific Palisades: Goodyear.

Harding, S. (2004). *The feminist standpoint theory reader*. New York: Routledge.

Haynes, J. M. (1994). *The fundamentals of family mediation*. Albany: State University of New York Press.

Klages, M. (2003). *Postmodernism.* Retrieved from http://www.colorado.edu/English/ENGL2012Klages/pomo.html

Kurtz, P. (2000). *Humanist manifesto 2000: A call for a new planetary humanism*. Amherst: Prometheus Books.

Lang, M. D., & Taylor, A. (2000). *The making of a mediator: Developing artistry in practice*. San Francisco: Jossey-Bass.

Lascoux, J. (2001). *Pratique de la mediation: Une methode alternative a la resolution des conflicts*. Issy-les-Moulineaux: ESF editeur.

Leopold, A. (1949). *A sand county almanac and sketches here and there*. New York: Oxford University Press.

Lorenz, K. (1996). Keynote: Innate bases of learning. In K. H. Pribram & J. King (Eds.), *Learning as self-organization* (pp. 1–56). Mahwah: Erlbaum Associates.

Mays, J. M. (2006). Feminist disability theory: Domestic violence against women with a disability. *Disability & Society, 21*, 147–158.

Minsky, M. (1975). A framework for representing knowledge. In P. H. Winston (Ed.), *The psychology of computer vision* (pp. 211–277). New York: McGraw-Hill.

Moore, C. W. (2003). *The mediation process*. San Francisco: Jossey-Bass.

Moore, C. W., & Woodrow, P. J. (2010). Facilitation and mediation. In C. W. Moore (Ed.), *Handbook of global and multicultural negotiation* (pp. 407–433). San Francisco: Jossey-Bass.

Morineau, J. (1998). *L'esprit de la mediation*. Ramonville Saint-Agne: Editions Eres.

Ritzer, G. (2000). *Modern sociological theory*. Boston: McGraw Hill.

Schellenberg, J. A. (1996). *Conflict resolution: Theory, research and practice*. Albany: State University of New York Press.

Society for Neuroscience. (2011). Retrieved from http://www.sfn.org/index.aspx?pagename=whatIsNeuroscience

Straus, R. A. (2002). *Using sociology: An introduction from the applied and clinical perspectives* (3rd ed.). Lanham: Rowman & Littlefield.

Sweet, W. (2004). Herbert Spencer (1820–1903). In *Internet Encyclopedia of Philosophy*. Retrieved from http://www.iep.utm.edu/spencer

Taylor, A. (2002). *The handbook of family dispute resolution*. San Francisco: Jossey-Bass.

Turner, J. H. (2001). Sociological theory today. In H. T. Turner (Ed.), *Handbook of sociological theory* (pp. 1–17). New York: Kluwer.

Van Wyhe, J. (2002). *The complete work of Charles Darwin online*. Retrieved from http://darwin-online.org.uk/

Vraneski, A. (2004). Al di la dell'arte e della scienza (Beyond art or science). In L. Luison & J. M. Fritz (Eds.), *La mediazone come strumento di intervento sociale (Mediation as an instrument of social intervention)*. Milano: FrancoAngeli.

Wan, A. H., & Wan, P. M. (2008). Clinical sociology and community mediation: Training grassroots leaders in multiethnic Malaysian communities. In J. M. Fritz (Ed.), *International clinical sociology* (pp. 208–227). New York: Springer.

Wendell, S. (1989). Toward a feminist theory of disability. *Hypatia, 4*(2), 104–124.

Wennerstrom, E. (2000). Address by the director for international relations, Ministry of Justice, Sweden. Social Mediation and New Methods of Conflict Resolution in Daily Life. In: *Proceedings of the seminar organized by the Interministerial Delegation for Urban Affairs under the French Presidency of the European Union-Oisin Program, Paris-Creteil, 21-22-23 Sept 2000*. Paris: Les editions de la DIV.

Wilson, E. O. (1975). *Sociobiology: The new synthesis*. Cambridge: Belknap Press of Harvard University Press.

Winslade, J. (2006). Mediation with a focus on discursive positioning. *Conflict Resolution Quarterly, 23*(4), 501–515. doi:10.1002/crq.152.
Winslade, J., & Monk, G. (2000). *Narrative mediation: A new approach to conflict resolution*. San Francisco: Jossey-Bass.
Winslade, J., & Monk, G. (2002). *A narrative approach in mediation*. Retrieved from http://narrative-mediation.crinfo.org/docuemnts/mini-grants/narrative_mediation/Context_narrative_mediation.pdf
Winslade, J., Monk, G., & Cotter, A. (1998). A narrative approach to the practice of mediation. *Negotiation Journal, 14*(1), 21–41.
Zaki, J., Hennigan, K., Weber, J., & Ochsner, K. N. (2010). Social cognitive conflict resolution: Contributions of domain-general and domain-specific neural systems. *The Journal of Neuroscience, 30*(25), 8481–8488.

Part II
Selected Applications

Chapter 5
Community Mediation in the United States

Cheryl Cutrona

Introduction

This chapter presents an overview of the community mediation movement in the United States as it developed beginning in 1976. It outlines the history and background of community mediation; identifies its proponents and critics; and discusses the purpose, benefits and hallmarks of the movement. Community mediation programs, including governmental, faith-based, court-annexed and grassroots neighborhood justice centers and their innovative applications, are highlighted. The chapter concludes with a discussion of the impact of the institutionalization, professionalization and legalization of mediation on the future of community mediation in the United States.

What Is Community Mediation?

Community mediation is a process for resolving disputes with the help of a third-party, impartial mediator. The mediator does not give legal advice or representation, or provide the parties with counseling or therapy. The mediator's role is to facilitate the process and help the parties reach a mutually satisfactory resolution of the matter that brought them to mediation. People involved in disputes can select community mediation as an alternative to filing a civil action in court.

The author would like to thank Adrian Sagan for his invaluable contributions to the sections on restorative group conferencing and peace circles.

C. Cutrona (✉)
Executive Director of the Good Shepherd Mediation Program in Philadelphia, Pennsylvania, USA
e-mail: ccmed8r@aol.com

J.M. Fritz (ed.), *Moving Toward a Just Peace: The Mediation Continuum*,
Clinical Sociology: Research and Practice, DOI 10.1007/978-94-007-2885-1_5,

What Is a "Community Mediation Center"?

A "community mediation center" is a community-based organization that offers free and low-cost mediation services to a particular neighborhood or region. The centers, envisioned in 1976, are in nearly every state in the United States. The community mediation movement began, in earnest, in the 1980s as one way to provide access to justice to people who could not afford to go to court or wait years for their cases to reach litigation because of the court's backlog of cases (Hedeen and Coy 2000, p. 353). Centers hope to build community and empower citizens to work out their own disputes without police or court intervention.

Centers typically handle disputes involving neighbors; family members; friends; consumers and businesses; and landlords and tenants.

Some of the benefits of community mediation centers are that they are:

- **Community-based**: Centers are located in the parties' own neighborhood or nearby.
- **Convenient**: Mediation can be scheduled within a few days or weeks of the initial request, typically at the parties' convenience, including evenings and weekends.
- **Inexpensive**: Community mediation is free or less expensive than going to court. Some community mediation centers charge fees based on a sliding scale but as non-profit charitable organizations, they never turn away anyone for inability to pay. Fees are either hourly or per session. Other community mediation centers do not charge a set fee; they request donations or offer free mediation services.
- **Diverse**: Community mediation centers typically train their own mediators, usually community volunteers who reflect the diversity of the surrounding neighborhood.
- **Boot camps for private mediators**: A center with a reputation for providing excellent mediator training and enough cases to apprentice new mediators serves as a "boot camp" for private practitioners. This is a win-win arrangement; the center gains volunteers and the would-be private practitioners receive the experience they need to have their names added to mediator rosters or meet the experience requirements mandated by court rules so they can accept court-referred cases.

History and Background

The genesis of modern community mediation in the United States is the "Pound Conference on Popular Dissatisfaction with the Administration of Justice" held in St. Paul, Minnesota in 1976 (Levin and Wheeler 1979). The conference was convened by the then Chief Justice of the U.S. Supreme Court, Warren Burger, and sponsored by the American Bar Association and the Conference of State Chief Justices to commemorate the 70th anniversary of a famous speech to the American

Bar Association made by Roscoe Pound (1936). Pound was an American legal theorist who served as the dean of the law school at Harvard University from 1916 to 1936.

The legal community had gathered to discuss its concerns about the rising cost and delays involved for those seeking their "day in court." Because of America's litigious nature, the courts were too crowded, litigation too adversarial and often prolonged, and access to justice was denied to those who could not afford it.

Chief Justice Warren Burger said (Goldberg et al. 1999):

> The notion that ordinary people want black-robed judges, well-dressed lawyers and fine-paneled courtrooms as the setting to resolve their disputes isn't correct. People with problems, like people with pains, want relief and they want it as quickly and inexpensively as possible. People want alternatives to the adversarial process of litigation that reduces crowded court dockets, and is more efficient, less formal, less expensive, less stressful, and takes less time than the traditional system.

Sander (1994) intrigued colleagues with his vision of the "multi-door courthouse" – one building with an intake process designed to perform legal triage where incoming cases would be assessed and channeled to the most appropriate dispute resolution forum. For example, parties might be led to Door #1, where they could negotiate resolution, or Door #2, where mediators could facilitate a collaborative dispute resolution process. Or perhaps the case might be better suited to Door #3, where an arbitrator would decide the dispute. And, the few remaining parties desiring "judicial vindication or a legal precedent to apply in future situations" (Sander 1996) would go through the "Door of Last Resort," to litigate their dispute before a judge or jury.

As a result of the Pound Conference, a task force was formed for the purpose of developing proposals for judicial reform in the United States. The task force recommended funding a pilot project that resulted in the Department of Justice establishing neighborhood justice centers in Atlanta, Georgia; Kansas City, Missouri; and Los Angeles, California in 1978, and two more in Dallas, Texas and Honolulu, Hawaii in 1980 (Hedeen and Coy 2000). The courts diverted small claims and criminal disputes to these non-profit, community-based centers staffed by trained, volunteer mediators. Over the next 25 years, community mediation centers cropped up all over the country (Hedeen and Coy 2000).

In 1993, the National Association for Community Mediation (NAFCM) (2009) was founded "to support the maintenance and growth of community-based mediation programs and processes; to present a compelling voice in appropriate policy-making, legislative, professional, and other arenas; and to encourage the development and sharing of resources for these efforts." According to NAFCM (2012), there are 408 community mediation programs in the United States with approximately 1,300 full-time equivalent staff members, 20,000 volunteer community mediators nationwide receiving 400,000 case referrals annually. NAFCM (2012) also indicates that "the typical CMC has three full-time-equivalent staff members, an averages of 50 volunteer mediators, and an annual budget between \$150,000–\$200,000."

Over the last 20 years, court backlogs have decreased now that Alternative or Appropriate Dispute Resolution (ADR)[1] processes, such as community mediation, have been institutionalized across America. In contrast to the Pound Conference in 1976, recent bar association meetings and journal articles have centered on the "vanishing trial," discussing the sharp decline in both the percentage and number of claims that reach a court trial (Galanter 2004) and a concurrent increase in the length of the trials that do occur. The sharp decline is due, in part, to the ever expanding array of ADR options, including community mediation, available to settle a dispute short of a full-blown trial.

Criticisms of Community Mediation

Albie Davis, an early proponent of mediation, stated in an interview that community mediation is the "soul" of the ADR movement (Merry 1994, p. 247). There are some, however, who have criticized mediation in general, and community mediation in particular, characterizing them as both a pacifier and a dumping ground for the courts. Some critics claim that community mediation centers provide "second class justice" rather than "access to justice" (McEwen and Williams 1998, p. 865).

Laura Nader (1993), for instance, a professor of anthropology at the University of California at Berkeley, has criticized ADR, particularly mediation, calling it "second class justice." Nader asserts that ADR is a "coercive mechanism of pacification" created because of society's intolerance for conflict. She suggests that the preference for "peace through consensus" is a reaction against the adversarial nature of litigation. She contends that this "harmony ideology," exalting compromise and agreement over rights, has reframed conflicts about rights and values into issues about communication problems, feelings and relationships (Nader 1993). She accuses the courts of diverting important legal cases from their dockets and claims that the veil of secrecy that surrounds mediated issues prevents important information from being publicly known (Menkel-Meadow 2000). Other critics claim that the community mediation movement has failed because it has been co-opted by the legal system (Kovach 2007), turning to a more legalistic model (Senft and Savage 2003; Zumeta 2000) of mediating rather than the original intent which was to teach people how to resolve their conflicts constructively.

Other critics claim that non-lawyer community mediators are practicing law without a license, particularly when they help the parties generate and evaluate options (e.g., reality testing), and draft the mediated settlement document. In fact, there have been cases where non-lawyer mediators have been charged with the unauthorized practice of law (Young 2008).

[1] ADR is so well established now that some commentators prefer "appropriate" dispute resolution, suggesting that it is more than just an alternative (Menkel-Meadow 2001).

Trainers of community mediators typically caution would-be mediators not to give legal advice, but there is a fine line between giving "legal information" (which some mediators, particularly in divorce and custody mediation, are often required to do) and giving "legal advice." It is generally accepted in community mediation that mediators may give legal information (e.g., copies of statutes or materials prepared by local bar associations or other groups) and discuss parties' rights. However, mediators should not apply the law to the parties' situation because that would constitute legal advice.

In response to opponents' claims of unauthorized law practice, the 2002 American Bar Association Dispute Resolution Section (2009) passed a "Resolution on Mediation and the Unauthorized Practice of Law." The resolution makes it clear that mediating and drafting settlement agreements is not the practice of law, and that a mediator's discussion of a party's legal rights does not constitute giving legal advice. The resolution also suggests that the mediator explain the mediator's role and encourage the parties to seek independent legal advice both during the mediation process and prior to signing the settlement agreement.

Community Mediation Models

Despite its critics, community mediation has taken root in the American system of justice, and grown into several models. The two basic models are: (1) nonprofit "community mediation centers" and/or "neighborhood justice centers" and (2) mediation programs institutionalized within larger entities, such as courts and government agencies (office of children and youth, or human relations commissions) (Hedeen 2003). Community mediation centers typically only provide mediation services. Neighborhood justice centers provide a panoply of other social justice programs, conflict resolution training and consulting services, in addition to mediation services. Institutionalized community mediation programs are designed to serve a particular need of the parent organization.

Nonprofit Community Mediation Programs

Community Mediation Centers (CMC) are typically small, grassroots, community-based centers with one or two employees and a stable of volunteer mediators. The mission of the CMC is peacemaking and community building by providing mediation as a way to deescalate and resolve conflicts. CMCs rely on word-of-mouth referrals to survive, and they often struggle to find disputing parties willing to mediate. They spend lots of time publicizing the availability of their services and educating the public about the benefits of mediation, as well as raising enough funds to keep the centers open. Many centers are housed in donated space to minimize overhead.

Neighborhood justice centers (NJC) usually rely on the courts to divert minor disputes for resolution. NJCs typically boast a multitude of dispute resolution services that provide access to justice. For example, NJCs may have developed various fee-based training services to generate income, or programs created in response to the needs of local schools, courts and other community-based organizations. Some NJCs collaborate with family court (Press 2003, p. 47) to provide domestic relations mediation, delinquency prevention and diversion programs for juveniles, and permanency mediation for dependency issues involving child abuse, neglect or abandonment. Some NJCs have expanded their services to include school-based conflict resolution education and peer mediation training and implementation to assist young people in resolving conflicts precipitated by miscommunication, vandalism, petty theft, minor assault, boy-girl relationships and other school-based issues.

The majority of private community mediation and neighborhood justice centers in the United States are nonprofit corporations under 501 (C) 3 of the tax code.[2] Many centers were started by faith-based institutions, particularly peace churches like the Mennonites and the Quakers, because of the natural connection between resolving conflict and the Christian concept of reconciliation. Some centers with religious roots have reorganized independently. Examples include the Montgomery Conflict Mediation Center in Pennsylvania, which was originally a Mennonite organization, and the Center for Conflict Resolution in Delaware County, Pennsylvania, which was originally organized by Quakers and reorganized in the 1990s. Others offer services to the community, but also herald their roots. These include the Mennonite Conciliation Service in Lancaster, Pennsylvania and the Good Shepherd Mediation Program in Philadelphia, owned by a Catholic order of nuns, the Sisters of the Good Shepherd.

Institutionalized Community Mediation Programs

Mediation programs also are housed within large institutions. These include government agencies, colleges and universities, and faith-based institutions. Some courts have taken community mediation out of the hands of community mediation centers and started in-house mediation programs to handle small claims, landlord-tenant and private criminal complaints (Arnold-Burger 1998; Hedeen 2003). Because the courts have the cases, some creative court-community collaborations have ensued. Some courts contract with community mediation to administer the mediation of these minor disputes. All the programs rely on pro bono attorney mediators and other volunteer mediators who have completed a training and apprenticeship program. Only a handful of programs, court or community-based, actually pay their mediators.

[2]The 501(c) 3 label is a U.S. tax code designation for organizations that are tax exempt, nonprofit organizations that may be, for example, charitable, educational or religious organizations. These organizations can accept donations and receive grant funding.

Funding for these programs is varied. Some programs have line item funding designated in state or county budgets. Surcharges on court filing fees are often used to generate revenue to support in-house as well as community mediation of court-referred cases. In a few cases, the parties pay to mediate. Such programs have been instituted in Alabama, Alaska, Arizona, California, Colorado, Florida, Georgia, Hawaii, Illinois, Maine, Maryland, Minnesota, New Hampshire, North Carolina, Ohio, Oklahoma, Oregon, Utah, Virginia, Washington, and Wisconsin (National Center for State Courts, 2013).

Community mediation also is housed in various government agencies. For example, the Philadelphia Commission on Human Relations Community Relations Service trains its community relations staff as mediators. The Human Relations Commission handles disputes involving discrimination. In addition to staff members using their street mediation skills while they are deescalating neighborhood disputes, formal mediations take place at the agency's office.

Colleges and universities have started community mediation programs in connection with their sociology, religion and peace studies programs. Over 200 colleges and universities have campus mediation programs that deal with conflicts between students (similar to peer-mediation in K-12 schools). In some universities, students trained as mediators may be eligible to mediate for local court programs. For example, at Marylhurst University (outside Portland, Oregon), students who complete the university mediation coursework mediate for the Multnomah County Court Small Claims Mediation Program. Law school mediation programs typically connect with local courts to provide clinical programs for their students.

And some colleges and universities offer mediation programs to the community using volunteer student mediators. One such program is the Howard Community College Mediation and Conflict Resolution Center in Columbia, Maryland which mediates landlord-tenant, interpersonal, organizational, employment, and consumer-business disputes. Another example is the University of Minnesota Extension, a service which has managed a Farmer-Lender Mediation program since 1986.

Common Characteristics

Regardless of the community mediation model, NAFCM (2009, 2012) defines community mediation as having nine common characteristics:

> (1) the use of trained community volunteers as the primary providers of mediation services; volunteers are not required to have academic or professional credentials; (2) a private non-profit or public agency, or program thereof, with a governing/advisory board; (3) mediators, staff and governing/advisory board are representative of the diversity of the community served; (4) providing direct access of mediation to the public through self referral and striving to reduce barriers to service including physical, linguistic, cultural, programmatic and economic; (5) providing service to clients regardless of their ability to pay; 6) initiating, facilitating and educating for collaborative community relationships to effect positive systemic change; (7) engaging in public awareness and educational activities about the values and practices of mediation; (8) providing a forum for dispute resolution at the early stages of the conflict; and (9) providing an alternative to the judicial system at any stage of the conflict.

Challenges

Community mediation shares the frustration of dealing with the obstacles endemic to mediation, but also has its own challenges. These include getting parties to the table, the care and feeding of volunteer mediators, funding, and a lack of research to guide program choices.

Getting Parties to the Table

Getting parties to come to the table is a common challenge that is discussed whenever community mediation people gather to talk about their programs. Unless the referral source threatens negative consequences for failure to participate (e.g., juvenile courts mandating mediation as an alternative to seeing a judge), participation depends on the willingness of the parties to face each other and engage in a difficult conversation. Consequently, not all inquiries result in mediation. In fact, at least one center reports that only about one-third of the mediation inquiries find their way to the mediation table (Cutrona 2002).

When a call comes in to a mediation center, there is typically someone, often called the "intake worker," who interviews the initiating party to determine if the case is appropriate for mediation. If the case is appropriate and the initiating party wants to proceed, the intake worker contacts the responding party. More often than not, the responding party does not want to mediate because she/he (1) does not want to pay; (2) wants more time to think it over; (3) does not have time available; (4) feels uncomfortable talking about the issue in public; (5) does not believe the promise of confidentiality and does not want his/her "dirty laundry" aired in public; and/or (6) is ashamed of his/her role in the conflict or feels guilty and makes up some excuse not to mediate because she/he does not want to confront the other party. While most of these excuses are surmountable, because mediation is voluntary and it would be contrary to the philosophy of mediation to coerce parties to mediate, there are often fewer cases to mediate than there are volunteer mediators. That leads to another challenge: dealing with the frustration of eager volunteers who want to mediate and rarely have the opportunity.

The Care and Feeding of Volunteer Mediators

Community mediators are a diverse cadre of trained volunteers who consistently give of their time and effort to help others resolve their problems. Many of them not only serve as mediators, they also use their skills to help train others, participate in professional development activities designed to enhance their mediation skills, and offer their peacemaking skills to the community in other capacities. In urban areas, volunteer mediators are often so plentiful some centers have more mediators than they have cases. Some centers need to hire translators because they do not have enough trained mediators who speak languages other than English. In rural areas, some centers have a difficult time finding volunteer mediators who are willing to travel long distances.

When unemployment is high and conflict appears to be a growth industry, it seems like everyone wants to be a mediator. Mediator trainers joke about "keeping your day job," but there is some truth to it. While the number of paying, mediation-related jobs are more plentiful than ever, the number of people who want to become mediators also appears to be at an all-time high. So community mediation centers must find creative ways to engage and affirm their volunteers, whether they can keep them busy mediating or not. To do that, centers must have someone dedicated to coordinating volunteers.

It is the job of the Volunteer Coordinator to provide volunteer mediators with engaging, meaningful work as well as to affirm them for their dedication. For example, centers that provide basic mediation training may use their volunteers to assist the trainers by coaching role-plays and mentoring new mediators. Providing continuing mediation education opportunities for their volunteers encourages networking and builds mediation skills, as well as offering a benefit for those mediators who are seeking advanced practitioner status through the Association for Conflict Resolution or need continuing education to maintain their status on mediation rosters. Centers may invite guest speakers who can present on topics of importance to mediators.

Volunteer coordination involves providing opportunities for affirmation. Savvy centers provide inexpensive "perks" and recognition to keep their mediators happy, such as reimbursement for parking, food, advanced training opportunities, and opportunities for networking. Centers may recognize their volunteer mediators publicly for their contributions to the community by holding award ceremonies and sending out press releases naming dedicated volunteers, or listing them on the center's website (with permission, of course).

Asking volunteers to help with outreach will keep them engaged and help bring in more referrals. Centers may provide volunteer mediators with business cards and brochures that they can distribute when the volunteers have an opportunity to recommend mediation, present information about the center at community events, and represent the center at public meetings. This involves keeping volunteers educated about the center's programs and activities. Centers may even involve their volunteers in fund-raising activities[3] and special events.

Funding

In this shrinking economy, most community mediation centers struggle to balance shoestring budgets with no guarantee of money up ahead. According to Baron

[3]While this is beneficial, it also runs the risk of volunteers feeling like they are only called upon when the center needs money.

(2004), “Centers have managed to survive, but for most centers seeking funding consumes a significant portion of the energies of center staff and volunteers, and funding is always precarious.”

Only a handful of states provide funding for their community mediation programs. New York provides funding to the mediation centers serving all 62 counties. Michigan does the same, providing funding for 29 mediation centers. And, Nebraska has six regional community mediation centers supported by the state (NAFCM 2009). But these states are the exception, not the norm.

Because community mediation providers offer mediation at low or no cost, and no one is turned away for inability to pay, one of the major obstacles faced by nonprofit community mediation programs is funding. The income generated by mediation fees never seems to be enough to balance even a shoestring budget. Providing low or no-cost mediation requires public subsidies and sources of revenue. To balance the budget, some centers have added fee-for-service training, consulting services and government contracts to subsidize grants from private foundations and fund-raising through individual contributions and special events.

Community mediation centers also are adversely impacted by diminishing grant opportunities. Foundation grants and soliciting contributions are directly impacted by the health of the economy. In the 1990s, it was fairly easy to obtain grants from private foundations in the United States. Interest rates were high and foundations had a lot of money to spread around. After the tragedy on September 11, 2001, the stock market declined and interest rates plummeted leaving foundations much less money to distribute to non-profit agencies. Private foundations are typically limited to dispersing the interest earned on principle. When interest rates are high, foundations have more money to distribute. When interest rates are low, the amount of money they have available for grants to nonprofit organizations, like community mediation centers, is less. Furthermore, following the bombing of the World Trade Center towers in New York City, the number of nonprofit organizations rose dramatically. So in addition to there being less money available for grants, there were more organizations vying for it. And, community mediation competes with organizations that provide food, shelter and other necessities. The bottom line is that nonprofit community mediation centers, with even bare minimum overhead costs, are struggling to find new revenue sources to survive.

Those centers that rely on successful annual appeals and special events have also seen a reduction in the amount of funds generated. Centers are scrambling to market themselves more effectively and inexpensively using websites and social networking sites.

At the same time as financial resources are dwindling, administrative costs are rising (Cutrona 2006). Centers that must pay for staff salaries, health insurance (an employee benefit), professional liability insurance, utilities, printing, office supplies and facility management have seen their cost of doing business increase. Many centers are reluctant to pass this cost on to the community because the community cannot bear the increase and it will make it even more difficult to encourage people to mediate.

To secure federal funding and grants from national foundations, grantees must typically engage in research and evaluation to prove that the project for which they are receiving funds have met their stated goals and objectives. This leads to another challenge faced by community mediation: a lack of research measuring the effectiveness of community mediation.

Lack of Research

Most people involved in community mediation strongly believe that it works, but proving that it does is another matter. While anecdotal data abounds, there is a dearth of evaluation research available demonstrating the success of community mediation (Hedeen 2004, pp. 119–128) as an efficient, cost effective process for resolving disputes.

One of the problems involves defining "success." Does success only occur when the parties reach a mediated settlement? Is it a failure when the parties engage in meaningful conversation, address issues of concern, but don't reach agreement? Some community mediation proponents argue that settlement rates are not the only way to measure success. However, that is the focus of much of mediation research available.

Centers that keep statistics report that community mediations result in a settlement about 85 % of the time. While that is a noble result, it is derived from a self-selected participant base. Critics point out that because of the voluntary nature of community mediation, the parties have already demonstrated a willingness to settle. Certainly the settlement rate should be higher than if the parties were mandated to mediate, which by the way is contrary to the spirit of community mediation. This "catch-22" demonstrates the need to find other characteristics to assess.

There is some research gauging the parties' satisfaction with the process, the mediators and the outcome, and the durability of the settlement, but there is almost no comparative research on cost effectiveness (i.e., between community mediation and other alternatives). It would be wonderful to prove that community mediation allows private parties, the courts, the police and other organizational consumers to save time and money, and that mediation contributes to community-building and peacemaking.

Innovative Applications

Despite the challenges outlined in the previous section, community mediation has prevailed. Community mediation is a fertile ground for developing creative dispute resolution applications in response to the needs of local communities.

Community mediation programs have expanded their repertoire of services in response to community needs and as a way of generating income so that they may continue to offer free and low-cost mediation to the community. Most of the centers provide peer mediation training and implementation in the schools and conflict resolution training and consulting in their community. Some centers have developed innovative projects and services that have been replicated in the private sector and expanded the core mission of conflict resolution, peacemaking and social justice. Centers have applied mediation to an ever-expanding array of community disputes including custody, permanency of children in dependency situation, foreclosure, elder issues, prisoner reentry, and the reintegration of military families. Some of these innovative applications[4] are described here, but this is by no means a comprehensive list.

Conflict Coaching

Conflict resolution coaching is an innovative extension of the services provided at neighborhood justice centers that developed as a way to serve the initiating party when the responding party declines the invitation to mediate. Conflict coaching serves those clients by having them meet with a conflict coach to make a plan for addressing the conflict on their own, when the other party does not want to engage in the mediation process.

Conflict resolution coaching is a conflict assessment and planning process involving a neutral "coach" and the person experiencing conflict. The goals are to: (1) examine the client's views about conflict and how the client deals with it; (2) prepare mentally and emotionally to approach the other person involved in the conflict; and (3) develop a plan for how to address the conflict situation and achieve the optimal outcome.

In addition to serving people whose desire to mediate is thwarted by reluctant respondents, conflict resolution coaching also may be used when:

- A person involved in a conflict is unsure how to approach the other person.
- A person involved in a conflict is concerned about possible negative outcomes because of (1) a perceived power imbalance; (2) inexperience dealing with the other person; (3) fear of confrontation; or (4) other concerns preventing open communication.
- A person involved in a conflict seeks guidance from a person trained in conflict management and is open to receiving this help.[5]

The "coach" is an impartial person, usually a trained mediator or "conflict manager," who is not involved in the conflict and who is trained to help people involved in conflict assess the situation and prepare to address the situation in a constructive manner. The coach is a combination of personal consultant, supporter, advisor, motivator, agent of reality and trainer.

---

[4]Unfortunately, program discontinuance is also a reality due to lack of funding – even for successful projects.

[5]The coach is not going to "do it" for the client.

The coach meets with a person involved in a conflict to:

- Establish conflict as "normal"
- Serve as a process consultant to assess the situation and select an appropriate conflict management style for approaching the other person
- Offer guidance in knowing when to confront
- Engage in perspective-taking (how other people see things or might respond)
- Focus on conflict management rather than recommend outcomes
- Help develop a plan for addressing the conflict constructively
- Give the disputant an opportunity to practice what he/she will say when addressing the other person involved in the conflict
- Offer affirmation and encouragement

Inafa' Maolek in Guam and the Good Shepherd Mediation Program in Philadelphia, Pennsylvania were introduced to conflict resolution coaching by Tricia Jones, a professor at Temple University and co-author of the book, *Conflict Coaching* (Jones and Brinkert 2008). Both centers now offer conflict coaching to initiating parties when the responding party declines the invitation to mediate.

Mosaica, The Center for Consensual Conflict Resolution in Jerusalem,[6] and the U.S. Embassy in Israel's American Center, invited the Good Shepherd Mediation Program to Israel to train community mediators to use conflict coaching in 2009 and in 2012. Mosaica, in cooperation with the Multicultural Center for Jerusalem, operates the national program, Gishurim. As such, Mosaica provides "consultation, accompaniment and guidance to mediation and dialogue centers throughout the country and provides assistance in establishing such centers (Mosaica 2013)." In addition, the program assists the centers to be more professional and tailor the mediation and dialogue to the varied cultural needs of the communities within which they operate. This international collaboration (in English and Hebrew) introduced conflict coaching to 70 community mediators representing 16 community mediation centers across Israel. Mosaica offers occasional refresher and advanced training to fully institutionalize conflict coaching.

Restorative Practices

Many of the issues handled by community mediation centers involve private criminal complaints involving property crimes and minor assaults. The problem with using mediation to "resolve" victim-offender issues is that there is no real "dispute" involved in a criminal act. Crime is not negotiable. So victim-offender "mediation" is a misnomer. The goal is "dialogue"; not settlement so many centers

[6]The program was founded by the Masad Klita in cooperation with Joint Israel, the Ministry of Social Affairs and Social Services, the Ministry of Absorption, the Ministry of Education and the Ministry of Construction and Housing" (Mosaica 2013).

have reframed programs from "Victim-Offender Reconciliation Project (VORP)" and "Victim-Offender Mediation" to "Victim-Offender Dialogue" and "Victim-Offender Conferencing" (Umbreit et al. 2003). Whatever it is called, the restorative justice approach has caught on among community mediation centers as a way to address criminal complaints because it resonates with the mission of community-building and peacemaking. Restorative practices involve the community, gives a voice to the victim, and – while it does not resolve a dispute – its goal is to make things as right as possible.

A criminal offense is more than a violation of law. Crime directly impacts the individuals involved in the incident, those closest to them and the larger community. Restorative justice is a way of looking at the criminal justice system in a different way. Traditional justice systems view crime as a violation of the law and the state, and its focus is on punishment and retribution. Restorative justice views crime as a violation of people and relationships and its focus is on the harm done to individuals and the community, the victims' needs, the offenders' obligation to the victims and the community and engaging the victim, the offender and the community in the justice process. Restorative justice explores the impact of crime, the victim's needs, and ways offenders can be held accountable using a variety of dialogue models that allow for secure and balanced engagement (Zehr 2002). Restorative practices do not determine guilt or innocence; offenders must take responsibility for their role in the matter to participate in this process.

The first North American victim-offender program was established in Kitchener, Ontario by the Mennonite Central Committee in 1974. Shortly thereafter, the first Victim-Offender Reconciliation Program (VORP) in the United States was established in Elkhart, Indiana. There are more than 300 victim-offender programs in the United States and more than 1,200 in Canada, Europe, Israel, Japan, Russia, South Korea, South America and the South Pacific (Umbreit et al. 2004).[7]

Victim-Offender Processes

Neighborhood justice centers have embraced Victim-Offender Dialogue and related restorative justice projects to provide diversion programs for first-time juvenile offenders. Victim-offender dialogues offer juvenile offenders and those they have harmed an opportunity to meet face-to-face in a structured, secure environment to facilitate restoration, healing, reconciliation and/or negotiate restitution (monetary or symbolic). In some programs, if the victim declines the invitation to conference with the offender, the offender's family participates in parent-youth meetings where the discussion centers on the consequences of the youth's actions to the youth, the victim, the family and the community.

[7]New Zealand uses Family Group Conferences for all youth crimes except murder and homicide. In Germany and Austria, victim offender mediation is used for both adult and juvenile violent crimes (Kurki 2000).

Victim-offender dialogue is a very old and well-respected tradition, dating back to tribal customs of the Maori people from New Zealand. Howard Zehr (1990), in *Changing Lenses*, explains:

> The Western juvenile justice system was widely recognized to be working poorly, and many Maori argued that it was antithetical to their traditions. The system was oriented toward punishment rather than solutions, was imposed rather than negotiated, and left family and community out of the process. In the new juvenile system adopted in 1989, all juvenile cases except a few very violent crimes are diverted from police or court into Family Group Conferences (FGSs). As a result, judges report substantial drops in case loads as high as 80 %. New Zealand Judge Fred McElrea has called it the first truly restorative approach to be institutionalized in a Western legal framework.

In 1974, the first formal Western model using the mediation process to bring victims and offenders of crime together for a face-to-face dialogue began in Elmira, Ontario (Peachy 1989). Two Mennonite Probation Officers, Mark Yantzi and Dave Worth, with the approval of the judge, decided that two young men who had gone on a neighborhood-wide vandalism spree, should go door-to-door (with a probation officer or volunteer coordinator) to each home that they had vandalized and ask what each of these property owners needed from the young offenders. Both Yantzi and Worth admitted that this was a "pie-in-the-sky" idea, but it actually worked. Of the 22 vandalized properties, all but two victims (who had moved from the neighborhood) met with the boys and the court representatives and came up with restitution agreements. Within months, repayment occurred and thus, the VOC process began.

Since the late 1970s in the United States, restorative justice programs have had many different names (e.g., victim offender reconciliation programs, victim-offender mediation, victim-offender dialogue, victim-offender conferencing), but the heart of the process has remained constant. A crime occurs, harm is done to a person and a community, so who better to decide what is needed than the victim(s) themselves? And, who better to listen to the human consequences and offer ways of reparation but the person who committed the offense? The question becomes: If a face-to-face meeting is possible, amenable to both parties and can be in a safe environment with impartial parties facilitating the dialogue, can true justice be done? Can this victim and this offender remain in the same community, only this time repairing the damage and building new respect? These are the questions behind all the victim-offender processes, regardless of their names.

Restorative Group Conferencing

Community mediation centers, including the Good Shepherd Mediation Program in Philadelphia, have embraced Restorative Group Conferencing (RGC), a voluntary, facilitated dialogue attended by the offending person, the victim and members of the community. Led by a trained, impartial third party called a "facilitator," the dialogue focuses on the offense, the harm caused by the incident and how to make things right to the greatest extent possible.

RGC is a forum for victims to increase their understanding of the incident, ask questions, express how they have been directly impacted, work towards healing and be a central part of a just process. RGC gives offenders a venue to learn how their actions impact themselves and others and an opportunity to be directly accountable to the individuals they harmed. Community members learn how to best support victims and offenders and what steps to take to prevent similar violations in the future. Conferences are often completed with a written agreement, reached by consensus, which memorializes the meeting and identifies what the offender must do to repair the harm to the greatest extent possible.

- *Diversion Program for Young Adults ages 18–24* – As a meaningful alternative to the traditional justice process, RGCs have been convened to address offenses that affect the quality of community life. Offenses that have been diverted to restorative conferences include: underage drinking, public intoxication, low-level drug possession, vandalism and destruction of property. Cases that involve a direct crime victim such as assault, reckless endangerment, terroristic threats, theft and auto theft are also prime candidates for RGC.
- *Pre-sentence Investigation* – RGC has been used to convene parties to learn more about the offense, identify offender deficits, address community needs and increase the voice of victims during sentencing. The contract developed during the conference may be delivered to the judge as a sentencing recommendation.
- *Post Sentencing* – RGC can be a tool to discuss symbolic or financial restitution, community service, and offender competency development. This provides offenders with the opportunity to be held directly accountable to their victim and community of care.
- *Direct Victim Support* – In situations where offenders are not suitable to participate in the RGC, victim advocates can use RGC to provide victims, and their community of support, a forum to discuss the offense, identify current needs and develop a plan of action.
- *Strategic Offender Community Re-entry* – An offender's transition from supervised probation to self sustainability can be unsettling. A Restorative Group Conference can provide the offender and the offender's support community an opportunity to actively plan the necessary steps for a successful transition by identifying delinquent triggers and a plan of action to ensure healthy decision making as well as roles that are effective and supportive.

Peace Circles

Peace circles are a restorative practice used by community mediation centers to address multi-party criminal offenses that arise in neighborhoods. With its roots in Native American culture, the Circle process involves the offending person, the victim and any support people the parties would like included (Pranis 2005). The dialogue focuses on the offense, the harm people have experienced and what actions should be taken to repair the harm to the greatest extent possible.

Like other restorative processes, Circles place as high a priority on listening as outward participation. The dialogue is led by trained facilitators called "Keepers." A Keeper will offer a question to the group. A "talking piece" is passed around to each member in the Circle. The person holding the talking piece has the floor to speak uninterrupted. Members of the Circle may choose to speak or pass their turn.

The restorative Circle process has been used successfully to facilitate dialogues, particularly in inter-group situations. For example, Good Shepherd Mediation Program used a Circle to address a neighborhood "terrorized" by a roving "gang" of young people who enjoyed scaring homeowners by running across the flat-top roofs in a block of row-houses. The neighbors were concerned that someone would fall off and get hurt, about their liability if someone did get hurt, and complained about noise and damage to the roofs. The young people and the homeowners came together in a Circle process to discuss the situation. The young people agreed to stop running across the roofs once they heard the concerns of the neighbors and the neighbors realized the young people were "just having fun" to pass the time; the adults agreed to put pressure on the Department of Recreation to open the community pool which had been closed due to budget cutbacks. At the end of the conversation, everyone reported that they believed they understood each other, and that the situation of concern was resolved in good faith.

Peace Theater

Peace Theater is an interactive performance featuring audience warm-up, activities, skits and cooperative games designed to introduce conflict resolution through drama. The performers are actors, often former peer mediators, who are specially trained in conflict resolution in general, mediation and improvisation. The performers develop the material for the skits based on their own experiences. This theater workshop encourages young audiences to become peacemakers, teaches practical tools for resolving conflict, and entertains, all at the same time. Good Shepherd Mediation Program in Philadelphia and Inafa' Maolek in Guam, both developed Peace Theater programs as an offshoot of their comprehensive package of school-based services (Inafa' Maolek website; Jones and Compton 2003, pp. 163–167).

The Good Shepherd Mediation Program's Peace Theater performed mainly in summer camps and featured age-appropriate skits focused on getting along. Peace Theater was developed in 1991 as a way to "teach peace" by encouraging young people to use communication and problem-solving skills rather than fighting to settle their disputes. Each summer the troupe, which consisted of teens and young adults, would schedule performances at summer day camps throughout Philadelphia, usually reaching about 4,000 young people between the ages of 5 and 12 each year. The camp counselors received a packet of cooperative games and other short exercises suitable for summer camps to use to reinforce and advance the skills introduced by the Peace Theater performance. Because of the interactive, improvisational approach, each performance was different as it was based on audience contributions. Like many successful community mediation programs, after 12 years of performances, lack of funding lowered the curtain on the Good Shepherd Mediation Program's Peace Theater.

In contrast, Inafa' Maolek Mediation Center, on the beautiful island of Guam, has been performing for 23 years. In addition to performing in schools on Guam, Peace Theatre has been invited to perform on the United States mainland, most recently at the Association for Conflict Resolution annual conference. Inafa' Maolek's Peace Theatre troupe is geared toward the older student featuring topics such as dating violence, bullying, rumors and gossip, sexual harassment, hate crimes, peer pressure, bulimia, drinking and drugs.

Quality Assurance

In the United States, there is no federal or state licensing or certification of mediators. However, many courts and other organizations that maintain mediator rosters have prescribed eligibility requirements for mediators wishing to be listed as a qualified mediator for that entity. As a field that is largely unregulated, many centers have developed internal policies and procedures to ensure quality.

In 2002, with funding from the William and Flora Hewlett Foundation, the National Association for Community Mediation (NAFCM) developed a Community Mediation Center Self-Assessment Manual (Broderick and Carroll 2002) which presents a set of questions to stimulate dialogue and encourage self-reflection and analysis and help centers determine how to best serve their communities. This checklist has given centers a starting point for developing policies and procedures.

Many centers maintain strict mediator eligibility requirements, apprenticeship guidelines, and on-going assessment of their volunteer mediators and their training programs in order to meet the national standards outlined by professional organizations. Most centers require that their mediators complete a minimum of 20 hours of training consisting of a combination of lecture, discussion, practice and processing that includes the following substantive content: information gathering; communication and facilitation skills; relationship and interaction skills; problem solving; decision making; agreement writing; a minimum of five hours of coached role-playing; and a review of mediator standards of conduct including ethical and legal considerations regarding self-determination, neutrality and confidentiality.

Most centers indicate that they also require their volunteer mediators to successfully complete an apprenticeship, typically including observation and co-mediation with experienced mediators who will provide feedback and guidance, and a set number of hours per year of documented continuing mediation education. "Continuing mediation education" is defined as advanced mediation training; refresher training; related training (e.g., domestic violence, multi-party mediation, child development); mediation coursework at an accredited university; and professional association conferences. Other requirements for the mediators include: criminal and child abuse clearances, particularly if they will facilitate mediations involving children; a minimum number of mediation hours each year; a copy of a mediator's training certificate of completion if the volunteer was trained through another organization; and specialized training to qualify to mediate divorce and child custody, victim-offender, dependency, elder, or multi-party disputes. Based on the credentials that many community mediators are required to have, they may be better qualified than a private practitioner who hangs a "shingle" after completing one course!

The Future of Community Mediation

Despite its grassroots focus, a community mediation center, with its finite resources, must operate as a business to survive. These days, free community mediation may be the exception rather than the rule, as centers charge fees[8] as they scramble to balance their budgets. And even though community mediation centers have high-quality, impeccably trained volunteer mediators and develop innovative applications to respond to community needs, centers face a number of challenges. The exponential growth of mediation has inevitably led to professionalization requiring community mediation centers to compete with private practitioners while struggling to survive with fewer resources than ever. Gaining credibility and visibility with a shoestring marketing and public relations budget necessitates keeping up with the latest technology to take advantage of social networking and online marketing. And documenting success through research and evaluation continues to be a pressing, and expensive, need.

In spite of the challenges, conflict resolution is a growth industry in America. The *U.S. News & World Report* ("Mediator" 2009) has identified mediation, arbitration and conciliation among the 50 best careers over the next decade: "Employment in arbitration, mediation, and conciliation is expected to expand by 1,400 jobs, or 14 percent, between 2008 and 2018—a growth rate above the average for all occupations." Does that prediction include community mediation? If centers can survive the economic lows and the professionalization of mediation, community mediation centers can be an important contributor in the movement to build community, encourage peace, and prevent, deescalate and resolve conflict.

References

American Bar Association Section of Dispute Resolution. (n.d.). *Resolution on mediation and unauthorized practice of law*. Retrieved 15 Mar 2009, from http://www.abanet.org/dispute/webpolicy.html#3

Arnold-Burger, K. (1998). Municipal court mediation: Reducing the barking dog docket. *Court Review, 35*, 50–54.

[8]This is typically done on a sliding scale and without turning anyone away for inability to pay.

Baron, L. (2004). Commentary: The case for the field of community mediation. *Conflict Resolution Quarterly, 22*, 135–144.

Broderick, M., & Carroll, B. (Eds.). (2002). *Community mediation center self-assessment manual*. Washington, DC: NAFCM.

Cutrona, C. (2002). Reflections on past successes and future challenges: Good Shepherd Mediation Program. *Mediation Quarterly, 17*(4), 324–328.

Cutrona, C. (2006). La mediazione di comunita negli Stati Uniti: Il Good Shepherd Mediation Program (Community mediation in the United States: The Good Shepherd Mediation Program). In L. Luisan (Ed.), *La Mediazione come Strumento di Intervento Sociale: Problemi e prospettive internazionali (Mediation as a tool for social intervention: Perspectives, challenges and practical aspects)* (pp. 252–272). Milano: FrancoAngeli.

Galanter, M. (2004). The vanishing trial: An examination of trials and related matters in state and federal courts. *Journal of Empirical Legal Studies, 1*(3), 459–570.

Goldberg, S. B., Sander, F. E. A., & Rogers, N. H. (1999). *Dispute resolution: Negotiation, mediation and other processes*. Gaithersburg: Aspen Law & Business.

Hedeen, T. (2003). Institutionalizing community mediation: Can dispute resolution, 'of, by and for the people' long endure? *Penn State Law Review, 108*(1), 265–276.

Hedeen, T. (2004). The evolution and evaluation of community mediation: Limited research suggests unlimited progress. *Conflict Resolution Quarterly, 22*(1–2), 101–133.

Hedeen, T., & Coy, P. C. (2000). Community mediation and the court system: The ties that bind. *Mediation Quarterly, 19*(4), 351–367.

Jones, T. S., & Brinkert, R. (2008). *Conflict coaching: Conflict management strategies and skills for the individual*. Los Angeles: Sage.

Jones, T. S., & Compton, R. (Eds.). (2003). *Kids working it out: Stories and strategies for making peace in our schools* (pp. 163–167). San Francisco: Jossey-Bass.

Kovach, K. K. (2007). Centennial reflections on Roscoe Pound's *the causes of popular dissatisfaction with the administration of justice*: Foreword: Article: Pound revisited. *South Texas Law Review, 48*, 1003–1050.

Kurki, L. (2000). Restorative and community justice in the United States. *Crime and Justice, 27*, 235.

Levin, A. L., & Wheeler, R. (Eds.). (1979). *The Pound conference: Perspectives on justice in the future*. St. Paul: West.

McEwen, C. A., & Williams, L. (1998). Legal policy and access to justice through courts and mediation. *Ohio State Journal on Dispute Resolution, 13*, 865–883.

Mediator: As one of the best careers in 2010, this should have strong growth over the next decade. (2009, December 28). *U.S. News and World Report*. Retrieved 1 May 2010, from http://www.usnews.com/money/careers/articles/2009/12/28/mediator-mediator.html

Menkel-Meadow, C. (2000). Mothers and fathers of invention: The intellectual founders of ADR. *Ohio State Journal on Dispute Resolution, 16*, 1–37.

Menkel-Meadow, C. (2001). Ethics in mediation: The many "Cs" of professional responsibility and dispute resolution. *Fordham Urban Law Journal, 28*, 979.

Merry, S. E. (1994). Albie M. Davis: Community mediation as community organizing. In D. Kolb (Ed.), *When talk works: Profiles of mediators* (pp. 244–277). San Francisco: Jossey-Bass.

Mosaica. (n.d.). *Mosaica – Center for consensual conflict resolution*. Retrieved 8 August 2013, from http://www.mosaica-gishur.org.il

Nader, L. (1993). Controlling processes in the practices of law: Hierarchy and pacification in the movement to re-form dispute ideology. *Ohio State Journal on Dispute Resolution, 9*, 1–25.

National Association for Community Mediation. (2009). *Home page*. Retrieved 15 Mar 2009 from www.nafcm.org/pg1.cfm

National Center for State Courts. (2013). *Small claims courts: Who pays for small claims mediation?*. Retrieved 31 July 2013, from http://www.ncsc.org/Topics/Civil/Alternative-Dispute-Resolution-ADR/State-Links.aspx?cat=who%20Pays%20for%20Small%20Small%20Claims%20mediation

Peachy, D. E. (1989). The Kitchener experiment. In M. Write & B. Galaway (Eds.), *Mediation and criminal justice*. London: Sage.
Pound, R. (1936). The causes of popular dissatisfaction with the administration of justice, 29 *ABA Report* 395 (1906). (Reprinted in *Journal of the American Judicial Society, 20*, 178)
Pranis, K. (2005). *The little book of circle processes: A new/old approach to peacemaking*. Intercourse: Good Books.
Press, S. (2003). Institutionalization of mediation in Florida: At the crossroads. *Penn State Law Review, 108*, 43–66.
Sander, F. E. A. & Goldberg, S. (1994). Fitting the Forum to the Fuss: A user Friendly Guide to selecting an ADR Procedure 10 Negs 49 (pp. 49–68).
Sander, F. E. A. (1996). Foreword. In D. Golann (Ed.), *Mediating legal disputes: Effective strategies for lawyers and mediators* (p. xxiv). Boston: Little Brown.
Senft, L. P., & Savage, C. A. (2003). ADR in the courts: Progress, problems, and possibilities. *Penn State Law Review, 108*, 327–348.
Umbreit, M. S., Coates, R. B., & Vos, B. (2003). *Facing violence: The path of restorative justice and dialogue*. Monsey: Criminal Justice Press.
Umbreit, M. S., Coates, R. B., & Vos, B. (2004). Victim-offender mediation: Three decades of practice and research. *Conflict Resolution Quarterly, 22*(1–2), 279–303.
Young, P. M. (2008). A Connecticut mediator in a kangaroo court? Successfully communicating the "authorized practice of mediation" Paradigm to "Unauthorized Practice of Law" Disciplinary Bodies. *South Texas Law Review, 49*, 1047–1293.
Zehr, H. (1990). *Changing lenses*. Scottdale: Herald Press.
Zehr, H. (2002). *Little book of restorative justice*. Intercourse: Good Books.
Zumeta, Z. (2000). A facilitative mediator responds. *Journal of Dispute Resolution, 2000*, 335–341.

Chapter 6
Police and Mediation: Natural, Unimaginable or Both

Maria R. Volpe

Mediation is a universal intervention process whose roots are as old as the dawn of civilization (Folberg 1983; Moore 2003). While complex definitions have been developed and they can vary markedly depending on the context, in its simplest characterization, mediation is commonly referred to and recognized as an intervention process where third parties provide assistance to disputing parties by helping them to have a difficult conversation and perhaps reach some understandings. As mediation's visibility, utilization, and acceptance have grown worldwide, its diverse applications have become increasingly creative (Mayer 2004). This chapter will address one of the most challenging contexts in which mediation can be and, to a limited extent, has been applied, namely the police context (Cooper 1997; Volpe 1989; Volpe and Phillips 2006), using the United States as a primary example. Depending on circumstances, mediation in the police context can be seen as natural, unimaginable, or both.

Framing the Context for Police Mediation

For starters, how is mediation a natural part of policing? Quite simply, since police work has always involved the handling of a variety of conflict situations, historically mediation related interventions have been a part of routine police work (Goldstein 1977). For the most part, those officers who have felt comfortable serving as a go-between for disputing parties have done so quite naturally, usually by using their intuition and without specific mediation training. They often brought a skill set that was well suited for listening to parties and helping them to move on. Even though their communication and intervention practices can be unique to their work,

M.R. Volpe (✉)
Professor, Department of Sociology, Director, Dispute Resolution Program,
John Jay College of Criminal Justice, City University of New York, USA
e-mail: mvolpe@jjay.cuny.edu

J.M. Fritz (ed.), *Moving Toward a Just Peace: The Mediation Continuum*,
Clinical Sociology: Research and Practice, DOI 10.1007/978-94-007-2885-1_6,

in fact, their practices would be recognizable by those who specialize in mediation in other contexts. Given this impromptu but widespread use of informal intervention between parties, a strong case can be made that mediation has been a natural part of policing worldwide.

On the other hand, an equally compelling case can be made that the use of mediation is unimaginable in the police context. In virtually every part of the world, as an arm of the state, police are authorized to use force to compel parties to comply with their directives and to make crucial decisions that can adversely impact the people involved. For the most part, police are also expected, if not required, to prepare official reports documenting their interventions. Moreover, much of their traditional intervention work occurs in public spaces where control of the situation is an essential component of their routine response efforts. These types of police actions collide against such core mediation principles as self-determination by the parties, voluntary consent by parties to participate in mediation, and confidentiality of communications during the mediation sessions (American Arbitration Association et al. 2005).

The incongruity between police work and general mediation practices is evident in other instances as well, including where the mediation sessions are held and how much time is allocated for the intervention efforts. For police, it is common for interventions to be undertaken in public areas where there is virtually no opportunity for them to manage the physical layout of the surroundings or who else might be present. Moreover, since the number and gravity of the calls for police services are unpredictable, police are unable to plan how much time they can spend when responding to any matter. For mediators in other contexts, more often than not, their mediations occur at deliberately chosen meeting spaces and at scheduled times, all arranged by the mediator with the parties. They have much greater control over who participates, when, where, and how. Given all of the differences between police mediating when responding to calls for assistance and conventionally accepted practices in mediation, it is plausible to argue that any notion of mediation in the police context is an oxymoron and hence totally unimaginable.

Despite the aforementioned contrasts, mediation and policing can and, in fact, do coexist. Mediation has emerged as an invaluable tool for police officers in improving relations with citizens and in helping to create and sustain more peaceful communities. Imagine police using mediation to respond to a situation where a person's loud music has resulted in clashes with his neighbors and repeated calls to the police. Mediation also has been viewed as particularly useful in a variety of situations where conflict situations involve misunderstanding and miscommunication over perceptions in diverse communities. Imagine police using mediation to intervene in a situation where unwanted congregating activity among some new members of the community has resulted in assaults. While mediation is not a panacea and it is unacceptable for police officers to use mediation in response to many situations they are asked to address, especially domestic violence related incidents, in fact, mediation is increasingly recognized as a useful component of the police landscape. Not only do police serve as mediators themselves between disputing parties, they also refer cases to other mediators and participate as parties in mediation sessions for employment related matters.

Police Landscape

Since police work around the world varies depending on where it is performed, there is no simple or uniform characterization of how it has been or is undertaken. Different organizational structures, philosophical approaches, cultural expectations, and leadership practices have all influenced how police officers carry out their work. Despite all of the differences, a unifying theme of virtually all police work, regardless of context, is that police officers universally work for hierarchical, quasi-militaristic organizations and that they have the ability to utilize authoritative power to contain and control situations. Departure from this norm has left officers in a position to draw on their own natural talents, intuition, and cultural traditions especially when intervening in conflict situations.

In the United States, one of the most important developments in policing that arose as a result of the pervasive rethinking of police approaches in the 1960s and 1970s was the introduction of community-oriented policing, a new philosophy about policing that began to take root in the 1980s and has consistently gained popularity around the world (Skolnick and Bayley 1988). Depending on the department, community policing policies, procedures, and practices can vary significantly. Despite all of the variations, generally speaking, community policing values a deeper engagement by police officers in the everyday life of a community, creative ways of partnering with citizens and groups, and identification of resources to assist those who live, work, worship, and play in their respective communities (Trojanowicz et al. 1998; Community Policing Consortium 1994). Officers are expected to examine and address problems even when seemingly intractable. As such, community policing is a distinct departure from rapid response police practices where officers who respond to a call quickly gather the facts, make decisions, and move on to the next call. The expectation for community police officers is that they will take the time to proactively and resourcefully intervene with the assistance of others in the community.

While it could be argued that community-oriented policing is like old wine in new bottles and hence offers nothing new, it could also be argued that this approach to policing subscribes to a philosophy that deliberately immerses police in the community to resourcefully manage situations. The important word here is deliberately. As mentioned earlier, police have a long history of serving as problem solvers on the beat and of being connected with their respective communities, but their interventions were often left to the discretion of officers. With community policing, immersing police in the community is not only accepted practice, but assigned and expected practice.

Of particular note, community policing has provided the infrastructure, context, and philosophy needed for non-adversarial police intervention processes like mediation to begin to have presence in police departments. It allows officers to walk the talk of being creative partners in managing problems in the community. In their study on the changing role of police officers involved in community policing, Buerger et al. (1999, p. 132) have noted that "The community policing movement is creating an institutional context where long-term mediation efforts are encouraged".

Another philosophical framework closely allied to community policing and mediation is restorative justice (Nicholl 1999a, b). While there are many definitions of restorative justice and it can refer to different things depending on context, central to most understandings is the involvement of victims, offenders, and the community in face-to-face meetings designed to address the harm(s) that have resulted from crimes, the feelings about what happened, and the ways to hold offenders accountable (e.g., see Johnstone and Van Ness 2007). Among some of the better known approaches used are victim offender mediation first used in Kitchener, Ontario, Canada in 1974 (Peachey 2003), peacemaking circles popularized in Canada (Pranis et al. 2003) and family group conferences originally developed in New Zealand (Morris and Maxwell 1998).

How police are involved in restorative programs varies (Hoyle 2007; Hines and Bazemore 2003; Restorative Justice Online; Umbreit 2000), in some instances they serve as facilitators, in other instances as participants. The New Zealand family group conferencing model, which was started by social workers in 1989, served as the impetus for police-led restorative conferencing. By 1991, police in Wagga Wagga, New South Wales, Australia established a restorative conferencing model that was subsequently embraced by police organizations in England, Northern Ireland, and North America. Police were trained to lead restorative conferencing sessions with offenders, victims and members of the community (Hoyle 2007).

Intersection of Policing and Mediation: Natural or Unimaginable

At about the same time that community-oriented policing began gaining traction in the 1980s, particularly in the United States, another significant development was emerging, the introduction of mediation as a means of resolving conflicts. One of the settings in which mediation gained visibility early on was in the community context where a wide range of initiatives started to flourish. Over the years, the community-based mediation programs began to creatively and energetically reach out to local organizations and groups, including their local police departments in an effort to identify ways of partnering with them (McGillis 1997). While it is still challenging to find readily accessible data about the many creative mediation-related undertakings involving the police, there is evidence that a significant nexus between community mediation and the police exists. (e.g., see Volpe and Phillips 2003). More so than mediators in any other setting, those in the community have reached out to the police, usually in their local jurisdiction. Among the most visible community mediation efforts with respect to policing are: mediation training for officers, availability of mediation programs for referral of police cases, and mediation of a variety of citizen complaints against the police. Of particular note, the community mediation programs have played a significant role in increasing the number of police officers who have been made aware of mediation and in making mediation resources available to police departments (Volpe and Phillips 2003).

Overall, the convergence of community policing and community mediation efforts has been the singularly most important development in increasing the use of mediation in the police context. Without community policing, it is highly questionable if mediation could have made inroads within police structures, particularly in the United States. Community policing stresses the need for police officers to work with members of the community. Community mediation programs have provided their local police departments with ways in which mediation could be a useful component of the police officers' toolbox.

With increasing emphasis on police officers to demonstrate sensitivity in their interactions and interventions in culturally diverse communities, mediation emerges as an invaluable process (e.g., see Syeed-Miller 2006). Central to mediation are skills and techniques that stress the importance of listening, respect for others, keeping an open mind, finding common ground, and resourceful problem solving. In instances when the police have tried to mediate, refer cases to mediation, or participate in mediation processes, the message sent to the community is that they are trying to use a more collaborative, non-adversarial approach. It may also send a strong signal that mediation related initiatives suggest a more humane approach when police respond to situations.

Applications of Mediation in Policing: Where Mediation Fits in Policing

Despite the fact that the police have been able to apply mediation and related skills in a wide range of ways, there continues to be a dearth of research on police use of mediation. Nonetheless, the anecdotal information, assorted postings online, and limited research provide sufficient evidence that allows for identification of numerous applications of mediation in the police context including collective bargaining, contract negotiations, interventions as mediators, referrals of cases to mediators in other contexts, in specialized contexts, participation in the mediation process, and working alongside mediation experts.

Collective Bargaining

Historically, mediation has been used to resolve collective bargaining between police unions and local governments in the United States. This use of mediation is consistent with how it is used in other collective bargaining contexts, namely, to negotiate compensation packages and working conditions. In Canada, for instance, a detailed examination of the history of police bargaining in Vancouver shows that mediation has been combined with arbitration (Fisher and Starek 1978). The third party initially attempts to mediate contract differences, but when unsuccessful in reaching consensus, serves as an arbitrator.

General Policing: Mediation Skills for Everyday Police Work

While police have always intervened as informal mediators during the course of their patrol work in the community, as noted earlier (Goldstein 1977), recently officers have received mediation training. Depending on where they are trained, the nature and duration of the training will vary from superficial to intense (Volpe and Phillips 2006).

At the superficial end, the training sessions are brief, usually focused on information sharing presentations providing mediation awareness. Police officers learn about how mediation works and how to refer cases to mediators, usually at local community mediation programs. Part of these initiatives can include distribution of information flyers or palm cards. At the more intensive end, officers are trained in in-depth mediation skills, sometimes at sessions where all attendees are police officers, at other times with non-police personnel at department organized trainings or at other settings such as educational institutions or community based mediation programs.

As trained mediators, police officers gain knowledge and techniques that help them to listen to the parties, sort through concerns, identify issues, reflect information, brainstorm options, consider solutions, find creative ways of problem-solving and bring closure to situations. The mediation training also offers officers with knowledge about values that support mediation, including empowerment of the parties, creative ways to make talk work, respectful listening, self-determination by the parties, and non-adversarial interactions. As a result, officers are able to more skillfully and sensitively respond to conflict situations they encounter during the course of their work.

One of the earliest mediation services set up as part of a community policing program that integrated mediation into its police practices was the Hillsboro Police Department in Oregon. In 2007, the Hillsboro Police Mediation Program reported that 10 years after it started offering mediation training to the Hillsboro police officers, all of the officers in the department had been trained as mediators (Cadonau and Williams 2007).

Mediation training for police also can be used as a means of remediating harsh police practices. In a study on the use of force by police in Gauteng Province, South Africa, one of the recommendations made to reduce use of force incidents, as well as their occurrence and severity, was training in mediation skills (Minnaar and Mistry 2006). In 2005, as part of the G8 Action Plan on Expanding Global Capability in Peace Support Operations, the United States and Italy launched the Center of Excellence for Stability Police Units (CoESPU) in Vicenza, Italy, an international police training mission run by Italian Carabinieri. Among the topics included in the CoESPU curriculum are conflict analysis, negotiation and mediation "to improve the capacities of law enforcement professionals and contributors to peacekeeping operations working in vulnerable societies" (USIP 2009). In 2009, participants came from Burkina Faso, Egypt, Cameroon, Indonesia, Jordan, Mali, Nepal, Nigeria, Pakistan, Senegal, Serbia, and Ukraine.

Police Officers as Referrers of Cases to Others for Mediation

On a daily basis, police encounter a wide range of conflicts that they typically do not have the time to process as mediators. In many communities in the United States where mediation programs have been established, police officers can refer selected cases to them, particularly in those instances where there are disputing citizens who have an ongoing relationship or where police must make repeat calls. Rather than spending time on the scene, the police have been able to refer disputing parties to trained mediators who are able to convene more traditional protracted, sit down mediation sessions. In New York State, for example, the recent statewide data for the Community Dispute Resolution Centers Program show that 4.2 % of the cases referred to mediation centers are by police and sheriffs (NYS UCS 2011–2012, p. 2).

Police Use of Mediation in Specialized Contexts: Domestic Situations and Hostage Negotiations

Police have historically used mediation-related skills in specific contexts. Most common have been those situations involving responses to domestic situations and when negotiating hostage situations. In the case of responding to domestic violence situations, the use of mediation has been the subject of much debate (see Thoennes et al. 1995; Lerman 1984; Maxwell 1999). Among the concerns raised by experts has been the power disparity between perpetrators and victims, and the resulting potentially dangerous situation created for victims who would not be able to share their concerns in a face-to-face mediation session.

How to address the use of mediation by police in domestic violence situations has been the focus of significant concern to the law enforcement field. A well-known research study conducted in the 1980s examined police responses to simple assault in domestic violence situations (Sherman and Berk 1984). Officers were randomly assigned to one of the following three options, to arrest, give advice to the suspect, or ask the suspect to leave the premises for eight hours. The researchers found that arrest was more effective in reducing recidivism than removing the suspect from the home for the evening or giving advice, also referred to as informal mediation. As a result, the study had a chilling effect on the use of mediation even when circumstances might otherwise be suitable for its use in domestic situations. The study was often relied on and cited by those who supported mandatory intervention or "pro-arrest" policies in domestic violence situations. It was not until the study was replicated that mandatory arrest policies were questioned since the researchers found that arrests did not effectively deter violence (Sherman et al. 1992). In fact, they found that in some instances violence increased and that other options should be considered.

Despite the challenges raised by women's advocacy groups particularly in the United States, the use of mediation by police in handling domestic violence situations can be found elsewhere. For example, in Jamaica, in 1994, the then

Commissioner of Police established a Police Mediation Unit with 15 police officers trained in conflict resolution to address the problem of domestic violence. These officers then trained other officers (New measures 2001). In Tamil Nadu, India, the all-women police stations provide dowry-related domestic violence victims with an opportunity to negotiate and mediate their issues (Natarajan 2005). The officers, who are trained in dispute resolution, bring all of the parties, wife, husband and family members together to discuss their conflicts over dowry related matters. Natarajan (2005, p. 102) concludes that "it is evident that women from traditional backgrounds are comfortable bringing their problems to women officers for resolution and that, where there is no immediate threat to life, these officers can often help to resolve domestic disputes through negotiation and mediation." In India, there is precedence for community-based dispute resolution efforts through the use of elders and panchayats, a group of five respected village members who are chosen by the community members to assist with their conflicts (Vincentnathan and Vincentnathan 2007; Wall et al. 2008).

When responding to hostage situations, police negotiators must simultaneously engage the other side and slow down the interactions. Jack Cambria, commanding officer of the New York City Police Department Hostage Team has noted that "Most policing looks to resolve a situation quickly. Negotiation has a different dynamic. People have to work through their emotion" (Ford 2007). In the protracted police hostage negotiation context, a variety of opportunities for mediation occur. For example, since hostage situations and police responses to them can impact the surrounding community, officers often find themselves in the position of informal mediators among all of those on the scene including other police personnel, the media, onlookers, political officials, neighbors as well as the family and friends of those involved in the hostage situation itself.

Police Officers as Participants in Mediation Processes: Civilian Complaints

Many communities have introduced mediation to provide citizens who have a complaint against the police with an opportunity to meet with the officers they have accused (Baker 2006; Berger 2000; Hatch 2005–2006; Patterson 2006; Walker et al. 2002). This option can be an alternative to official investigation by internal affairs. Police departments have different policies about which types of complaints are permitted to go to their respective mediation programs. Generally speaking, the complaints that involve improprieties like rude behavior, insensitive interactions, and, depending on the department, matters involving racial profiling. Complaints involving use of force and arrests are usually not mediated. The mediation sessions are voluntary for both the police and citizens, however if police officers refuse to participate, the police department may take any number of actions including pursuit of a more formal investigation of the charges, taking some other actions to address the situation, or perhaps even order the officer to attend the scheduled mediation sessions.

Mediation of complaints against the police mirror the use of mediation in other contexts. The sessions are confidential and parties themselves play a significant role in defining what is included in any agreements that may be reached (Berger 2000). In their study on level of satisfaction of citizens and police officers whose cases were mediated, Bartels and Silverman (2005) found that complainants who participated in mediation were more satisfied than those whose cases were investigated. They found that police officers who participated in mediation were also highly satisfied.

Working with Mediation Experts: Use of a Mediation Liaison

At the local level, mediators and police departments are developing some innovative initiatives. For instance, the Community Mediation Program (CMP) in Baltimore, Maryland and two districts of the Baltimore Police Department have partnered to create positions known as Police Mediation Liaison to "to assist officers and screen and refer cases that may be more appropriate for community-based mediation than arrest." A lengthy job description that was posted online (University of Baltimore CNCM) outlines a variety of tasks that will enhance the officers' ability to make use of mediation in their interventions. The Police Mediation Liaisons would be expected to:

> *Help officers educate the community about nonviolent conflict resolution and mediation*
>
> Police Mediation Liaisons will ride along with officers 1–2 times per week to assist them in de-escalating conflict and to introduce a referral to mediation in a way that will be well-received.
>
> *Help provide trainings or presentations*
>
> With the CMP Director of Community Education, train designated officers about mediation on a semi-annual basis, using a one-hour mediation role play, followed by a referral training and question and answer session. Update incoming recruits on the project as they arrive at the District.
>
> *Make timely, complete referrals to CMP and educate CMP staff*
>
> Referrals to mediation will be completed daily using [repeat call statistics, officer referral pad carbons or cases left by officers in a designated box]. The invitation to mediation will consist of a letter to potential participants directly from the Police Department and signed by the District's Community Affairs Supervisor, asking participants to contact the CMP Mediation Coordinator directly at the CMP office. An intake form will be generated for CMP staff, and delivered on a twice-weekly basis to the office in person, so that CMP staff can be briefed quickly on any special circumstances that might help bring the participants to the mediation table.
>
> *Follow-up on referrals and continually communicate with officers about mediation case status*
>
> The Baltimore City Police Department's Northern and Southwest District Community Affairs Supervisor will act as the Site Supervisor for the Mediation Liaisons, giving them initial orientation and occasionally checking in to educate or head off problems. Detailed

records and a case status matrix will be kept to update officers. Cases which may benefit from a third resource rather than mediation will be referred to appropriate services such as Community Conferencing, large group facilitation, counseling and/or domestic violence services.

Evaluate successes

Liaisons will track the number of referrals, mediation sessions, agreement rates, and 3-month agreement durability.

Attend monthly Community Coordinating Council meetings

Community Coordinating Council Meetings are a monthly opportunity to spread the word about mediation, and educate the community about conflict resolution strategies.

The Challenges to Police Mediation

While there are many diverse efforts underway worldwide that are beginning to formally address how mediation can be used to enhance police work when managing conflict situations, the challenges mediation faces remain omnipresent. Foremost is the inherent clash between values central to mediation and police practices.

Among the most prominent challenges are the following.

(a) Police mediation: an oxymoron

Police officers have the authority to take control, compel parties to comply with their directions, and make decisions about circumstances they encounter. Their initial contact with parties may well occur while the parties are emotionally charged and in need for immediate intervention. Moreover, they encounter the parties on the latter's physical setting where the differences are occurring, the conflicts are potentially ripest for escalation to violent behavior, and the police on the scene are not able to utilize time or space in creative ways. If parties do not follow instructions, police are authorized, and even expected, to take action and use as much force as is needed to control and contain situations. Moreover, given the more authoritarian approach used by police, they can extract information from parties that they might not otherwise reveal. Parties may well fear that not providing information may result in the police taking some action against them.

On the other hand, mediators in other contexts subscribe to key principles including self-determination, confidentiality, and voluntary participation by the parties. For them, the process is subject to careful crafting of conditions to ensure that best practices are followed, even if it means conducting multiple sessions and significantly delaying the process into the future. The mediators pay considerable attention to preparing the parties as well as the setting for bringing the parties together. In short, unlike police practices, mediation relies on parties to voluntarily consent to participate in the process since mediators have no authority to impose solutions on anyone.

Quite simply, when police officers mediate, the core principles valued by mediation can be challenged and compromised. As a result, a strong case can continue to be made that policing and mediation are not a good fit, even when policing is more community-oriented (e.g., see Hoyle 2007, pp. 303–305).

(b) Emerging Professionalization of Mediation

As the practice of mediation becomes more popular, acceptable, and even institutionalized, there are increasing efforts underway to identify the criteria for professionalization of the field. This will mean a growing emphasis on standards of practice that embrace principles maximizing control of the process by the parties. Given the nature of police practices, this emerging professionalization of the mediation field will continue to present ongoing tension between the professional practice of mediation and police use of mediation on the scene.

(c) Police organizational structure and culture

While police have always engaged in some form of go-between when responding to conflicts between citizens, the dominant culture and organizational structure of policing are not designed to be supportive of such interventions. Police are expected to respond rapidly and move on, and the reward system in place for promotions and recognition supports this kind of police culture and organizational structure. It is virtually unheard of for police departments to release news headlines to report on the successful resolution of a conflict between neighbors engaged in ongoing complaints over noise that has included repeated police interventions. More common headlines are those that focus on the police solving a burglary, murder or robbery case. How personnel are recognized is a measure of what kind of police activity is more likely to be valued.

(d) The public's expectations

While the public expects the police to be respectful and understanding, they also expect the police to make decisions when they call upon the police to respond to a situation. The public is not accustomed to police arriving and asking them to play active roles in handling the matter that triggered the need for the call, especially when retributive climates have defined how police should operate. Such would require a significant paradigm shift in how the police role is defined for and by the public. For police to be viewed as mediators, a major public awareness initiative would have to be undertaken. For instance, after many decades, it is now part of conventional wisdom that police hostage negotiators can spend protracted time at a hostage situation by slowing down the process in order to rescue hostages and ensure everyone's safety. Similarly, in other contexts, officers would have to be trained and the public educated to expect a more collaborative problem solving approach in responding to more common conflict situations.

(e) Existing societal belief systems

Mediation's viability gets challenged in societies that do not subscribe to democratic principles. Worldwide there are vast discrepancies over the role of police. Presumably, the more authoritarian the context, the more challenging it will be to introduce a form of policing that empowers the citizens.

In addition to the aforementioned, specific concerns have been raised about police-led restorative conferencing sessions popularized by the police in Wagga Wagga, Australia. While these efforts are not specifically referred to as mediation undertakings, in fact they are mediation-like. Umbreit and Zehr, (1996, pp. 27–28) have identified the following potential dangers of the Australian approach:

1. Inadequate preparation: Lack of preparation prior to a restorative conference could notably impact on the parties' participation during the dialogue.
2. Victim insensitivity and coercion: Since sessions begin with the offenders' story, victims may feel uncomfortable and perceive the session as not addressing their needs.
3. Young offenders feeling intimidated by adults: When officers appear in uniform at the session, the offenders may feel uncomfortable.
4. Lack of neutrality – shaming of offender: Police may not be able to serve as neutral facilitators given the nature of their authoritarian role, thereby leading to shaming and blaming of offenders rather than reintegrative shaming.
5. Inflexibility and assumed cultural neutrality of process: The police conferencing model is highly scripted and may be too inflexible for restorative processes in diverse and multicultural communities.
6. Net-widening: Since minor cases may be identified, labeled and handled as a result of early intervention efforts, more offenders can be taken into the criminal justice system whose offenses might have otherwise been ignored.

The Future of Police Mediation: Some Observations

The use of mediation in the police context has tremendous potential worldwide. By its very nature, mediation provides police with precisely the kind of process and relationship building tools that they need to engage their communities in problem solving. With growing numbers of citizens around the world knowledgeable about mediation, it is safe to say that even if mediation is not fully integrated into police organizations globally, the inclusion of the kinds of techniques and skills integral to the mediation process will be of value to police organizations seeking to demonstrate their responsiveness in their communities. For some police organizations, the potential of incorporating mediation is greater when the mediation efforts can draw on the traditional culture. In their study on Navajo peacemaking, for example, Meyer et al. (2009) noted how the emphasis on restoring harmony in the Navajo culture can play a role in including peacemaking in Navajo peacekeeping work.

Concurrently, mediation in the police context will continue to experience significant challenges and resistance. Police organizational structures, policies, procedures, and culture suggest that the law enforcement setting does not provide the optimal milieu needed for mediation. This is especially true in those cultures where police are expected to maintain a social distance from the public and to assume unchallenged presence in the community. In fact, the informality of mediation-like processes can in fact be misused and abused by more coercive law enforcement agencies.

Finally, understanding and tracking mediation-like developments and initiatives in the police context globally present researchers with enormous challenges. Since many of the mediation efforts occur at the local level, data are not readily available or accessible. Any innovative effort that is undertaken can be overly cited and relied upon as an example of what is transpiring, thereby creating the illusion that more is occurring than is. Moreover, the varied terminology used to describe mediation makes it very difficult to track or compare mediation efforts longitudinally or across cultures. As a result, ascertaining what the police mediation landscape consists of is confusing and complicated. What is sorely needed is a systematic analysis of police mediation efforts that have been undertaken around the world. Among the beneficiaries would be the police organizations themselves since the information would provide insights about the potential and challenges of mediation in the police context.

References

American Arbitration Association, the American Bar Association's Section of Dispute Resolution, and the Association for Conflict Resolution. (2005). *The Model Standards of Conduct for Mediators*. Retrieved from http://www.abanet.org/dispute/news/ModelStandardsofConductforMediatorsfinal05.pdf

Baker, A. (2006, September 20). Settling disputes across a table when officer and citizen clash. *The New York Times*. Retrieved from http://www.nytimes.com/2006/09/20/nyregion/20mediation.html?_r=1&scp=3&sq=ccrb%20mediation&st=cse

Bartels, E. C., & Silverman, E. B. (2005). An exploratory study of the New York City Civilian Complaint Review Board mediation program. *Policing: An International Journal of Police Strategies and Management, 28*(4), 619–630.

Berger, V. (2000). Civilians versus police: Mediation can help to bridge the divide. *Negotiation Journal, 16*(3), 211–235.

Buerger, M. E., Petrosino, A. J., & Petrosino, C. (1999). Extending the police role: Implications of police mediation as a problem-solving tool. *Police Quarterly, 2*(2), 125–149.

Cadonau, D., & Williams, C. (2007). Policing and mediation: Common ground. *Hillsboro Mediation Program Newsletter, 16*, 2 [as cited in Meyer, J. F., Paul, R. C., & Grant, D.R. (2009). Peacekeepers turned peacemakers: Police as mediators. *Contemporary Justice Review*, 12(3), 331–344].

Community Policing Consortium. (1994). *Understanding community policing: A framework for action*. Washington, DC: US Department of Justice, Bureau of Justice Assistance. Retrieved from http://www.ncjrs.gov/pdffiles/commp.pdf

Cooper, C. (1997). Patrol police officer conflict resolution processes. *Journal of Criminal Justice, 25*(2), 87–101.

Fisher, E. G., & Starek, H. (1978). Police bargaining in Canada: Private sector bargaining, compulsory arbitration, and mediation arbitration in Vancouver. *Canadian Police College Journal, 2*(1), 133–161.

Folberg, J. (1983). A mediation overview: History and dimensions of practice. *Mediation Quarterly, 1*(1), 3–13.
Ford, E. (2007, July 26). An officer with the gift of the gab: Jack Cambria talks about the skills he needs as a hostage negotiator with the New York Police Department. *Times Online.* Retrieved from http://business.timesonline.co.uk/tol/business/career_and_jobs/graduate_management/article2138151.ece
Goldstein, H. (1977). *Policing a free society*. Cambridge: Ballinger.
Hatch, R. P. (2005–2006). Coming together to resolve police misconduct: The emergence of mediation as a new solution. *Ohio State Journal on Dispute Resolution, 21*(2), 447–484.
Hines, D., & Bazemore, G. (2003). Restorative policing, conferencing and community. *Police Practice & Research, 4*(4), 411–427.
Hoyle, C. (2007). Policing and restorative justice. In G. Johnstone & D. Van Ness (Eds.), *Handbook of restorative justice* (pp. 292–311). Portland: Willan Publishing.
Johnstone, G., & Van Ness, D. (Eds.). (2007). *Handbook of restorative justice*. Portland: Willan Publishing.
Lerman, L. (1984). Mediation of wife abuse cases: The adverse impact of informal dispute resolution on women. *Harvard Women's Law Journal., 7*, 57–113.
Maxwell, J. P. (1999). Mandatory mediation of custody in the face of domestic violence: Suggestions for courts and mediators. *Family and Conciliation Courts Review, 37*(3), 335–355.
Mayer, B. (2004). *Beyond neutrality: Confronting the crisis in conflict resolution*. San Francisco: Jossey-Bass.
McGillis, D. (1997, July). *Community mediation programs: Developments and challenges*. US Department of Justice, Office of Justice Programs. NIJ, Washington, DC: GPO.
Meyer, J. F., Paul, R. C., & Grant, D. R. (2009). Peacekeepers turned peacemakers: Police as mediators. *Contemporary Justice Review, 12*(3), 331–344.
Minnaar, A., & Mistry, D. (2006). Dealing with the use of force and stress-related violence by members of the police: Observations from selected case studies in Gauteng Province. South Africa. *Acta Criminologica, 19*(3), 29–63.
Moore, C. W. (2003). *The mediation process: Practical strategies for resolving conflict* (3rd ed.). San Francisco: Jossey-Bass.
Morris, A., & Maxwell, G. (1998). Restorative justice in New Zealand: Family group conferences as a case study. *Western Criminology Review, 1*(1). [Online] Retrieved from http://wcr.sonoma.edu/v1n1/morris.html
Natarajan, M. (2005). Women police stations as a dispute processing system: The Tamil Nadu experience in dealing with dowry-related domestic violence cases. *Women & Criminal Justice, 16*(1/2), 87–106.
New measures to combat domestic crime. (2001, January 16). *The Jamaica Gleaner*. Retrieved from http://www.jamaica-gleaner.com/gleaner/20010116/news/news2.html
New York State Unified Court System (NYS UCS). (2011–2012). *Community Dispute Resolution Centers Program Statistical Supplement 2011–2012*. Retrieved from http://www.nycourts.gov/ip/adr/Publications.shtml#stats
Nicholl, C. G. (1999a). *Community policing, community justice, and restorative justice. Restorative justice: Exploring the links for the delivery of a balanced approach to public safety*. Washington, DC: U.S. Department of Justice, Office of Community Oriented Policing Services.
Nicholl, C. G. (1999b). *Toolbox for implementing restorative justice and advancing community policing*. Washington, DC: U.S. Department of Justice, Office of Community Oriented Policing Services.
Patterson, R. W. (2006). Resolving civilian-police complaints in New York City: Reflections on mediation in the real world. *Ohio State Journal on Dispute Resolution, 22*(1), 189–225.
Peachey, D. (2003). The Kitchener experiment. In G. Johnstone (Ed.), *Restorative justice reader: Texts, sources, contexts* (pp. 178–186). Portland: Willlan Publishing.
Pranis, K., Stuart, B., & Wedge, M. (2003). *Peacemaking circles: From crime to community*. St. Paul: Living Justice Press.
Restorative Justice Online. Retrieved from www.restorativejustice.org/police

Sherman, L., & Berk, R. (1984). The specific deterrent effects of arrest for domestic assault. *American Sociological Review, 49*(2), 261–272.
Sherman, L. W., Schmidt, J. D., & Rogan, D. P. (1992). *Policing domestic violence: Experiments and dilemmas*. New York: Free Press.
Skolnick, J. H., & Bayley, D. H. (1988). *Community policing: Issues and practices around the world*. Rockville: US Department of Justice, NIJ.
Syeed-Miller, N. (2006). Developing appropriate dispute resolution systems for law enforcement and community relations: The Pasadena case study. *Ohio State Journal on Dispute Resolution, 22*(1), 83–103.
Thoennes, N., Salem, P., & Pearson, J. (1995). Mediation and domestic violence: Current policies and practices. *Family and Conciliation Courts Review, 33*(1), 6–29.
Trojanowicz, R., Kappeler, V. E., Gaines, L. K., Bucqueroux, B., & Sluder, R. (1998). *Community policing: A contemporary perspective* (2nd ed.). OH: Anderson Publishing.
Umbreit, M. (2000). *Family group conferencing: Implications for crime victims*. Washington, DC: U.S. Department of Justice, Office of Justice Programs.
Umbreit, M., & Zehr, H. (1996). Restorative family group conferences: Differing models and guidelines for practice. *Federal Probation, 60*(3), 24–29.
United States Institute of Peace. (2009, May 27–28). *CoESPU Workshops on Negotiation and Mediation for Police in Peacekeeping Environments*. Retrieved from http://www.usip.org/in-the-field/coespu-workshops-negotiation-and-mediation-police-in-peacekeeping-environments
University of Baltimore CNCM Student Info Blog (UBCNCM). Retrieved from http://ubcncm.wordpress.com/2007/12/20/job-opportunities-police-mediation-liaison-two-positions-2/
Vincentnathan, L., & Vincentnathan, S. G. (2007). Village courts and the police: Cooperation and conflict in modernizing India. *Police Practice and Research, 8*(5), 445–459.
Volpe, M. R. (1989). The police role. In M. Wright & B. Galaway (Eds.), *Mediation and criminal justice: Victims, offenders and community* (pp. 229–238). London: Sage.
Volpe, M. R., & Phillips, N. (2003). Police use of mediation. *Conflict Resolution Quarterly, 21*(2), 263–267.
Volpe, M. R., & Phillips, N. (2006). Police mediation: Research survey themes. In N. Phillips & S. Strobl (Eds.), *Dispute resolution: Managing conflicts in diverse contexts* (pp. 15–26). New York: CUNY Dispute Resolution Consortium.
Walker, S., Archbold, A., & Herbst, L. (2002). *Mediating citizen complaints against police officers: A guide for police and community leaders. Web Version*. Washington, DC: Government Printing Office.
Wall, J. A., Arunachalam, V., & Callister, R. R. (2008). Third-party dispute resolution in India and the United States. *Journal of Applied Social Psychology, 38*(12), 3075–3100.

Chapter 7
Intervening in Special Education Cases

Jan Marie Fritz

A number of intervention strategies (e.g., coaching, mentoring, resolution session, conferences, court hearing, outside assessment) can be used, alone or in combination, for a dispute between a parent or guardian of a student with special needs and the student's school or school system. Since the 1997 reauthorization of one particular law in the United States (U.S.), the Individuals with Disabilities Education Act (IDEA), mediation is also available in the U.S. to a disputing party for any matter related to the identification, evaluation, educational placement or provision of a free and appropriate public education related to a child's disabilities.

This chapter is based, in part, on my experience as a mediator of special education cases over the last nine years in two U.S. states.[1] It also is based on interviews (e.g., Gruber 2006; Højsteen 2011; Scully 2006; Thorin 2010); site visits (e.g., Finland, Kazakhstan, United States, Denmark, Brazil, Ukraine, Nigeria, South Africa, Sweden); written exchanges with those involved in special education in a number of countries (e.g., Gefen 2006; Gunvall 2006; Iarskaia-Smirnova 2011; Moses 2011; Philpot 2011) and a review of relevant literature.

Although the focus of this chapter is special education mediation in the United States, the chapter also covers several other approaches that are being used alone or in combination with mediation. Before discussing these approaches, some basic

---

This chapter is based on "Improving Special Education Mediation" which appeared in the *International Review of Sociology* (Fritz 2008) and "Special Education Mediation in the United States" (Fritz 2010), which was published in both Ukrainian and English.

[1]I would like to thank those involved in the special education process – parents, children, school administrators, those running mediation programs, mediators, advocates, attorneys and analysts – who took the time to share their ideas with me.

J.M. Fritz (✉)
Professor, University of Cincinnati, USA and Senior Research Fellow, Centre for Sociological Research, University of Johannesburg, South Africa
e-mail: jan.fritz@uc.edu

J.M. Fritz (ed.), *Moving Toward a Just Peace: The Mediation Continuum*, Clinical Sociology: Research and Practice, DOI 10.1007/978-94-007-2885-1_7,

information is provided about inclusive education, special education in a number of countries, and mediation. The chapter concludes with some points to consider for those who are interested in effective mediation in special education cases.

Inclusive Education

Nicholas Burnett was the Assistant Director-General for Education for the United Nations Educational, Scientific and Cultural Organization in 2009 when he wrote that inclusive education is (UNESCO 2009, p. 4):

> . . . a process that involves the transformation of schools and other centres of learning to cater for all children – including boys and girls, students from ethnic and linguistic minorities, rural populations, those affected by HIV and AIDS, and those with disabilities and difficulties in learning and to provide learning opportunities for all youth and adults as well. Its aim is to eliminate exclusion that is a consequence of negative attitudes and a lack of response to diversity in race, economic status, social class, ethnicity, language, religion, gender, sexual orientation and ability . . . Inclusive education is not a marginal issue but is central to the achievement of high quality education for all learners and the development of more inclusive societies. Inclusive education is essential to achieve social equity . . .

The international legal frameworks that support inclusive education (from 1948 to 2007) are the Universal Declaration of Human Rights (United Nations 1948), Convention against Discrimination in Education (1960), International Convention on the Elimination of All Forms of Racial Discrimination (1965), Convention on the Elimination of All Forms of Discrimination against Women (1979), Convention concerning Indigenous and Tribal Peoples in Independent Countries (1989), Convention on the Rights of the Child (1989), International Convention on the Protection of the Rights of All Migrant Workers and Members of their Families (1990), Convention concerning the Prohibition and Immediate Action for the Elimination of the Worst Forms of Child Labour (1999), Convention on the Protection and Promotion of Diversity in Cultural Expressions (2005), Convention on the Rights of Persons with Disabilities (2006) and United Nations Declaration on the Rights of Indigenous Peoples (2007) (UNESCO 2009, p. 9). Article 24 (See Appendix 2) of the 2006 Convention on the Rights of Persons with Disabilities (http://www.un.org/disabilities/convention/conventionfull.shtml) indicates that States Parties are to guarantee an inclusive education system and at all levels of education.

According to UNESCO (2009, p. 8), "the major impetus" for inclusive education came from discussions at a world conference, Special Needs Education: Access and Quality, held in June, 1994, in Salamanca, Spain. The Salamanca Conference, as it is known, underscored that special needs education should include all children regardless of their condition and that this initiative could not happen in isolation. It had to be part of a new inclusive education strategy in regular schools.

Inclusive education can be a high priority and an important component of a "culture of acceptance." There is, for instance, a culture of acceptance at Søholmskolen, a school for some 170 children from grades 0–8 (ages 5–12) located outside the city of Ringsted in Denmark.[2] The teachers and the headmaster (principal) are called by their first names, as is typical in Danish schools. In this school, children learn how to listen to each other and how to handle anger, impatience and conflicts. Beginning with zero grade, children work together in different pairs so they learn the importance of cooperation with all kinds of people and, as they enter the higher grades, they also will start working in teams of 4 or 5. First graders each have an "umbrella friend" (a sixth grader who is a mentor and support person), some fifth graders have been trained to help the second graders who need assistance with their reading and all kinds of systems are used so that each child will have a friend with her/him when the children are using the playground.

In Søholmskolen, children speak up. Discussion and disclosure are encouraged; students are expected to ask for help when they want it. Children will tell you of the difficulties they are facing (e.g., "I have tics because of Tourette Syndrome.", "My father died.")[3] and they expect and receive each other's support (e.g., an empathetic comment, a touch on the arm). One story is told of a teacher who admonished a child for eating in a sloppy way and was then publicly reminded by a second child that the first child was dealing with a problem and was not able to control that behavior.

When someone enrolls with special needs, Søholmskolen staff say they figure out what is needed to help the child.[4] Parents are welcome to visit the school at any time and discussion between parents and teachers is encouraged. The door to the resource classroom (for students needing special assistance) is always kept open during school hours and students know that anyone can come there for help.

There are different definitions for and approaches to inclusive education, however, and sometimes this has been problematic. For instance, for some U.S. school districts inclusive education has meant including certain kinds of special education programming (e.g., for students who are autistic or blind) within the school system, but not in all or most of the schools. That means many students without disabilities are in schools that have no exposure to the range of challenges (autism, for example) faced by students with certain kinds of special needs. Miles and Singal (2010) also have cited research that indicates inclusive education has been used in England to describe activities within special schools and in some places in the United Kingdom

[2]Information about Søholmskolen was obtained during a site visit (including discussions with the resource teacher, classroom teachers, a parent and students) on November 16, 2011. Additional information came from discussions with Anne Marie Østergaard Andersen (2011), the Ringsted municipality's udviklingskonsulent (development consultant for inclusion in education) and a copy of a presentation made by Torben Lyster (2010), the former director of the Department of Children and Culture in Ringsted Kommune. Lyster noted that "We are putting together a programme of courses, networks, and competency development for childcare workers and teachers under the theme of 'Towards More Inclusion.'"

[3]While the resource persons and teachers don't like to classify the difficulties faced by a student (e.g., autism), they will do so if the parents think it is useful to have a diagnosis.

[4]Admittedly, Søholmskolen is a small school and, in 2011, does not have any students with severe mental and physical needs. There also is a question about whether students who graduate from Søholmskolen will find a culture of acceptance at the next school.

"it is no longer associated with disability or special needs, but rather with school attendance or behaviour."

As many who write about special needs have noted, inclusion is not just about school placement or school culture. Without an individual, needs-based approach, "inclusion is nothing more than another label and students will continue to experience exclusion" (Lynch and Irvine 2009, p. 846) and not be able to progress to a high degree within a classroom setting. This means there has to be real commitment to the process, sufficient financial support and an ongoing interest in finding and using the best methods for each student. If a school system does not do it all well, a modified or incremental approach[5] might be necessary at times or continuously. As AbleChildAfrica (2011, p. 6) has noted:

> We need to see an education system across Africa which is focused on the best outcomes or 'best fit' for the child. We believe that this means inclusion in mainstream settings for the majority of children where possible but we also believe that there are some disabled children for whom specialised provision may be a better fit, usually due to the severity of their disability and/or the current lack of capacity in the system to support them.

There have been some initiatives to develop indicators for effective monitoring of the inclusive education process at school system, country, region and international levels. For instance, at the regional level the European Agency for Development in Special Needs Education (Kyriazopoulou and Weber 2009) developed a set of indicators for use at national and European levels. The 14 areas covered included value statements underlying the curriculum; clear national policy on inclusive education and inter-sector cooperation. From four to six requirements were then developed in three key policy areas – legislation, participation and financing. Finally, up to ten indicators were identified for the requirements that were identified for each of the three key policy areas. One of the four indicators for one of the requirements in the area of financing, for example, is "essential and adequate funding for full access to inclusive education for all pupils/students is provided by governments and does not depend on voluntary/charitable organizations" (Kyriazopoulou and Weber 2009, p. 31).

---

[5] According to the *World Report on Disability* (World Health Organization and World Bank Group 2011, p. 211): "Deaf students and those with intellectual impairments argue that mainstreaming is not always a positive experience. Supporters of special schools – such as schools for the blind, deaf, or deafblind – particularly in low-income countries, often point to the fact that these institutions provide high-quality and specialized learning environments. The World Federation of Deaf argues that often the best environment for academic and social development for a Deaf child is a school where both students and teachers use sign language for all communication. The thinking is that simple placement in a regular school, without meaningful, interaction with classmates and professionals, would exclude the Deaf learner from education and society."

Special Needs Education in Global Perspective

Special education or *special needs education*[6] is defined here as a "customized instructional program designed to meet the unique needs of an individual learner" (Gargiulo 2006). This is a broad definition, including all children (e.g., those who are gifted; have disadvantages because of gender, ethnicity, war trauma, or being orphans) who need some kind of additional support, although the focus usually is on students who have learning difficulties. Learning difficulties may be due, at least in part, to one or more problems/disorders (e.g., physical, psychiatric, emotional, behavioral and minority status) and might require an educational program with special materials, services, teaching approaches and/or equipment.

Children in the United States receiving special education services sometimes are referred to as "exceptional children," an inclusive term that refers to those who would receive special education services as well as children who are gifted. Forlin and Forlin (2000) note that Australia has a definition of special education which focuses on special needs and includes gifted and talented as well as those who are from diverse cultural backgrounds, geographically isolated or at risk of not achieving their potential. Forlin and Forlin also say that this is an "extremely broad" definition of the term and that services usually are limited to those receiving designated funding.[7]

Countries use different kinds of classification systems to decide who shall receive services. For example, Denmark uses two categories – "special needs and extensive special needs" (Højsteen 2011). Some countries consider two points: the extent to which a child has a low educational performance and the type of medical disability (usually 4–10 categories). Poland and the United States have more than 10 categories of disability (Peters 2007, p. 118). Some countries may include children who are not medically disabled in the special needs category (e.g., refugees, gifted, disadvantaged). A tripartite system for explaining difficulties in learning – based on clear biological reasons, no particular reason and difficulties arising from disadvantages – is being used by a growing number of countries (Peters 2007, p. 118).

It is easier to make general statements about special education in one country than to characterize it globally. In many countries children's special needs are not identified, while in others children's needs are supposed to be identified, appropriate services should be delivered and the aim is to integrate (rather than segregate). As one might expect, economically developing countries frequently have not been able to identify or meet the special needs of children.

---

[6]The International Standard Classification of Education, in 1997, replaced the term *special education* with *special needs education*. This change was made to distinguish the 1997 approach which focused on intervention in any place from the earlier definition which connected special education with a place – special institutions, schools or classrooms (Florian 2007).

[7]The authors indicate that special education in Australia, like other forms of education, is the responsibility of the individual jurisdictions and that each state and territory has its own Education Act.

The following notes about experiences in three countries – *Russia*, *Malaysia* and *Uganda* – allow the reader to begin to think about some of the differences around the world regarding special education. I begin here with Elena Iarskaia-Smirnova and Pavel Romanov's (2007, pp. 91–92) description of special education in *Russia*:

> Special education in the late Soviet period may be characterized by the following developments: children were classified as 'capable and incapable of learning;' a concept "disabled child" (rebionok-invalid) was introduced in 1979 following the ratification of international legislation. In the rhetoric of the official agenda of the post-Soviet period, there is a recognition of the necessity to move from equal rights to equal opportunities (and) from institutionalization to integration. During this period the terms 'children with special educational needs,' 'children with limited abilities' are discussed; a term 'special education' is sometimes used instead of 'defektologia.'
>
> ... The shortcomings of the Russian system of educating children with disabilities are reported ... by the Russian and international human rights and disability NGOs. According to many experts, disabled children with developmental disabilities are often marked as 'uneducable;' the majority of teachers and administrators have little or no understanding of disability issues or training to deal with them; there is very little accessible transportation and very few accessible school buildings, the institutionalization of children harks back to the Soviet era.
>
> Over the past 10 years in Russia, with the emergence of disability advocacy NGOs and NGOs serving parents of disabled children and the passing of new federal and regional disability legislation, some significant social changes have occurred to improve the quality of life of persons with disabilities ... At the present time, integrated education could be considered as the priority of state educational policy in Russia. The transition to inclusive education is predetermined by Russia's ratification of the U.N. Convention of children and disabled rights ...

According to Curtis and Roza (2002), "Kremlin officials have publicly acknowledged the huge problem of inaccessibility and the lack of federal support provided to the disability community." Though integrated education is now a priority, more than 70 % of the 1.6 million Russian children with some kind of disability receive little or no formal education (Vershbow 2004; Roudik 2007). Roudik (2007) also indicates that "the dropout rate among the disabled is much higher than among students of regular schools and only one percent of people with disabilities continue to study at institutions of higher education."

There has been some improvement in recent years. Moscow, for instance, now has "140 public schools and a dozen ... kindergartens" that can teach children who have disabilities (Okorokova 2011). And Iarskaia-Smirnova (2011) notes that while "development is very slow" there are now "some cases of real success, real inclusion ... in Moscow ..., Petrozavodsk and other Russian regions."

The situation in *Malaysia* was described by a Malaysian consultant (Anonymous 2006) in the following way:

> Schools in Malaysia are Federal agencies with incredible bureaucracies. They are not sensitive or responsive to the needs and demands of parents or children. In Malaysia, school is considered as something beyond reproach – teachers are treated as almost demigods, at least among the less educated. The idea of telling teachers how to teach is unthinkable. Furthermore, many parents are not aware of their children's needs – much less their rights.

> It's unthinkable for parents of special children to put pressure on schools in any way. Even in normal schools, this does not happen. Parents are happy enough that their children have a place to go while they work – they are not too concerned with what happens in the schools. Besides the special classes in normal schools where only special children who are not too severe are accepted, there are residential institutions set up by the government. I found these residential government institutions for special children dismal – they are not well run. Abuse does happen, but I do not think the public is aware of it. They are placed under the welfare department, not the education department. Once in a while well-informed parents may make a police report when they believe their child is abused in the schools and institutions. That's about it

In *Uganda*, "education is one of the... Government's key priorities" and an "Act in 1954... granted education for people with disabilities" (Kristensen et al. 2006, pp. 139–40). While 3.2 % of students in primary schools in Uganda have an identified learning disability, the figure might be higher because students with mild or moderate challenges might not be identified (Kristensen et al. 2006) or they might not be in school.[8] In fact, AbleChildAfrica (2011, p. 4), a non-governmental organization (NGO) based in London, "found rates of childhood disability in Uganda to be as high as 16 %." Uganda's commitment to providing education for all has been characterized as "progressive" and "considerable" (Miles and Singal 2010) and selected programs for deaf children enrolled in inclusive schools and programs for their parents have been showcased (Wilson, Miles and Kaplan 2008, pp. 51–52, 104–105), but other research has highlighted problems in the schools.

AbleChildAfrica (2011, pp. 8–9) sponsored a survey, in 2005, conducted by its partner, the Uganda Society for Disabled Children. The USDC survey found:

> Integrated education was suitable for children with mild impairments who have supportive parents, but blind and deaf children with sensory impairments struggle to thrive in the large class sizes found in the average Ugandan school, which allow for only minimal teacher attention to the individual needs of each child. The assessment and examination system rarely allows extra time for students with impairments. While current thinking in Uganda supports inclusive education, in practice the USDC study did not find any fully inclusive school. Inaccessible latrines... lack of specialist teachers (especially for deaf and blind children) and the lack of specialist educational material all remain barriers to the full participation of disabled children. The teacher training colleges that were surveyed did not adequately prepare teachers to deliver inclusive education. This included even specialist training institutions...

Special schools (those that are exclusively for students who are disabled, physically handicapped, deaf, blind or mentally handicapped) were found to be problematic. AbleChildAfrica (2011, p. 8) noted that they were "few and far between" and "most were established and continue to be supported by NGOs and faith-based organizations, and... receive little or no government support."

[8] AbleChildAfrica (2011), p. 8 says "based on the latest data there may be 2 m disabled children in Uganda and perhaps only 20 % of them are in school."

Kristensen et al. (2006) conducted a study of 15 special schools in Uganda and found:

> Most of (the) special schools are boarding schools... (and are) far from homes and... families. Special schools in Uganda do not meet the minimum educational standards set by the Education Standards Agencies.

Kristensen et al. (2006) said the majority of those interviewed thought that the standards of their buildings were poor. Eleven of the 15 schools, for instance, had electricity, but also had frequent power problems. Two of the 15 schools had toilets with flush systems. The researchers also found:

> Financial constraints; lack of teaching materials, negative attitudes from parents, (children) not properly assessed before admission; no assessments... carried out of learners' progress; and some parents abandoning their children once the children were admitted to special schools.... Teachers were, in many cases, not adequate, not interested or unqualified. (Only 3% of the 264 teachers in the 15 schools had degrees in special needs education.) Nine out of the 15 schools had ramps. In most of the schools, four or five learners had to share a bench meant for three persons. This made it difficult for the learners to get space for writing.

Teachers indicated that the majority of the students had not been "properly assessed" making it difficult to address their needs. It also was noted that 313 of the 2,172 students in the special schools did not have any disabilities. In some cases, parents sent their children to the schools because of the nearby location.

– – – – – – – – – –

Four points should be made about special education from a global perspective. First, there are differences in how special education is defined (e.g., separate schools, inclusion, categories or no categories). Second, there is a movement toward inclusion but, in many countries, this is still a very distant goal. Even if some of the more economically-developed countries have rather good objectives, they may not come close to meeting expectations in all areas or in all parts of their countries. Countries that are less developed economically may need an incremental strategy that is tied to resource availability (e.g., teachers with sufficient training, accessible buildings, necessary equipment and materials).

Third, better data are needed to understand the extent of disability.[9] While the first *World Report on Disability* discussed this problem at great length, it also indicated (World Health Organization and World Bank Group 2011, p. 44) there are approximately 785–975 million persons (15.6–19.4 %) in the world, 15 years and older, who are disabled. Of these, some 110–190 million (2.2–3.8 %) have severe disability. Estimates of disability for children between the ages of 0–14 range from

---

[9]UNICEF's *State of the World's Children 2011* did not even include disability in its statistical table because "new, comparable data are unavailable for a significant number of countries" (Anthony 2011, p. 86).

93 to 150 million (World Health Organization and World Bank Group 2011, p. 205). *Disability World* (2003) estimates only 2 % of disabled children are in school.[10]

Fourth, there are just a few countries in which families know they have the right to have individual programs for students with special needs and where special education mediation also is widely available. One of these countries is the United States.

Special Education in the United States

Before passage of the Education for All Handicapped Children Act in 1975, the 50 states were not required to enroll students with disabilities in the public schools and, according to the Federal Education Budget Project (n.d.) "a majority of the then four million children with disabilities were denied meaningful participation in public education... (and) nearly half of these children were excluded entirely from public schools." Responsibility rested with families and many children were put in residential institutions which frequently lacked educational programs. The situation is quite different now as 9.1 % (more than six million students) of enrolled students (6–21 years of age) receive special education and related services (U.S. Department of Education 2010, p. xviii).

Provisions of the United Nations Universal Declaration of Human Rights[11] in 1948, the 2006 United Nations Convention on the Rights of Persons with Disabilities[12] (see Appendix 2) and Optional Protocol are pertinent. In the U.S., the landmark Civil Rights Act of 1964[13] has been followed by four main pieces of U.S. legislation that deal with special education: Section 504 of the Rehabilitation Act of 1973, the Americans with Disabilities Act of 1990, the Individuals with Disabilities Education Act of 1975 and the No Child Left Behind Act of 2001.

Section 504 of the Rehabilitation Act of 1973, a civil rights law, protects children and adults against discrimination because of a disability. While Section 504 states that students with disabilities (broadly defined) can participate in educational programs, schools are not compelled to provide expensive or substantial kinds of services. Schools only must provide "reasonable accommodations."

---

[10]Rousso (2004) and Nagata (2003) also noted that even within this already terrible situation, disabled boys have more educational advantages than disabled girls.

[11]Education is defined as a universal right by Article 26.

[12]The Convention opened for signature on March 30, 2007 and entered into force on May 3, 2008. Article 24 is about education (e.g., "without discrimination," "on the basis of equal opportunity," "ensure... inclusive education," "lifelong learning," "learn life and social development skills," "qualified teachers," and "incorporate disability awareness."

[13]The Civil Rights Act of 1964 (CRA), a very important piece of civil rights legislation, indicates that all persons are entitled to be free of discrimination. Although people with disabilities are not specifically named in the Act, the principles that underlie the CRA also are the principles framing later legislation about the rights of individuals with disabilities and many of the early special education cases cited the Act (Applequist 2006).

The Individuals with Disabilities Education Act (IDEA) of 1990, replacing the 1975 Education for all Handicapped Children Act, provides educational rights and benefits for children with disabilities and also protects them from discrimination. Under IDEA, an eligible child has more rights and benefits than under Section 504. The eligible child has the right to a free appropriate public education (FAPE) in the least restrictive environment, an Individualized Educational Program designed to address the child's individual learning needs and certain procedural safeguards.

The Individuals with Disabilities Education Act Amendments of 1997 (reauthorized in 2004 with final regulations published in August 2006 and in September 2011) identified 13 categories of disability (2004, Section 300.8)[14]: autism, deaf-blindness, deafness, emotional disturbance, hearing impairment, mental retardation, multiple disability, orthopedic impairment, other health impairment, specific learning disabilities, speech or language impairment, traumatic brain injury and visual impairment including partial sight and blindness.

The No Child Left Behind Act of 2001 (NCLB) is the renamed and amended Elementary and Secondary Education Act, first passed in 1965. Under the NCLB, schools are held accountable for the achievement of all children, including those who have disabilities.

Some general points may be made about students (ages 6–21) in the United States who are designated and receiving special education services, based on available data (US Department of Education 2010) and the legislation. First, American Indian/Alaska Native and black students are over-represented in the population of special education students. According to Beth Harry (2007), the pattern for black students has been noticed since the 1975 Education of All Handicapped Children Act.[15] Harry goes on to note that a particular area of concern is that:

> disproportionate placements (are) confined to the 'high incidence' disability categories, which are determined by clinical judgment, rather than the 'low incidence' categories, which rely on evidence of biological or organic anomalities.

Second, a little more than half (53.6 %) the students spend most of the school day in regular classes. Third, 4 % of the students are educated in separate environments (public or private residential facilities, public and private separate schools, and homebound or hospital environments). Fourth, the graduation rate for all students served by IDEA was 54.4 %; the graduation rate for black students was the lowest at 39.2 %. Fifth, boys are over-represented in special education. This has raised questions about whether "all girls with disabilities are appropriately identified" as those who are identified tend to be older and more disabled (Coutinho and Oswald 2005, pp. 7–8).

Sixth, the federal government has set the standards (students with disabilities are entitled to a fair, appropriate and inclusive education) and raised parent expectations, but has not financed what is required. Many special education disputes focus on or include issues related to financing (e.g., out-of-district school placement,

---

[14] http://idea.ed.gov/

[15] According to Harry (2007), research from many countries indicates that it is the historical status of a minority group within a society (rather than race) that accounts for low educational attainment.

transportation to an out-of-district program, a more effective educational program given the child's particular needs). The policies currently in place need adequate financial resources.

Mediation as an Approach for Resolving Special Education Conflicts

Families and schools in the U.S. have at least four ways to resolve special education disputes. The first is a state complaint procedure, a review by a state educational agency to determine if there has been a violation of IDEA by the state or a local school district. In the second approach, a due process hearing is held. This is an administrative procedure in which an impartial hearing officer reviews evidence, conducts examinations, cross-examines witnesses, issues findings and then makes a decision. The third approach, a resolution meeting, is required if either the local educational agency (LEA) or the parents have requested a due process hearing. This meeting is considered "a final opportunity for a face-to-face meeting before the formality of the due process hearing begins"[16] (Bar-Lev and Serak 2006). The last approach, less costly and less adversarial than a hearing, is mediation. Voluntary mediation must be offered to parties when a due process request has been filed.

Mediation is defined here as a humanistic and creative process in which one or more impartial individuals help disputants discuss an issue or issues that concern one or more of the parties. This process is sometimes referred to as facilitated negotiation. The mediator establishes an open, trusting environment in which parties are encouraged to discuss facts as well as their personal feelings about the issue or issues that brought them to the table. Mediation is usually conducted as a flexibly-structured process and can be free-flowing or more controlled. If the outcome of this process is an agreement, it would be shaped by the parties and satisfactory to them.

Mediation is used to settle a wide variety of disputes between individuals, organizations, communities and governments as well as combinations of these disputants (e.g., community residents might have a dispute with a company that they believe is polluting their neighborhood as well as the government agencies that are supposed to protect their interests). Mediation can be an excellent method for resolving some kinds of disputes in part because it can be faster and less expensive than the alternatives. Most importantly, the parties can create their own resolution to a dispute rather than have a decision imposed on them.

Mediation is not used or offered regularly by most countries for special education disputes. For instance, according to Gunvall (2006) most disputes in Sweden are resolved with the local school or higher levels of educational administration. Thorin (2010) coordinates special education in her district in Sweden and she said she talks with people and resolves the matters. Mediation is not offered. A special education

[16]The resolution meeting may be waived if both parties agree and sign a written document. The parties can then proceed to a due process hearing or, instead, request mediation.

expert in Israel said she did not know of any special education mediations, but an Israeli mediator (Gefen 2006) says his consulting organization has worked with the Ministry of Education in different ways and that their group has mediated special education cases. Denmark (Højsteen 2011; Klagenævnet for vidtgående specialundervisning 2011) does not use mediation but has a national complaint board as a last resort for cases regarding children who have extensive special needs. The board consists of six members appointed, for four-year terms by the Minister of Education. The chair of the board must by a lawyer and, in 2011, was headed by a judge. There are two members from a national coalition that represents organizations dealing with disability, two representatives from municipalities and, according to the board office (Klagenævnet for vidtgående specialundervisning 2011) one representative of the organization that represents the five regions in Denmark.[17]

A few countries (Scotland, England, Wales and the United States) do offer the mediation process for special education cases. The Additional Support for Learning Act of 2004 in Scotland (with an implementation date of November 2005), for instance, authorized mediation for "parents/carers and young people who are in dispute with education departments regarding issues related to additional support needs" (Scottish Mediation Network 2003; Mitchell 2006).

A Special Education Case in the United States

When the Individuals with Disabilities Education Act (IDEA) was reauthorized in June 1997 by the U.S. Congress, it required more collaborative problem-solving from parents and schools. The law also required that all states offer mediation as a possible way to resolve special education disputes. According to Philip Moses (2006, 2011),[18] CADRE's assistant director, there are four general approaches taken by the 50 states to mediation: (1) a state list (roster) of approved mediators, (2) a particular university program or center that offers mediation, (3) mediators available from the state's department of education or perhaps from a state panel such as administrative law judges and (4) mediators that are made available through a state's community mediation centers. According to Moses, the most popular approach is for a state to have an approved list of mediators. Even when a state chooses option 2 or 4, rosters are developed by those organizations under contracts with the state's department of education.

[17] The board meets every three weeks for five or six hours to review cases. The review is of all the written documents that have been submitted and it is rare that people appear before the board or that attorneys are involved. In 2010, "the board closed 630 cases." Cases are closed for a number of reasons including that they are sent back to the municipality/region or the parties came to an agreement on their own (Klagenævnet for vidtgående specialundervisning 2011).

[18] CADRE, the Consortium for Appropriate Dispute Resolution, is a project of Direction Services in Oregon (USA).

Each of the state approaches to mediation has strengths and weaknesses; none is seen as the best model. Many states have used one model (e.g., roster, working with community mediation centers) for a long time while others have changed their basic model. One state, for instance, started by offering mediation by its special education staff, but found that the staff did not know enough about mediation. The state moved to a system of selecting experienced mediators and provided a short program about special education and training in special education mediation for this select group.

Over the last nine years, I have mediated more than 70 special education cases in the United States. Most of these cases were completed with one meeting, but ten of them each required two meetings.[19] The special education cases were filed with a state's Department of Education because of allegations such as a principal gave unfair treatment to a child with special needs, inappropriate categorization of a child, inappropriate exclusion rather than mainstreaming of a child, lack of appropriate services, transportation not provided to an appropriate school outside of the district, controversy about an Individualized Educational Program and/or payment for an appropriate school placement outside of the home school district.

Cases were most frequently initiated by parents, but at least one was filed by the school system and four were jointly initiated.[20] More than half of the cases were difficult and complicated. Some involved as few as five persons, but a few had 15 or more people involved. Most cases included just the parties and their close associates (e.g., teachers, school consultants, attorneys, advocate, family members and friends) but several involved (in person or through conference calls) program experts, representatives of disability organizations, physicians, and one involved a representative of a hospital program. Some cases had no attorneys, but several cases had a number of attorneys as well as new attorneys or attorneys-in- training.[21] The usual length of a mediation meeting (not including pre-mediation conversations) was six or seven hours but some took considerably longer. In many of the cases, somebody on one side was initially resistant to settling the matter and/or sitting down to talk at length about the issues. Almost all of the cases resulted in signed agreements. Here is an example of one such case:[22]

The Adams family filed a due process complaint against their local school system but said, rather than go directly to a hearing, the family would like to try to resolve the case through

---

[19]In one of these instances, a terrible car crash involving five students occurred during a mediation. The superintendent and assistant superintendent of the small rural school district were involved in the mediation and, because they needed to immediately deal with the emergency, the mediation required a second meeting the following week. Another case involved two siblings and so it took more time than one day. The other cases were continued because both sides felt it would be useful to continue the conversation after some additional information was obtained.

[20]Parents, a public agency or the child – when he or she reaches the age of majority – can request mediation.

[21]This was the first mediation of any kind that I had handled in which the attorneys (including the one in training) outnumbered the other participants.

[22]The names and details of two actual cases have been changed and combined to avoid identifying the parties.

mediation. The case was filed on behalf of their 12-year-old daughter, Rachel, a white, first-year student in a large middle (junior high) school. Rachel is categorized as Other Health Impaired (OHI) but there was a discussion of a Specific Learning Disability in written expression.[23] *The two other children in the family have no special education needs and so, when Rachel entered kindergarten, it was the first time the family had dealt with special education.*

The mediator called each of the parties not only to set the date and time of the meeting, but also to hear what each might have to say about the issues and what might resolve the situation. In the course of these confidential conversations, the mother, identified here as April, indicated that one particular book about dyslexia (specific reading disability)[24] *has been very important to her. The mediator asked the mother if that information could be shared, in advance of the mediation, with the school representatives and she agreed. The school representatives noted the name of the book and both reviewed it before the meeting.*

The parents were accompanied to the mediation by an advocate (a parent who had dealt with school systems on behalf of children with special needs) and the school system was represented by the director of special education and the principal of the middle school. The mediation began after introductions were made and discussion about the forms that would be used (e.g., release to allow school records to be viewed by the mediator, agreement or no-agreement forms). The parents had been asked to "introduce" Rachel (though she was not attending the mediation), including the challenges and their (and her) aspirations for the benefit of those attending the mediation session. The parents began by showing pictures of their family and particularly their daughter. The parents then talked about Rachel from the time she was born until the present.

The mother, April, said Rachel was born a week late and always had ear infections. By the time Rachel was 4 months old, they suspected that something was wrong. April said she knew Rachel's written skills were not developing when she was in pre-school and she wondered about promoting Rachel to kindergarten. When she asked the kindergarten teacher about this, April remembers being told to enroll her and "turn off the TV and teach her." April said the whole family had been working with Rachel at home, but she just "wasn't catching on." April read to Rachel every day, but "Rachel did not want to read." April said that she had done "everything she could as a parent."

April said that Rachel was unsuccessful in school and even the bus ride was overwhelming because of the distance and noise. Rachel refused to take the bus and frequently would not get out of the car to go into the school. Rachel would not get out of April's arms.

The parents decided to enroll Rachel in private school for first grade. She started writing in cursive. Another child was now expected and the financial sacrifice for private school tuition for Rachel was too high. Because of financial considerations and because the parents thought Rachel now had a higher platform for learning, they sent her back to the public school and held her back one grade. They thought maturity was a factor in Rachel's performance in school.

Now, five years after Rachel returned to the public school, she is in some advanced placement classes (because she is very bright) and periodically has been offered special assistance (a reader and a scribe). But the parents say she still is unable to comprehend

---

[23]Other Health Impairment is defined in IDEA 2004 (Section 300.8, http://idea.ed.gov) as "having limited strength, vitality, or alertness with respect to the educational environment, that (i) is due to chronic or acute health problems . . . and (ii) adversely affects a child's educational performance." Specific Learning Disability is defined as "a disorder in one or more of the basic psychological processes involved in understanding or in using language, spoken or written . . . "

[24]Dyslexia, an unexpected difficulty in reading, is "characterized by difficulties with accurate and/or fluent word recognition and poor spelling and decoding abilities" (Lyon et al. 2003, p. 2). It is the most common learning disability "affecting over 80 % of those identified as learning disabled" (Shaywitz et al. 2008, p. 453).

and write. They are concerned that if the present situation continues, Rachel will "fall flat on her face" once she leaves school. The parents think that Rachel will "be able to talk her way through life for so long" and they think it is wrong "to just push her through school."

April says that Rachel talks with adults, but has a hard time making friends of her own age. Every morning Rachel's mother gives her a "pep talk" before going to school about how to talk to kids and keep things organized. After a recent classroom disagreement between Rachel and another girl, the school counselor interviewed other students to find out what happened. The school did not contact the parents before doing the interviews and, for Rachel, this was a terrible, public event. After this incident, Rachel has had a few emotional breakdowns at school and, at one point, told her mother that she did not think she should be alive.

April says that she thinks one of the problems her daughter is facing is dyslexia. She says she suspected this was a problem and had her tested by an expert in a large city about three hours away. April and the advocate both say that the school should have noticed this problem a long time ago. The expert confirmed that Rachel is dyslexic and started working with her. There have been improvements and April would like the school system to pay for a summer program for Rachel that the expert is offering.

After the initial statements from the parents and some questions by the school system representatives, we enter into a general discussion. It becomes apparent that the advocate is angry about the school system's lack of attention to this situation and thinks this school system has acted this way with other students. The mother had enlisted the aid of the advocate and trusts her advice and approach. The special education director says he is concerned about Rachel's situation, but seems focused on the advocate's anger more than the issues faced by the child. After about four hours, the advocate says she thinks the discussion is not going anywhere and that she is going to leave. The advocate says the parents can continue talking if they want to do so, but the advocate says she doesn't think any resolution is possible.

The parents decide to continue talking with the school representatives. As the discussion proceeds, it becomes apparent that the father would like to focus more on the current situation and the future rather than the past and also that the principal, known in her community as someone who had turned around a school with problems, was unaware that this new student was facing so many problems. The principal makes it very clear that she was unaware that a counselor had dealt with a problem in a way that did not follow correct procedures and that neither she nor the parents had been informed about the situation in advance of taking action. She said she knew that Rachel had learning difficulties, but thought that the issues were being addressed. She was unaware of the extent of the problems facing Rachel and the concerns of the parents. She asks the parents to give her a chance to correct the situation.

The school system representatives and the parents did come to an agreement. Among the outcomes: (1) Rachel would have a dyslexia assessment that would be completed within six weeks. (2) The school system would hire an assistant for the school and that person's primary responsibility would be to work with Rachel. If there were any problems with this assistance, the parents were to ask the principal to immediately address them. (3) The school counselor and the parents will meet to discuss the handling of the previous incident involving the counselor and how future communication would be handled. (4) The school will provide a draft meeting agenda at least one week in advance of any Individualized Educational Program (IEP) meetings for Rachel. The parents will be invited to make suggestions for the IEP before the draft has been written, after the draft has been reviewed and as well as during the meeting. (5) The next IEP meeting will be held at an agreed date and time during a one-week period that is three weeks away. (6) The parents and the special education director will continue to discuss dyslexia and information that may be useful in providing assistance to Rachel. Both parties are interested in learning about evidence-based approaches to dyslexia. (7) The principal agreed to make the school lab available to

Rachel for one month during the summer. (Rachel and her family will be away the other two months.) (8) The school agrees to contact both parents if something unusual happens at school regarding Rachel. (9) The principal and the parents agree to communicate directly about successes and concerns.

The day after the mediation, the principal called the mediator to ask what she should do to make this agreement work. The principal says she had been so focused on school changes, that perhaps she had missed giving enough personal attention to certain individual cases. We discussed the testing that needs to be done, the resources that might be needed and the immediate need to build a relationship with this family. The principal decided to call the parents to thank them for giving her the opportunity to help Rachel and to put their first meeting in place. As the mediator had talked with a school representative, the mediator also called the parents. They told the mediator how pleased they were that the principal took the initiative to call them and that they were looking forward to meeting with her.

The advocate also called the mediator to say that she thought this agreement should be thrown out. The mediator talked with the advocate about giving the agreement a chance and to continue giving the parents help on issues that they need to address with the school. While the advocate might be seen by some as impeding the process, she has been and can continue to be very helpful to the parents.

Additional Intervention Strategies

Mediators are involved in special education settings in a variety of ways. In addition to conducting mediations, they may be involved in *prevention activities, coaching, facilitating,* and *conducting research. Prevention activities* help analyze and address situations before they become very problematic. Mediators run workshops, help design material for websites and serve as consultants about the design and improvement of conflict intervention programs. Workshops which include parents as well as school system personnel can help provide information and suggest ways to deal with situations. Websites can be resources that help people to find out about support groups and services. Mediators also give lectures and run discussions about preventing and resolving disputes.

Coaching, in this case, is a process for helping a disputant or disputants as well as a person or group (e.g., managers) dealing with those involved in disputes. In the late 1980s and in the 1990s the term became a popular one for working with executives or those who needed to manage conflicts (Brinkert 2006, pp. 518–519). A mediator could make coaching part of the mediation process by working with parties before, during or after mediation. Coaching also can be done separately from a mediation to help people prepare for a negotiation, mediation or conflict resolution meeting. Mediators also can coach during the training of mediators (White and Agne 2009).

Facilitating is the process of enabling groups to run their meetings cooperatively and efficiently. It is a rather well-known activity for mediators in special education settings in some states. A number of states (e.g., Delaware, Minnesota, Oklahoma,

Wisconsin, Iowa[25]), now offer mediators trained in facilitation to school systems to facilitate Individualized Educational Program (IEP) meetings. As Alliance/CADRE (2004) has noted, "a facilitator helps keep members of the IEP team focused on the development of the IEP while addressing conflicts and disagreements that may arise during the meeting." The mediator/facilitator also can help the system design or revise the IEP process for the system or train people in the school system and parent community to be facilitators.

Mediators also can facilitate resolution meetings. Alaska and Wisconsin, for instance, contract with organizations to provide mediation services and those same organizations provide facilitation services for resolution meetings. Oklahoma, through the Special Education Resolution Center at Oklahoma State University, offers their mediators to serve as facilitators for the resolution meetings "with a goal of at least half the meetings to be facilitated" (CADRE 2010a, p. 7) and Wisconsin, in its guide to resolution meetings, notes that the parents and the school can request a facilitator from the Wisconsin Special Education Mediation System (Bar-Lev and Serak 2006).

Conducting research is something that only some special education mediators have been trained to do. Those with sufficient training may, for instance, develop case studies, study the effectiveness of various approaches or examine systems in which special education mediation is offered. Other mediators may participate in the research process by discussing their work or allowing others to observe it.

Some Ideas for Consideration

The following points are offered for consideration by those who might be interested in starting, improving or analyzing a special education mediation system.

1. **Mediation can work.** According to the U.S. General Accounting Office (2003):

   > State officials (in selected states) told us they found that mediation was successful in resolving disputes, strengthening relationships between families and educators, saving financial resources, and reaching resolution more quickly. The University of the Pacific reported that 93 percent of the mediation cases in California resulted in agreements between families and schools during the 2001–02 fiscal year; the cost of a mediator was about one-tenth that of a hearing officer.

   Mediation can be an effective way for parties in a dispute to shape their own solutions relatively quickly and quietly. If both parties want to settle the matter and/or improve their relationship, this approach can be very helpful. If a mediation system is not found to be working, the state and its stakeholders need

[25] There are times when local and area educational agencies ask for a mediator to act as a facilitator when a parent or advocate files a state complaint. There also have been times when parties "request that the state mediator return to facilitate the revision of the IEP to reflect the written settlement agreement, prior to the parent signing the agreement" (CADRE 2010b, p. 6).

to discuss and address the problems.[26] One way of doing this might be for the state to have a stakeholder advisory council.[27]

2. **Mediation can be made less difficult... and that may mean we need to discuss the attorneys.** Attorneys can be very helpful in the mediation process. In many cases,[28] they have expertise in special education law and can help the parties understand how this case might be seen in a hearing or a court. They also can help to creatively resolve the situation.

   Some attorneys, however, don't understand and/or don't accept that the purpose of mediation is to see if the matter can be resolved creatively at the lowest level and improve the way schools and parents deal with each other. They may be counseling their clients that they could win in a hearing and should not try to resolve matters at this level. Some attorneys use the same approach in mediation (e.g., making the strongest case for the client) that they would use in court. Some attorneys think only other lawyers should be mediators[29] or that there is one set way of conducting the mediations.[30]

   Doreen Philpot (2007), an attorney who represents parents in special education disputes, has identified what she sees as the worst reasons for a school district to use mediation and some of them involve their attorneys:

   – To go through the empty procedures so that they look reasonable and willing to work things out, when, in fact, they're not.
   – To secure information that they can use against the parent in a hearing.

[26]Doreen Philpot (n.d.) is an attorney representing children with special needs and their parents in Indiana and Texas. She says the following about the mediation system in one of the states: "Neither parents nor school districts have found the mediation system to be all that beneficial, as evidenced by the fact that schools and parents actually prefer to hire and pay for private mediators, rather than using the no-cost DOE (Department of Education) mediators. This has been going on for several years... and this is the sign of a broken system."

[27]The Oklahoma State Department of Education (OSDE) uses the Special Education Resolution Center (SERC) at Oklahoma State University to manage the state's special education mediation services (CADRE 2010a). SERC develops policies and procedures with the advice of the advisory council and presents them to OSDE as possible changes. The advisory council has 11–13 members. The council includes not less than 51 % of parents whose children have disabilities, an OSDE representative, school district representatives, a community representative and a special education mediator.

[28]In some case, attorneys have a background in the law but have never or infrequently dealt with special education cases.

[29]As one attorney (Philpot, n.d.) noted, it "is especially helpful (that all the special education mediators in one particular state are attorneys) because the language and terminology inherent in special education matters can be a stumbling block for someone not familiar with them." Special education mediators from all backgrounds, not just attorneys, should have training and experience regarding relevant language/terminology.

[30]According to Philpot (n.d.), "after the mediator gives the opening ground rules talk, he or she will put the school in one room and us (the parents and their representative) in another and will shuttle back and forth between the two rooms." The order of when things happen varies in mediations as well as whether there are any or many small meetings.

- To get a handle on parent/parent advocate/parent attorney's way of operating/style... because they've been ordered by the school board and/or outside insurance carrier.
- To see if there's some way to avoid the cost/hassle of a hearing and possible appeal and federal court litigation.

Some state systems have found ways to make the mediation process less difficult. Some allow mediators the freedom to spend time with attorneys in advance of the mediation to make sure they understand the process and how to be helpful. Some might ask mediators to advise attorneys and advocates that the parties, in most cases, are to do most of the talking (in order to strengthen their relationships) and that attorneys and advocates are there for advice and to help develop, if possible, a collaborative agreement. The state mediation system or the local school district may have as a general approach that school systems will not bring an attorney if the parent does not bring an attorney or a state system might discourage or rule out the participation of attorneys in mediation.

3. **Mediation can be affected by outside factors such as politics, finances or the system.** Artiles (2003) has discussed how cultural politics and a "neoconservative tide of (educational) reforms" has influenced special education. Mediation of special education disputes (e.g., the system adopted or mediation practice) also can be affected in a negative way by politics, finances or a state department of education's usual way of doing things.

   A state's mediation system, for instance, may be too close to law firms or some of the attorneys that regularly undertake special education work for the school systems. A state may have a selection process for mediators that allows certain law firms to keep certain mediators from being hired. That can lead mediators to think they have to pay particular attention to certain influential legal representatives if they want to be considered as a mediator in future cases. Mediation systems also serve as gatekeepers (e.g., picking mediators, deciding how assignments are made, and how a mediation is to be handled) and these processes may be run in a closed way. A state budget for mediation may be so limited that it won't pay mediators or that it won't pay for mediators to work with the parties before actual mediation meetings. Safeguards of some kind (e.g., review processes, advisors and discussions that compare values, best practices, program goals and actual practices) are needed to protect the integrity of the system.
4. **Information about mediation should be easily available.** Information needs to be clear, easily available and publicized, and an easy way to do this is to have an excellent website. School system representatives and parents need easy access to information about the parent information centers, local representatives/advocates and links to relevant information and organizations. Sometimes advocacy groups and attorneys have not recommended mediation because they think that parents don't know enough about their rights. The information on a mediation program's website starts to address this potential problem.

The website for the U.S. state of Oklahoma developed by the Oklahoma Special Education Resource Center http://serc.okstate.edu is an example of a good start for a state website. For instance, under its "Resources" section there is a list of attorneys who might be consulted; contact information for relevant organizations in Oklahoma, the US Department of Education and other places (e.g., organizations like CADRE and those that monitor data on educational outcomes); and a list of common abbreviations. There also is a section on mediation which includes brief descriptions of the state's five mediators. A review of other state websites can provide some good ideas. Some, for instance, contain documents translated into a number of languages (e.g., Minnesota), a discussion of ombudsperson services (Virginia) and minutes of the state's special education Advisory Council meetings (e.g., North Carolina).[31]

A mediation website should consider linking to a variety of helpful sites. Here are three for consideration. The Center for Appropriate Dispute Resolution in Special Education (CADRE) (http://www.directionservice.org/cadre/) provides names of contacts in all 50 U.S. states and territories, information for family members, articles in Spanish, many useful articles in Spanish and English and a calendar of upcoming conferences and trainings. Another is Wrightslaw (www.wrightslaw.com), put in place in 1998 by Pete Wright, an attorney who represents children with special educational needs, and Pam Wright, a psychotherapist working with children and families (Wright and Wright 2004). The site provides advice about special education cases and gives dates and places of their training programs. Finally, KIDS London http://www.kids.org.uk was established in 1940 and has "pioneered a number of approaches and programs for disabled children and young people." Under "Mediation" and then "Help and Resources," (http://www.kids.org.uk/information/100885/100924/101697/help_and_resources) there is an interesting video of a special education mediation, links to various publications, Parent Partnership contact information (they provide independent advice) and even a link to CADRE.

5. **Creativity needs to be fostered.** Mediation is a creative endeavor. While an agency certainly needs to have boundaries for its mediation process, it periodically needs to review its approach to see if its limits are unnecessarily affecting the creativity of the process. For instance, an agency may be making mediations unnecessarily difficult if it asks the mediators to try to conduct mediations within a two-hour time frame, requires the mediators to use a narrow approach, reduces pre-meeting contact to briefly setting the time and place of the meeting, or decides there never is a good reason for parties to have a second meeting. Agencies and mediators need to work together to identify ways to foster and support the creative process.

[31] One expert (Anonymous 2011) who has reviewed all the U.S. state websites said that "many states have, well, horrible websites which is to say that virtually ALL states could improve" in areas such as ease of use, parent friendliness, content, availability of all forms and search capacity.

6. **Training and early intervention need to be high priorities.** Mediation is an important intervention tool, but agencies, programs, and parents are recognizing the importance of excellent communication from the beginning of a parent-school relationship, some schools (like Søholmskolen in Denmark) have developed a culture of acceptance and some school systems want early intervention when difficulties are just becoming apparent. Some school districts in different countries provide training for all (rather than one for parents and another for school personnel) as a step in the right direction. Some districts in the U.S. facilitated Individualized Educational Program (IEP) and resolution meetings and training in facilitation to improve the general quality of those meetings. A goal can be to reduce the need for mediation. Iowa, a U.S. state, is particularly interested in doing this. It has offered "low-cost or free conflict resolution and communication training for hundreds of stakeholders" (CADRE 2010b, p. 5). Iowa "wants to resolve differences as early in the process as possible" and believes the state has "created a strong statewide culture of early dispute prevention and resolution" (CADRE 2010b, pp. 4, 6).
7. **Share good ideas.** Parents and their support organizations as well as managers of mediation systems need to identify good ideas and regularly share them with all those involved. The U.S. state of Kentucky, for instance, has a fund to help its roster mediators attend advanced training at special education mediation conferences and workshops (Brown 2005) and Oklahoma's (CADRE 2010a, p. 7) mediators/facilitators "are invited to attend national mediation and facilitation conferences." The conflict resolution program in the U.S. state of Delaware runs workshops about facilitated IEP meetings and has found that mediations take less time (because issues have been narrowed) if there has been a facilitated IEP process (Fletcher 2006).

Conclusion

The world is beginning to identify and meet the needs of those who require additional support to be successful in educational systems. As we publicize the goals of inclusive, fair and appropriate education for all, we can expect parents and school systems to have differences of opinion about whether a child is receiving the promised fair, appropriate and inclusive education. When there are these disagreements, a creative mediation process is one way to help parties not only settle a dispute but improve future communication and even contribute to better school system policies and practices. Mediation, however, is not a static, one-approach-fits-all way of dealing with conflict. The process requires periodic reviews – emphasizing values and best practices in relation to existing policies and practices – and possible changes that can foster creativity and maximize effectiveness.

References

AbleChildAfrica. (2011). *Still not going to school: A review of the state of disabled children's access to education in Africa*. London: AbleChildAfrica.

Alliance/CADRE. (2004). *Facilitated IEP meetings: An emerging practice*. November. http://www.directionservice.org/cadre/facilitatediep.cfm

Andersen, A. M. Ø. (2011, November 16 and 22). Interviews with the Ringsted municipality's consultant for inclusive education. Ringsted/Denmark.

Anonymous. (2006, May 21). *Correspondence from a Malaysian consultant*.

Anonymous. (2011, September 27). *Correspondence*.

Anthony, D. (2011). *The state of the world's children 2011: Adolescence, an age of opportunity*. www.unicef.org/sowc2011/fullreport.php

Applequist, K. (2006). Special education legislation. In E. Fletcher-Janzen & C. R. Reynolds (Eds.), *The special education almanac* (pp. 537–562). Hoboken: Wiley.

Artiles, A. J. (2003). Special education's changing identity: Paradoxes and dilemmas in views of culture and space. *Harvard Educational Review, 73*(2), 164–202.

Bar-Lev, N., & Serak, J. (2006). *The resolution meeting: A guide for parents and educators*. http://www.wsems.us/resmeeting/index.html

Brinkert, R. (2006). Conflict coaching: Advancing the conflict resolution field by developing an individual disputant process. *Conflict Resolution Quarterly, 23*(4), 517–528.

Brown, K. (2005, May 18). *Interview with the assistant general counsel with responsibility for the coordination of special education mediation in Kentucky*.

Center for Appropriate Dispute Resolution in Special Education (CADRE). (2010a). *Oklahoma ~ An exemplary dispute resolution system in special education*. Eugene: CADRE.

Center for Appropriate Dispute Resolution in Special Education (CADRE). (2010b). *Iowa An exemplary dispute resolution system in special education*. Eugene: CADRE.

Coutinho, M. J., & Oswald, D. P. (2005). State variation in gender disproportionality in special education. *Remedial and Special Education, 26*(1), 7–15.

Curtis, B., & Roza, D. (2002). Access to an equal education for children and youth with disabilities in Russia, *Disability world, 15*. http://www.disabilityworld.org/09-10_02/children/russia.html

Disability World. (2003). World bank supports growth of inclusive education in Brazil. *Disability world: A bimonthly web-zine of international disability news*, 18. Retrieved 5 May 2006 from http://www.disabilityworld.org/04-05_03/children/brazil.shtml

Federal Education Budget Project. (n.d.). Individuals with disabilities education act overview. http://febp.newamerica.net/background-analysis/individuals-disabilities-education-act

Fletcher, F. (2006, May 30). *Interview with the Assistant Policy Scientist with responsibility for special education mediation*. Conflict Resolution Program of the Institute for Public Administration, University of Delaware.

Florian, L. (Ed.). (2007). *The sage handbook of special education*. London/Thousand Oaks/New Delhi: Sage.

Forlin, C., & Forlin, P. (2000). Special education research in Australia. *Exceptionality, 8*(4), 247–259.

Fritz, J. M. (2008). Improving special education mediation. *International Review of Sociology – Revue Internationale de Sociologie, 18*(3), 469–480.

Fritz, J. M. (2010). Special education mediation in the United States. In O. Dikova-Favorskaya (Ed.), *People with health limitations in modern society* (pp. 268–297). Zhitomar: DZHIVIES.

Gargiulo, R. M. (2006). *Special education in contemporary society: An introduction to exceptionality*. Belmont: Thomson Wadsworth.

Gefen, O. (2006, May 21). *Correspondence from a mediator with Gevim, a mediation center in Israel*.

Gruber, D. (2006, May 22). *Interview with the director of the Michigan Special Education Mediation Program*.

Gunvall, P. (2006, May 14). *Correspondence from a special education expert with the Swedish Institute for Special Needs Education.*

Harry, B. (2007). The disproportionate placement of ethnic minorities in special education. In L. Florian (Ed.), *The sage handbook of special education* (pp. 67–83). London/Thousand Oaks/New Delhi: Sage.

Højsteen, S. (2011, September 19). *Interview with a consultant for The Danish Council of Organizations of Disabled People.*

Iarskaia-Smirnova, E. (2011, September 18). *Correspondence with a Russian special education expert.*

Iarskaia-Smirnova, E., & Romanov, P. (2007). Perspectives of inclusive education in Russia. *European Journal of Social Work, 10*(1), 89–105.

Klagenævnet for vidtgående specialundervisning (The Special Education Appeals Board in Denmark). (2011, September 29). Correspondence.

Kristensen, K., Omagor-Loican, M., Onen, N., & Okot, D. (2006). Opportunities for inclusion? The education of learners with special educational needs and disabilities in special schools in Uganda. *British Journal of Special Education, 33*(3), 139–147.

Kyriazopoulou, M., & Weber, H. (Eds.). (2009). *Development of a set of indicators – For inclusive education in Europe*. Odense: European Agency for Development in Special Needs Education.

Lynch, S. L., & Irvine, A. N. (2009). Inclusive education and best practice for children with autism spectrum disorder: An integrated approach. *International Journal of Inclusive Education, 13*(8), 845–859.

Lyon, G., Shaywitz, S., & Shaywitz, B. (2003). A definition of dyslexia. *Annals of Dyslexia, 53*, 1–14.

Lyster, T. (2010) *Presentation about Mithras Policy in Ringsted Kommune*. Former director of Children and Culture in Ringsted. Unpublished.

Miles, S., & Singal, N. (2010). The education for all and inclusive education debate: Conflict, contradiction or opportunity? *International Journal of Inclusive Education, 14*(1), 1–15.

Mitchell, S. (2006, December 8). *Interview with the Mediatio and Services Development Officer, Children in Scotland.*

Moses, P. (2006, May 15 and 16) *Interview with CADRE's assistant director.*

Moses, P. (2011, September 26) *Correspondence from CADRE's assistano director.*

Nagata, K. K. (2003). Gender and disability in the Arab region: The challenges in the new millennium. *Asia Pacific Disability Rehabilitation Journal, 14*(1), 10–17.

Okorokova, L. (2011). Parents plead for children's rights. *Moscow News* Available on the website of the Regional Society of Disabled People PERSPEKTIVA. http://eng.perspektiva-inva.ru/index.php?1438

Peters, S. J. (2007). Inclusion as a strategy for achieving education for all. In L. Florian (Ed.), *The sage handbook of special education* (pp. 117–130). London/Thousand Oaks/New Delhi: Sage.

Philpot, D. J. (2007). *Special education mediation*. Retrieved 21 Jan 2007 from http://www.dphilpotlaw.com/html/mediation.html

Philpot, D. J. (2011, September 26). *Correspondence.*

Philpot, D. J. (n.d.). *Everything you ever wanted to know about mediation but were afraid to ask.* Retrieved 24 Sep 2011 from http://www.dphilpotlaw.com/html/mediation.html

Roudik, P. (2007). *Children's rights: Russian federation.* http://www.loc.gov/law/help/child-rights/russia.php

Rousso, H. (2004). *Education for all: A gender and disability perspective.* Background paper prepared in 2003 for the Education for All Global Monitoring Report 003(4): Gender and Education for All: The Leap to Equality.200.

Scottish Mediation Network. (2003, November 10). *Notes from the meeting of special education Mediation groups and the Scottish Mediation Network.*

Scully, J. (2006, May 15). *Interview with the president of the International Association of Special Education and dean of admissions at Maplebrook, a private school for students with a primary diagnosis of learning disability.*

Shaywitz, S. E., Morris, R., & Shaywitz, B. A. (2008). The education of dyslexic children from childhood to young adulthood. *Annual Review of Psychology, 59*, 451–475.
Thorin, I. (2010). *Interview with the coordinator of special needs education*. Sweden: Sigtuna kommun.
United Nations. (1948). *Universal declaration of human rights*. New York: United Nations.
United Nations Educational, Scientific and Cultural Organization. (2009). *Policy guidelines on inclusion in education*. Paris: UNESCO.
United States Department of Education, Office of Special Education and Rehabilitative Services, Office of Special Education Programs. (2010). *29th Annual Report to Congress on the Implementation of the Individuals with Disabilities Education Act, 2007* (Vol. 1). Washington, DC: US Department of Education.
U.S. General Accounting Office. (2003). *Special education: Numbers of formal disputes are generally low and states are using mediation and other strategies to resolve conflicts*. Report to the ranking minority member, Committee on Health, Education, Labor and Pensions, U.S. Senate. September. GAO-03-897.
Vershbow, A. (2004). *Toward greater educational access for the disabled, inclusive education: problems and perspectives, conference*, Moscow, 24 June, http://moscow.usembassy.gov/bilateral/statement.php?record_id=100
White, C. H., & Agne, R. R. (2009). Communication practices of coaches during mediation training: Addressing issues of knowledge and enactment. *Conflict Resolution Quarterly, 27*(1), 83–105.
Wilson, K., Miles, S., & Kaplan, I. (2008). *Family friendly!: Working with deaf children and their communities worldwide*. United Kingdom: Deaf Child Worldwide.
World Health Organization and the World Bank Group. (2011). *World report on disability*. Geneva: World Health Organization.
Wright, P., & Wright, P. (2004). *The wrightslaw story*. Hartfield: Harbor House Law Press, Inc. Retrieved 28 May 2004, from www.wrightslaw.com/us.htm Accessed IDEA 2004.

Chapter 8
Problem-Solving Mediation in Israel

Ariella Vraneski

> *Israel is a vibrant society where people tend to argue a lot, but desire to mend things just as much.*
>
> (Bekenstein and Syrquin 2007)

Introduction

The practice of Alternative Dispute Resolution (ADR),[1] particularly problem-solving mediation in Israel started during the 1990s. A comprehensive study of the process introducing mediation, and the dynamics of its absorption into the Israeli conflict-ridden society, seems crucial to future coping with conflicts there.[2] It might foster endorsement of mediation and ADR as a philosophy of life based upon a

[1]This chapter spotlights the introduction and practice of modern mediation in Israel. Other forms of ADR, particularly arbitration exist here as well. Arbitration was well known and widely practiced long before the introduction of mediation, and, by the beginning of 2012, parties still seem to trust and use it much more than mediation and other ADR processes.

[2]Unfortunately a comprehensive study of Israeli mediation has not been done and research on mediation in Israel is still scarce. I am a mediator and researcher and have worked in Israel for many years. Hence, the sources of much of the documentation are conversations with knowledgeable persons, conferences, workshops and seminars, as well as my own field experience and observations. This chapter might contribute towards further research.

A. Vraneski (✉)
Head of the Conflict Resolution Research Group, The Center for Urban and Regional Studies, Technion IIT, Haifa, Israel
e-mail: ariellav@tx.technion.ac.il; avraneski@yahoo.com

J.M. Fritz (ed.), *Moving Toward a Just Peace: The Mediation Continuum*, Clinical Sociology: Research and Practice, DOI 10.1007/978-94-007-2885-1_8,

broad social vision, as was envisioned by those who introduced mediation.[3] Lessons from the Israeli experience are relevant for many nations worldwide.

Advocates of ADR approaches and tools portrayed them as educational means towards a way of life based upon mutual respect, openness and tolerance. Nevertheless, numerous controversies and clashes have developed in the course of introducing ADR. In addition to brief historical and comparative overviews, this chapter will focus on Israeli ADR-related processes and initiatives, particularly practices and debates linked to courts' referred mediation.[4]

Tens of thousands of Israelis have studied mediation and know about related skills and "language". Only several hundred actually practice mediation, and just few earn a living at it. Since the 1990s, several hundreds of thousands of young students also have been exposed to peer mediation concepts and practice in schools. In this chapter I try to assess the effects on young and mature students, their environment and Israeli society in general.[5]

Israel and the Continuum of Mediation: The Background

Israel is a developed country that shares many cultural features with Western countries in Europe and North America and possesses features of a traditional society. It also is extremely small, yet well known internationally due both to its antique history and its turbulent current times. Since declaring independence from the British Colonial Protectorate in 1948 and the first Israeli – Arab war that followed,[6] Israel has absorbed millions of Jewish immigrants including Holocaust

---

[3]Those who introduced mediation in Israel were: previous Supreme Court president, the Hon. Aaron Barak; Dr. Peretz Segal, the head of the Department of Legal Counsel and Legislation in the Ministry of Justice; psychologist Susan Zaidel; professor Mordechai Mironi; attorney Yoram Elroi and a few more prominent individuals (Israeli Ministry of Justice 2012).

[4]Evaluations included in this chapter rely on official publications and partial reports as well as interviews, discussions and observations conducted by my colleagues and students and myself over the past two decades.

[5]For example, did mediation skills and language have an impact on the 2011 Israeli social justice protest? The 2011 Israeli social justice protests, known also as "the tents protest" and "the middle class protest" are a series of demonstrations in Israel beginning in July 2011 involving hundreds of thousands of protesters from a variety of socio-economic and religious backgrounds. Demonstrations addressed the continuing rise in the cost of living (particularly housing) and the deterioration of public services and also issues relating to the social order and power structure in Israel. A common rallying cry at the demonstrations was the chant "The people demand social justice!" Prominent communication, collaboration and dialog skills; eminent order; and the use of social networks characterize this social movement. Following the large-scale protest, the government responded with attempts to negotiate, and a line of measures to meet expressed demands and underling needs.

[6]For some perspective on the Israel-Palestinian conflict, see Vraneski 2003.

survivors and refugees from Arab countries.[7] By 2011, Israel's permanent population was about 7.8 million citizens.[8] About 80 % of the citizens are Jewish, 16 % are Muslims, and 4 % are Christians. These numbers don't include a temporary population of about 200,000 work immigrants.

The surface of Israel is about 20,000 km^2 and so Israel is one of the smaller and most densely populated countries worldwide. It is also connected to the Palestinian territories – the West Bank and the Gaza Strip, which span 7,000 km^2, have 4.2 million inhabitants, and among the highest birth rates worldwide (Government of Israel. The Central Bureau of Statistics 2012; UNSD 2012; United States CIA 2012). Israel has a very diverse society, and is tremendously conflict-ridden on several levels. It is indeed an excellent laboratory for the study of conflicts and conflict resolution.

The practice of mediation in Israel is distinctive due to the extensive interest and involvement, for a number of years, of a central agency – the Ministry of Justice (MOJ) – in the introduction and implementation of this tool. Since the 1990s, preeminent individuals in the MOJ and in the judicial system led a difficult initiative to introduce non-adversarial conflict resolution approaches and tools. They hoped for positive influences on local communities. Notably, former Supreme Court President, Aharon Barak, viewed the introduction of mediation as an opportunity to transform Israel from an adversarial, zero-sum oriented civic culture into a more consensus, "win-win" guided society. In 1997, MOJ created the National Center for Mediation and Conflict Resolution (NCMCR) (http://www.justice.gov.il/MOJEng/The+National+Center+for+Mediation+and+Conflict+Resolution/). Although it was located in the Ministry of Justice, NCMCR addressed a range of sectors and issues, including the endorsement of community mediation and peer mediation programs. The center encouraged people and organizations to view mediation as a way of leading a common life together based upon agreement.

While in the US and other western countries mediation practices originally occurred outside the legal systems and were only later incorporated into these, the Israeli mediation started "top down"[9] following legislative initiatives. Israel is characterized by extremely centralized governmental systems. Therefore, this kind of development was possible there, unlike in typical decentralized democracies.

The official start of mediation in Israel coincided with two processes of international significance. The first was the absorption of almost one million Jewish

[7]Some 80 % of Israel's Jewish population are immigrants or sons/daughters of immigrants. About half originated in Africa (mostly North Africa); Asia (mostly the western parts of the continent); and about half in Europe and America (mostly Eastern and Central Europe). (http://www.cbs.gov.il).

[8]This compares to 1.2 million in 1949, 3 million in 1970, and 4.8 million in 1990. (http://www.cbs.gov.il).

[9]Some mediation processes were practiced in modern Israel for many years in planning and community settings, in some labor and business disputes, and, since the late 1980s, within the framework of the Israel Family Therapy Association (Vraneski 1994; Zaidel 2002; Sassoon–Buras 2000).

immigrants from Russia and other previously Soviet states to join Israel's five million citizens. This unexpected immigration was a catalyst for economic growth, environmental problems and social tension. Second, there was the start of the historic Israeli-Palestinian reconciliation process, accompanied by a local burst of renewed hope and optimism, and by much interest in conflict resolution processes.

An overwhelming number of new lawsuits plus awareness of alternative tools to address disputes and the vision of several prominent individuals allowed this exceptional movement to begin. Encouraging alternative dispute resolution programs is a major challenge for every enlightened society, even more so for Israeli society, which for ages has been involved in deep-rooted, intractable conflicts as well as many "regular" disputes such as workplace conflicts, neighbors' disputes, and family controversies.

Launching mediation in Israel induced hope and enthusiasm. Unfortunately, frustration soon emerged, and patterns that enabled a fast and massive introduction of mediation[10] turned into potential roots of failure. Bringing the communal, social, and mental readiness for mediation into the Israeli heterogeneous, zero-sum oriented society developed into an awkward and frustrating process. Additionally, mediation, particularly an interest-based style of this generic approach, has been "imported" into the Israeli society. Little has been done to apply methods to local cultures and needs, or to integrate them with local cultures, characteristics and traditions (Sassoon–Buras 2000). Creative, synergetic trends surrendered to the urge to obtain fast results. Once mediation training programs appeared, thousands studied mediation, but demand for mediation was still very low. Mediators had little opportunity to practice their new skills.

Due to limited training and procedural rigidity, many mediation processes failed to deliver expected outcomes. Potential clients didn't trust mediation suppliers or the process. The trust and reputation essential for adoption of conflict resolution concepts and tools were missing. Additionally, instead of collaborating to build a new profession, providers of mediation services became locked in competition for a limited market, and that was counterproductive, or even destructive.

By the mid-2000s, more than a decade after it's formal introduction in legislation, the number of actual mediated cases was very small in spite of the efforts of its promoters, the mediation centers, and the large numbers of trained mediators. The number of claims asking for Israeli court decisions was continually rising.[11]

Since the early 2000s, mediation and other conflict mitigation and resolution methods have been addressed in more inclusive ways when compared to the 1990s. Several institutes of higher education have added conflict resolution to their programs and related research. For example, the Interdisciplinary Program

---

[10]For example, mediation could be easily introduced nationwide by an existing legal amendment, the centralized governmental system and the relatively small size of the country.

[11]The number is about 50 % higher than 14 years beforehand, and more than 10 times higher than in 1950 (Vacknin 1991, Israeli Judicial Authority 2007).

in Conflict Management and Negotiation at Bar-Ilan University, launched in 2001, focuses on graduate level (M.A. and Ph.D.) studies.[12] Moreover, the Evans Program at Tel Aviv University initiated its International MA Program in Conflict Resolution and Mediation in 2009 (Ferber 2011). Besides, most Israeli universities and colleges now include courses related to dispute resolution, in addition to the few offered previously (e.g. Planning and Environmental Dispute Resolution taught by the author since 1995 at the Architecture and Town Planning faculty at the Technion in Haifa). Gradually, *realistic perceptions and expectations about the promises and premises of mediation, with related professional responsibility and ethics, are penetrating and stabilizing this essential field.*

Dialogue initiatives and other programs aimed at conflicts have been conducted in Israel since the 1950s, due probably to the features of Israeli geo-political situation (Givat 2012; Maoz 2000; Suleiman 2004), These programs have dealt with intercultural, interreligious and interethnic cleavages. They have been attended by students of different ages through formal and non-formal studies and meetings. Although very important on the Israeli mediation continuum, I will not emphasize them here since they are not yet associated with the current Israeli Mediation Movement, the focus of this chapter.

Several cross-border mediation initiatives, including joint training and practice, also have occurred in the region – e.g., IPCRI, founded in Jerusalem in 1988, a joint Israeli-Palestinian public policy think-tank devoted to developing practical solutions for the Israeli-Palestinian conflict (IPCRI - Israel Palestine Center for Research and Information 2012). Although these could not transform the geo-political situation, they helped construct foundations for positive long-lasting social infrastructures, inter alia by general dispute resolution and environmental dispute resolution courses. These practices overlap with and strengthen the current Israeli Mediation Movement.

In my view, the endorsement of research and development programs to integrate ADR studies and practices and peace studies and initiatives in our region should be a high priority. These would serve to promote a culture of peace in the region, and provide precious related lessons for other nations worldwide.

[12]Dissertations there include titles such as: *The Tradition of Aaron, Pursuer of Peace between Man and Man as a Rabbinic Model of Reconciliation* (Daniel Roth under the supervision of Professor Moshe Rosman 2009). *The Accomodational Society: The Civil Society Organizations – Reconcil-iation Attempts of the Religious-Secular Conflict* (Bat-Chen Weinheber under the supervision of Dr. Asher Cohen 2006) and *Perspectives on the Use of Power by Mediators and its Influence on Mediation Outcomes: A Legal, Philosophical and Psychological Analysis* (Omer Shapira under the guidance of Dr. Michal Alberstein 2003) (Program in Conflict Management and Negotiation at Bar-Ilan University 2012).

Holy Land = Conflict Land? An Historical Overview

Israel is consistently featured in the conflict analysis and resolution literature (e.g., Kriesberg 2002; Bar-Tal 1998). Interconnected territorial, ethnic, cultural and political issues certainly are involved in conflict dynamics there. However, Israel also is a relevant case study regarding "regular" conflicts. This chapter focuses on the "regular conflicts" within the society.

In the modern state of Israel, police and the courts sustain the functions of maintaining law and order in the community. The mediation roles played previously by religious leaders and other respected members of the community have decreased in importance, although they are still influential (Zaidel 2002; Tarabeih et al. 2009).

Mediation is not a new concept for Israeli people in both Jewish and Arab cultures. Traditionally these cultures placed a high value on managing conflict and on agreement between parties as the basis for resolving disputes. Both had their own "alternative" methods of dispute resolution to maintain peace and harmony within the community[13] (Kasdan 1990; Abu-Nimer 1996; Melamed 2002).

Mediation is actually the preferred method of conflict resolution used by Jewish courts in a process called *psharah* (compromised settlement). The Torah mandates "to do that which is right and good in the sight of the Lord." The Talmud states that only *pshara* constitutes the ideal justice of judgment of peace and judgment of righteousness. It expressed the unique nature of mediation to provide an integrated justice balancing the values of fairness, peacefulness and compassion. It seems the first and foremost mediator was Aharon HaCohen, the brother of Moses. The Talmud extols Aharon as one who "loved peace and pursued peace and made peace between man and man . . . " (Sanhedrin 6:72). For many centuries among Jews, the local rabbi was the mediator and often acted as an arbitrator if "reason" did not prevail (Kasdan 1990).

Among Arabs, an elaborate peace-making method called "sulcha" was used for all kinds of conflict. In Islamic law, sulh is a form of contract ('akd), legally binding on both individual and community levels. Similar to the private sulh between two believers, the purpose of public sulh is to suspend fighting between two parties and establish peace, called muwada'a (peace or gentle relationship), for a specific period of time (Khadduri 1997; Al-Krenawi and Graham 2003). Notably, the extensive Israeli Mediation Portal http://www.sulcha.co.il/, launched in 2000, is named "Sulcha". It publishes, for instance, news and articles about mediation and lists of mediators. The founder and chief editor is Dr. David Silvera – mediator, journalist and former head of the Israeli Mediator's Organization.

---

[13]This, as other traditional dispute resolution mechanisms, may include negative impacts besides the positive ones (e.g., with regard to discrimination between males and females). This is particularly true when transferring conservative tools into modern societies without proper adaptation.

Modern Mediation in Israel

From Rule-Making to Actual Mediation

In the late 1980s, the capacity and efficiency of the Israeli courts was challenged by an unexpectedly high number of civil disputes looking for resolution.[14] The initial introduction of modern mediation in 1992 was a result of experience gathered throughout the world in court-related implementation of ADR methods (Gaddot 1998, 1999). This experience, according to Gaddot, indicated that among various methods being applied, mediation was the most effective for quality of solutions and efficiency of procedure in terms of cost and time.

Mediation was formally institutionalized in Israel in February 1992, when the Knesset, Israel's parliament, passed amendment 15 to the 1984 Courts Act (Consolidated Version) authorizing courts to refer civil disputes to mediation or arbitration. Before then, there was only limited experience with arbitration and conciliation, mostly in organized labor settings. This amendment, Sub-section 79C of the Courts Act, conferred legal status on mediation defining it as "a procedure in which the mediator consults with the parties involved in order to bring them to an agreement to resolve the conflict without having the power to decide in the matter." (Israeli Judicial Authority 2012). In 1996, attorneys and judges who favored conventional court-ruled decisions over mediation advocated annulment of Sub-section 79C because it was being virtually unused. In response, the Manager of the Courts, the Hon. Pres. Revivo nominated Tel-Aviv municipal courts judge Sarah Gaddot to head an Advisory Committee for Mediation in Courts (the "Gaddot Committee") to generate guidelines for court-connected programs (Gaddot 1998, 1999).

At first, mediation in the Israeli court system was a voluntary option for judges to suggest to litigants in any civil lawsuit. Soon thereafter, regulations were enacted that determined the scope of confidentiality, the training requirements for mediators, and mediator duties and responsibilities. However, more than three years after mediation had been put in place, judges were not making use of the new regulations although these had been designated to assist their overburdened courts. For one thing, most judges did not trust mediation. Their education contrasted with mediation's basic concepts. Moreover, it took several years to provide instructions aimed at integrating mediation concepts with the more conventional dispute resolution system. In addition, trained mediators to whom courts could refer cases were almost nonexistent in Israel in these early years. (Zaidel 2002; Vraneski 2006b).

In recent years the field of mediation and conflict resolution has begun to gain momentum within the courts. A much more impressive jump has been seen in the number of practitioners offering their services in the field. I will expand on this issue later in this chapter.

---

[14]In 1990,122 out of 1,000 Israeli citizens were involved in civil lawsuits as compared to about 17 per 1,000 in 1950 (Vacknin 1991).

Parties and Processes

The aim of the initial introduction of mediation into Israel was to release the pressure that impacted negatively the activity of the courts system. Therefore, since the very beginning Israeli modern mediation focused mostly on issues related to court-refereed mediation.[15] Yet, as stated before, leaders in the judicial system viewed bringing mediation into Israeli society through a values-driven, transformative prism, and as an opportunity for deliberate, immense improvement.

As a result of the influence of Aharon Barak, the Supreme Court President, the Ministry of Justice (MOJ) created in February 1998, the National Center for Mediation and Conflict Resolution (NCMCR), an internal sub-division chaired by Dr. Peretz Segal, the head of the Department of Legal Counsel and Legislation in the MOJ, perhaps the most influential and enthusiast promoter of ADR. NCMCR was designated to regulate matters concerning mediation and conflict resolution and to promote the ADR practice, both in the court system and within the community. Notably, although located in the Ministry of Justice, NCMCR addressed an extensive number of sectors and issues. The Center encouraged people and organizations to view mediation as a way of life, a way of leading a common life together based upon agreement.

NCMCR had several key objectives:

Heighten awareness of the concept of mediation and alternative dispute resolution, and the advantages of their use within a community framework, the business sector, academia and the general public.

Development of professional knowledge and appropriate tools for resolving different types of disputes such as civil and business disputes, workplace disputes, public disputes, disputes within the family and the community, and disputes in the criminal field (Restorative Justice).

Promotion of initiatives and provision of professional assistance to frameworks developing mediation and ADR services both in the public and private sectors.

Initiation of pilot programs to imbue the use of mediation and ADR in government offices, district attorney departments, and amongst litigants and lawyers.

Development of professional standards and rules of ethics for those involved in the field of mediation and ADR.

Development of mediation training programs in various fields, including practical experience programs in mediation (practicum), in cooperation with the Court's administration and mediation trainers.

It is easy to see NCMCR fingerprints on most Israeli ADR initiatives. NCMCR has written guidelines and directives on how to establish and operate municipal

[15] Although the initiative to introduce mediation into Israeli court system is definitely credited to the Ministry of Justice, many in the legal community were against it and still prefer the traditional processes. In the Bar leaders' view, mediation of court cases should only be conducted by mediators who are lawyers.

mediation centers. With NCMCR's professional guidance, community mediation centers have been developing throughout the country, using trained volunteers to mediate disputes. In 2003, following NCMCR's initiative, a business mediation treaty was signed by major relevant stakeholders in Israel. NCMCR also collaborated with the Ministry of Environment and others to introduce environmental dispute resolution and with scholars in Israel and other countries to promote research and conflict resolution curricula. NCMCR initiated conferences, training programs, and research projects (http://www.justice.gov.il/MOJeng/default.htm).

In 1997, only 5 years after mediation received legal status, there were mediation courses, mediators, and mediation centers appearing gradually and then followed by a rapid increase in the number of mediators and private and community organizations providing mediation services. Similarly, there was expansion in the number of private organizations offering mediation training courses and advanced courses in specialized fields such as family mediation.

By 1998, the expectations of most individuals who attended mediation courses focused on making a living in this new and promising profession. Less than 10 years later, the number of "trained mediators" was assessed at about 28,000 and roughly 6,500 of them were included in court rosters. Many began to attend mediation courses for general knowledge and personal development. The courses are recognized by employers and taxation authorities as "further education," are well structured, and include play-like simulations (Vraneski 2006b).

But demand for mediation among private and public entities and the general public was slow to rise. By 2000 only a handful of people earned a living as full-time mediators. It was common to earn more by conducting mediation courses and "producing" additional mediators than through mediation practice. More recently, many mediators claimed that they did work, but it was mostly on a voluntary basis and courts tend to refer well rewarded cases to retired judges and a small number of lawyers.

Within the courts, case management pilot programs were developed in 1998, spearheaded by Edna Bekenstein, a Tel Aviv District Judge and Head of the Tel Aviv Courts (http://www.justice.gov.il/MOJeng/default.htm), with the support of Judge Dan Arbel, then Chief Administrator of the Courts. Case Management Departments (MANAT) also were established.

Yet, in 2003, about one decade after mediation had been formally introduced in Israel, parties seldom sought mediators to assist in solving their controversies unless told by courts to proceed in this manner. Moreover, the rate of refusal to mediate among court referrals was high. There were claims of superficial and even unjust agreements due to mediators' lack of substantive knowledge and/or limited experience.

As criticism mounted, the Minister of Justice, Joseph Lapid, nominated a Commission on Mediation in Courts, headed by Judge Michal Rubinstein. The commission was asked to investigate the feasibility of turning court-referred, voluntary mediation into a mandatory process, and to explore other means of promoting mediation in courts.

The commission studied mandatory mediation experience worldwide (particularly in northern California and Canada). Following the commission's recommendations, in 2007, Israeli Justice Minister Daniel Friedman gave the green light for an experimental mediation program, called MAHUT to address claims exceeding NIS 50,000 – about $12,000 (Bekenstein and Syrquin 2007). It required all sides in civil cases to hold one free mediation session before a trial could begin so that they could decide if they wished to solve their dispute through mediation. Since September, 2008, MAHUT has been carried out in a few magistrate courts as a pilot program. MAHUT only employs exceptionally skilled mediators, is accompanied by built-in research and evaluation, and provides ongoing feedback and further training to the mediators. The MAHUT program started with less than 100 mediators; by mid-2011, another 30 joined this elite group. Notably, MAHUT mediators are chosen through a competitive process.

Development of this new, fragile enterprise has been hampered by disagreements within and between Institutes concerned with the promotion of mediation and disputes within the mediation community. In 2008, responding to criticism of some mediators' performance, the Ministry of Justice canceled the regulations regarding criteria for listing mediators on court rosters. In 2009, MOJ decided to close NCMCR – the National Center for Mediation and Conflict Resolution, despite harsh protests from the mediation community (Israeli Mediation Portal 2012). The closing of NCMCR coincided with the nomination of MOJ highly-ranked officials who did not support mediation.

NCMCR was providing guidance and coordination, which still seemed vital for the development of mediation in Israel. Yet these events sparked the start of a mature, serious and responsible Israeli Mediation Movement. Dozens of private "centers" and hundreds of individuals of varying professional backgrounds now offer their services as mediators. The Chamber of Israeli Mediators, the mediation division of the Israeli Bar Association, University departments, dozens of Community Mediation Centers countrywide, and many others are working harder than ever to back-up, promote and improve mediation in numerous ways and in many fields (Chamber of Israeli Mediators 2012; Israeli Mediation Portal 2012).

By 2012, most Israelis know much more about mediation, but in most matters the parties still do not try mediation until they have appealed to the Courts' rule. An exception is in the area of divorce, where people do seek out mediators as an alternative to court proceedings and often arrive in courts with divorce contracts agreed upon through mediation processes.

I now often meet students who have been familiar with mediation and its "language" since their childhood. Courts are no longer the main opportunity to get acquainted with mediation. People hear about it from their children, who are trained as young mediators in schools. The Ministry of Public Security has embraced mediation as part of its efforts to prevent violence. Activities of many community mediation centers now are sponsored by the Ministry of Social Affairs and Social Services, municipalities, national and local NGOs and more.

Several coalitions have been created to sustain dispute resolution programs. For example "Gishurim" aims to help solve disputes and increase dialogue and understanding, and to instill values of multi-cultural mediation. Its facilities and programs are tailored to fit the needs of minority communities, including Arabs and new immigrants. http://www.gishurim.org/, http://www.jicc.org.il/. Entities collaborate formally and ad-hoc to conduct mediation and other ADR processes. New mediation practices are much more flexible, aware of cultural differences, and applied to the characteristics of cases and parties. These practices contrast with court-refereed mediation, which still dominates the Israeli arena.

Critical Insights

The contemporary Mediation Movement presents some favorable as well as troubling features as it is being integrated into Israel's diverse and dynamic society. Should the problems that accompany this process, as portrayed above, be viewed as "infant's maladies" or as a "chronic incurable sickness"? Notably two interconnected issues feature these problems: (1) Destructive rivalry between prospective mediators, in particular between lawyers and non-lawyers and (2) Non-appropriate training processes.

- Rivalry between prospective mediators, particularly between lawyers and non-lawyers. The Israeli Bar currently has more than 30,000 members which boils down to one lawyer for every 200 people. By comparison, in the United States, long said to lead the world in litigation, there is one lawyer per approximately 360 capita. Israeli lawyers opposed mediation from the beginning, perhaps because many viewed it as a threat to their financial interests. Later they claimed that attorneys do not need mediation training or practice as preconditions for practicing mediation in court-referred cases.

After mediation was actually being endorsed by the courts, the Israel Bar Association (IBA) started running its own training courses. In the leaders' view, mediation of court cases should only be conducted by mediators who are lawyers. Many attorneys refused to take their cases to mediation unless the mediator was an attorney. Judges tend to prefer mediators who are attorneys, due to similar background and common language. On the other side, many non-attorney mediators claim that lawyer skills and experience differ from the skills needed to mediate. Since most rewarded mediation cases in Israel are still related to courts, this struggle persists. Yet we also witness much mutual respect and collaboration between individual mediators – lawyers and non lawyers alike.

- Training processes. For several years after mediation legislation was introduced in 1992, there were virtually no mediators in Israel, courts did not refer parties to mediation, mediation was not practiced and no curricula for studying it were created. Once the first mediation courses were launched in 1997 at the Israeli Center of Mediation (ICM) of the Neaman Institute for National Policy Research at the Technion, Harvard's Program on Negotiation (PON) mediation syllabus was translated into Hebrew. The first trainers here had been previously trained in the 1980s in Harvard's PON. By 1998, about a dozen public and private organizations joined the new trend of teaching mediation. The 1980s PON model, became the Israeli mediation training "bible." Not much was done to update the curriculum, not even with the changes introduced in the PON syllabi themselves, for example, with regard to cultural competency. The need to translate and adopt training materials from English to Hebrew, matched with a small audience within Israel's small population and high competition among many actual and potential training providers, resulted in stagnation. Moreover, lawyers with limited mediation skills and experience kept leading most of the mediation processes. Adaptations of different models according to the background and wishes of the parties, as well as the context and the conflict's issues have scarcely been considered.

The way mediation was introduced implied a structural transformation of Israeli dispute resolution approaches and styles. Structural transformations are rare in all systems. Israel is customarily engaged in geo-political and development tensions and constraints rather than in deliberate structural transformation. However, by the late 2000s, as the Mediation Movement matured, further learning and accumulated experience changed practice. Well-trained mediators and mediation success stories are now finally building trust in ADR processes and changing related public attitudes (JPOST Editorial 2011).

A few interconnected factors are responsible for the tough adaptation of Modern Mediation to Israel. First, many in Israel's diverse society – including Jewish immigrants from Eastern Europe and from Moslem countries, Orthodox religious Jews, as well as Arab Israelis and Palestinians – have cultural and traditional ties within communal, non-individualistic backgrounds. Accordingly, the North-American contractual, interest-based mediation style introduced into this society through a top-down process does not make much sense to most of Israel's inhabitants.

Emergent or hybrid styles of mediation could better meet their needs. Scholars and practitioners tend to distinguish between contractual-mediation, which is practiced mainly in individualistic cultures where an impartial outsider is favored, and emergent-mediation, which prefers inside mediators, and is inclined to resolve conflicts in group settings, and/or by highly respected members of a relevant family, community or tribe (Kressel et al. 1989; Folberg and Taylor 1986; Jandt and Pedersen 1996; Shook 1985; Vraneski 1994, 2006b; Fritz 2008; Bercovich et al. 2009).

When comparing the state of mediation in Israel and in the United States, one should take heed of the fact that U.S. mediation developed organically, culminating in general federal laws after 70 years of experience, whereas mediation in Israel covered the distance between non-existence and significant institutionalization in roughly 10 years (Vraneski 2006b).

A basic criticism of the adopted Western conflict resolution techniques is that they are either too mechanistic or based on therapy-oriented formulas. Although the selected Western techniques and skills are relevant and useful, they ought to be better adapted to indigenous realities (Irani 1999). For instance, cultural competency and sensitivity to variances is crucial for mediation in general and in non-western and heterogeneous communities in particular. Commonly having local/indigenous members as mediators or part of a mediation team might be an advantage. A colleague of mine, Arch. Dr. Mohamad Shibeli, serves in court referred mediation cases of land disputes in Israeli Arab villages. Due to his multifaceted knowledge and understanding of middle-eastern and western mediation dispute resolution approaches and tools; Israel land legislation and local Arab traditions; and about planning needs and constraints, he often mediates successfully and helps bring forth quick and creative resolutions to harsh disputes that were trapped in courts for ages and divided communities and even families.

Ironically, the introduction of classic contracted, problem-solving mediation in Israel coincides with the strengthening of more relationship-oriented and emergent-like mediation styles in the US and other individualistic societies. Notably, these developments create appropriate options for diverse needs, and may expand the mediation "market" itself.

My insights with regard to the pros and cons of the applicability of mediation to the Israeli communities partly rely on interaction with highly-ranked, mid-career Israeli graduate students who were in classes that I taught in the 1990s and 2000s. "How can I separate the problem from the parties, when the parties **are** the problem" was the typical response to "rules" my students were reading in *Getting to Yes*.[16] They simply didn't buy into this kind of rule; their experience was contraindicative. When I invited a young mediator to simulate mediation in class, several students secretly informed me that they would not rely on such a young woman to deal with a real case. Age correlated in their view with experience, and they were sure a mediator needs life experience, not just process skills, to assist others in solving their problems. Notably, in Israel, retired judges mediate many court-referred cases, although their styles are often poles apart from most basic definitions of mediation. It seems that parties often look for patriarchal/matriarchal-style knowledgeable resolutions, and rely on these far more than on the outcomes of a facilitated collaboration with their combatants, the way contemporary mediation preaches.

Besides the early 1980s problem-solving mediation model used in the United States, other approaches to mediation and additional processes of dispute resolution have scarcely been considered within the Israeli practice, although advanced training includes mentioning the existence of more than one approach to address disputes. Among those to be considered are transformative mediation, which aims to better address future relationships and empower the parties (Bush and Folger 1994, 2005); narrative mediation, which seeks to de-construct the parties'

---

[16]Fisher and William (1981) in their famous book *Getting to Yes* suggested several outstanding rules and a sequence of rational steps aimed at solving conflicts and creating sustainable agreements.

conflict-saturated stories and co-construct alternative stories (Monk and Winslade 2000); or applied integrations of patterns and futures from several mediation models, such as the interactive mediation model (Vraneski 2006a) Additionally, several conflict prevention/mitigation/resolution approaches, applied in conjunction with or instead of mediation, might better address particular arenas and/or kinds of disputes. For example, "Consensus Building" for public policy disputes (Susskind et al. 1999) or Dispute Resolution Boards (DRB) for construction project disputes http://www.drb.org (Hunt and Reich 2002).

Finally, some malfunctions of the initial attempts to introduce mediation to Israel are connected to mediators' superficial training and to limited process and general experience. The initial standards set in Israel for court lists of mediators played a role in the induction of faulty mediation. In the rush to get things moving, these standards were rather minimalist: a 40-hour training course, a college degree in any field, and five years' work experience of any kind for non-family civil disputes; or 60 hours of training, a law degree or a master's degree in one of the helping professions, and five years' work experience in the person's specialized field as qualifications for the family court rosters. As options for internships or supervised practice were virtually non-existent, the initial standards didn't require mediation experience.

As a result of the limited requirements, the situation moved quickly from one of not having mediators at all to having up to 10,000 so-called qualified mediators. Most had no practical experience in mediating beyond the simulations provided in their training courses. Many new trainers have little more knowledge of mediation than the course materials that were disseminated, and very little practical experience. It is not surprising that in the first period the average outcomes of court-referred cases were not successful. Yet, not only the related cases and parties were damaged, but also the fragile reputation of the newly introduced dispute resolution tool.

Fortunately, since the mid-2000s, mediation and other conflict mitigation and resolution methods have been addressed in Israel in more comprehensive and serious ways, particularly when compared to the early days. Several institutes of higher education have included conflict resolution within their studies, at graduate and undergraduate levels, as diploma studies and as further education for practicing mediators. Related research and curriculum building are underway.

Gradually, realistic perceptions and expectations with regard to the promises and premises of mediation and with related professional responsibility and ethics penetrate and stabilize this most essential field. However, many resources and much creativity have yet to be invested to build a mediation practice in Israel that is both appropriate and reliable.

Conclusion

Tens of thousands of Israeli citizens now possess mediators' diplomas. Only several dozen of these work as full-time mediators. Hundreds work as part-time mediators, combining their professional careers (such as psychologists, social workers, attorneys, and engineers) and dispute resolution. Hundreds practice their mediation skills voluntarily – in community mediation centers and other NGOs. Yet, the study of conflict resolution has had an impact on the lives of tens of thousands of graduates of mediation training programs as well as their relatives, friends and coworkers.

Mediation concepts such as win-win/all-gain situations, vis-a-vis the zero-sum games we were used to since early childhood, and mediation skills such as active listening and reframing, have penetrated the lives of hundreds of thousands. The new practices bear possibilities to help make better connections between people, respect differences, cheer tolerance, and, finally, promote and sustain a culture of peace. I believe they had an impact on the Israeli social justice protest that started in the summer of 2011 and its outcomes.

References

Abu-Nimer, M. (1996). Conflict resolution approaches: Western and middle eastern lessons and possibilities. *American Journal of Economics and Sociology, 55*(1), 35–52.

Al-Krenawi, A., & Graham, J. R. (2003). Principles of social work practice in the Muslim Arab world. *Arab Studies Quarterly (ASQ), 25*(4), 75–91. Fall.

Bar-Tal, D. (1998). Societal beliefs in times of intractable conflict: The Israeli case. *International Journal of Conflict Management, 9*(1), 22–50. January.

Bekenstein, E., & Syrquin, A. (2007). Mandatory mediation – The Israeli pilot. Israel Bar Association. (Viewed Feb 2012). http://www.israelbar.org.il/english_inner.asp?pgId=59929&catId=246

Bercovich, J., Kremenyuk, V., & Zartman, I. W. (Eds.). (2009). *The SAGE handbook of conflict resolution*. London: Sage.

Bush, R. A. B., & Folger, J. P. (1994). *The promise of mediation*. San Francisco: Jossey-Bass

Bush, R. A. B., & Folger, J. P. (2005). *The promise of mediation: The transformative approach to conflict*. San Francisco: Jossey-Bass.

Ferber, A. (2011). *Studying conflict resolution, living the conflict* Haaretz 29 May 2011 http://www.haaretz.com/jewish-world/studying-conflict-resolution-living-the-conflict-1.364744

Fisher, R., & Uri, W. (1981). Getting to yes: Negotiating agreement without giving. In Boston: Houphton Mifflin.

Folberg, J., & Taylor, A. (1986). *Mediation*. San Francisco: Jossey-Bass.

Fritz, J. M. (2008). Clinical sociological contributions to the field of mediation. In J. M. Fritz (Ed.), *International clinical sociology*. New York: Springer.

Gaddot, S. (1998 & 1999). *Report of the advisory council for mediation in courts a & b. Jerusalem: Israeli Ministry of Justice* (In Hebrew).

Givat, H. (2012). *National education center of the Kibbutz federation in Israel* (Viewed Feb 2012). http://www.givathaviva.org.il/english/

Government of Israel. The Central Bureau of Statistics. (Viewed Feb 2012). http://www.cbs.gov.il, http://www.cbs.gov.il/engindex.htm

Hunt, R., & Reich, N. (2002). The use of dispute review boards and similar processes as dispute avoidance tools for dams and related projects in the Asia-Pacific region. *The Arbitrator and Mediator, 21*(1), 1–24.

IPCRI – Israel Palestine Center for Research and Information. (Viewed Feb 2012). http://www.ipcri.org/IPCRI/Home.html

Irani, G. (1999). Islamic mediation techniques for middle east conflicts. *Middle East Review of International Affairs, 3*(2) 1–17. (June 1999).

Jandt, F. E., & Pedersen, P. B., (Eds.). (1996). *Constructive conflict management: Asia-Pacific cases*. Thousand Oaks: Sage.

JPOST Editorial. (2011). "Medical mediation" *The Jerusalem Post*. 12 June 2011.

Kasdan, I. Y. (1990). A proposal for P'sharah: A Jewish mediation/arbitration service. *Jewish Law Articles*. Examining Halacha, Jewish issues and secular law. http://www.jlaw.com/Articles/psharah1.html

Khadduri, M., (1997). In C. E. Bosworth et al. (Eds.). *The encyclopedia of Islam*, Vol. 9. Leiden: E. J. Brill.

Kressel, K., Pruitt, D. G., & Associates. (1989). *Mediation research*. San Francisco: Jossey-Bass.

Kriesberg, L. (2002). The relevance of reconciliation actions in the breakdown of Israeli-Palestinian negotiations, 2000. *Peace & Change, 27*(4), 546–571.

Maoz, I. (2000). *Evaluation of Jewish-Arab coexistence programs funded by the Abraham fund*. http://www.abrahamfund.org/main/siteNew/?langId=1

Melamed, N. (2002). *The mediation – A Jewish outlook*. http://www.bhol.co.il/forums/topic.asp?cat_id=4&topic_id=144192&forum_id=771&upd=1, first published in www.sulcha.co.il (In Hebrew).

Monk, G., & Winslade, J. (2000). *Narrative mediation: A new approach to conflict resolution*. San Francisco: Jossey-Bass.

Program in Conflict Management and Negotiation at Bar-Ilan University (Viewed Feb. 2012). http://www.biu.ac.il/interdis/pconfl/english/index_eng.html

Sassoon–Buras, R. (2000). Introducing alternative dispute resolution to Israel's planning practice – The applicability of mediation to the investigation procedure. M.A. thesis supervised by A. Vraneski, Technion, Haifa.

Shook, E. V. (1985). *Ho'oponopono: Contemporary uses of a Hawaiian problem-solving process*. Hawaii: University of Hawaii Press.

Suleiman, Y. (2004). *A war of words: Language and conflict in the middle east*. Cambridge: Cambridge University Press.

Susskind, L., Sarah, M., & Jennifer, T-L. (Eds.). (1999). *The consensus building handbook: A comprehensive guide to reaching agreement*. Thousand Oaks: Sage.

Tarabeih, H., Shmueli, D., & Khamaisi, R. (2009). Towards the implementation of Sulha as a cultural peacemaking method for managing and resolving environmental conflicts among Arab Palestinians in Israel. *Journal of Peacebuilding and Development, 5*(1), 50–64.

(The) Chamber of Israeli Mediators. (2012). (Viewed Feb 2012). http://www.megashrey-israel.org.il/

(The) Israeli Judicial Authority. (2012). (Viewed Feb 2012). http://elyon1.court.gov.il/eng/home/index.html. http://www.court.gov.il/heb/home.htm

(The) Israeli Mediation Portal. (2012). (Viewed Feb 2012). www.sulcha.co.il

(The) Israeli Ministry of Justice. (2012). (Viewed Feb 2012). www.justice.gov.il

(The) United Nations Statistics Division (UNSD). (2012). (Viewed Feb 2012). http://data.un.org/

United States. Central Intelligence Agency. (2012). *The world fact book*. (Viewed Feb 2012). http://www.cia.gov/cia/publications/factbook

Vacknin, S. (1991). Judges LTD. *The Globes Magazine, 1*(11), 2–3. (In Hebrew).

Vraneski, A. (1994). *Conflict resolution in urban and regional planning: The applicability of alternative dispute resolution*. Haifa: CURS Technion. (In Hebrew).

Vraneski, A. (2003). Reframing involuntary population displacement and resettlement. The case of the Palestinian refugees: Causes, consequences, and prospects for an impoverishment processes reversal. *Peace and Conflict Studies, 10*(1), 40–71. http://shss.nova.edu/pcs/journalsPDF/V10N1.pdf

Vraneski, A. (2006a). Beyond art or science: Creativity and culture in interactive mediation". In L., Luison (Ed.), 2006. *Mediation as a tool for social intervention: Perspectives, challenges and practical aspects in different societies* (pp. 58–80). Milano: FrancoAngeli. http://www.ccrs.technion.ac.il/cv/Vraneski_cv_files/Beyond%20Art%20or%20Science-%20vraneski2006.pdf

Vraneski, A. (2006b). The introduction of mediation in Israel: Difficulties, challenges and prospects. In L., Luison (Ed.), *Mediation as a tool for social intervention: perspectives, challenges and practical aspects in different societies* (pp. 184–197). Milano: FrancoAngeli. http://www.ccrs.technion.ac.il/cv/Vraneski_cv_files/mediation%20in%20israel%20-%20vraneski2006.pdf

Zaidel, S. (2002). Mediation in Israel. *ADR Bulletin, 5*(2), 21–24.

Chapter 9
The Art of Facilitation

Jan Marie Fritz

Introduction

There are a number of ways to successfully facilitate (assist a group with) activities. Facilitators are expected to learn different techniques/styles/methods such as probing, reframing, positive reinforcement, design, use of resources,[1] problem analysis (Hartwig 2010, pp. 18–19), and methods of decision-making. The use of such techniques is only a part of a facilitated activity; facilitation is an art,[2] a creative undertaking in which the facilitator needs to continually act,[3] focusing on what is currently happening while taking into account a group's setting, participants, aims, relevant history, current situation and future opportunities. This chapter discusses the creative facilitation of meetings and provides a case study which points to some of the problems that can develop when not enough attention is given to effective facilitation.

[1]Nielsen (2012, p. 87) wrote about how "a range of semiotic resources (whiteboard, colored cards, speed markers, re-usable adhesive putty, body posture, gestures, gazes, pauses and talk) is used in a facilitated meeting.

[2]Shaw et al. (2010, p. 4) indicated "the true art of an effective facilitator is often not always about the methods, tools or techniques that they employ but on the internal condition of the facilitator" which allows the facilitator to "create transformation in groups."

[3]According to Shaw et al. (2010, p. 4), "as scholars and practicing facilitators have emphasized, facilitators work intuitively, and often need to act in the moment... deciding if, when and how to intervene..."

J.M. Fritz (✉)
Professor, University of Cincinnati, USA and Senior Research Fellow, Centre for Sociological Research, University of Johannesburg, South Africa
e-mail: jan.fritz@uc.edu

J.M. Fritz (ed.), *Moving Toward a Just Peace: The Mediation Continuum*,
Clinical Sociology: Research and Practice, DOI 10.1007/978-94-007-2885-1_9,

Defining Facilitation

The term *facilitation* basically refers to the act of making something easy or, at least, easier. The concept is known in many countries, but not all. Japan, for instance, has no word for facilitation in Japanese, but the idea of facilitation, particularly in the areas of education and training, is "increasingly gaining attention and acceptance" (Kato 2010, p. 694).

Because facilitation is such a general term, one finds it used in different ways in many fields including neuroscience (increase in postsynaptic potential evoked by a second impulse), business (running meetings), ecology (for instance, when a plant provides shade for a seedling) as well as areas such as human trafficking (facilitators are the people who are engaged in illegal trafficking across international borders). There also are "practice facilitators" (PFs) who are health care professionals – in England, the Netherlands, Australia, Canada and the US – who assist primary care clinicians with "a variety of activities, including enhancement of documentation and delivery of clinical interventions, particularly preventive services; improvement of office systems; and implementation of Health Information Technology" (Nagykaldi et al. 2005, p. 583). There is "facilitative dialogue" (Smock and Serwer 2012, pp. 1–2), a conversation, moderated by a third-party, to help those involved in a discussion overcome any barriers to effective communication. While this approach can be used in many situations, Smock and Serwer (2012) discuss its use in conflict and post-conflict areas.[4] And "facilitative leadership," "a skilled approach to leading that's based on the core beliefs and practices of group facilitation" (Bens 2006, p. 8), is frequently discussed (e.g., Kato 2010, p. 694; Fryer 2012; Subramaniam 2011). Finally, there is "guerilla facilitation," techniques to be used by a meeting participant when a meeting is not going well and the participant is not managing the meeting (Wilkinson n.d.).

Facilitation is a concept that is frequently used by mediators and many others to characterize some or all of the work they do. Haskell and Cyr (2011, p. 5) defined facilitation, in a group facilitation journal, "as the design and management of structures and processes that help a group do its work and minimize the common problems people have working together." Amnesty International (2011, p. 20), in its training manual about facilitation, has provided a useful definition of the term that has much less of a management focus:

> Generally speaking, facilitation is defined as making things occur easily, or making something possible. Facilitation is an enabling and guiding process which creates and supports a space for purposeful engagement and participation.

Mie Femø Nielsen (2012, p. 89) indicated that a facilitator is a "content neutral" person "working to enable… [a group or organization] to collaborate, work more

---

[4]Smock and Serwer (2012, p. 2) indicate that the three components of facilitated dialogue in conflict and post-conflict situations are (1) being sensitive to situations and intervening as needed to make conversations productive, (2) focusing on underlying interests and (3) organizing topics to achieve early consensus on less-difficult topics.

effectively and achieve synergy," or to think in a deeper way about its assumptions, beliefs, values, processes, or other areas by using a rather informal, flexible alternative "to constricting formats like parliamentary procedure or *Robert's Rules of Order*."[5] Facilitators LISTEN, encourage participation, draw out the opinions of participants, ask questions, clarify communication, keep a meeting on task, guide groups through difficult discussions, test assumptions, are optimistic, give as well as receive feedback, have no substantive decision-making authority and periodically summarize progress.

In discussing facilitation, there are differences of opinion about where one usually finds facilitation being used and how it should be done. According to Nielsen (2012, p. 89), for instance, facilitators "are frequently used in innovation projects and change management projects; but usually not used in 'ordinary,' intraorganizational idea development meetings." Others would think facilitation is also valuable in idea development meetings. And according to Smock and Serwer (2012, p. 163), a skilled facilitator in conflict zones should be "actively engaged in directing the discussion and helping the participants reach consensus;" this kind of facilitator would not be a "neutral traffic cop." Others might see this as an option in many kinds of facilitation (not just in conflict zones) while some others might think that this characterization opens the door to a facilitator being directive or opinionated.

Stephen Thorpe, in an editorial for *Group Facilitation* (2011, p. 3) lovingly described the role of the facilitator:

> A facilitator "in the moment" might be likened to the metaphor of a swan that skillfully and gracefully glides on the surface of a pond: guiding the group towards their purpose, making subtle interventions, and cutting through blockages and conflict with precision. The group [members] may find that they are achieving [the group's] goals, are becoming empowered, and participants are amazed at how easy it all seemed to flow – even through those tough bits they had been avoiding. Yet, just beneath the surface of the water, that facilitator's feet are paddling away, drawing on a number of inner resources, picking up on subtle currents and bringing deeper awareness to all that is happening. This I call the *inner practice* of a group facilitator... There is a need now... to further expore and write about these subtle aspects of the group facilitator role... [so that others] can truly see the magic in the things we are... doing *while we are facilitating*.

Amnesty International (2011, p. 22) emphasized that a facilitator's qualities include "resourcefulness and creativity:"

> Each group is as different as the people who make it up. A good facilitator needs an overall programme and objectives but may also adapt these to fit changing conditions and opportunities...

---

[5]*Robert's Rules of Order* is a widely used parliamentary authority in the U.S. The first edition of the procedures was published in 1876.

Mediation and Facilitation

Mediation is a humanistic and creative process in which one or more impartial individuals help disputants discuss an issue or issues that concern one or more of the parties. This process is sometimes referred to as *facilitated* negotiation. The mediator will establish an open, trusting environment in which parties are encouraged to discuss the facts of the matter as well as their personal feelings about the issue or issues that brought them to the table. Mediation is usually problem-centered with a flexibly-structured process that can be free flowing or rather controlled or directed. If the outcome of this process is an agreement, it would be shaped by the parties and mutually satisfactory.

The U.S. Institute for Environmental Conflict Resolution (n.d.) indicates that mediation and facilitation "are the cornerstone of the U.S. Institute's services." The Institute indicates that mediation is a negotiation process in which "'resolution' is the goal" while facilitation is a collaborative process that aims to "seek a shared understanding of the issues at hand, and to explore how they might work together to meet their common goals." The Institute's definition tries to draw a strong line between the two processes... but that is actually hard to do. Both mediation and facilitation can be broadly defined and are overlapping. For instance, New Zealand's guidance note (Sefton 2009) for environmental disputes sees the role of mediator and facilitator as the same except that "outcomes of facilitated meetings are summarized at the conclusion" and "at closure, the agreement of a mediation is nailed."

Mediators, for a number of reasons, may refer to some or all of their work as facilitation. It may be that the term mediation is not understood by most or some segment of the public or it may be that some think if the term "mediation" is used that it means there is a severe problem. Facilitation may be a more acceptable term for those reasons. Also, a mediator may feel that the work she or he is doing – perhaps because it involves many people or a number of groups[6] – really is facilitation, although she or he uses many mediation skills.

Mediators in the U.S. who regularly work with large groups usually have been trained in and have experience with facilitation. However, not all mediators (particularly those working with individuals or small groups) have been trained in facilitation. Increasingly, there has been an interest in and opportunities for these mediators to have this training. For instance, some large civic discussions (e.g., about national health options or problems facing women who wish to fully participate in society) offered facilitation training to mediators and asked them to serve as table or group facilitators. Also, special education mediators in the U.S.

---

[6]According to The State of Queensland, Department of Justice and Attorney-General (Australia) (n.d.), "mediation doesn't usually involve large numbers of people... [and] facilitation is used for large-scale disputes, often involving several parties, an organization, a department or entire community."

are being trained or have been trained by a number of state education departments to serve as facilitators. These individuals are increasingly being made available to school systems to run meetings or develop models for running meetings when parents and school system representatives are trying to develop an individualized education plan for a student with special needs. The thinking is that if the initial meetings between parents and school system representatives are successful, there will be less problems in the future and less need to have mediators deal with special education disputes.

Mediators and facilitators often belong to the same professional organizations. They may be active, for instance, in the International Association of Facilitators or the Environment and Public Policy Section (or other sections) of the Association for Conflict Resolution. The US Institute for Environmental Conflict Resolution (n.d.) frequently uses "contracted private-sector" mediators and facilitators in addition to its own small staff in dealing with environmental disputes. The Institute maintains a national roster of dispute resolution and consensus building professionals who all are third-party professional facilitators and/or mediators.

The selection of mediators and facilitators generally should be acceptable to all the members of the groups. However, sometimes mediators and facilitators are assigned and it is only after assignment that a person or organization might question if the person is appropriate for the assignment.

Both mediation and facilitation involve creativity. The situations of groups involved in mediation and facilitation may often be unclearly defined (what have been called "ill-defined domains"). Particularly when that is the case, creativity may not just be a contribution of the mediator or facilitator; the creativity may be in the collaboration/sharing of the participants as well as the contributions of the facilitator or mediator (see Reilly 2008).

Novice, Experienced and Artisan Facilitation

Facilitators may not be needed in particular situations. The authors of a book about collaboration (Dukes and Firehock 2001, p. 29) noted that when a group has low conflict and "the meeting process is not terribly demanding," a meeting can be managed by a chair or a member of the group. And Andy Williams (2012, p. 137) studied student learning when an open facilitation approach was used regarding "solo camping" (camping on your own). He concluded (p. 153) "that soloists can and do attach important meanings to their experiences without the need for a facilitator to guide or structure the learning process on their behalf." Williams (p. 154) underlined, however, that he was not saying that "facilitator-led solo activities should become a thing of the past" but, rather, that all should be aware of the "potential of a more open mode of facilitation (a learner-centered approach in) which participants (solo campers) have more ownership of the process and outcomes of their own learning because facilitators were encouraged to take a step back."

When facilitation can be useful, what level of facilitation skill is needed? Facilitators do have different levels of expertise (see, for example, Bens 2000, p. 35; Rees 2005, pp. 261–283).[7] Modifying Berkvens' typology of facilitators (2012, p. 360), this chapter discusses the following levels: *novice facilitator* (little or no training in facilitation; uses more authoritarian style that she or he probably has experienced without checking the backgrounds and needs of participants; no continuing support offered to participants); *experienced facilitator* (training, some experience after training and some feedback from more experienced facilitators; has thought about background and needs of participants and sometimes has done a needs assessment; provides support for participants by asking how they are doing) and *artisan facilitator* (has training and periodically is given feedback by experienced and artisan facilitators; can use many different techniques in facilitating meetings; continually adjusts what is being done by taking into account the context and needs of participants; optimizes full participation of all participants). Holborn (2002), Hogan (2002), and Jenkins (2004) have noted the complex skills (such as clear communication, neutrality, process and participation skills) required in facilitation. All levels of facilitation require not only continuing training and/or discussion of facilitations, but also ongoing support and resources.

Amnesty International (2011, pp. 20–22) discussed experienced and particularly artisan facilitation when it described what facilitators should do:

- Promote inclusion and active participation of all members of the group.
- Promote dialogue in a constructive way.
- Emphasize process, as well as outcomes.
- Manage tensions.
- Recognize and address power imbalances.
- Inspire!

Is there any evidence that experienced and artisan facilitation is better than novice facilitation? The general expectation is that experienced or artisan facilitation is better. Dukes and Firehock (2001, p. 30), based on their experience with environmental conflicts, noted that "the more diverse the group, the greater the scope of the group's purpose and potential impact, and the more complex or conflictual the issues, then the more likely you will need a skilled and experienced facilitator or mediator who will take an active role in all elements of the group's process." Espiner and Hartnett (2011) also noted the value of a skilled facilitator. In discussing person-centered facilitation of planning with adults who have intellectual disabilities, they (Espiner and Hartnett 2011, p. 63) wrote that "the facilitation of a person's aspirations requires a skilled facilitator who is a clear communicator giving priority to the aspirations and choices expressed by the person." The researchers

[7] Shaw and his colleagues (2010, p. 5) have defined intentional facilitator in the following way: "we use the label 'intentional' to distinguish a purposeful (or formal or professional) facilitator from one who facilitates a group meeting with only a tacit awareness of the reasons or motives behind actions or with limited knowledge of facilitation tools and techniques."

(Espiner and Hartnett 2011, p. 69) concluded that "skilled facilitation in the planning process will be essential to honour the adult's voice and to promote a greater sense of ownership and control." This study, however, did not discuss the different levels of skilled facilitation.

Two studies are mentioned here because of their interest in both effectiveness and different levels of facilitation. One study of electronic meetings – by Wong and Aiken (2003, p. 125) – concluded that "automated facilitation was as good as expert-human and better than novice-human facilitation for simple idea generation and ranking tasks." One of the big limitations of this study was that "no attempt was made to automate more cognitively complex facilitation tasks such as ensuring that parties are heard, that one 'faction' does not take over the meeting, that all ideas are discussed fairly, intimidating or derisive comments are discouraged, and that new ideas are considered."

The other study – by Kolfschoten et al. (2007) – compared facilitators who had different levels of experience. For their research (Kolfschoten et al. 2007, p. 353) *novice* facilitators were those who had facilitated less than 25 workshops, *experienced* facilitators had facilitated between 25 and 100 workshops and *expert* facilitators had conducted over 100 workshops. The researchers (Kolfschoten et al. 2007, p. 347, 354, 359) concluded that "generally, the time to prepare diminishes when experience increases," novices and experienced facilitators regularly use less (facilitation) techniques than experts," "novices have less access to a consulting team" and novices "are more likely to encounter surprises (e.g., unexpected outcomes or conflict) yet they are less equipped to handle (by adapting their facilitation designs) these surprises."[8] These findings lend support to the value of experienced and artisan facilitation and also provide some suggestions about how facilitation can be improved.

Steps to a Better Meeting

Facilitators, whether external (outside of the group making decisions) or internal (a member of the group making decisions who is taking on the role of a facilitator), are expected to improve the processes and outcomes of group meetings.[9] The meetings may differ in substantial ways such as the emotional connection of some or all participants to issues being discussed, different power of participants, or

[8]Dukes and Firehock (2001, p. 32) noted that "a volunteer facilitator, or even a paid agency staff person with minimum training, may not have the skills required to help parties negotiate the twists and turns of a highly political and/or highly technical issue . . . Innocent mistakes by an untrained person may result in parties leaving the group or other adverse outcomes."

[9]Nielsen (2012, p. 89) indicates that "a workshop facilitator is often an external consultant, working to organize and lead events like meetings, seminars, workshops and group sessions in order to help their participants reach a certain goal or conclusion defined in advance (by the participants or the management)."

group traditions including usual approaches to making decisions. The purpose for the meeting also can be quite different. Retreats,[10] for instance, may be for developing a strategic plan, changing organizational culture, building relationships or encouraging creativity/innovation. Because of these differences, no one set way of facilitating a meeting is the only way to do things.

Even though meetings can be quite different, there are some general considerations (e.g., Frediani 2009; Bens 2000, pp. 39–44; Doyle and Straus 1976) that can be put forward as basic for most business-type meetings in the United States (with varying applications in other countries). The following section of this chapter is divided into five parts – before, beginning, during, ending and after the meeting.

Before the Meeting

1. ***Plan the meeting carefully***. *Meetings often require a great deal of advance work. Among the questions to be answered: Who should attend? What will be discussed? When will the meeting be held? (In some situations, the timing of when a meeting will be held is extremely important.) Where will the meeting be held? What will be the best seating arrangement for the meeting room? Will there be refreshments? Why is the meeting being held? What is the desired outcome or outcomes of the meeting? If a series of meetings might be needed, how many will there be? Will the meeting be a safe environment? Will guests or the public be invited/allowed/encouraged to attend the meeting? How much notice needs to be provided before the meeting? Will a quorum be needed? Will Robert's Rules of Order (Robert* 2011*) or some other format need to be followed? Management representatives (at the highest level) should be involved in the planning meeting or meetings to make sure that there is agreement about the process, content and goals.*
2. ***Collect needed background information***. *This may involve interviews. (Sometimes you learn surprising information in individual interviews. In advance of a small meeting, I learned that two participants had not spoken to each other in 10 years and that junior members of the work group were afraid to say anything in front of senior people.) A review of documents (including records and accounts of previous meetings) also may need to be undertaken. Some documents may need to be distributed at and/or in advance of the meeting.*
3. ***Prepare and send out a tentative agenda in advance of the meeting***. *The tentative agenda should identify the kind of meeting that will be held, the proposed topics for discussion and the tentative amount of time that will be devoted to each item. (The facilitator's copy of the draft agenda also should include process notes indicating how each agenda item will be handled –* e.g., *each person will give one story, brief report from three people, or establish*

[10] See, for instance, *Retreats that Work* (2006) by Liteman, Campbell and Liteman.

evaluation criteria.) Comments/suggestions should be invited about the topics, the order of the topics and amount of time required for discussion. Depending on responses, a revised agenda may need to be sent out in advance of the meeting.

4. ***Arrive early at the meeting site and set up the meeting room***. *Make sure that there is sufficient time to set up your room before your meeting begins. I have found that sometimes arrangements made in advance do not result in what is expected. Be prepared, for example, to move tables and locate extra seating.*
5. ***Plan and check all technical aspects of the meeting***. *This should be done well in advance of the meeting and again just before the meeting. Have plans in place about what will be done in the event that some equipment is not there or does not function.*
6. ***Have a troubleshooter poised and in position***. *If you are greeting those attending the meeting or are the facilitator, you probably will not have the possibility of dealing with a security issue (*e.g., *threatening person) or other problem. It always is best to have one or two people identified as troubleshooters who know it is their job (if you indicate) to solve any problem that develops.*

At the Beginning of the Meeting

7. ***Greet those attending the meeting***. *Make people feel welcome when entering the meeting room and ask if they have any questions. This might be done just before or at the beginning of the formal meeting or, if people are attending who are not known to the facilitator, as each person enters the room. This might be a point to ask what people are expecting from the meeting or why they are attending. This gives the facilitator some sense of who is in the room and why people are attending the meeting.*
8. ***Identify the type of meeting***. *Indicate if the meeting will be, for instance, all or in part informational, planning, advisory, relationship-building or decision-making. This is good to do at a beginning of a meeting and also may need to be done during the meeting.*
9. ***Establish ground rules?*** *Some meetings can progress very nicely without establishing any ground rules. If ground rules or stated principles (*e.g., *confidentiality) are needed, they can be developed (with the help of the participants) at the beginning of the meeting or at any point during the meeting.*
10. ***Start on time***. *The announcement of the meeting and the agenda indicate the starting and ending times for the meeting. Those attending generally expect that these times are accurate.*
11. ***Have participants introduce themselves and perhaps state their expectations for the meeting***. *Don't assume everyone knows everyone else. Set a process in place that lets everyone hear what is being said but doesn't let anyone monopolize the introduction process. The last two meetings I attended were problematic from the very beginning. In one a rather large number of people were asked by the novice facilitator to introduce themselves (without a*

microphone) and nobody heard or understood the information because most of the names and affiliations were mumbled. One of the meetings had people introducing themselves with a microphone but the novice facilitator also asked each person to say a little something about her or his project. Many of the people talked for a rather long time about their projects while the novice facilitator did nothing (but wring his hands and look pained) while this was going on. Introductions can be a very good idea at the beginning of the meeting but the approach that is used, the directions that are given and the handling of this process by the facilitator are very important. (In a large meeting, it may be that only small numbers of people can be given the opportunity to introduce themselves to each other and/or people can introduce themselves as they contribute to the meeting.)

12. ***Clearly define roles.***[11] *The facilitator should use an approach that makes clear the expectations for all those participating in a meeting. It may be that each person is expected to speak and also that each person should encourage others to contribute. Participants should understand the role of the facilitator and whether a recorder (writing a public display of notes) will be used rather than a secretary (with private notes). Who will be acting as the timekeeper? Will roles possibly change (*e.g., *people sharing the recorder role) during the meeting? If a top manager or official is there, what will be her or his role during the meeting?*
13. ***Review, revise, and order the agenda (including times).*** *The agenda already has been through at least one review and may have been resubmitted to those attending the meeting. This would be a final review, even though topics and times still may be changed during the meeting.*
14. ***Review action items, if any, from previous meetings.*** *This can bring participants up-to-date, note accomplishments or progress, identify problems and help bring closure on some issues.*
15. ***Explain the process that will be used.*** *In addition to explaining the roles of those participating in the meeting, explain (or discuss) the process that will be used for any discussion and decision-making (*e.g., *ranking and evaluating, multi-voting, ranking/prioritizing, nominal group, force-field analysis).*

During the Meeting

16. ***Focus on an issue (all in the same way and the same time).*** *The facilitator, with the help of all participants, has to keep the meeting on track. The process that has been explained at the beginning of the meeting will help the facilitator do this and also to handle new topics or difficult points that may emerge during the discussion.*

---

[11] Those who want more information about defining roles in meetings will find it useful to look at *How to Make Meetings Work* (1976) by Michael Doyle and David Straus.

17. ***Consider using small groups***. *This approach can bring involvement/energy or renewed energy to a discussion. Groups need concrete directions and a time limit.*
18. ***Consider having one or more breaks***. *Breaks can be an excellent way to get people to talk or caucus with each other, change the seating arrangements and/or have the meeting easily go in a different direction. Participants do need to know when the meeting will reconvene. While this can be a very effective tool, I have seen meetings where participants did not return on time and some used the break as an opportunity/invitation to leave.*

At the End of the Meeting

19. ***Review the group memory***. *This is easily done if there is a public version (*e.g., *overhead or poster sheets on walls) rather than a private record (personal notes). It is most important that* ***action items are established or confirmed*** *including who will take an action, what will be done and when it will be done.*
20. ***Set the date, time and place of the next meeting (if one is needed) and develop a preliminary agenda***. *It may be that only suggestions for dates, times and places can be mentioned if one also has to consider the preferences of those who were not able to attend this meeting.*
21. ***Evaluate the meeting***. *This can be done casually or in a formal way. Information obtained at the end of a meeting can be helpful to those who may put another meeting in place.*
22. ***Close the meeting on time – crisply and positively***. *Unless the whole group has agreed to extend the meeting, it is best to close the meeting at the announced time. After this formal ending, a group or groups may be given encouragement to meet.*
23. ***Clean up and rearrange the room***. *People in charge of a space appreciate some help in getting a room ready for the next meeting. The amount of help that is appreciated will vary depending on the administrators (*e.g., *hotel manager, school principal) and/or the regular set-up people for the space.*

After the Meeting

24. ***Evaluate the meeting/write and file a report***. *Review any comments given orally or in writing by participants and add your own comments. Even if there will be no additional meetings, at least a brief report (including the agenda, any action items and evaluations) should be developed based on the meeting as well as the preparatory and evaluation sessions. This will serve as guidance to others who may eventually hold a meeting of these participants or run a meeting dealing with the same or similar topics.*

25. ***Follow-up on any action items and, if there will be a next meeting, begin to plan it****. A plan needs to be put in place dealing with the completion of action items.*
26. ***Give praise (as deserved) for those who helped develop and run the meeting****. It is important to thank people by name for their assistance. It also may be a good idea, in some cases, to write notes of thanks that will be included in personnel files.*

Two examples of facilitated meetings might be useful at this point. The first, an initiative in a Minnesota county (CR Planning, Inc. n.d.), required a permanent stakeholder advisory commission be established for decisions involving parks, trails and open space. A consulting group, CR Planning, used a facilitated public participation process (during a one-year period) to "engage citizens, landowners and public officials in a respectful dialogue" at the start of the planning process and then facilitated discussion of the Park Advisory Committee. A policy plan was adopted by the County Board and this was followed by an implementation plan.[12]

As a second example, I facilitated a series of meetings (every two weeks for several months) for a "blue ribbon" citizen advisory group that had been put in place by a large city's school board. The school board had been "encouraged" by community groups to get input from civic and business organizations representing minorities (as well as unions) regarding inclusive, local hiring in connection with new construction that the school system was going to undertake over a 10-year period. The facilitator, in this case, was involved in the process after the participants already had been selected, helped design the process that would be used for each meeting, facilitated each session, provided research and perspective for the head of the advisory group and assisted in developing the Committee's report to the board.

Mediators also serve as advisers or mentors about facilitation processes. For example, SwissPeace (n.d.), which describes itself as a "practice-oriented peace research institute," has a coaching program (2012–2013) for women in Myanmar who are engaged in peace processes. In another instance, I advised the head of a chapter of a national NGO in developing a process for bringing together parts of a community that was deeply divided. I also helped a community organization revise its process for a public forum that would bring together members of the community to discuss a multi-service center that was proposed by a religious organization based outside of the community. The religious group thought that the center was an excellent idea but had not collaborated with community organizations in developing its project. Many community organizations (and many members of the community organization sponsoring the forum) were skeptical or opposed to the project. The

---

[12]Full implementation did not happen. According to Brian Ross (2012) of CR Planning, the implementation work was to be managed by an employee of the small parks department and not the consultants. Most of the plan was not implemented because the parks department employee who was to manage the implementation was hired away by another organization and county officials disbanded the parks department and shifted the responsibility for parks to another county department that had a different focus.

community room in which the meeting was held was packed and included local residents as well as sign-carrying members of the outside church.

Some mediators and facilitators, run meetings dealing with environmental, community or public policy issues. Frequently such meetings are part of a series of meetings that may take place over a long period of time (e.g., months or years). Depending, in part, on the importance and urgency of the issue to those attending the meeting, the need to agree on a process, the level of controversy and the number of sectors and groups involved, the facilitator (or facilitation team) may organize a set of planning meetings to arrange the actual decision-making meetings. Those planning meetings could cover topics such as number of organizations that will be represented in the meetings; how many representatives each group will have; how decisions will be communicated to the public (if needed); who will facilitate the actual meetings; how representatives will communicate and get the involvement of the organizations they represent; how absences will be handled; what topics will be covered and how decisions will be made.

Some mediators facilitate sessions in conflict zones or post-conflict situations (see Asuni 2012, pp. 113–126; Smock and Serwer 2012, pp. 163–169). Smock and Serwer (2012) provide advice about a number of difficult issues including getting minority representation in meetings and getting minority representatives to have full and accepted participation from those with more power. They also caution that if discussions involve national policies, that there need to be links to Track One (official) diplomacy. And they discuss that frequently participants want to represent themselves rather than their organizations which can have consequences in moving things forward in a country or region. While Smock and Serwer's advice is based on working in conflict zones, the points are true (or can be adapted) for many other kinds of mediation and facilitation settings.

Dealing with Facilitation Difficulties: The Well City Experience

The hearings described below were held in Well City,[13] a medium-sized community in the U.S. The first hearing was in a court room and run by the elected mayor. The second hearing was in a university building and run by an experienced facilitator.

Aurora Punch, Well City's Health Commissioner, knew that tobacco use was a preventable cause of disease and death. She also knew the American Cancer Society and the American Lung Association were encouraging communities to put tobacco use prevention regulations in place and she wanted to do that in Well City.

[13]The example described here is based on an actual case that is discussed at length in "The Bumpy Road to a Tobacco-Free Community: Lessons from Well City" (Fritz et al. 2000). Pseudonyms are used here and in the original article for the names of the city and individuals.

In September, Commissioner Punch sent letters to selected organizations, including the city council, indicating that she was forming a "task force of community leaders" to study the tobacco problem. She wanted representatives from each group to "actively participate" in the work of the task force.

The task force first met eight months later (in May) with 18 representatives, including the mayor, two city council members, the clerk of court, three city board of health members, a county health department employee, a representative from the hospital, an employee of the county commissioner' office, and a member of the business community. One of the task force members, a representative of the American Cancer Society, was a retired regulatory technologist and familiar with the indoor air standard accepted by the American Society of Heating, Refrigerating, and Air-conditioning Engineers (ASHRAE). The American Cancer Society representative along with the city health commissioner and two other task force members formed a smaller working group – the Clean-Air Regulation Subcommittee. In July, the subcommittee recommended a clean air regulation to the city board of health that incorporated the ASHRAE standard of ventilation.

The proposed regulation stated that "lighted smoking materials in public places is declared a public nuisance and hazardous to the public health." It prohibited the possession of lighted smoking material in any form in any commercial establishment (including bars, restaurants, and bowling alleys), public vehicles, restrooms, elevators, and selected public facilities (libraries, educational facilities, museums, auditoriums, and art galleries). The proposed regulation did allow an owner of a facility to permit smoking if the owner installed a ventilation system based on the ASHRAE standard or have a hearing if the owner wanted a variance.

It was anticipated that owners would not attempt to meet the ASHRAE standard, as this would be an expensive undertaking, and also that few variances would be given. Any owner or operation that failed to comply with the regulation could be charged with a minor misdemeanor and fined up to $100. Essentially what was being proposed was a total smoking ban for public places.

The city health commissioner proposed the regulation at a city board of health meeting in October and the city's first public hearing (meeting) was held in November. That hearing, by all accounts, was bedlam. About 250 people jammed a small courtroom and the group heard more than 50 speakers. The meeting lasted more than four hours. While no smoking was allowed in the courtroom, smoking was allowed in the hall just outside the courtroom. Tobacco smoke from the packed corridor poured into the hall every time the court's doors opened.

The mayor, who served as head of the city's health board, facilitated the public hearing. The mayor indicated that anyone who wanted to speak could do so. He allowed speakers to go beyond the prescribed time limits and speakers frequently repeated what others had said. Hecklers were not controlled. Most of those opposing the proposed regulation were bar, restaurant, or small business owners.

One of the speakers was Marge Can, a well-known, realtor in the community, who had owned her own business for more than 10 years. She was smart and energetic. While not frequently active in the public life of the community, she had headed the committee (whose members all were smokers) that organized the American Cancer Society's annual (fundraising) golf tournaments for the two years prior to Well City's tobacco-control initiative.

Each morning Marge went for coffee at P.T.'s, a local restaurant, and joined the regulars for a discussion of local events. One morning the talk turned to the story on the front page of the local paper, the city and county's proposed tobacco control regulations. After considerable discussion, Marge, who smoked two to four packs of cigarettes a day, and a farmer decided to form an organization, BADLAW, to fight the proposed regulations. The core group of organizers also included the owner of a restaurant and the non-smoking owner of a travel agency. They spoke at the public hearing and Marge gave interviews to the city newspaper.

Marge said the main issue was one of freedom. She pointed out that the health boards were not elected and had no right to be making tobacco-control rules. Marge felt that if she and a client wanted to smoke in the conference room of her office, they should be able to do so without government interference.[14]

After the shock of the chaotic public hearing, the city health department began licking its wounds, and four months later, in January, the city and county health boards started working together on revising the proposed regulation. The new proposal dropped the term "clean air" and the list of exemptions and variances began to grow to include (1) bars, bowling alleys, and pool halls (if they have signs stating that a no-smoking area is not available; (2) an employee vehicle where the driver and all the passengers consent to smoking; and (3) retail tobacco stores.

More than one year after the first hearing, in October, the city and county boards of health held a joint public hearing at the Well City campus of a state university to collect feedback on the revised proposal. The university building was chosen because it was removed from city departments and offices and no smoking was allowed in the whole building. This time there would be no smoke coming in from the corridors.

This public hearing was held in a large auditorium, much larger than the expected number of participants, and it was run by a trained facilitator. The facilitator gave a rather complete informational presentation that began the meeting. After the presentation, audience members were able to speak, but they had to follow guidelines. Speakers had to sign up in advance and no more than one speaker was allowed from an organization. Length of speaking time and heckling were now

[14]Five years after Marge's group (BADLAW) lost its last court battle against the city, Marge Can, 52, died of lung cancer. During the 20 years she had lived in Well City, Marge unsuccessfully tried many methods to quit smoking, including acupuncture, hypnosis, and the patch. She did not try to quit smoking while she was the spokesperson for BADLAW. One year before she died, Marge learned she had lung cancer and would have to have surgery. She stopped smoking. During her last year, she established a website to let others follow her progress in dealing with cancer. When she became too weak to type her own website entries, family members made the entries for her. The obituary that appeared in the local paper noted Marge's community service, particularly her volunteer work on behalf of the American Cancer Society.

under control. Security personnel were available if needed, and the organizers of the hearing had agreed in advance that if the event got out of control in some way, it would be ended early. The meeting ended at the announced time.

The facilitator has to be in control of a meeting, in this case, a community hearing. Well City's first public hearing was a disaster. It was led by an elected official who did not want to upset any of his constituents; he allowed people to speak too long and repetitively, did not control heckling, and held the hearing in a place where tobacco smoke could pour into the hearing room. By the time of the second hearing, Well City public health officials had learned a lesson. The hearing was held in a building that was smoke-free on a college campus (neutral territory). The meeting room was much larger than the number people that would be in attendance. This setting – a large room with many empty seats rather than a crowded court room – means that the setting will not easily add fuel to any controversy. There was visible security and the hand-picked, experienced facilitator had a long, thorough, informative introduction about the main topic and established a speaking process that was inclusive, orderly and calm. The second hearing gave the public the opportunity to take part in the discussion, but, unlike the first hearing, there was no chaos.

Conclusion

Mediation and facilitation often are broadly defined and the definitions can be quite similar. This certainly is seen when mediation is described as "facilitated negotiation." And when Hampson and Zartman (2012, p. 35, 51) refer to "triple talk" (when a mediator becomes involved with parties who have been negotiating) as "mediated negotiation" or say a mediator is "by any other name [a] facilitator, good offices, third party, etc." While there are some differences between mediation and facilitation, sometimes the definitions don't reflect these differences because the definitions are not detailed enough or the differences are differences in emphasis (rather than absolute differences).

One general difference between mediation and facilitation is that facilitators need to be able to work with large meetings (as well as small ones) and mediators, based on their special area of work, may not have to work with large groups. Also, mediators have to be able to write formal agreements while facilitations often do not have such an outcome. Some think that a facilitator's main task is to improve the process or structure of a group while a mediator most frequently is working on resolving an issue. (While this may generally be true, there are many exceptions.) Finally, facilitators, because they are expected to have the capacity to work with large groups of people, may have exposure to many different techniques (particularly ones that encourage participation) as part of their training while some mediators, depending on the area of practice, may not have this training or experience. Professional mediators who work with large groups usually also are facilitators; some mediators who work with individuals and small groups are facilitators, and, increasingly, the others are being trained in the art of facilitation.

Business-type meetings need to be prepared carefully and, if a mediator/facilitator or facilitator team is involved, the mediators/facilitators need to be part of the planning as well as the implementation effort. As noted in the Well City case, meetings that are not well-prepared may not accomplish goals, can reinforce initial positions and anger as well as lose participants.

There is evidence that facilitated processes can be very effective. Shaw and his colleagues (2010, p. 9), based on their research of facilitator impact during a quality improvement process, concluded that external facilitators, who are experienced or artisan, "are able to ask critical questions, hold people accountable, and even 'see' processes or dynamics that the insider may not." The art of facilitation can help meeting participants work through difficult issues; really involve people in their organizations and communities; help people who have had difficulty participating in groups as well as those who think that others should not be full participants; and develop creative, inclusive long-range plans. All groups do not need professional facilitators, but experienced and artisan facilitation often can make a central contribution to a group's progress.

References

Amnesty International. (2011). *Facilitation manual: A guide to using participatory methodologies for human rights education*. London: Amnesty International.

Asuni, J. B. (2012). Nigeria: Dialogue in the delta. In D. R. Smock & D. Serwer (Eds.), *Facilitating dialogue: USIP's work in conflict zones* (pp. 113–126). Washington, DC: United States Institute of Peace Press.

Bens, I. (2000). *Facilitating with ease! A step-by-step guidebook with customizable worksheets on CD/Rom*. San Francisco: Jossey-Bass.

Bens, I. (2006). *Facilitating to lead! Leadership strategies for a networked world*. San Francisco: Jossey-Bass.

Berkvens, J. (2012). What international aid organizations can learn from international adult learning: Experiences from Cambodia. *The Journal of Agricultural Education and Extension, 18*(4), 347–368.

CR Planning Inc. (n.d.). Retrieved from www.crplanning.com and www.crplanning.com/pdfs/crowwingparks.pdf. Accessed 15 Oct 2012.

Doyle, M., & Straus, D. (1976). *How to make meetings work*. New York: Jove Books.

Dukes, E. F., & Firehock, K. (2001). *Collaboration: A guide for environmental advocates*. Charlottesville: Institute for Environmental Negotiation.

Espiner, D., & Hartnett, F. M. (2011). 'I felt I was in control of the meeting': Facilitating planning with adults with an intellectual disability. *British Journal of Learning Disabilities, 40*, 62–70.

Frediani, J. A. (2009). *Sharing the floor: Some strategies for effective group facilitation*. Unitarian Universalist, Association of Congregations. Retrieved from www.uua.org/re/adults/151805. Accessed 15 Jan 2013.

Fritz, J. M., Bistak, P., & Auffrey, C. (2000). The bumpy road to a tobacco-free community: Lessons from Well City. *Sociological Practice: A Journal of Clinical and Applied Sociology, 2*(2), 113–126.

Fryer, M. (2012). Facilitative leadership: Drawing on Jürgen Habermas' model of ideal speech to propose a less impositional way to lead. *Organization, 19*(1), 25–43.
Hampson, F. O., & Zartman, I. W. (2012). *The global power of talk: Negotiating America's interests*. Boulder/London: Paradigm Publishers.
Hartwig, R. T. (2010). Facilitating problem solving: A case study using the devil's advocacy technique. *Group Facilitation: A Research and Applications Journal, 10*, 17–31.
Haskell, J. E., & Cyr, L. F. (2011). Community facilitator education: How training can lead to positive impacts at the community level. *Group Facilitation: A Research and Applications Journal, 11*, 5–14.
Hogan, C. (2002). *Understanding facilitation: Theory and principles*. London: Kogan Page.
Holborn, S. (2002). The value of measuring person-centered planning. In J. O'Brien & C. O'Brien (Eds.), *Implementing person-centered planning: Voice of experience* (pp. 79–97). Toronto: Inclusion Press.
Jenkins, J. (2004). *Facilitation, training, consultation or do it yourself? Handout for ADR institute meeting 5 November 2004*. Retrieved from masterplan.co.za/resources/documents/facilitationis.pdf. Accessed 15 Jan 2013.
Kato, F. (2010). How we think and talk about facilitation. *Simulation & Gaming, 41*(5), 694–704.
Kolfschoten, G. L., den Hengst-Bruggeling, M., & de Vreede, G. J. (2007). Issues in the design of facilitated collaboration processes. *Group Decision and Negotiation, 16*, 347–361.
Liteman, M., Campbell, S., & Liteman, J. (2006). *Retreats that work: Everything you need to know about planning and leading great offsites* (Expandedth ed.). San Francisco: Jossey-Bass.
Nagykaldi, Z., Mold, J. W., & Aspy, C. B. (2005). Practice facilitators: A review of the literature. *Family Medicine, 37*(8), 581–588.
Nielsen, M. F. (2012). Using artifacts in brainstorming sessions to secure participation and decouple sequentiality. *Discourse Studies, 14*(1), 87–109.
Rees, F. (2005). *The facilitator excellence handbook* (2nd ed.). San Francisco: Pfeiffer.
Reilly, C. R. (2008). Is expertise a necessary precondition for creativity? A case of four novice learning group facilitators. *Thinking Skills and Creativity, 3*, 59–76.
Robert, H. M. (2011). *Robert's rules of order. Newly revised*. Philadelphia: Da Capo Press.
Ross, B. (2012). *Telephone interview*. November 27.
Sefton, E. (2009). *Resource Management Act Amendment 2009 Guidance*. New Zealand. October.
Shaw, E., Looney, A., Chase, S., Navalekar, R., Stello, B., Lontok, O., & Crabtree, B. (2010). 'In the moment': An analysis of facilitator impact during a quality improvement process. *Group Facilitation: A Research and Applications Journal, 10*, 4–16.
Smock, D. R., & Serwer, D. (Eds.). (2012). *Facilitating dialogue: USIP's work in conflict zones*. Washington, DC: United States Institute of Peace Press.
SwissPeace. (n.d.). Retrieved from http://www.swisspeace.ch. Accessed 16 Oct 2012.
Subramaniam, M. (2011). Grassroots groups and poor women's empowerment in rural India. *International Sociology, 27*(1), 72–95.
The State of Queensland, Department of Justice and Attorney-General (2010–2012). (n.d.). Dispute resolution: Facilitation. Brisbane: The State of Queensland. Retrieved from http://www.justice.qld.gov.au/justice-services/dispute-resolution/facilitation. Accessed 16 Oct 2012.
Thorpe, S. (2011). Editorial introduction. *Group Facilitation: A Research and Applications Journal, 11*, 3–4.
U.S. Institute for Environmental Conflict Resolution. (n.d.). Retrieved from http://www.ecr.gov/HowWeWork/Services.aspx. Accessed 16 Oct 2012.
Williams, A. (2012). Taking a step back: Learning without the facilitator on solo activities. *Journal of Adventure Education & Outdoor Learning, 12*(2), 137–155.
Wilkinson, M. (n.d.). *Guerilla facilitation: What to do if the meeting leader is not leading*. Retrieved from www.inifac.org/articles/arGuerillaFacilitation.pdf. Accessed 18 Oct 2012.
Wong, Z., & Aiken, M. (2003). Automated facilitation of electronic meetings. *Information & Management, 41*, 125–134.

Chapter 10
Conflict Intervention on Behalf of Widows: Notes from Enugu State in Nigeria

Eleanor Ann Nwadinobi

Introduction

A *widow,* a female whose husband has died, can experience a great deal of change in her living circumstances after the death of her spouse. In many parts of the world, a widow may face more difficult financial circumstances and a loss of at least some of her social network, but the *status* of a widow is not seen as a problem. Widowhood and remarriage are acceptable, in other parts of the world, however, widowhood can be seen as punishment and a widow can be subjected to restrictions and terrible circumstances. For instance, in the Caprivi Region of Namibia, widows are no longer forced off the land, but there is a more subtle form of property disinheritance (Thomas 2008). And, the previous practice of Sati in India meant that during the cremation of a husband's corpse, it was an honor for the widow to climb on the funeral pyre and die (Malathi 2008; Ahmad 2009). Though this practice has been banned, there have been instances of it from 1987 to 2008 (Ahmad 2009).

This chapter focuses on the problems faced by widows in Enugu State, an Igbo-speaking area in the South East region[1] of Nigeria, and the work of WiDO, a local organization, to try to solve or reduce those problems. The chapter begins with a brief discussion of Nigeria and its conflicts. This is followed by a discussion of the status of widowhood in Nigeria. The Widows Development Organization

[1]Nigerians frequently refer to the country's six regions: North East, North West, North Central, South West, South South and South East (ActionAid Nigeria 2009, p. ii). The South East region includes Enugu State.

E.A. Nwadinobi (✉)
President of the Widows Development Organisation (WiDO), Nigeria
e-mail: elenwad@yahoo.co.uk

J.M. Fritz (ed.), *Moving Toward a Just Peace: The Mediation Continuum*,
Clinical Sociology: Research and Practice, DOI 10.1007/978-94-007-2885-1_10,

of Nigeria (WiDO) is discussed next and an example of a mediation is provided. The conclusion includes some recommendations for those conducting mediations or putting mediation programs in place.

The History of Nigeria in the Context of Conflicts

The Federal Republic of Nigeria, located in western Africa on the Gulf of Guinea, is the most populous country in Africa with approximately one-sixth of Africa's people. The land is about twice the size of Sweden or the state of California. Some 48 % of the population lives in urban areas and about half of those people live in the 24 cities that have more than 100,000 inhabitants. The median age of the population is 19. The country is the world's second highest in terms of numbers of people living with HIV/AIDS and second highest in terms of deaths (UNAIDS 2007).

Nigeria, a country of 36 states and one federal territory, has a great deal of cultural diversity[2] as there are approximately 250–390 ethnic groups. The most numerous group,[3] in the northern part of the country, is the Hausa-Fulani (mostly Muslim). The Yoruba are most numerous in the southwest. Over half of the Yoruba are Christian, about a quarter are Muslim and the rest follow traditional beliefs. The Igbo, the largest group in the South East region, is predominantly Christian. Other ethnic groups include the Nupe, Tiv and Kanuri in the North and the Ijaw, Efik, Ibibio, and Annang in the South. English is the country's official language, but many other languages (e.g., Hausa, Yoruba, Igbo (Ibo), Fulani) also are spoken.

Nigeria has a long and difficult history that is filled with conflict (e.g., Suberu 2001; Falola 2009; Achebe 1984; Nigeria 2007; Institute for Peace and Conflict Resolution 2002).[4] People were living in southern Nigeria as early as 9000 B.C. and, by the eleventh century, city states, kingdoms and empires were formed including the Hausa kingdoms and Borno dynasty in the North and Oyo and Benin kingdoms in the South. In the sixteenth, seventeenth, and eighteenth centuries, millions of slaves were sent to the Americas. This Trans-Atlantic Slave Trade, connected, in part, to the slavery that existed at the time as a result of inter-tribal warfare, has negative effects to this day on relations between some Nigerian groups (Simpson 2004).

While civil wars were fought in Yoruba areas in the middle and late 1800s, the British established a presence around Lagos and, on January 1, 1901, Nigeria became a British protectorate. In 1914, the area was known as the Colony and Protectorate of Nigeria, but remained divided into the Lagos colony and southern and northern provinces.

---

[2] Horowitz (1993, p. 37) has described this as "irrepressible pluralism."

[3] No percentages for the ethnic groups are provided here. The percentages frequently presented are not consistent and have been controversial.

[4] According to Diamond (2001, p. xii), "over the past four decades, no country in the world has had a more turbulent and tragic democratic experience than Nigeria."

After World War II, the educated indigenes still were excluded from the governance of the country. There was growing Nigerian nationalism and demands for independence. Economic hardship in the post-war period also contributed to a series of conflicts including the General Strike of 1945, the Burutu Strike of 1947, and the Enugu Colliery Strike. The Zikist movement became famous for organizing demonstrations, strikes, and boycotts. This was followed by the Kano disturbances in 1953. All these afforded people the opportunity to agitate against the colonial regime.

In October 1960, Nigeria gained her independence under a constitution that included a measure of self-government for the country's three regions and a bicameral parliament. The federal government had exclusive power in terms of fiscal policy, foreign relations and defense. Executive power was under a prime minister and cabinet and judicial authority was in a Federal Supreme Court. The political parties were each connected primarily to an ethnic group.

On October 1, 1963, Nigeria became a Federal Republic and severed its last ties with Britain. Nigeria did remain, however, in the British Commonwealth of Nations. The Governor-General's position was, therefore, renamed as President. The disputed result of the 1965 national election put the country on the road to a civil war. In January 1966, a group of army officers overthrew the government and the prime minister and premiers in the northern and western regions were assassinated. Another coup took place in July. Thousands of Igbo were massacred and many Igbo wanted to secede from Nigeria. In 1967 a military governor of the eastern region became a leader of the Igbo secessionist movement. After he declared the independence of the eastern region, civil war broke and more than one million died in the war before it ended in 1970.

Economic development followed the end of the civil war but, in 1975, a general and a group of officers staged a coup and delayed the promised return to civilian rule. The general announced a timetable for the return of civilian rule, but was assassinated before that happened. A new constitution was finally put in place in 1978. The 1979 election was marred by violence and accusations of voting irregularities.

In the following years, the military governments were overthrown in 1983 and again in 1985. The government that emerged promised to restore civil rule by 1990. In early 1989, an assembly completed a new constitution and political activity was permitted again. In 1990, there was an unsuccessful coup and 69 people were executed after secret military trials. That same year, elections were held, without violence, at the local government level. After a number of voting issues (e.g., fraud, disqualification of all candidates for president), a presidential election was finally held on June 12, 1993. Although some observers thought it was a fair election, the election results were annulled, some 100 people were killed in riots and an interim government was put in place.

The next years saw continued military leadership. Some labor leaders were arrested in 1994 and there was an alleged coup attempt in 1995 that resulted in a secret tribunal and death sentences. Also in 1995, Ogoni activist Ken Saro-Wiwa and eight others were, as a result of a politically motivated and unfair process, executed for their alleged roles in the killings of four Ogoni politicians. In 1997, the government arrested a general, ten other officers and eight civilians on charges of plotting a coup. Nine were sentenced to death. These death sentences were commuted under the next head of government.

Democracy emerged in Nigeria in 1999. Local elections were successfully held and 16 consecutive years of military rule finally came to an end. The head of government was now a former general who wanted civilian rule and to represent all Nigerians rather than one religious group. Under his leadership, however, community violence continued. For instance, in May 1999, there was violence in Kaduna State that resulted in more than 100 deaths. In November 1999, the army destroyed a town and killed many civilians in retaliation for local gang members having murdered 12 policemen. In Kaduna, from February through May 2000, over 1,000 people died in rioting. In September 2001, more than 2,000 people were killed in religion-based rioting in Jos. In October 2001, hundreds were killed and thousands displaced in communal violence that spread across the states of Benue, Taraba, and Nasarawa.

Other examples of conflicts include the Dumne crisis in Adamawa State in 2002, Bambam crisis in Gombe State in 2003, Jukun-Tiv crisis of 2004 in Taraba State, Taliban uprising in Borno and Yobe States toward the end of 2005, and church burnings and murders in Maiduguri in 2006. In April 2007, a Muslim religious leader/state official and a disciple were killed in a mosque during early-morning prayers and, in November, there was a riot on the campus of the University of Maiduguri that resulted in the closure of the university.

Pro-democracy tensions in Nigeria have resulted in an end to military dictatorship, but there are still daunting problems. While Nigeria is an oil-rich country, it is plagued with huge problems that stem, at least in part, from the fact that the wealth from the oil is not widely shared by the local communities or the country. Other issues include widespread corruption; longstanding ethnic and religious tensions that have resulted in many bloody confrontations; rape[5]; failed leadership (e.g., Achebe 1984); HIV/AIDS; pollution; longstanding poverty; desertification; the Niger Delta environmental crisis (e.g., Courson 2007); and insufficient economic growth.

The Situation of Widows in Nigeria

There are a large number of widows in Nigeria as a result, in part, of wars and conflicts. The recent pandemic of HIV/AIDS also has increased the number. The actual number of widows is hard to determine as many remain largely uncounted due to lack of disaggregated data.

---

[5] According to Amnesty International (2006), rape is an "endemic" problem in Nigeria requiring immediate action and the government's response "has been, and continues to be, woefully inadequate."

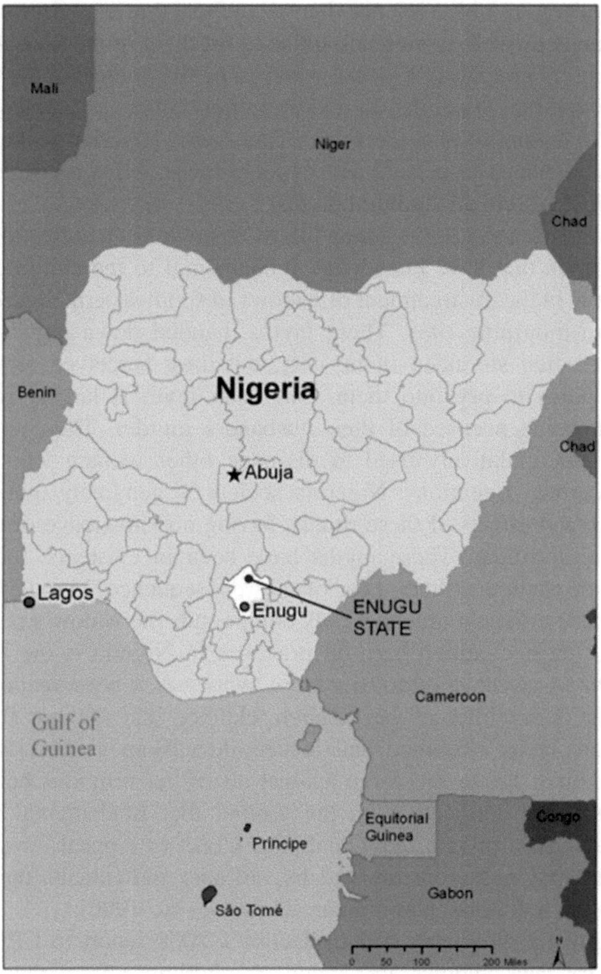

Fig. 10.1 Enugu State in Nigeria

Widows in Enugu State, an Igbo area in southern Nigeria, encounter conflict, mainly due to cultural and socio-economic circumstances. Certain harmful traditional rites are meted out to widows by her in-laws. These harmful practices have their historical origin in widows being labeled as witches and blamed for causing the death of their husbands. Widows undergo dehumanizing cultural practices such as forced hair shaving, differing periods of confinement and loss of their property (Aruna and Fasoranti 2007). Conflicts arise when the violated widows register their displeasure at the treatment and pursue their rights. In the process of intervening in such cases of conflict at the household and community levels, one cannot assume a generic fit considering the different cultural and social influences; in other words, each case has to be treated on its own merit (Fig. 10.1).

Widows undergo double violence due to conflicts that may have caused the loss of their husbands as well as violence inflicted on them at the household level due to harmful cultural practices. Widows, who can be the poorest of the poor, are most vulnerable in conflict situations. In addition, most times, as women, they bear an extra burden in having to play the role of caregivers. Nigerian widows continue to be plagued by problems associated with disinheritance, AIDS transmission, a slowly responding legal system and cultural myths.

Fleisher and Krienert (2009) define the word myth as "a collection of culturally rational narratives that have knowledge fundamental to the culture itself." Myths play a large role in the mistreatment of widows in southeastern Nigeria, particularly with regard to mourning rites. These myths, handed down largely through oral traditions, are often shrouded in mystery, entailing perceived repercussions for anyone who dares to pry into them. One such myth is largely responsible for widows often being accused of their husband's murder. These openly punitive practices are manipulatively used to dissuade other women who might harbor similar 'murderous' intentions. Nigerian society is genuinely ignorant as to the actual dangers and effects of these rituals, having no knowledge of their historical significance or meaning. These myths have been in existence for so long that few question or challenge them. Fear of the "consequences" brought about by not adhering to these mythical practices only compounds the widow's plight.

One of the most common harmful practices in Nigeria is the forced shaving of hair. In Onwo v. Oko (1996), a widow, who was a born-again Christian and member of the Assemblies of God church, claimed that she was forced to shave her hair before being assaulted and locked in a room as part of a traditional mourning practice. These acts were against all of her religious beliefs. The trial court dismissed the application on the ground that fundamental rights are not enforceable against a private individual. The Court of Appeal however, held that where fundamental rights are invaded by ordinary individuals, the victims have rights against the individual perpetrators (Onwo v. Oko 1996).

According to the Women's Aid Collective's 2008 report to CEDAW,[6] "under most customary laws widows are denied in inheritance from the estate of their deceased husbands (and) even where they are allowed inheritance, the share is not equal to that of a man." In some instances, following the death of a husband, relatives drive the widow out of her home and confiscate all her property in the suppositional belief that it was all acquired solely by the husband. In other instances, widows are deprived of a husband's inheritance simply because they do not have male children (Dimkpa 2007). Ironically, in situations where a widow does have a son, she can be subject to the custom known as "Okpala" (first son) custom, whereby the eldest son in entitled to the property of the deceased father even though the widow survives. In 1989, the Nigerian Supreme Court (in Nzekwu et al. v.

[6]The Committee on the Elimination of Discrimination Against Women (CEDAW) is the body of independent experts that monitors the implementation of the Convention on the Elimination of All Forms of Discrimination Against Women.

Nzekwu et al.) condemned the Okpala custom, commenting that is "a barbarous and uncivilized custom which should be regarded as repugnant to equity and good conscience and therefore unacceptable" (Nweze 2006, p. 21).[7] In general, children suffer along with their widowed mothers since widows are left to fend for their children without benefit of any inheritance. As a result, children are often forced to drop out of school, ending up as hired hands and laborers. Worse, girls become particularly vulnerable to violence.

The harmful widowhood practices found in Nigeria put widows at increased risk of contracting HIV/AIDS. A common widowhood practice is that of sexual cleansing, entailing a sexual act as a means of symbolic cleansing and breaking of marital ties with the deceased. Other practices having a direct relationship to HIV/AIDS transmission include early marriage and widow inheritance (also known as wife inheritance or levirate), in which the widow is 'passed on' to the next surviving male in the family. In such situations, widows might be forced into an arrangement with an infected heir, brother-in-law or any surviving male relation. The widow is thus put at risk of either becoming infected or transmitting the virus to her inheritor. This inheritor may in turn transmit the disease to his other sexual partners, including new co-wives in cases of polygamous marriage. In addition, widows are often not informed of the cause of their partner's death, or may not find out until they themselves become ill. The practice of early marriage means that young brides are facing widowhood at an earlier age because their older husbands are dying of AIDS.

A widow's exposure to HIV/AIDS often entails devastating consequences for her family as well. When infected, widows are not as likely to live as long as men with AIDS since they bear the burden of familial care and are less likely to have access to treatment. The lack of legal access to inherited household resources, due to customary or religious laws, means that a woman widowed because of AIDS loses the ability to provide for herself and her family. On World AIDS Day, 1999, Kenyan journalist Esther Muoso (1999) noted that "Wife inheritance - where a widow becomes the property of her late husband's brother - also contributes to the spread of HIV. After the death of a breadwinner, the widow cannot provide adequate care, food, clothing and above all school fees, so many women see wife inheritance as a solution to financial constraints."

Enugu State and Widows' Rights

Enugu State, located in the South East region of Nigeria, was established in 1991 when Anambra State was split into Anambra and Enugu States. Subsequent political and administrative partitions have reduced Enugu's size further than its original

[7]In should be noted, however, the court held, in this case, that a widow who has "no male issue by the deceased husband... has the right to reside in the matrimonial home... in the absence of the widow's misbehaviour or misconduct" (Uzodike 1990, p. 402). The widow is not entitled to any absolute ownership rights.

1991 form. The current population of Enugu State is approximately 3,257,000, while the city of Enugu, the State's capital, has a population of 2,388,862 (National Bureau of Statistics 2006). The Igbo people are the largest ethnic group in Enugu State (approximately 95 %); most are Christian, nearly half of whom are Roman Catholic. Outside of the city of Enugu, Enugu State's economy is predominantly rural and agrarian.

Widows in this part of Nigeria are often subject to oppressive and dehumanizing cultural rituals. Many of these widowhood rites, which are not applicable to widowers, are in breach of both constitutional and international law (Williams 2004). Legal protection for widows in Enugu State is evolving, though the process is cumbersome and slow. Presently, most of the extreme practices, such as drinking the water used to bathe a husband's corpse, or sleeping with the corpse in the same room, have been eliminated in Enugu State (Nwadinobi 2008, p. 8). A bill called "Prohibiting the Infringement of a Widow's and Widower's Fundamental Rights" (Enugu State 2001) has provided protection for widows, and increased public awareness of harmful widowhood rites. On its surface, the bill represents a step forward for widowhood rights; awareness of this law has undoubtedly influenced some Traditional Rulers who have made declarations outlawing or abolishing some of the widowhood practices. However, the bill is not properly enforced and the prescribed punishment is very lenient. Widows having the courage to fight and go to court often find that the process is very expensive and laborious. Court cases are lengthy and judgments often remain, it is said, at the discretion of biased male judges or magistrates.

According to Ewelukwa (2002):

> New laws still reflect the deep seated cultural biases against women. What is more, in the day-to-day application of these laws, widows have experienced a disregard of even the minimal protection accorded them.
>
> A Nigerian judge, writing with regard to the position of women under the customary law of succession, rightly cautions that 'it is necessary to appreciate that rules and customary law on the subject are unwritten. Our source is mere oral traditional history and testimony of men in leadership of their community. . . . Men played a dominant role in the formulation of customary law and practice. They are the judges and witnesses.'

A study carried out by the Widows Rights Coalition (WRC) showed that while most of the harmful, traditional widowhood rites are on the decline, disinheritance and forceful shaving of hair are still prevalent (Nwadinobi 2008, p. 6).

For all of the above reasons, mediation is often a widow's best platform for dispute resolution. The primary organization in Enugu State, whose role it is to lobby for and promote widowhood rights, publicize harmful cultural practices, provide safe havens, and conduct mediations, is the Widows Development Organisation (WiDO).

The Widows Development Organisation (WiDO)

The Widows Development Organisation (WiDO) is a non-governmental organization (NGO) based in Enugu, the capital of Enugu State. WiDO is represented in all 17 Local Government Areas of the state through its Community Focal Persons (CFPs); WiDO's interventions are in over 100 communities.

WiDO has been in existence for over 15 years and provides support for widows whose rights are violated. WiDO has so far intervened on behalf of widows in cases involving eviction, disinheritance, abduction of children, and wrongful arrest. When necessary, WiDO has collaborated with a sister organization, the Civil Resource Development and Documentation Centre (CIRDDOC), for the services of lawyers. WiDO's activities include the following:

Widow Support Centre. This quiet and secluded facility was the administrative office as well as the mediation office. It also served as a safe, temporary shelter for widows and their children in situations where the widow was thrown out of her matrimonial home or when her life has been threatened. Counseling was provided and clients, researchers and other civil society organizations also had access to resource materials. (The shelter is now closed due to a lack of funding but will be discussed in this chapter as it existed.)

Information. WiDO has the names of over 5,000 widows from the 17 Local Government Areas in our database. The database comprises those who have reported cases to us for mediation, as well as those who have attended our activities. We have additional information because WiDO has participated in two State-wide research initiatives about the prevalence of harmful traditional practices. The first was conducted in 1998 and the second in 2005. We also have carried out a community research project about the health consequences of widows and their children in one of our focal communities.

Widows' Clubs. There are presently five functioning clubs for widows in five communities. All widows are encouraged to form Widows' Clubs in their respective communities. The clubs provide a platform for peer counseling and serve as a rallying point for sharing experiences on coping strategies. A club also enables widows to have collective protection of their human rights as well as to facilitate the forming of thrift co-operatives to assist themselves. A club also serves as a platform for WiDO to reach the widows as a group, as opposed to seeking them out individually. The widows have been encouraged to keep minutes of their meetings and start thrift systems of savings otherwise known as "isusu."

Sensitization Programs. We have been able to impact the lives of widows through a series of sensitization meetings in the three Senatorial Zones of Enugu State. The targeted groups include widows, representatives of the Nigeria Police Force, priests from various Christian denominations, representatives of the Muslim community, daughters of the lineage (Umuada)[8] and representatives of the media.

Legal Initiatives. After six years of working in this area, a bill was passed in Enugu State outlawing widowhood practices. We also have made some copies of the Widowhood Rights Laws and distributed to them to community members. They have information and skills now to assert their rights as well as they know where to report whenever their rights are abused or violated.

Publicity. We have used many ways to publicize our work. For instance, we printed the 2001 law[9] about widows' rights in pictorial form in both English and Igbo, the local language. We also distributed many copies of the law to communities. The publication is an important tool that is used during mediation sessions when intervening on behalf of widows whose rights have been violated.

We have organized *Widow Friendly Days* and these are usually held during a period called the 16 days of activism (25 November to 10 December). These days serve as a forum for the widows from the various communities to share their experiences and coping strategies with each other.

August is a month set aside by churches for women to meet. We use this unique opportunity to *visit the churches* and sensitize their members about the rights of widows.

We also have developed an effective campaign of *radio jingles*. Our radio jingles have reached over 10 million people through our prime-time broadcasts using Radio Nigeria, Enugu National Station. The signals of the Federal Radio Corporation of Nigeria, Enugu National Station are received in six states including Enugu, Benue, Anambra, Abia, Ebonyi, and Cross River.

We have used mock *Tribunal Sessions* to disseminate information about the plight of widows. A mock Tribunal consists of the widow testifying before a panel of judges followed by audience participation.

We have participated in international meetings including the Panel on Widows Rights of UNGASS in 2000, the First International Conference on Widows in 2001, International Widows Day in the United Kingdom in 2006 and Parallel Events connected to the UN Conference on the Status of Women (CSW) in New York City in 2007 and again in 2008.[10]

---

[8]Umuada refers to Women of the Igbo tribe. In this context, umuada includes the daughters, sisters, aunts and female cousins of the deceased, but does not include females who have married into the family of the deceased as they may perpetuate harmful widowhood practices.

[9]The Enugu State 2001 bill number 3 is about "The Prohibition of Infringement of Widows and Widowers Fundamental Rights."

[10]The United Nations General Assembly recognized 23 June as International Widows' Day. The declaration calls on "Member States, the United Nations system and other international and regional organizations, within their respective mandates, to give special attention to the situation of widows and children" (http://www.un.org/en/events/widowsday). WiDO put out press releases as well as provided a news commentary on national radio to commemorate the first International Widows' Day in 2011.

Lobbying and Advocacy: WiDO belongs to a number of Advocacy Groups that are campaigning for various legal reforms. We participated in lobbying for the passage of the 2001 bill that protects widows in Enugu State.[11] We also were involved in advocating for a bill about stopping violence against women and contributing to a shadow report for the Commission on the Elimination of Discrimination against Women (CEDAW).

We collaborated with the Legislative Advocacy Coalition on Violence Against Women (LACVAW) in a Legislative Consultation in March 2004. We also belong to the Gender and Constitutional Reform Network (GECORN). GECORN and WiDO are part of a group that is advocating for legal reform of CEDAW before the Enugu State House of Assembly. WiDO is also a member of the Centre for the Eradication of Violence Against Women (CEVAW).

Awards. WiDO has presented awards to some notable organizations that are champions in the fight for widows' rights. Those named have included the International Federation of Women Lawyers (FIDA) and Nigerian Association for Women Journalists (NAWOJ). Awards also have been given to Traditional Rulers as well as some individuals who have played key roles in support of widows. Additionally, some widows have been named "Champions" in their communities.

Intervention by WiDO

Conflicts generally arise when people are disenfranchised and disenchanted. Innovative approaches and interventions have been shown to be successful in dealing with the certain problems faced by widows. The success of these interventions is largely dependent on the system that is put in place for identifying, reporting, verifying and intervening in these conflicts.

There are many approaches that can be used for preventing and addressing problems faced by widows. Among these are negotiation, arbitration, reconciliation, resolution, litigation and mediation. Mediation is considered to be a major instrument for conflict/dispute resolution, peaceful co-existence and sustainable democracy and it can be particularly useful in dealing with some of the problems faced by widows.[12]

Conflict and dispute mediation are often carried out by Civil Society Organizations (CSO). These non-governmental organizations may be thematic groups such as human rights organizations; professional groups such as associations of lawyers or doctors and/or faith-based organizations. CSOs, in part because of their grassroots approaches, are capable of coming up with *innovative approaches* that best

[11] This bill eventually was passed with the support of the Nigerian Association for Women Journalists (NAWOJ).

[12] However, very little has been written on the topic of mediation and widows (Edemikpong 2005).

suit their beneficiaries. The mediation approach described below is the basic one employed by the Widows Development Organization.

WiDO's mediations can be held in the community, at the NGO office or in a Traditional Ruler's residence. We put a system in place to ensure the smooth running of the mediation services. The office-based team is called the Vanguard team and the community-based team is called the Community Focal Persons.

The Vanguard Team.[13] This is a five-member team that handles reports of violation by screening, verifying and investigating the reports submitted by widows themselves, a team member, a relative of the widow or a Community Focal Person (CFP). The team members and their functions are as follows:

(1) *The investigator*. As soon as a report of victimization is received, the investigator documents it at the office and then visits the specific community to investigate the genuineness of the claim; (2) *The counselor*. The widow will need to be reassured and she will need a detailed explanation of the aim of the intervention and what it covers. The widow will be advised that she may benefit from a combination of interventions such as rehabilitation, shelter, skills, and coping strategies; (3) *The scribe*. The scribe takes verbatim notes at the support centre, or in the community, through a direct translation of the local language, Igbo, into English. The scribe works closely with the Investigator to ensure proper data entry both at the community and at the support center; (4) *Para-legal officer*. This is the WiDO legal resource person who is trained to do preparatory and follow-up legal work and is the liaison between WiDO and lawyers and will attend the court sessions if the need arises; and (5) *The photographer*. The photographer captures still or motion pictures of the event. This is done with full permission of the widow.

All the members of the team are trained in basic human rights as well as Alternative Dispute Resolution (ADR). The team members carry out investigations and arrange for mediation meetings – with the relatives and in-laws of the widows – both within the communities as well as at the widow support centre. This usually is a long process as it involves several visits and preliminary meetings with the all the relevant parties.

The Vanguard Team determines which of the dispute resolution methods to apply. The choice depends on the nature of the case and what seems appropriate for the situation.

Community Focal Persons (CFPs): The CFPs are volunteer indigenes (indigenous people) of their communities. They are selected by the Vanguard Team and trained to represent WiDO in the communities as a link between the widows in the Local

[13]The Vanguard intervention described here is an expensive approach that needs regular and substantial funding. (Much of the expenditure is for transporting team members to remote areas.) WiDO lost its funding for the full approach in 2008 and has been forced to be innovative to make sure that mediation is still offered. Current interventions take place with at least two WiDO members in the company of a focal person (someone already in the community who has been trained in mediation by WiDO). For cases where a lawyer is needed, we approach lawyers who provide pro bono services. We also might ask for assistance from other NGOs that have more resources or already are working in a particular community.

Government Areas and WiDO. These are people of integrity who have been selected based on their passion and commitment to community service as well as their literacy level. They live in the community and, as such, understand the behavior, attitudes, customs and traditions of their people and community. They also are well respected and held in high esteem. They are, therefore, well positioned to help their own people.

The presence of a CFP facilitates the monitoring of the widows in the rural communities as well as easy reporting of cases when there are violations. The CFPs are allocated mobile phones and trained in their use.[14] They also are periodically provided with top-up units (pre-paid units to a card for cell phone calls or gas). This facilitates the exchange of information between the CFPs and the widows and also between CFPs and the WiDO base office. This system has ensured the fast reporting of cases, especially those cases in which someone's life is threatened.

WiDO is represented in all the Local Government Areas of Enugu State through the CFPs. Widows and other members of the community bring their complaints and concerns to the CFPs who in turn forward the complaints to the Vanguard Team. In minor cases, the CFPs carry out the initial mediation.

The CFPs serve as point persons whenever there is need to enter the communities, assist in community mobilization and outreach programs and generally make local arrangements to facilitate interventions. They hold periodic meetings with members of their community to pass information to them as well monitor feedback. WiDO also holds periodic review meetings with them to assess the progress and status of various interventions.

The Procedure for Application and Processing

The steps below describe the process that is generally followed regarding mediation:

- Applications are received by WiDO in writing or by oral testimony.
- If the application is oral, the Counselor to whom the application is made will hold a counseling session.
- If the application is oral, the Scribe will produce a verbatim, written report.
- On receipt of the oral or written application, the Investigator will invite the applicant for an interview.
- The Counselor, in the company of the Vanguard Team, will go on a fact-finding mission.
- On confirmation of the report, the Investigator and the Vanguard Team will commence mediation efforts. (This effort would be on-going). If this avenue is fully exhausted without reaching settlement, litigation is inevitable.

[14] Some areas of the country are very remote and lack mobile phone services. Setting up meetings in such communities takes longer as it involves a lot of traveling.

Mediation Considerations: Intervention Decisions and Gatekeepers

Once victimization is confirmed, the first line of action would be a mediation process that involves dialogues with the relatives and/or local communities. When discussions fail to persuade relatives to discontinue acts that infringe on a widow's rights, we would have cause to move on to the next level of intervention. This means we would facilitate redress through litigation or seek injunction restraining the relatives or community from carrying out further victimization. We would do this with the advice and guidance from formal legal institutions such as the Legal Aid Council and the National Human Rights Commission.

While this is in process, we would mount a systematic awareness campaign in the local communities to enlighten them about the need for a change of attitude and modification of the social and cultural patterns of their customary laws and culture. We would let them know that a law – "The Prohibition of Infringement of a Widow's and Widower's Fundamental Rights Law, 2001" is already in place in Enugu State and that it prohibits such harmful cultural practices.

In selecting or deciding the cases in which to intervene, certain criteria are employed which include:

- Seriousness of the case
- Likelihood of loss of life
- Likelihood of serious damage to property
- Breach of fundamental rights
- The fact that a widow is the primary victim
- The fact that the case involves oppressive acts of relatives
- That there is probability of loss of livelihood
- The effect on the widow's children

Conflict resolution is made easier by gaining the confidence of the community gatekeepers. These are individuals who have some position of leadership at the community level and who will provide a safe and conducive environment for the resolvers of the dispute.

These gatekeepers include the Traditional Ruler or Igwe. The Traditional Ruler is an elected head of an Autonomous Community. The majority of Traditional Rulers are men. They are natives of the community and have a cabinet of chiefs. The home of the Traditional Ruler/Igwe is regarded generally as neutral ground for resolving conflicts. However, in some cases the Igwe has been known to take sides and, therefore, may have a biased view which may further fuel the conflict.

Another gatekeeper is the Religious Leader, who may be the parish priest, or pastor. The vast majority of Nigerians in the South East are Christians. They attend church and are dues-paying members in their respective churches. A lot of importance is placed on one receiving a good funeral. This is measured by the involvement of the church and the feeding of mourners. Citizens therefore like to have a good reputation with their priests and generally will have paid all church dues and levies. A priest can therefore be approached to wade in to a matter in the process of mediation as the individual's spiritual head. A good opportunity is provided at the annual "August" meetings. The August meeting is a church-based meeting that takes place in the South East part of Nigeria. All daughters of a particular community are expected to travel from different parts of Nigeria and sometimes from abroad for this meeting. Those who fail to attend have to pay very heavy fines. Issues are raised at these meetings such as community development problems. We use this unique opportunity to visit the churches and sensitize people about the rights of widows. During these programs, the participants are taught basic human rights and the various ways to protect their rights.

The previous beneficiaries of successful conflict resolution also serve as good gatekeepers. Happiness Odoh, for instance, received her property back through mediation and she served as a good reference point for introducing another widow to the program. The story of her success had been spread in her community. When another widow, Uche Oguenyi, was victimized, she approached Happiness to ask for an introduction to WiDO. Uche's case was successfully handled and she became a volunteer Community Focal Person. Today she intervenes on behalf of other widows. This is just one example of the cascade or ripple effect.

Summary of a Mediation Meeting

In order to understand our approach to mediation, I will describe a mediation session that was held with the Okoro family.[15] WiDO provided a mediator (Ms. Chika Okoh, the Investigator/Program Officer for WiDO) and Mrs. Theresa Akpata, the scribe for WiDO. The participants in the mediation were:

1. Mrs. Geraldine Okoro, Widow
2. Mr. Joseph Okoro, Brother-in-law
3. Ezemadu Okoro, the young man purported to be Mr. Romanus
4. Okoro's son, born out of wedlock
5. Chimsom Okoro, Geraldine Okoro's son
6. Ameze Okeke, Geraldine Okoro's sister

After introductions, the family members were all warmly welcomed to WiDO[16] by the Program Officer. They were reminded that the purpose for coming to our organization was for a peaceful resolution of their case.

The two parties, Geraldine and Joseph, also were reminded of the facts they had presented previously, since both Geraldine and Joseph had been interviewed by WiDO. The facts were:

> Geraldine's husband (Romanus Okoro) and Joseph Okoro jointly owned a property at Ugbo Odogwu. The house had five rooms. A room was given to the Caretaker while the remaining

[15]The names of the family members have been changed in order to respect the family's privacy.

[16]Geraldine and her children lived in Onitsha, about 1½ hours away from the WiDO office where the mediation was held and the property in question was located.

four were shared between Joseph and Ezemadu Nimonbe. Ezemadu was introduced by Joseph as Romanus' son whom he fathered out of wedlock. Geraldine was not given any part of the money and has never collected the rent since her husband died four years before this mediation. Also, Joseph had gone ahead and added a house on the land without Geraldine's consent.

After listening to the facts, Joseph agreed that he had never given any money to Geraldine but that he gave two rooms to Romanus' son, Ezemadu, which he felt made up for Romanus' share of the house. He maintained that his brother Romanus left a lot of property including some vehicles and a motorcycle after his death and that the family had never asked Geraldine about any of the property. He thought that Ezemadu Okoro had the right to his father's property.

The issue of Ezemadu led to outbursts from the parties. Geraldine denied ever knowing the boy or of ever being told by her husband that he had an illegitimate child. She said she knew the young man just as a member of their community. Geraldine's son, Chinson, also denied knowing Ezemadu.

Ezemadu himself was near tears as a result of all the denials. He revealed that he was told by his mother who his father was, and how his late father accepted him and treated him as his son. He claimed Romanus sponsored his education while he was alive and Ezemadu also spoke about how he often stayed with the family at Onitsha.

Joseph said the whole community acknowledges that Ezemadu was Romanus' son and that Geraldine just wanted to deny the fact. He revealed that his brother Romanus got Ezemadu's mother pregnant when they were both in secondary school, but he did not tell anybody until the child was in primary 6.

Concerning the issue of the new house he was building on the land, Joseph claimed he did not consult Geraldine before doing that because he knew she couldn't contribute financially towards the project. He said he did not want to disturb her knowing the enormous responsibility she had on her hand with respect to raising seven children all alone.

When asked how he would want the house and land to be shared among them, Joseph maintained the house had already been shared since Ezemadu was collecting rent from two rooms out of five. As for the new building which he had built, Geraldine could refund him half of the money he used in building the house and then she could share it with him. After being reminded of the rent he had been collecting for many years and that he had not given any share to Geraldine, Joseph kept quiet.

Geraldine agreed that the old building should be shared – one half for herself and the other half for Joseph. She also said the new building would be shared between them also and that she had nothing to refund to Joseph.

Finally, they agreed that even if Ezemadu was Romanus' son, it was Geraldine, his wife, who should be given his property. Joseph and Ezemadu promised to stop further collection of rent from the house.

Ezemadu asked how he would be expected to fend for himself and whether he would be denied his father's property just because Geraldine was denying him. Joseph agreed to consider letting Ezemadu have part of the new buildings he had put up on the jointly-owned land.

Further mediation sessions were planned during which the WiDO Vanguard Team would go to Ugbo Odogwu. The team would learn about the sharing of the building.

Reflections/Interpretations: This case is typical of the type of family situations that come up which require mediation. This case depicts the following:

- Joint property ownership between two brothers, this brings conflict about inheritance when one brother dies
- Lack of a will, thus no legal claimants to the property
- Presence of a child born out-of-wedlock and unknown to the formal family, leads to a problem of recognition
- Decision by the brother-in-law not to recognize the widow as a beneficiary of the property because she is a woman
- Recognition and priority granted to the first son in customary fashion even if this son is born out-of-wedlock
- Without the intervention of WiDO, the parties would probably not have had an opportunity to come to the negotiating table. In addition, Geraldine would be disenfranchised and not be able to secure income-generating property for her family.

Epilogue: This case was one of our most difficult. The meetings (including pre-mediation meetings) took place over 1 year. (Usually we try to complete cases in 2½ day sessions.) Following the mediation, Geraldine, who had malignant breast cancer, was admitted to a hospital. Sadly, she passed away several months later leaving seven young children. The family did not return to mediation, but we did learn about some of what happened after Geraldine passed away. Joseph said he had no choice because the children were orphans; he automatically inherited the children and it fell to him to look after them. He gave them some money following Geraldine's death and he asked the children to come for the rent at intervals of 6 months. Joseph continued to manage the property and is renovating it. Joseph also continues to support Ezemadu who is living in Lagos.

Success Stories and Challenges

WiDO has had many successes and these should be noted. They include the reinstatement of widows who were evicted from their homes, return of abducted children, and rebuilding of a widow's demolished home. These successes, however, have not been recorded without challenges.

We have found that it is crucial to have the Traditional Rulers, the custodians of culture, on our side. The reason is that the belief system greatly influences judgment. For example, in matters of inheritance, traditional law and custom most often do not allow a woman to inherit land if she has no male child. The presence of a Traditional Ruler who is forward-looking, however, helps to change the status quo.

One example which I personally encountered was that of the Traditional Ruler of Ugwu Ogo Nike Autonoumous Community in Enugu State. This particular community was one in which female genital mutilation was practiced, women were not included in the Traditional Ruler's cabinet and harmful widowhood practices were prevalent. However, with our targeted advocacy toward the Traditional Ruler, HRH Igwe Linus Ekete, he was able to make a proclamation outlawing female genital mutilation and widowhood practices in his community. In addition, he insisted on having scouts who would inform him of any cases of non-adherence to his proclamation. The Traditional Ruler also appointed ten women to his cabinet; this was the first time in the state that there were women chiefs in a cabinet.

Some government officials may make matters worse depending on their own beliefs. In one case, a pension officer refused to pay the pension to a wife and was of the opinion that the pension should instead go to the first son. In another case, it took the timely intervention of an employer to ensure that a widow had access to her husband's pension when the brother-in-law snatched the full amount, while the widow and her children were starving.

Some communities are difficult to access due to difficult terrain. Inaccessible roads may require the use of motorcycles. In one case, a community was completely inaccessible due to heavy rains that had washed out the only bridge leading to the community. This led to delays in conducting a mediation.

Sometimes we encounter uncontrollable relatives on the widow's side who make the mediation sessions difficult. We also have experienced situations where a widow tries to capitalize on the fact that we are an organization for widows by expecting us to be on her side even when she is wrong. Such cases are easily discovered due to the thorough investigations carried out by the Vanguard Team.

Other Interventions in Nigeria

Awareness about the problems facing widows has heightened in the media and movies,[17] and widows now know that they can come to us in case of violations. We have moved from being the only NGO acting on behalf of widows, to being one of a number of organizations. Those offering help to widows include the Human Development Initiative (Lagos State); Widows in Development (Lagos State); Society for Women Development and Empowerment of Nigeria (SWODEN, Kano State); the International Federation of Women Lawyers (Lagos and nationwide); Widow Support Centre (Lagos State); Academic Associates Peace Work; Widows Concern (WICON, Anambra State); and the Widows Association of Nigeria (Rivers State). I particularly would like to note the work of two organizations: Action Aid and Widows for Peace through Democracy.

[17]"Till Death Do Us Part," produced by Communicating for Change in 1998, is a 30-minute documentary film that profiles the lives of three widows in eastern Nigeria. The film was produced for the 50th Anniversary of the Universal Declaration of Human Rights and has been shown (with panel discussions) in a number of Nigerian communities.

ActionAid Nigeria

ActionAid Nigeria, one of international ActionAid's 45 country programs, is headquartered in Abuja. Its primary mission is "to work with the poor and excluded people to eradicate poverty and injustice in Nigeria" (ActionAid Nigeria 2008). In order to achieve this mission, the programs of ActionAid Nigeria (2009, p. 18) are implemented according to six rights-based thematic priorities. The first is women's rights and the others are rights to just and democratic governance, education, health, food, and human security in conflict and emergency.

ActionAid Nigeria (2009, p. 16) says it was involved in the movement for the successful passage of the violence against women and widowhood act in three states – Enugu, Kaduna and Rivers – and has "recorded great improvement in our struggle for the rights of women to participate in decision-making process(es) and to inherit landed property (2008, p. 10)." According to the 2009–2011 strategic plan (ActionAid Nigeria 2009), the work on women's rights will continue to "focus on challenging patriarchy and systems that inhibit women's rights to resources including land."

Widows for Peace Through Democracy

Widows for Peace through Democracy (WPD 2004)[18] is a London-based umbrella organization for widows' groups in South Asia, the Middle East and Africa, including Nigeria. WPD establishes partnership networks to facilitate the exchange of information, helps raise awareness of widowhood issues with the European Union and United Nations, and provides training on how to utilize national and international laws in order to protect the human rights of widows.

The focus of WPD is on widowhood issues in areas of conflict as well as the rights of widows in developing countries where they can face discrimination, poverty, abuse, violence, and the lack of legal protection. WPD also is concerned that widows may be denied access to justice systems simply because of their widowhood status. WPD "continues to share information, experience and training with partners in countries ostensibly at peace" and also has worked with widows who have been victims of internal conflicts in countries such as India, Kenya, Sudan, Kashmir, Bosnia, Kosovo and Nigeria.

WPD wants to ensure that the voice of widows at peace negotiation tables is heard since the widows of those who have disappeared in post-conflict situations endure problems that are not like those of other women. To support this mission, WPD developed a model widows' charter to influence legal reform and new constitutional drafts in post-conflict areas. The *Model Charter for the Rights*

[18]http://www.widowsforpeace.org

of Widows (Widows for Peace through Democracy 2009), a "draft proposal for adaptation to specific country, legal, social, cultural and economic situations... demands the elimination of all discrimination against widows." The 10-article document includes the following:

- Calls all actors involved in negotiating and implementing peace agreements to address the special needs of widows and wives of the missing (as required by UN Security Council Resolution 1325) and ensure the protection and respect for their human rights.
- Calls on all actors to support widows to band together in associations so that they can collectively undertake mapping and profiling projects to fill the gap in statistics on their situation.
- Calls on all actors to ensure that widows are represented in these negotiations so that (all have heard) their particular concerns, for example:

  (i) Rights of safe return (of displaced widows to former homes)
  (ii) Inheritance and property rights, land allocation and owner ship
  (iii) Protection of widow witnesses at national and international tribunals
  (iv) Personal status guarantees in constitutional and legislative reform...

Conclusions and Recommendations

The application of the laws governing marriage and inheritance in Nigeria often causes great distress and injustice to widows. There is a big gap between the word of the law and its reality, and many customary laws and practices undermine widows' statutory rights.

In Enugu State, where most of our work has been done, a State law was passed about widows' rights in June 2001. The law is aimed at ameliorating the plight of widows as well as strengthening their legal protection. The law makes it illegal for anyone to compel a widow to perform any of the widowhood rites. However, the law is slow to be implemented and enforced and cases that go to court are very costly and take a long time (years, in some cases) to be resolved. Despite the law on harmful widowhood practices in Enugu State and efforts by the government, churches and Non-Governmental Organizations in the State to educate the people about the harmful effects of such practices, these obnoxious and marginalizing widowhood practices still exist and remain a painful reality.

We have found that mediation can be a good approach for dealing with disputes faced by widows and our creative approach also deals with the conflict in the community. In discussing the value of such mediation, I would like to make the following points:

1. Mediation should give due consideration to the culture and belief system of the people while ensuring that dignity and human rights are respected.
2. It is necessary to involve the appropriate gatekeepers in mediation.

3. There is a need to have adequate representation around the table in the design of programs for widows. Therefore, widows should be involved in designing, implementing and monitoring such programs to ensure acceptance and sustainability.
4. Creative and innovative approaches that are employed in the process of mediation should be recorded for dissemination.
5. Interventions should be timely and the timing appropriate.
6. There is a need to engage in innovative partnerships such as those among traditional institutions, civil society and the private sector.

The fact that we have been unable to secure continued funding for the full Vanguard program has been unfortunate and shows the difficulty of sustaining the work of small but effective organizations in economically developing countries. While the treatment of widows has improved, there is still much work to be done regarding the (1) development and implementation of laws, (2) publicity for the problem as well as available resources; and (3) delivery of timely, adequately-funded and effective services, particularly in rural areas.

References

Achebe, C. (1984). *The trouble with Nigeria*. London/Exeter: Heinemann Educational Books.

ActionAid Nigeria. (2008). *ActionAid Nigeria Annual Report 2008*. Abuja: ActionAid. Retrieved 1 May 2010, from http://www.actionaid-nigeria.org/admin/ontrack/2008%20Annual%20Report1.pdf

ActionAid Nigeria. (2009). *Country strategy paper 2009–2013: Fighting poverty in the midst of plenty II*. Retrieved 1 May 2010, from http://www.actionaid-nigeria.org/admin/ontrack/AAN%20CSP1.pdf

Ahmad, N. (2009). Dying for the dead: A socio-legal examination of Sati in India. *Asia Pacific Journal on Human Rights and the Law, 9*(2), 1–10.

Amnesty International. (2006). *Nigeria: Rape—the silent weapon*. AI Index. Retrieved 7 Feb 2010, from http://www.amnestyusa.org/document.php?id=ENGAFR440202006&lang=e

Aruna, J.O., & Fasoranti, O.O. (2007). A cross-cultural comparison of practices relating to widowhood and widow-inheritance: Among the Igbo and Yoruba in Nigeria. *Pakistan Journal of Social Sciences, 4*, 525–533. http://medwelljournals.com/abstract/?doi=pjssci.2007.525.533

Courson, E. E. (2007). *The burden of oil: Social deprivation and political militancy in Gbaramatu Clan, Warri South West LGA, Delta State, Nigeria*. Economies of Violence Working Paper No. 15. Berkeley: University of California, Institute of International Studies. Retrieved 7 Feb 2010, from http://geography.berkeley.edu/ProjectsResources/ND%20Website/NigerDelta/WP/15-Courson.pdf

Diamond, L. (2001). Foreword. In R. T. Suberu (Ed.), *Federalism and ethnic conflict in Nigeria* (pp. xii–xviii). Washington, DC: USIP Press.

Dimkpa, D. I. (2007). Influence of in-laws on inheritance rights as perceived by widows in Port Harcourt Municipality, Nigeria. *The Nigerian Journal of Guidance and Counselling, 11*(1), 93–103.

Edemikpong, H. (2005). Widowhood rites: Nigeria women's collective fights a dehumanizing tradition. *Off Our Backs, 35*(3–4), 34–36.

Enugu State. (2001). *Law prohibiting the infringement of a widow's and widower's fundamental rights*, No. 3, 2001.

Ewelukwa, U. (2002). Post-colonialism, gender, customary injustice: Widows in African societies. *Human Rights Quarterly 24*(2), 424–486. Retrieved 29 Nov 2009, from http://muse.jhu.edu.proxy.libraries.uc.edu/journals/human_rights_quarterly/v024/24.2ewelukwa.html

Falola, T. (2009). *Colonialism and violence in Nigeria*. Bloomington: Indiana University Press.

Fasoranti, O. O., & Aruna, J. O. (2007). A cross-cultural comparison of practices relating to widowhood and widow-inheritance among the Igbo and Yoruba in Nigeria. *Journal of World Anthropology: Occasional Papers, 3*(1), 53–73.

Fleisher, M. S., & Krienert, J. L. (2009). *The myth of prison rape: Sexual culture in American prisons*. Lanham: Rowman & Littlefield.

Horowitz, D. L. (1993). Democracy in divided societies. *Journal of Democracy, 4*(4), 18–38.

Institute for Peace and Conflict Resolution (IPCR). (2002). *Strategic conflict assessment of Nigeria*. Consolidated Report, Federal Government of Nigeria. October. Retrieved 3 May 2010, from http://www.usaid.gov/ng/downloads/rfa/consolidated%20report.pdf

Malathi, K. (2008). *Empowerment of widows: A three generations study*. New Delhi: Serials Publications.

Muoso, E. (1999, December 1). *Aids in Kenya: A social disease*. BBC News. Retrieved 11 March 2009, from http://news.bbc.co.uk/1/hi/world/africa/545033.stm

National Bureau of Statistics, Nigeria. (2006). *2006 Population Census*. Retrieved 7 Feb 2010, from http://www.nigerianstat.gov.ng/

Nigeria. (2007). *The World Factbook* [online]. Retrieved 29 Jan 2010, from U.S. Central Intelligence Agency: https://www.cia.gov/library/publications/the-world-factbook/geos/ni.html

Nwadinobi, E. A. (Ed.). (2008). *Widowhood: Facts feelings and the law*. Enugu: Booklet, A Publication of the Widows Development Organisation.

Nweze, C. C. (2006, May 25–25). *Domestication of CEDAW: Points to consider for customary laws and practices*. Paper presented at the Commonwealth West Africa Colloquium of Gender, Culture and the Law, Yaounde.

Nzekwu and others v. Nzekwu and others (1989) 2 NWLR (pt.104) 373, 395.

Onwo v. Oko, (1996) 6 NWLR (Pt.456) 584.

Simpson, A. (2004). *Oral tradition relating to slavery and slave trade in Nigeria, Ghana and Benin*. Paris: United Nations Educational, Scientific and Cultural Organization. Reprinted in the *African Diaspora Archaeology Newsletter*, March 2007, Retrieved 22 April 2010, from http://www.diaspora.uiuc.edu/news0307/news0307.html#9

Suberu, R. T. (2001). *Federalism and ethnic conflict in Nigeria*. Washington, DC: USIP Press.

Thomas, F. (2008). Remarriage after spousal death: Options facing widows and implications for livelihood security. *Gender and Development, 16*, 73–84.

UNAIDS (Joint United Nations Program on HIV/AIDS). (2007). *AIDS Epidemic Update*. December 2007. Geneva: UNAIDS. Retrieved 3 Dec 2009, from http://www.unaids.org/en/KnowledgeCentre/HIVData/EpiUpdate/EpiUpdArchive/2007/default.asp

Uzodike, E. (1990). Nigeria: Defining the ambit of custom. *Journal of Family Issues, 29*(1), 399–406.

Widows for Peace through Democracy. (2004). *Model charter for the rights of widows*. Retrieved 2 May 2010, from www.gaps-uk.org/docs/WPD%20widows%20charter.pdf

Widows for Peace through Democracy. (2009). *Model charter for the rights of widows*. Retrieved 2 May 2010, from www.gaps-uk.org/docs/WPD%20widows%20charter.pdf

Williams, S. (2004). Nigeria, its women and international law: Beyond rhetoric. *Human Rights Law Review, 4*(2), 229–255.

Women's Aid Collective (WACOL). (2008). *CEDAW and accountability to gender equality in Nigeria: A shadow report*. Compiled by the Nigeria NGO Coalition on CEDAW Report for the forty first (41st) Session of the Committee on the Elimination of All Forms of Discrimination Against Women. Retrieved 7 May 2010, from http://www2.ohchr.org/english/bodies/cedaw/docs/ngos/NigeriaNGOCoalition41.pdf

Chapter 11
Promoting Positive Peace One Block at a Time: Lessons from Innovative Community Conferencing Programs

Lauren Abramson and David B. Moore

Introduction

This chapter describes principles and practices of Community Conferencing, a process in which a group of people meet to address a common concern. The process is most often used with a group of people affected by interpersonal conflict. Participants in a Community Conference reach a shared understanding about the causes and consequences of the conflict. They then devise a plan of action.

Conferencing is used in a variety of settings, including schools, youth and adult criminal justice systems, neighborhoods, and workplaces. It asks different questions than those asked by adversarial processes. Adversarial processes typically ask: "Who did it?" and "What are those in authority entitled to do to them?" In schools, the justice system and elsewhere, authorities tend to administer some form of punishment.

In contrast, Conferencing asks: "What has happened?" "Who has been affected; and how have they been affected?" and, "What can be done to repair the harm and to make things better in the future?" Where people have disengaged from each other, or have engaged destructively, Conferencing creates the potential for *constructive* engagement. The *primary* emphasis is not on entitlements and rights. The primary emphasis is on responsibilities and resolution. In this way, Conferencing can help restore, maintain, or create positive connections between and among people.

The authors have collaborated to incorporate theory and practice from a range of disciplines and from international experiences. We have aimed to create a

L. Abramson, Ph.D. (✉)
Assistant Professor at Johns Hopkins School of Medicine and Founding Director of the Community Conferencing Center, Baltimore, Maryland, USA
e-mail: labramso@jhmi.edu

D.B. Moore, Ph.D.
Communication Consultant and a Principal with Primed Change Consulting, Australia
e-mail: david@primed.net.au

J.M. Fritz (ed.), *Moving Toward a Just Peace: The Mediation Continuum*,
Clinical Sociology: Research and Practice, DOI 10.1007/978-94-007-2885-1_11,

"learning organization," by continually furthering our understanding of theory and principles that guide how the Conferencing process is facilitated and programs are implemented. The resulting principles and practices have helped bring this work to scale, while maintaining fidelity and quality.

We provide detailed examples from a Conferencing program with some unique features. Since 1998, a group of committed colleagues in the US city of Baltimore have developed an innovative approach to this work. (www.communityconferencing.org) The Baltimore Community Conferencing Canter has: (1) applied Conferencing in a variety of sectors and venues, (2) built a firmer understanding of core principles that guide the work, and (3) regularly reflected on each of these principles. This paper highlights key lessons we have learned, and possible next steps of reform.

Community Conferencing: An Inclusive Conflict Transformation Process

Brief General History of Community Conferencing

The first Community Conferencing programs were established in New Zealand. Reform activists among the indigenous Maori promoted a community process called (in English translation) "Family Group Conferencing". Pilot programs offered Conferencing as an alternative to state practice (Hudson et al. 1996). The success of these pilot programs in the 1980s led to national legislation in 1989. The use of Family Group Conferencing was extended across New Zealand, both in youth justice and in care and protection matters. Legislation was subsequently extended to cases involving adult non-violent offenders.

Various jurisdictions in Australia and Canada followed New Zealand's lead. The Conferencing process was adopted and adapted in neighboring Australia in the early 1990s. A group working in youth justice sought to develop a practical theory and an optimal format for the Conferencing process. Conferencing was initially used by community police in a border region of the state of New South Wales. In this pilot program, police diverted youth justice cases from the children's court to an official caution, which now involved a Conference (Moore and Forsythe 1995).

The training program developed for youth justice conveners in New South Wales was next offered in neighboring South Australia, and then more widely. Within a year, training was being provided for school teachers in Queensland and New South Wales, and for youth justice conveners in other Australian states. The same Conferencing format and generic training program evolved through the 1990s, bringing Conferencing to many other countries.

This emerging Conferencing movement was categorised early as part of the broader international "restorative justice" movement, which began in Canada and the US in the early and mid-1970s (www.restorativejustice.org). 'Restorative justice' promises a non-authoritarian response to crime (McCold 1997; Sharpe 1998; Van Ness and Strong 1997; Zehr 1990). Community Conferencing has been recognized as way of realizing principles of restorative justice. By the mid-1990s, Conferencing was routinely described as a "restorative justice process" and offered as an alternative or adjunct to *retributive* justice (Hudson et al. 1996; Chatterjee 1998; Trimboli 2000).

However, the archetypal restorative scene involves reconciliation between two individuals, one of whom has harmed the other. In contrast, the archetypal Conferencing scene is a group seated in a circle, reaching collective agreement. Furthermore, Conferencing shares values and practices with several other social movements. One such movement, with origins in North American (and other) indigenous traditions, promotes the use of "circles". The movement is well-described in publications from Minnesota's Living Justice Press (Pranis et al. 2003).

In part, because of convergence between the Conferencing and Circles movements, a delegation from Canada's Aboriginal Justice Learning Network and the Royal Canadian Mounted Police invited David Moore and John McDonald to bring the program developed in Australia to Canada in 1996 (Deukmedjian 2008). The same trainers later helped establish Conferencing programs in Norway and the UK (Sherman and Strang 2007)

Many similar Conferencing programs have been established since the mid-1990s. The larger programs are administered by established institutions such as departments of education, human services, youth justice or adult criminal justice. Far fewer programs operate as a community-based entity, as we will discuss below.

The Community Conferencing Process

The basic structure of a Community Conference is simple. A skilled facilitator brings together a group of people who are in conflict. Participants are seated in a circle. This arrangement maximizes direct conversation and non-verbal communication between participants. No person is in a position of power relative to others. No tables or other barriers interfere with communication around the circle. For similar reasons, we eschew co-facilitation. The working relationship between co-facilitators can distract participants, drawing their attention to questions such as which facilitator might speak next. Flipcharts or other visual aids are not usually necessary (unless to record a particularly complicated agreement). In most applications of Conferencing, agreements tend not to be lengthy or complicated.

To prepare a Conference, the facilitator meets with individual participants, describes the process, and addresses questions and concerns. Thus, participants attend the Conference voluntarily, with informed consent and an understanding of the Conference structure.

The facilitator leads the group through what we have traditionally described as *three* stages of a structured conversation. During the conference, each participant has a chance to:

1. Describe what they did, or observed, or had related to them.
2. Hear and feel how other participants have been affected. Individual contributions add to a shared understanding of what caused the conflict that affects everyone present. Participants can then:
3. Negotiate a plan to improve their situation. They can repair what can be repaired, work together to prevent something similar from recurring, and often also work together on some fundamentally positive change.

A Deepening Appreciation for the Power of Simple Questions

The following process overview combines elements of our initial understanding with lessons from our experiences of Conferencing in neighborhoods, workplaces and other community applications. Our initial explanation of the Conference structure or sequence was that it guides participants through three stages:

Stage I: What happened? The Conference begins with an examination of the origins of the conflict. Participants are invited to describe 'What has happened?' This question is important for several reasons. First, conflict cannot be transformed until it is understood and acknowledged. It is significantly more powerful for all of the people who have been affected to acknowledge the conflict than it is for any single individual to do so. Second, participants often attend the Conference with different understandings – derived from incomplete or false information – of what actually happened. Beginning the conversation with a detailed story of what happened can thus go a long way towards dispelling misinformation that has fueled the conflict. Third, when a Community Conference is held in a criminal justice setting, and victims, offenders and others address the harm that has resulted from a crime, there are several advantages to first "hearing the story" of what happened.

For an offender to describe the details of what happened can be the first step toward accountability and responsibility. It can be very challenging for offenders to face those affected directly and to describe what they did. Victims are often greatly relieved just to hear the details of what happened. Many victims believe they were targeted for the crime. Often, they learn that they were simply in the wrong place at the wrong time, and are victims of a random crime.

A slightly different logic applies when cases involve many disputes. After preparatory interviews, the facilitator typically suggests that the group revisit three key incidents and/or periods in the history of the conflict. The Conference facilitator assists participants to focus on concrete details. Revisiting three incidents or periods allows participants to see patterns that were not clear when the incidents are recalled in isolation. The exercise also restrains Conference participants from amplifying interpersonal conflict.

A natural and universal human tendency, when people experience conflict, is to: (1) judge the other people involved, (2) characterize their actions, (3) attribute motives to them, and/or (4) demand specific actions to solve perceived problems (Stone et al. 1999). These are *symptoms* of conflict, most often fueled by fear and anger, but they also *cause* conflict, generating fear and anger in others. Tendencies to judge, characterize, attribute motives and dictate solutions are all associated with what psychology calls the "fundamental attribution error". Most of us tend to accord too much explanatory weight to the character and motives of others, and not enough to the situation in which they find themselves.

When participants are invited to focus on specific events, and to describe their own experience in detail, they are helped to avoid judging others' characters, characterizing their actions, speculating on motives, or demanding unilateral action. Instead, as each describes what they alone could know, participants collaborate to paint a picture of their common situation.

Where conflict is the cause and consequence of many poorly resolved disputes, the facilitator may invite one participant to begin the Conference by describing what has happened. In these cases, the sequence in which people speak is rarely a point of contention. The conversation grows lively. Other participants soon engage. Again, the process provides a safe and structured forum for people to listen to each other's stories, rather than focusing on whose version of the facts is correct. Remarkably, once participants connect with each other as fellow human beings (rather than as an archetypal "offender," "bully", "heartless city official", and so on), the urge to dispute facts diminishes. The prospect of creating a better future emerges as people's keenest concern.

Stage II: How have people been affected? Participants are invited to examine the effects of the conflict. Each person is asked 'How have you been affected?' This stage of the Conference is often strongly emotional. Participants are encouraged to express how they feel – and this can involve rage, terror, surprise, disgust, or any other strong emotion. However, the facilitator minimizes the likelihood that participants attack others – verbally or otherwise. Should such an attack begin, the facilitator focuses attention more directly on how each participant has been personally affected by what happened. The effective technique here is thus not to rely on preliminary *talk* about ground rules for decent behavior. Rather, the facilitator *actively* fosters civility by encouraging people to contribute facts about their own experience to a collective picture. Constructive activity trumps the temptation to allow fear and anger to drive judgments about others and further encourage interpersonal conflict. A vital aspect of this stage of the process is that each person gets to "tell his or her story"; to give voice to pain, suffering, and distress; and to learn how others have also been affected. Participants provide narrative accounts, rather than formulaic responses.

Replacing formulas with stories tends to connect people (Tilly 2006). As each participant shares his or her story, the group collectively paints a broader, deeper picture of how conflict has affected them. Participants understand a variety of perspectives. They connect with each other as human beings – which they have previously been unable and often unwilling to do. To be *heard* is a fundamental human need. To be *understood* is better still.

We now understand what we initially called the first *two* stages of a Conference as a *single* stage. "What happened?" and "How have people have been affected?" are questions about the legacy of the past and about the present. Participants are thus "negotiating a shared understanding" of their present situation.

The facilitator helps people share "objective facts" about actions, and "subjective facts" about associated feelings and thoughts (reflecting values and beliefs). In some cases, feelings have been a response to actions or thoughts; in other cases, the feelings or thoughts came first, motivating actions. As participants discuss events in a structured sequence, they often articulate beliefs about the world, ways of thinking and feeling that influence their actions. In this way, participants gain insights about themselves and about others.

Stage III: How can the situation be made better? Once everyone's experience has been heard, the group is invited to consider the future. The facilitator asks: "How can we repair harm, and how can this be prevented from happening again?" In short: How can we make things better? By now, participants understand more, and *feel* differently about the situation and each other. They have reached a degree of "shared understanding".

Participants often reach resolutions dramatically different from what they might first have felt to be appropriate. Participants experience themselves as more connected to each other. They see their futures as interdependent. Individuals who were initially keen on severe punishment typically find themselves addressing the underlying causes of the conflict. For example, a woman seeking monetary compensation from three young men who stole her car learns during the Conference that they are jobless and have little family support. She reaches into her purse and gives them each her contact information. She says she knows where they can get good work and she expects to hear from them within 48 hours. Similarly, adults on a city block, who have repeatedly called police to stop boys playing ball in the street and thereby damaging their cars, finally learn during the Conference that these children have no safe place to play. The neighbors agree to create a youth football league run by adult volunteers – the same adults who previously wanted the children dealt with by police and even jailed.

The facilitator notes suggestions. The group deliberates whether each suggestion is fair, workable, and would achieve the agreed goals. The facilitator checks which suggestions are agreeable and drafts an agreement, which participants sign.

The facilitator then invites participants to enjoy refreshments with each other. This is more than a courtesy; it is an important part of the process. Now that their feelings and understandings about each other have changed, people use this opportunity beyond the formal circle to establish or re-establish relationships with each other. Contact details are often exchanged, plans made, and there is a general feeling of cooperation.

Innovative Implementation of Community Conferencing in a Mid-Sized American Inner-City

This deceptively simple Conferencing process is now used in many countries. It is used in education, justice systems, human services, neighborhoods and workplaces. Most programs are administered by an institution that refers cases – whether that be courts, corrections, human services, schools, or police.

The Baltimore, Maryland program remains unusual because it:

1. Is the first Conferencing program implemented in a large inner-city in the United States,
2. Applies Conferencing in a variety of institutions, neighborhoods and other settings, and
3. Is coordinated by a community-based organization created specifically to deliver Community Conferencing, rather than by a larger agency with a broader mandate (Abramson and Moore 2001).[1]

Baltimore as an Urban Context for Community Conferencing Programs

Baltimore is a mid-sized city located in the state of Maryland in the mid-Atlantic region of the United States (Fig. 11.1). As in other cities of the region, an exodus of automotive and related industries depleted Baltimore's economic base from the early 1980s. The city's population declined from one million to approximately 640,000 residents between the 1970s and the mid-1980s. Financial and social investment in neighborhoods suffered greatly. Over half of Baltimore's families now have annual incomes below the poverty level. (Baltimore Neighborhood Indicators Alliance, www.bnia.org.)

Baltimore has many strengths. Its hundreds of neighborhoods each have their own identity and sense of pride. But after years of economic and social disinvestment in low-income areas, many residents struggle to find living-wage jobs, accessible shopping for food and clothes, quality schooling, and recreational opportunities. Many are greatly concerned about crime and safety, particularly in the most disinvested neighborhoods. Baltimore has ranked as the second most violent city in the United States, with annual murders exceeding 300 during the 1990s. The 2009 murder rate was 238 (Fenton 2010). An estimated 60,000 residents are addicted to hard drugs, and this malaise contributes significantly to both crime and social decay. Juvenile arrests have numbered between 9,000 and 11,000 for the past decade. This is the challenging context in which the Baltimore Community Conferencing Center (BCCC) was established in 1998.

---

[1]For example, many conferencing programs are run within juvenile justice institutions, or by individual schools.

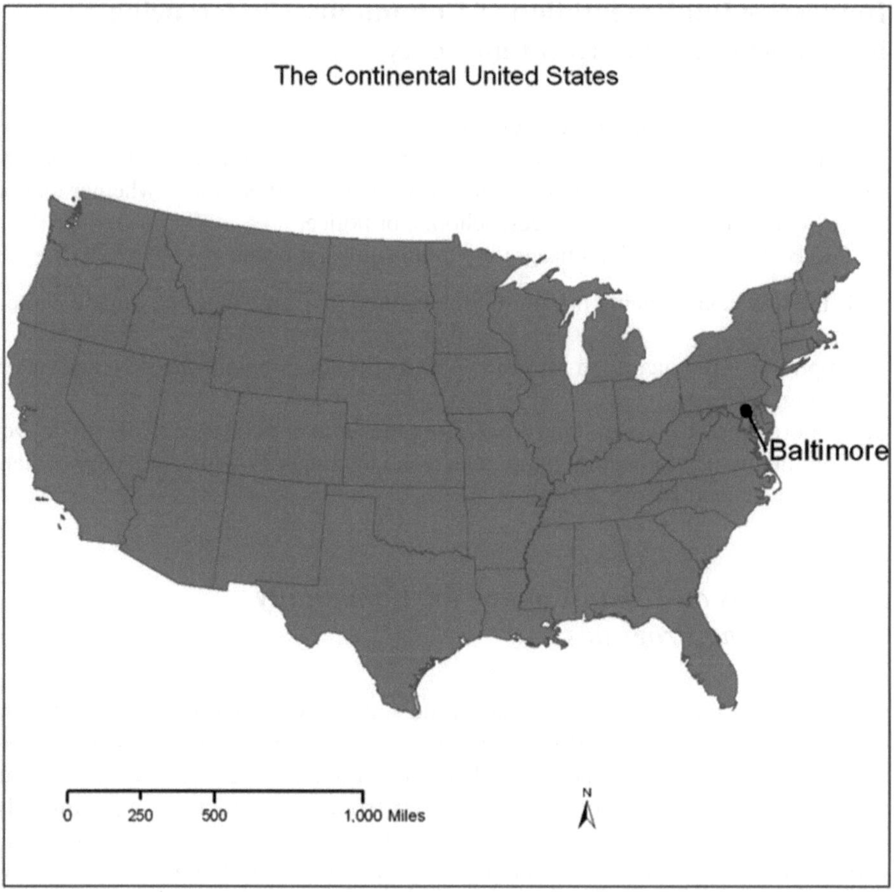

Fig. 11.1 The city of Baltimore, Maryland

The Community Conferencing Center provides most of its services in Baltimore's low-income neighborhoods. A founding aim of the Center was to fill the gap in available, effective, and community-based responses to interpersonal conflict and to crime. Many matters were being dealt with as crimes, drawing an authoritarian response from police and other justice system officials. Yet many of these incidents and issues could be resolved if understood and addressed more broadly as interpersonal conflict (Lipstein 2003).

Program Details

The BCCC currently operates with seven full-time staff and two part-time interns. Everyone on staff is a trained facilitator; however, some staff members also have administrative responsibilities. Approximately 85 % of the referrals are handled by staff facilitators. That said, each of the seven other Community Conferencing programs which have been established in other Maryland jurisdictions independent of the BCCC (though the BCCC provides ongoing training and technical assistance to all programs in Maryland), operate with a paid (usually part-time) Program Coordinator, and a pool of about 12 volunteer facilitators.

Every Community Conferencing facilitator has completed a two-part training program. The first part consists of a 22-hour Facilitator Training Workshop, with experiential and didactic learning focused on the principles of Community Conferencing, and the nuts-and-bolts of facilitating a Conference. Once training is completed, facilitators undergo an Apprenticeship, which consists of two Conference observations, three facilitations, with extensive debriefing/feedback after each activity. At the end of the Apprenticeship, the Program Director discusses strengths and challenges with the facilitator trainee, to determine whether the trainee's skills meet the requirements for facilitating Community Conferences.

Uses of Community Conferencing in Baltimore

The following are brief summaries of the various different ways Conferencing is used in Baltimore.

Criminal justice. The Community Conferencing Center uses Community Conferencing as a court diversion for misdemeanor and certain felony offenses. Criminal justice referrals are accepted only in cases where the offender "acknowledges involvement" in the crime. Participation in the process is always voluntary. Victims, offenders, and their respective supporters are invited to attend. An average conference involves 12 people.

Referrals include cases such as assaults, theft (including auto theft), and trespassing. The BCCC aims to receive the referral *before* the case has formally entered the court system. This is accomplished through strong partnerships established with police, juvenile justice, and the prosecutor's office. The Center currently receives referrals for misdemeanor and felony offenses, and encourages referral partners to send referrals for the *more* serious cases, rather than for the first-time offense. There are two reasons for this: First, research indicates that most first-time offenders will not re-offend even without intervention (Iyengar 1988). Second, whatever is currently being done is obviously not preventing the 12-year-old who has 10 prior offenses from re-offending, so why not refer to Community Conferencing? We have shown that Conferencing produces a recidivism rate 60 % lower than that for young offenders who go through the mainstream juvenile justice system (Irvine and Iyengar 2005). We therefore emphasize that sending more serious cases to Community Conferencing can truly reduce the labor and financial burden on the system.

Participants understand that if the case is referred to Community Conferencing and is successfully resolved, the matter will not be pursued by the courts. If, for any reason, the case is not resolved through Community Conferencing, it is simply referred back to the police or courts to be handled in the usual manner (e.g., court, probation).

Since 1998, the Center conducted over 400 of this kind of Community Conference, with a high level of success and reported satisfaction. Over 97 % of the conferences have resulted in an agreement, and the rate of compliance with agreements is over 90 %.[2]

Schools. Schools are targeted for referrals around suspension and truancy issues. Principals are asked: "Do you have any conflicts or incidents which have not been resolved in a way you that are happy with?" This question has prompted a growing number of school referrals. During each of the past several school years, over 400 students were referred to Community Conferencing. By 2009, over 5,000 students, parents, teacher and administrators had participated in a Community Conference. Again, over 95 % of the School Community Conferences resulted in a written agreement, with over 93 % compliance with the agreements. Thus, as a result of conferencing, many students have been able to stay *in* school – instead of being sent home as part of the standard authoritarian disciplinary arrangements. School conferencing has had powerful additional impact on the school climate, including increased teacher morale, improved parent-teacher relationships, and stronger connections between teachers and students. In addition, for each student that remains on the school rolls, that school is able to continue to receive the yearly dollar amount the state allocates for each student.

Re-entry from prison into families and communities. Cities in the United States are facing the challenge of thousands of people who have been incarcerated struggling to reintegrate into society upon their release (c.f., Re-entry Policy Council 2005). Hundreds of "re-entry" programs are now funded across the nation, providing a range of services to men and women trying to establish a decent life for themselves outside of prison. Recent research shows that a strong social support network is an important component of successful re-entry from prison (Coates et al. 2000). The BCCC began in 2003 to use Community Conferencing for individuals who are released from prison. Conferencing provides a structured process for ex-offenders to meet with family and friends, hear how these people have been affected by their incarceration, and work with the group to find ways to better support each other as the ex-offenders try to get their feet back on the ground.

Neighborhood unrest. The BCCC conducts extensive outreach in neighborhoods, to increase residents' awareness of an option other than calling the police or calling a lawyer in the event of conflict. Outreach takes place at community meetings,

[2]The Community Conferencing Center developed a customized database in 2003, which captures in-depth information about each referral, conference, and participants. These data are compiled quarterly, and can be obtained upon request at info@communityconferencing.org.

churches, schools, and any other venue that invites us. Residents experiencing ongoing and intractable conflicts in their neighborhood have now initiated several Community Conferences. These tend to be much larger than Conferences related to criminal justice referrals. An average Conference of this kind includes 30 participants. One such Conference, alluded to above, included 44 people. Residents tired of kids playing in the street and damaging people's property collaborated to create a volunteer-led football team for the children. The inspiring story was featured on the cover of Baltimore's city newspaper (Sullivan 2002).

Neighborhood planning issues. The BCCC also has conducted successful Community Conferences focusing on complex community and urban planning issues. One example was the case of a neighborhood that for years had angrily battled the businesses on their narrow street. Huge trucks used their street each day, endangering children on their way to school and damaging the foundations of their 50-year-old fragile homes. After a fruitless struggle for over 10 years, residents heard about Community Conferencing and decided to try it. Over 40 people attended, including business owners, city traffic planners, city officials, and community organizers. Their agreement included the city redirecting traffic and business owners helping neighborhood residents in a variety of ways.

Conflicts between and within organizations. It is now common for government-funded grant programs to require many community organizations to work in partnership. Once funding arrives, it is not uncommon for conflicts between these organizations to arise. Not everyone is in agreement with how to best conduct the project. The resulting conflicts can undermine project goals and jeopardize funding. The BCCC has facilitated several Community Conferences to address the conflicts between funded organizations. The situations are typically complicated and emotionally charged, yet Conferencing has been effective at helping the organizations to work through misunderstandings, clarify common goals, and create viable and lasting resolutions.

Serious crimes dialogue. The current criminal justice system rarely allows people an opportunity to talk directly to each other. In cases of serious crimes such as murder, this can have a lasting negative impact on victims, offenders, and their families. Many learn that time may not, in fact, heal wounds. For years and decades following an incident, victims and their families have lingering questions or wish they had been able to speak directly to the person responsible. In response to the need for dialogue between victims, offenders, and their supporters, the BCCC offers "Serious Crimes Conferencing" on a voluntary basis. Some exclusions for participation apply, including: (1) active drug use, (2) active gang activity, and/or (3) high psychopathology on the part of the offender. Most requests for these Conferences come from victims' family members. Many of the incidents occurred 10–30 years prior to the request for a Serious Crimes Conference.

Requests for Serious Crimes Conferences come mostly from victims' family members. The CCC has received over 40 referrals for Serious Crimes Conferences. The amount of time that has lapsed between the incident and the request for a

Serious Crimes Conference ranges from 8 to 27 years. For a variety of reasons, many cases do not end up with a Serious Crimes Conference taking place, (this is most typically because the offender is not interested, or the victim decides, at some point, to decline the service). However, in each case where the conversation did take place, participants reported that they were glad that they participated in the process, and that they felt a sense of healing as a result of the conversation.

The Growing Impact of Community Conferencing in Baltimore

It took a surprisingly long time to build a program that was well-established in, and well-used by, the institutions that refer cases to Community Conferencing. It took at least 5 years, from 1998 to 2003, before the BCCC received a steady rate of referrals from a variety of sources (juvenile justice, schools, court, neighborhoods). Encouragingly, from 2004 to 2009, the annual number of referrals averaged 850 young people. Over these five years, over 6,500 Baltimore residents safely resolved their own crimes and conflicts through Community Conferencing. Most of the cases handled by the CCC involve young people.[3] Research conducted by the Maryland Department of Juvenile Services in 2005 showed that young offenders who went through conferencing re-offended 60 % less often than a comparable group who went through the juvenile justice system (Irvine and Iyengar 2005).

Deliberate Effort to Keep the Program Community-Based

The Baltimore Community Conferencing Center (BCCC) uses a model of service delivery different to that offered by most agencies using the Conferencing process. The BCCC was founded as an autonomous community-based organization which partners closely with public agencies, receiving referrals from all of them, as well as from individual residents. There are at least four important reasons for maintaining the community-based identity.

First, the program's community-based identity helps demonstrate that justice can be fair *and* cost-effective when it is conducted "by and for the people." The community base sends the message that if residents and communities are provided with an appropriate structure, they can safely and effectively resolve crimes and conflicts themselves. It further promotes the idea that Conference outcomes belong to the participants themselves.

---

[3]This is because most of the funding is directed towards youth cases. However, the CCC readily accepts referrals for adult criminal cases, workplace and neighborhood conflicts – comprising 5 % of referrals to the CCC.

Second, the community base allows for flexibility in determining *how* and *where* Conferencing is offered. The Center is not "housed" with any single institution, nor is it overly identified with one area of state governance. Consequently, no institution has direct control over how or where the process is offered. Because the program is not limited to criminal justice interventions, Conferencing is not identified solely as a "Restorative Justice" intervention. From its inception, the program has been viewed more broadly as a program delivering conflict transformation and relationship management.

Community Conferences are typically convened in the neighborhood where the conflict or crime occurred, and at ***times*** (e.g., day, evening, weekend) and ***locations*** (e.g., library, recreation center, school) that are convenient for the participants. Because the program is independent of any particular institution, the choice of Conference locations is not delimited or restricted. The program strives to maintain the *voluntary* nature of participation. The independent status of the program protects against institutional pressure to mandate particular intervention options at certain times, for certain types of case.

Third, the community base allows for flexibility in funding sources. Funding flexibility has helped create the necessary degree of administrative flexibility. Early funding sources for the BCCC included the Maryland Judiciary (via their Alternative Dispute Resolution efforts), private foundations, the public school system, as well as a few, significant, private donors. This varied funding has allowed the BCCC to provide services in a variety of sectors.

For the first six years of operation, the bulk of BCCC funding came from private foundations. Foundation funders delivered a consistent message that public funding of this effort was needed in order to sustain these services. It was 6 years before the majority of BCCC funding shifted to public sources. The Maryland Department of Juvenile Services (DJS), which was a primary source of referrals, finally provided funding for a portion of the Community Conferencing diversion services which they were utilizing for 4 years. However, despite documenting 60 % reductions in recidivism, Community Conferencing funding was cut by DJS in the wake of recession-induced statewide budget cuts.[4]

After more than 15 years in operation, BCCC funding consists of fluctuating proportions of public sources, private sources, fundraisers, and fee-for-service income such as training and technical assistance. For the first six years of operation, most of CCC's funding came from private foundations. Funding from state agencies became the largest source of funding from years 7 to 11, with the exception of Maryland's judiciary having been supportive throughout. Revenue from training and technical assistance has grown over the years, contributing variably from 5 % to 20 % of CCC's annual operating expenses.

---

[4]The Maryland Department of Juvenile Services (DJS) has an annual budget of approximately $250 million. DJS funded 20 % of the diversion services provided by the Community Conferencing Center from 2004 to 2008, The CCC secured one-time-only funding from two sources to cover DJS, and other state-wide, funding cuts in FY10. More creative and diversified sources of funding are being explored for the future, including the application of dialogue circles and "Reintegration Conferences" with returning soldiers.

A fourth advantage of the community base is that it helps participants in conflict to move away from a punishment paradigm, and to experience Conferencing as a stepping stone to building relationships and community in the wake of crime. Conferencing engages the strong emotions of people in conflict, and provides a safe and effective structure for them to transform the negative emotions associated with conflict into the positive emotions associated with cooperation (Abramson and Moore 2002).

For this reason, in criminal cases, we prefer not to rely on designated victim representatives as a *substitute* for victims. Representatives can save *time* and increase *case volume*. Designated victim representatives are used in a variety of Restorative Justice programs in the United States and Europe, most-often when the program is sponsored by a state or governmental agency, and have been very helpful in supporting victims, especially in Conference preparation and follow-up. But *representing* rather than supporting victims limits the opportunity to *transform* conflict into cooperation, *heal/build* relationships and *strengthen community bonds,* all of which is possible when the people directly affected meet face-to-face.

Understanding the Vital Role of Emotion in Conflict Transformation

We have described elsewhere the transformation of emotions during the course of a Conference (Abramson and Moore 2002). In essence, once participants have shared their stories, and acknowledged conflict within and between themselves, their emotional state shifts, and their motivation shifts accordingly – from conflict to cooperation. Group members can now connect with each other, negotiate, and create lasting resolutions. In the language favored by the Harvard Negotiation Project, participants have first "gotten to peace", allowing them to "get to yes".[5]

We understand emotions to be a fundamental reason for the effectiveness of the Conferencing process. A key element of our understanding is the work of Silvan Tomkins, who extended Darwin's prescient work on the motivational and communicative functions of emotions (Tomkins 1962, 1963). The physiology of anger involves pupils constricting to bring a threat into sharper focus, and our heart pumping more blood to muscles to prepare for attack. In contrast, interest motivates us to "engage" in positive ways with our environment and the people in it. Table 11.1 outlines nine "basic emotions" and the specific ways that they motivate us.

[5]Fisher and Ury's classic text *Getting to Yes* (1981) is the widely-read and cited early formulation of interest-based negotiation theory, and has since been promulgated through the Harvard Negotiation Project. The theory of interest-based negotiation has informed mediation practice over several decades. A mediator assists disputing parties to negotiate an agreement that meets their interests.

Table 11.1 Basic emotions and motivation

Basic emotion	Motivation
CONTEMPT	Stay away!
DISGUST	Get rid of it
FEAR	Get away!
ANGER	Attack!
DISTRESS	Seek & provide comfort
SHAME	Seek to restore
SURPRISE	Stop, look. listen
INTEREST	Engage
JOY	Affiliate

In essence, the collective mood during a Community Conference shifts from the most strongly negative emotions associated with conflict (contempt, fear, anger, disgust), to less strongly negative emotions that motivate us to seek comfort and connection (distress, shame), and finally to the positive emotions that motivate us to cooperate and affiliate with one another (interest, joy). A Conference enables these emotions to be expressed and then transformed, and this drives the shift from conflict to cooperation.

This powerful theory linking basic emotions to motivation and group dynamics has subsequently helped us to develop guidelines for other facilitated processes. These processes are likewise informed by the principle that participants can successfully cooperate when they communicate within a structure that allows the negative emotions associated with conflict to be expressed and transformed into the positive emotions associated with cooperation. There is a clear a link between this practical theory and evolving fields of practice such as positive psychology and group decision-making – but this is the basis for another, broader discussion (e.g., Seligman 2002; Sawyer 2007; Senge et al. 2008).

All Conflicts Are Not Created Equal

In early Conferencing programs, the distinction was not well understood between Conferencing in those cases where there is *no dispute*, and Conferencing for situations where there are *many poorly resolved disputes*. In youth justice programs, there generally has to be to be no dispute about the nature of the case for Conferencing to be appropriate. Someone has offended against someone else. There are one or more clearly identified offenders, one or more victims, and their supporters. If an accused person denies an accusation against them, they retain the right to have their case heard before a court. The shortest Community Conferences, and by far the easiest to facilitate, involve cases of "undisputed harm." This type of Conference usually last from 45 to 90 minutes. The BCCC typically assigns volunteer facilitators to only this kind of case.

When Conferencing began to be used in schools, however, we encountered cases that were less clear-cut. There was frequently a history of destructive interaction between students. A person may have worn the label of "offender" in one of these interactions, but could be understood as the "victim" in some other interaction, and as a "bystander" in another, and may not have been involved at all in yet another interaction that affected fellow students.

As Conferencing began to be used to address conflict in schools and other settings beyond the justice system, this distinction between "no dispute" and "many dispute" cases became clearer. Dialogue between programs in Baltimore and in Australia greatly helped us to understand these differences.

Soon after it was established, the BCCC began running Conferences for neighborhood conflict. These cases often involved neighbors who were engaged in long-running, complex, seemingly intractable conflicts. There may have been many incidents, with little agreement on how conflict began and what had since transpired. Neighborhood conflicts were often maintained – even exacerbated – by a "professional pot stirrer". This person (or group of people) in the neighborhood can gain status in the local community by fomenting conflict – spreading misinformation through gossip and rumor. Community Conferencing has proven a powerful tool for helping everyone affected to collectively "cut through" this misinformation. If neighborhood residents are gathered in the same place, at the same time, they can hear the same collective story. A Community Conference facilitator provides the coordination that renders ineffective the "divide and conquer" strategy of a "pot-stirring" political entrepreneur.

While BCCC staff members were learning these lessons in the second half of the 1990s, colleagues in Australia had comparable experiences extending applications of Conferencing. John McDonald and David Moore (2001) partnered with a local law firm to form Transformative Justice Australia (TJA). Here they gained extensive experience convening Conferences in Australian community-, government- and corporate sector *workplaces* (Moore 2003, 2004).

As in schools, Conferences in workplaces and in neighborhoods typically addressed complex situations. These situations had developed over several years, even decades. And yet, with slight adjustment to language and format, the Conferencing process proved ideally suited to addressing these situations. This experience provided useful lessons on what sort of incidents to revisit, which additional participants to invite, and when to run parallel or subsequent mediation or training sessions.

BCCC staff members have learned over the years that the relative difficulty and labor intensity of facilitating Community Conferences for these different situations varies significantly. Table 11.2 summarizes basic differences between Conferences for the various types of cases. This summary is of the several hundred cases referred to the Center between 2006 and 2010. As the table indicates, half of the cases involve juvenile court diversion cases.

This table seems to suggest that the primary focus of most cases in Baltimore is still *remediation* – "responding to bad things". Closer analysis shows that much

Table 11.2 Characteristics of different types of community conferences

Referral from	% cases	How complex?	Requisite convenor skill level	Average hours to prepare	Typical number of sessions & length (hours)
Juvenile justice	30	Low	Beginner	3	1 @ 1
School suspension arrest	40	Low-med	Beginner	6	1 @ 1.5
Re-entry after prison	2	Low-med	Intermediate	10	1–2 @ 1.5
Courts: multiple charges	8	Med	Intermediate	12	1 @ 2
Ongoing community conflicts	14	High	Intermediate – advanced	20	1–2 @ 2
Planning/ environmental issues	2	Very high	Advanced	30	1–3 @ 2–3
Organizational conflicts	3	Very high	Advanced	30	1–3 @ 2–3
Serious crimes conference	1	Very high	Advanced	40	1–2 @ 1–2

more is happening. The program as a whole is having a *preventative effect* on crime and social disorder. By responding more constructively to cases that require remediation, Conferencing is reducing the total amount of social harm in affected neighbourhoods – and so is "stopping bad things from happening", in many cases, by making good things happen.

For example, participants in many of the larger Conferences are addressing more complex issues. Their agreements solve coordination problems such as how to organise recreational arrangements for young people, link local businesses with residents, and forge relationships and networking opportunities that fulfil an identified unmet need. In addition, *most* school-based Conference Agreements include a detailed plan for handling volatile situations more safely and effectively in future. These plans prove to be powerful tools for building positive relationships and school climate. Large fights among students typically begin as a result of some "s/he said, s/he said" incident (whether earlier in the week or several years ago). Most of these incidents are resolved through Conferencing, which allows participants to problem-solve about better ways to handle similar situations in the future. In short, these larger Conferences are fostering safe and supportive communities.

Whether this positive counterpart to remediation and prevention is called "flourishing", "building social capital", or some other term, it is perhaps the most promising element of this social movement. It leads us to reconsider early goals and assumptions, and to reconsider how to categorise the Conferencing process.

Changing How a Culture Deals with Conflict

The Baltimore Conferencing program illustrates the power and the importance of *informal referral sources* in expanding the awareness and use of Community Conferencing. For example, a police lieutenant who attended a Community Conference in her district was so impressed with the outcomes that, some weeks later, she referred a case to Community Conferencing that had been plaguing her for over a year. She had been seeking an effective response to a situation involving three feuding families on one block. Police had received more than 75 calls about the case during the previous 12 months. The families had forgotten *why* they were fighting. There had been a knife fight, a gun incident, and four court cases during the year, yet nothing was resolved. The lieutenant requested a Community Conference.

As the Conference unfolded, participants learned that the conflict had begun 14 months earlier, when two teenagers exchanged insults. It escalated over the following months as parents from the three homes sought to intervene. The adults were fed up with taking time off from work each month to attend court, and readily agreed to participate in a Community Conference. The Conference itself lasted a mere 75 minutes, yet in that time participants reached an agreement that was so effective that police logged no calls whatsoever from those homes over the following 12 months. Local police now use Community Conferencing regularly, with the support of area residents. This outcome exemplifies the way that an effective Community Conference gains advocates for the process.

Residents, court officials, counselors, police, teachers, principals, and policy makers have been helping transform conflict, Conference by Conference, across their neighborhoods. Community Conferencing has helped to build human and social capital. Each Community Conference helps improve and/or extend a network of relationships while individuals, communities and/or systems are transformed. And all this occurs without external experts and institutions doing things to or for people. Rather, the facilitator mobilizes resources within the community. A goal of the BCCC is to extend this work across the state and into other states.

Reflections and Lessons

Building Skills on Many Levels Using a Variety of Structured Processes

The delivery model developed by the Baltimore Community Conferencing Center allowed us to compare the application of Conferencing more broadly than in other programs. Conferencing in neighborhoods demonstrated how valuable these large scale, democratic meetings could be for coordinating local action where such coordination had been lacking.

Using Conferencing in the artificial, non-residential communities of schools and workplaces showed how Conferencing techniques came to be applied outside Conferences both in informal communication and in other formal processes. Students, staff and work colleagues have regularly reported that they apply, in their regular communication at school and in other workplaces, lessons learned during Conferencing. As educators, we sought ways to "fast-track" this outcome.

The slow path to cultural change in a school, workplace or neighbourhood was to train Conference facilitators, wait until they could address a suitable case with a Conference, and then hope that participants would apply more broadly some of the lessons learned. As more Conferences were convened, the likelihood of skills transfer and cultural change would increase. But there seemed to be a more rapid path to cultural change. This was to identify the techniques and principles learned by Conference participants, and to teach these directly.

For example, the BCCC provides a relationship-building tool for the classroom called the "Daily Rap." These sessions provide students with a regular, safe structure to talk about issues that concern *them*, and with an opportunity to come up with their own ideas about how to make things better in their lives. This circle training offers teachers an easy-to-implement, yet powerful, intervention to broaden and deepen the school's efforts to build better relationships among and between staff and students.

Thus, our work with Conferencing was suggesting we focus attention on the structure of conversations in groups. We observed participants in Conferences and mediations applying in more general communication many of the tactics from these processes. We also observed the value of coaching processes, which assist individuals to understand their working relations with others, and to change their own behaviour. Feedback, in the form of coaching or mentoring, influences the type of conversation one has with oneself.

We now see an immediate impact in schools when we build skills across these several levels of communication. With a combination of training workshops, mentoring, and group decision-making, we can improve the: (1) nature of observational feedback; (2) capacity of individuals to negotiate with each other, and (3) capacity of groups to engage proactively in true dialogue so that conversation generates new, creative, and helpful insights.

It is increasingly understood that the quality of feedback can be the most influential factor contributing to intrinsic motivation and to learning (Dweck 2006; Hattie and Timperley 2007). Likewise, the capacity to negotiate effectively is an invaluable skill – and the more individuals can negotiate without the need of a third party, the better their agreements and the greater the social harmony. Finally, it is increasingly understood that groups can be truly wise – but only if communication is structured to allow for creativity rather than groupthink (Surowiecki 2004). Like many insights, it then struck us as quite obvious that there should be a self-reinforcing effect from improving several modes of communication within a school community. We just hadn't seen it done in this way.

Re-categorizing Conferencing

The label of "restorative justice, though still applied to much work involving Conferencing and other circle-based processes internationally, is becoming less apt. Although the process is designed for fairness of process and outcome, much Conferencing occurs well clear of the justice system. Furthermore, in many cases the focus is not so much on "restoring" as it is on preventing harm, and on creating and/or coordinating social networks.

Schools were probably the first institutions to address this concern about terminology. Teaching staff in many jurisdictions spoke of restorative "practices" or "approaches" rather than restorative "justice". More recently, "relationship management" has emerged as preferred terminology to describe the use of Conferencing and related processes in school. The phrase *relationship management* contrasts with a traditional focus on *behaviour management.* It emphasises a shift from manipulating the psychology of individuals to negotiating the rules of social networks.

This shift had already begun in schools with initiatives like peer mediation, which was introduced well before Conferencing came to prominence. Peer mediation is part of the much broader movement for "Alternative", or "Appropriate" Dispute Resolution. That movement has offered victim-offender mediation to the justice system across North America, and elsewhere. When Conferencing began to be offered in schools and in those justice systems offering victim-offender mediation, there was a need to explain the relationship between these various processes in which a third party facilitates a negotiated agreement between participants.

A program that offers more than one process requires an intake system to identify which process will be most effective at addressing a particular conflict. The BCCC has asked the following simple questions to help determine whether Community Conferencing might be most appropriate:

1. ***How many people are affected?***

If many people are affected, Community Conferencing may provide the optimal process. It includes everyone who might be helpful in deciding *and* implementing the best resolution.

2. ***Are people in such conflict that some or all do not want to sit down with each other? Do some even feel that a meeting would not be safe?***

Sometimes people disagree with each other so strongly that they do not even want to sit at the negotiating table with the other person. When people are in such vehement conflict, a more appropriate approach is to allow them to get to *peace* before they try to get to *yes*. Community Conferencing encourages people to bring supporters and anyone else they feel has been affected by the conflict. In a "widened circle" of participants, people feel safer and more supported, and are often more willing to engage in a process to address the conflict. For high conflict situations, the familiar format of mediator-assisted negotiation between or among participants may not be ideal. Conferencing has been able to fill this gap.

The distinction between disputes and conflict helped us understand and explain which process was likely to be suitable for which situations.[6] This distinction, as the basis for determining when to use mediation and when to use Conferencing, proved invaluable in the late 1990s, when the Australian Defense Forces (ADF) was revising its own workplace relations practice, and looked to offer more than one process for addressing staffing issues (Cadd et al. 2002). The ADF then followed a Canadian lead and also began offering the process of conflict coaching as another method of addressing working relations among staff.

New Language to Reflect Shift in Focus

Lessons from work in schools and neighborhoods in the Baltimore program, and schools and workplaces in Australia, began to suggest a more fundamental shift in how we understood Conferencing and other processes for transforming conflict into cooperation. One broad lesson is that the shifting focus of our practice reflects a general trend in reform programs. We have seen the primary focus of our work shift from *remediation* – "responding to bad things" – through *prevention* – "stopping bad things from happening" – through to a more subtle and complex question: What promotes safe and supportive communities? This positive counterpart to remediation and prevention can be called, variously, "*pro*vention", flourish*ing*, or building social capital. Whatever it is called, "encouraging good things to happen" requires that we adjust our language, practice, and assumptions about the most effective pathways for reform.

When we combine the distinction between the aims of communication – *Reactive* (i.e., reacting to something bad); *Preventative* (i.e., seeking to prevent something bad); and *Proactive* (i.e., promoting something good) – with conversations that occurred – with *oneself* (prompted by observational coaching), *between individuals, between individuals with the assistance of a third party,* and *within a group* (with the assistance of a third party), we generate a fairly simple typology. The typology (Table 11.3) helps us categorize all the processes we had used and/or observed in communities, whether these communities were residential neighborhoods or artificial communities such as school or workplaces.[7]

---

[6]As it happens, the distinction had been made in international relations literature decades earlier, but had not been widely applied in the field of inter-personal and small group negotiation (Dunn 2004).

[7]"Circles" refers generally to a variety of inclusive and participatory dialogue processes which are convened by a "circle keeper" or facilitator, who is neutral (can also be thought of as being "equally caring of all participants") and who provides the structure for the dialogue. Circles can be convened for a variety of purposes, such as healing, conflict transformation and planning. Appreciative Inquiry (Cooperrider and Whitney 2005) refers to a collaborative approach to change that helps a group focus on those things that are working well, and using the existing successes and healthy dynamics to guide and envision an energized plan for the future.

Table 11.3 Typology of the range of relationship management processes

Mode ☟ Aim ☞	Reactive	Preventative	Proactive/creative
Observation	Counselling	Coaching, mentoring, advising	
Conversation	Problem-solving/self-resolution		Dialogue
Mediation	Assisted negotiation Relationship counselling		
Facilitation	"Conferencing"	"Conferencing" "Circles"	"Appreciative Inquiry" "Daily Rap" "Circles"

This framework helps us understand at a glance the set of processes for managing relationships in a school, a workplace or a neighbourhood. The framework is based on the assumption that decision-makers need a range of structured communication processes for collaborative problem-solving. It helps describe the skills and processes colleagues in communities can use to communicate constructively. It moves us beyond the language of "restorative justice" *and* "alternative dispute resolution." In this way, it has helped us and our colleagues shift the focus of our thinking and practice, from responding reactively using Community Conferencing, to the more complex question: How can we achieve more effective communication and constructive action in communities?

Conclusion

Community Conferencing is a process for responding to something bad that has happened in a particular community. The process begins as *remediation.* Participants determine together how best to respond to what has happened. But they then often focus on how to stop bad things from happening again in their community and how to make good things happen. Their focus shifts from *remediation* to *prevention* and *flourishing*.

We now see this shift occurring more broadly within the social movement that includes circles, Conferencing and other processes. This movement to improve the way we manage our own relationships in communities has implications for criminal justice, education, social welfare, and community development. It has implications for the way communities and organizations are governed.

Circles, Conferencing and related processes create a safe space for participatory decision-making. These processes are now frequently being applied in situations where the preferred approach would previously have been to engage an expert (e.g., judge, police officer, consultant) to make a decision. When the expert or Conference facilitator instead encourages/facilitate a group to reach a shared understanding and its own decision, conflict is transformed into cooperation, leaving individuals with greater control over their own lives and the life of their community.

References

Abramson, L., & Moore, D. B. (2001). Transforming conflict in the inner city: Community conferencing in Baltimore. *Contemporary Justice Review, 4*(3–4), 321–340.

Abramson, L., & Moore, D. B. (2002). The psychology of community conferencing. In J. Perry (Ed.), *Restorative justice: Repairing communities through restorative justice* (pp. 123–140). Lanham: American Correctional Association.

Cadd, N., Jakeman, L., Marks, H., & Moore, D. (2002). Dealing with conflict within the military: An evolving model for managing conflict and promoting good working relationships among defence employees. *Australasian Dispute Resolution Journal, 13*(3), 135–147.

Chatterjee, J. (1998). *A report on the evaluation of RCMP restorative justice initiative: Community justice forum as seen by participants*. Ottawa: RCMP Community, Contract and Aboriginal Policing Services.

Coates, R., Umbreit, M., & Vos, B. (2000). *Restorative justice circles in south St. Paul, Minnesota*. St. Paul: Center for Restorative Justice & Peacemaking, University of Minnesota, http://ssw.che.umn.edu/rjp/Resources/Documents/Circles.Final.Revised.pdf

Cooperrider, D., & Whitney, D. (2005). *Appreciative inquiry: A positive revolution in change*. San Francisco: Berrett-Koehler Publishers.

Deukmedjian, J. E. (2008). The rise and fall of RCMP community justice forums: Restorative justice and public safety interoperability in Canada. *Canadian Journal of Criminology and Criminal Justice, 50*(2), 117–152.

Dunn, D. J. (2004). *From power politics to conflict resolution: Assessing the work of John W. Burton*. Houndmills: Palgrave Macmillan.

Dweck, C. (2006). *Mindset: The new psychology of success*. New York: Random House.

Fenton, J. (2010, January 3). Baltimore homicides total 238 for 2009. *The Baltimore Sun*. Retrieved from http://www.baltimoresun.com/news/maryland/baltimore-city/bal-md.ci.yearend03jan03,0,73903.story

Fisher, R., & Ury, W. (1981). *Getting to yes: Negotiating agreement without giving in*. New York: Penguin.

Hattie, J., & Timperley, H. (2007). The power of feedback. *Review of Educational Research, 77*(1), 81–112.

Hudson, J., Morris, A., Maxwell, G., & Galaway, B. (1996). *Family group conferences: Perspectives on policy and practice*. Sydney: The Federation Press.

Irvine, J. & Iyengar, L. (2005). *Match-controlled study of young offenders: Community conferencing vs. juvenile services*. Report of the Maryland Department of Juvenile Services.

Iyengar, L. (1988). *A Review of recidivism rates among juvenile justice youth born in 1977*. Report of the Maryland Department of Juvenile Services.

Lipstein, D. (2003). *From conflict to cooperation* (video), from: http://www.communityconferencing.org

McCold, P. (1997). *Restorative justice: An annotated bibliography*. Monsey: Willow Tree Press.

McDonald, J., & Moore, D. (2001). Community conferencing as a special case of conflict transformation. In J. Braithwaite & H. Strang (Eds.), *Restorative justice and civil society*. Cambridge: Cambridge University Press.

Moore, D. (2003). *David Williamson's Jack Manning trilogy: A study guide*. Sydney: Currency Press.

Moore, D. (2004). Managing social conflict – The evolution of a practical theory. *Journal of Sociology and Social Work, 31*(1), 71–91.

Moore, D., & Forsythe, L. (1995). *Family conferencing in Wagga Wagga: A report to the Criminology Research Council*. Wagga Wagga: Centre for Rural Social Research. From: http://www.aic.gov.au/rjustice/links.html

Pranis, K., Stuart, B., & Wedge, M. (2003). *Peacemaking circles: From crime to community*. St. Paul: Living Justice Press.

Re-entry Policy Council. (2005). *Report of the Re-entry Policy Council: Charting the safe and successful return of prisoners to the community*. New York: Council of State Governments.
Sawyer, K. (2007). *Group genius: The creative power of collaboration*. New York: Basic Books.
Seligman, M. (2002). *Authentic happiness*. New York: Random House.
Senge, P., Smith, B., Kruschewitz, N., Laur, J., & Schley, S. (2008). *The necessary revolution: How individual organizations are working together to create a sustainable world*. London: Nicholas Brealey.
Sharpe, S. (1998). *Restorative justice: A vision for healing and change*. Edmonton: EVOMS.
Sherman, L., & Strang, H. (2007). *Restorative justice: The evidence*. London: The Smith Institute.
Stone, B., Patton, B., & Heen, S. (1999). *Difficult conversations: How to discuss what matters most*. New York: Penguin.
Sullivan, E. (2002). A league of their own. *City Paper*. 13–19 Nov 2002, from http://www.citypaper.com/2002-11-13/feature.html
Surowiecki, J. (2004). *The wisdom of crowds*. Norwell: Anchor.
Tilly, C. (2006). *Why? What happens when people give reasons and why*. Princeton: Princeton University Press.
Tomkins, S. (1962). *Affect, imagery, conciousness*. New York: Springer.
Tomkins, S. (1963). *Computer simulation of personality: Frontier of psychological theory*. New York: Wiley.
Trimboli, L. (2000). *An evaluation of the NSW Youth Justice Conferencing Scheme*. Sydney: NSW Bureau of Crime Statistics and Research, from http://www.lawlink.nsw.gov.au/bocsar
Van Ness, D. W., & Strong, K. (1997). *Restoring justice*. Cincinnati: Anderson Press.
Zehr, H. (1990). *Changing lenses: A new focus for crime and justice*. Waterloo: Herald Press.

Chapter 12
Capacity Building in Conflict Management at the Community Level: The Case of Burundi

Jenny Theron Kervarrec and Jerome Sachane

Introduction

Non-Governmental Organizations (NGOs) date back to the nineteenth century but it was globalization in the twentieth century that increased the importance of NGOs, allowing them to become more prominent and well-known. Though there are various definitions for NGOs, for the purpose of this chapter they will be described as "non-profit organization(s) dedicated to alleviating human suffering; and/or promoting education, health care, economic development, environmental protection, human rights, and conflict resolution; and/or encouraging the establishment of democratic institutions and civil society" (All et al. 2003, p. 89).

Today NGOs play an important role in the international arena especially when it comes to international responses to humanitarian emergencies, human rights abuses, physical and societal reconstruction needs, reconciliation challenges resulting from conflict, natural disasters and other emergencies. These organizations not only focus on rapid response in the face of natural disasters, ethnic and religious conflict, and human rights violations, but in addition are committed to long-term grassroots work within communities in developing countries. NGO involvement in conflict situations often continues through the life of a conflict from the first sign of violence or

J.T. Kervarrec (✉)
Director of Shades of Green, South Africa and the former Co-ordinator of the Peacemaking Unit at the African Centre for the Constructive Resolution of Disputes, South Africa
e-mail: jenny@sgevents.co.za

J. Sachane
Deputy Director of the African Centre for the Consructive Resolution of Disputes, South Africa
e-mail: jeromes@accord.org.za

J.M. Fritz (ed.), *Moving Toward a Just Peace: The Mediation Continuum*,
Clinical Sociology: Research and Practice, DOI 10.1007/978-94-007-2885-1_12,

unrest until reconciliation and reconstruction. The mandates of NGOs working in conflict areas or situations can, in general, be divided into four categories: rendering humanitarian assistance, promoting human rights, civil-society and democracy building, and conflict resolution. That said, some NGOs will focus on one of the above mandates, whereas others might focus on more than one or even undertake all of them (All et al. 2003, p. 89).

This chapter will focus on an NGO called the African Centre for the Constructive Resolution of Disputes (ACCORD). ACCORD is a South African-based organization, but works throughout Africa "to bring creative African solutions to the challenges posed by conflict on the continent" (ACCORD 2010). Its primary aim is to influence political developments by offering conflict resolution, dialogue and institutional development as alternatives to violent and protracted conflict. ACCORD specializes in prevention, analysis and management of conflict, and intervenes in conflicts through mediation, negotiation, training, research and conflict analysis.

ACCORD was established in 1992 and since then has trained over 15,000 people in conflict management and conflict resolution with a focus on all sectors of society namely, government and public service, business, military and police, and civil society (ACCORD 2010). ACCORD's approach of intervention, research, training and early warning has been recognized by the United Nations as a viable model for conflict prevention and transformation in Africa (United Nations Department of Public Information 1996). The experience gained by ACCORD over the years offers valuable lessons for the field of conflict management.

This chapter will focus on lessons learned by the organization in terms of capacity building in conflict management at a community level in a developing, post-conflict country. In this chapter, capacity building at a community level according to the authors refers to the process of developing and strengthening the abilities and skills of the leaders of local communities to peacefully manage the conflicts in their communities. The case to be presented is that of Burundi where ACCORD has been working since 1995. In 2010, ACCORD had five offices in Burundi staffed with 47 local staff and one Sierra Leonean team member. We are of the view that the lessons learned in Burundi, which will be outlined in this chapter, will provide other organizations or institutions with valuable considerations and guidance when undertaking conflict management capacity building at a community level in a developing, post-conflict country.

The chapter will provide the reader with a brief history of Burundi, a summary of ACCORD's work in Burundi, a description of the ACCORD Legal Aid Clinic Project and then the lessons learned. Whereas ACCORD's work in Burundi involves various state and grassroots level interventions, it is the ACCORD Legal Aid Clinic Project specifically that operates on a community level. The main focus of this chapter will be about this project.

The History of Burundi

Burundi is a small, landlocked country in central Africa, 27,830 km^2 in size,[1] with a population of approximately seven million people. It was an independent kingdom for hundreds of years and then became a German protectorate in the 1890s until the First World War, when it came under Belgium administrative authority. In 1962, Burundi gained its independence as a constitutional monarchy. The monarchy was abolished in 1966 and replaced with a republican system. The Belgian administrative authority systematically enforced the 'divide and rule' strategy by favoring the minority Tutsi ethnic group over the majority Hutu ethnic group. The Tutsi group was utilized to assist with the administering of the colony (Eggers 1997) resulting in Tutsis also having control of the government, the military and the economy during the post-independence period. Today, Burundian society consists of three ethnic groups: the Hutu (an estimated majority of 85 % of the population), the Tutsi (an estimated 14 % of the population) and the Twa (an estimated 1 % of the population) (Hatungimana et al. 2007).

Following Burundi's independence in 1962, the country has experienced on-and-off, latent and manifest conflicts between both ethnic groups and political factions. During the crises of 1965, 1972, 1988, 1991, and 1993 more than half a million people died. It was, however, during the crisis of 1993 that commenced following the assassination of the first democratically elected president, Melchior Ndadaye, that approximately 300,000 people died. This was by far the greatest death toll (Eggers 1997).

In 1996, the Arusha negotiations commenced between the government of Burundi and various armed and unarmed groups and opposition parties. The Arusha negotiations were first facilitated by Julius Nyerere, former president of Tanzania, and subsequently by Nelson Mandela, former President of South Africa. These negotiations resulted in the signing of the Arusha Peace and Reconciliation Agreement for Burundi in August 2000 (hereafter referred to as the 'Arusha Agreement'), after which the transitional government of Burundi was established (Eggers 1997). At the time the Arusha Agreement was signed, various opposition groups and armed movements still remained outside the formal peace process. The then Deputy President of South Africa, Jacob Zuma, with the backing of former South African President, Thabo Mbeki, and regional partner states, played an integral role in bringing these groups to the table. The result was that various ceasefire agreements were signed between the transitional government and these groups (Bentley and Southall 2005).

On 26 August 2005, Pierre Nkurunziza, leader of the former armed movement the National Council for the Defense of Democracy – Forces for the Defense of Democracy (CNDD-FDD), was inaugurated as the new President of Burundi, marking a new era for the country (Eggers 1997). However, at the time of his inauguration

[1] Burundi is about the size of Haiti.

there still remained one armed movement outside the peace agreement – the PALIPEHUTU National Liberation Forces (FNL). (The FNL later changed its name to the National Liberation Forces only). The then South African Minister of Safety and Security (and later Minister of Defense), Mr. Charles Nqakula, with the support again of former President Thabo Mbeki and regional partner states, played an important role as the facilitator of the Burundi peace process which resulted in various agreements and declarations being signed by the PALIPEHUTU – FNL and the government of Burundi. The FNL officially became a political party in 2009 (DFA 2006; UNSC 2009; ISS 2009).

It is tempting to simplify the Burundian conflict by focusing on ethnic divisions. However, ethnic diversity, as such, did not cause the conflict, rather it was the inequalities in the distribution of access to national resources and political and military power across ethnic groups (Ndikumana 2005). Regional and ethnic diversity were used as tools by the Tutsi (Hima) to control power. On the other hand, political actors lacking access to state resources manipulated ethnic solidarity to confront the regime, resulting in the political system discriminating along ethnic lines. Ethnic diversity thus became a tool in the pursuit of economic and political power and advantages. In other words, even though ethnicity was not a cause of the conflict, it was used as a vehicle of conflict. Moreover, there is a greater need to focus on the institutional failures that played a role in the conflict by creating and maintaining a divide between the state and the population. Until the early 1990s, the state, including political, economic and military power, was monopolized by the minority Tutsi, while the majority Hutu lacked access to these resources (Hatungimana et al. 2007). Following an intense negotiation process, the Arusha Agreement and, subsequently, the additional ceasefire agreements were signed.

A Brief History of ACCORD's Work in Burundi

1995–2000: ACCORD's Double Entry into the Burundian Peace Process

As an African conflict management organization, ACCORD monitored the situation in Burundi since the organization's establishment in 1992. ACCORD's involvement in Burundi, however, started at a later stage with a double entry into the peace process. The first entry consisted of a familiarization component, initiated by International Alert (IA), a London-based organization. In 1995, ACCORD was approached by IA to set up an exchange program between Burundian parliamentarians and diplomatic representatives and their South African counterparts to share the South African experience in relation to the national negotiations and the formation of the Government of National Unity. This initiative allowed Burundians to interact with their South African counterparts who had just come out of a protracted conflict, which had divided the country across racial, class and, to an extent, ethnic lines. It provided an opportunity for a valuable exchange of information and ideas between these groups and its success led to further exchange programs organized by ACCORD in partnership with IA between 1995 and 1997. These were followed-up in 1998 by further study tours and exchange programs for women and youth that were organized by ACCORD.

As mentioned, these exchange initiatives were the first of ACCORD's double entry into the Burundi peace process. The primary objective of ACCORD's involvement in these initiatives was to familiarize the organization with the dynamics in Burundi and to serve as a confidence-building mechanism between ACCORD and key stakeholders in Burundi, legitimizing the organization. The relationships built during this period permitted ACCORD to engage stakeholders during the peace process, allowing the organization to play a second-track[2] diplomacy role in the Arusha peace negotiations in 2000. ACCORD's involvement in Burundi was enhanced when it began to play a supporting role during these negotiations which were facilitated at the time by former South African President Nelson Mandela. ACCORD's role focused on creating space for interaction and dialogue between the facilitator and key stakeholders of organs of civil society which assisted with the negotiation between parties. The peace negotiations resulted in the Arusha Agreement which brought about the transitional period in Burundi. The overall objective of ACCORD's involvement was to ensure that the agreement reached would be embraced by the people of Burundi to assist with its effective implementation. Accordingly, while the first entry equipped ACCORD with knowledge about the situation in Burundi, the formal engagement of stakeholders served as the second entry of ACCORD's direct involvement in the Burundian peace process.

2001–2005: Consolidation of ACCORD's Commitment to Burundi

In 2001, ACCORD received support from the United Kingdom's (UK) Department for International Development (DFID) to continue with its activities in Burundi. With this support, ACCORD held several field research and consultative visits to Burundi and conducted capacity-building workshops in conflict management for a variety of stakeholders, including a coalition of women's organizations and armed movements, many of the latter, at the time, still outside of the Burundi peace process. Considering the importance of the inclusion of all stakeholders to ensure peace consolidation, it was critical for these armed movements to be brought into the process. Former President Mandela handed over this segment of the process to the then South African Deputy President, Jacob Zuma, to facilitate

[2]Second track or track-two diplomacy can be defined as unofficial, informal interactions facilitated between parties to the conflict or those who have an interest in the conflict with the aim of ultimately resolving the conflict. Track-two diplomacy aims to assist the official leaders or mediators of the conflict (Montville 1982).

the ceasefire negotiations between the transitional government in Burundi and the armed movements. During this process in 2002 and 2003, ACCORD consecutively assisted in the preparation of armed movements for the ceasefire negotiations. Capacity-building workshops in negotiation techniques and conflict management for the benefit of the leadership of these movements were conducted. These workshops aimed to build capacity to participate in ceasefire and peace negotiations and, therefore, contributed to the armed movements being included in the Burundi peace process and transforming themselves into political parties.

Throughout the period of 2001–2003, ACCORD operated from its head office in Durban, South Africa. However, given the importance of the political situation in Burundi, and noting the prospects and challenges that faced the country at the beginning of its transition, a decision was taken to open an office in Burundi with the assistance of the United Kingdom's DFID. The initial aim of this office was to monitor and track developments in the country and to design appropriate intervention strategies which acknowledged that the role of local Burundi players was vital in achieving sustainable peace in the country. In keeping with its principles of transparency, neutrality and impartiality, ACCORD's activities in Burundi for the period 2003–2005 focused on making a contribution to the political climate at the time, by conducting sector-specific capacity-building workshops in conflict management. These workshops were designed as both a skills transference exercise and a method to:

- Build local capacity within Burundi to deal with conflicts constructively;
- Facilitate interactions between key stakeholders in Burundi;
- Facilitate interactions between relevant stakeholders in Burundi with their counterparts in other African countries; and to
- Contribute to the on-going endeavor to find peace in Burundi through research that informed different policy makers in Burundi about what could be done to move the country forward in its peace efforts.

The overall aim of these initiatives was to bring about constructive collaboration of organs of civil society with the transitional government of Burundi towards the consolidation of peace and reconciliation.

In addition, in 2005, ACCORD played an integral role in building the capacity of former armed movements that had recently become political parties. ACCORD provided training in conflict management, leadership skills, strategy design and decision making. More specifically, ACCORD organized training workshops for senior leaders of recently formed political parties with the aim of creating capacity to address challenges relating to the transformation of a former armed movement into a political party. ACCORD's capacity-building work attempted to address the challenges faced by the Burundian political leadership during its transition period.

Finally, in addition to the above initiatives, in November 2004, with support from the United Nations High Commissioner for Refugees (UNHCR), ACCORD established its Legal Aid Clinic Project. Between 2004 and 2009, ACCORD opened four legal aid clinics in Bururi, Ruyigi, Rutana and Makamba Provinces and also worked in the provinces of Gitega and Cankuzo. The aim of the project, which is ongoing, is to help the local population, specifically the returning refugees, deal with the challenges in the repatriation process that are faced by both the welcoming communities and the returnees.

2006–2009: The Promotion of Peace, Reconciliation and Effective Governance

In 2006, ACCORD awarded the nation of Burundi the Africa Peace Award for the outstanding achievement of settling years of civil war through a negotiated settlement and the successful democratic election of a new government in 2005.[3] At the time it was decided that Burundi achieved a remarkable turnaround from a state of pervasive violent conflict and instability to a fledgling, but stable, democratic state.

In addition, ACCORD and the Ministry of Good Governance, on behalf of the Government of Burundi, signed a Memorandum of Understanding (MoU) relating to ACCORD's activities in Burundi for the period 1 July 2006 until 30 June 2010. This MoU reflected the importance for both parties to the agreement to work together to reinforce the capacity of Burundian cadres to carry out their mandate for the benefit of Burundi; to forge a partnership between the government of Burundi and civil society in the areas of peace making, good governance and reconciliation; and to conceptualize, develop and implement strategies for peace and reconciliation in Burundi.

Since 2006, various initiatives have been undertaken towards the completion of the MoU. These have focused mostly on building the capacity of government officials and civil society representatives in conflict management to ensure their understanding of the role of civil society in a post-conflict country; as well as to ensure that government and civil society view each other as partners, rather than opponents. ACCORD also has continued conflict management, reconciliation and legal matters training sessions for community leaders and local administrative authorities, while providing mediation services and legal assistance in selected communities, especially with regard to the resolution of land conflict. Special initiatives during this period worth mentioning include:

- Two special training sessions conducted in 2006 for what was, at the time, the newly established *Commission Nationale des Terres et Autres Biens* (National Commission for Land and Other Properties, CNTB) in conflict analysis, prevention and management in relation to land conflict in Burundi and Burundian legislation relevant to land conflict;
- A National Dialogue on Mechanisms for Transitional Justice: Special Case of Burundi undertaken in 2006 in collaboration with the South African Embassy in Burundi, and with the agreement of the Government of Burundi. The objective

[3]This was the sixth presentation of the award by ACCORD over a fifteen-year period. Previous winners include Nelson Mandela and the nations of Mozambique and Nigeria.

of the National Dialogue was to give Burundians the opportunity to express themselves about the transitional justice process taking place in their country and to create awareness of the different mechanisms of transitional justice at a grassroots level.
- A negotiations workshop conducted in 2008 for the benefit of the PALIPEHUTU-FNL to provide them with the skills needed to effectively participant in the peace process.

Furthermore, in line with the aforementioned MoU, ACCORD and the Royal Norwegian Ministry of Foreign Affairs signed a 3-year partnership agreement in 2007. The goal of this agreement was to contribute to post-conflict peacebuilding by promoting peace, reconciliation and effective governance in Burundi. More specifically, this agreement recognized that peace processes are fragile in nature. It is therefore imperative that systems and structures are established and skills developed to manage and resolve conflicts so as to mitigate instability before it develops into civil disorder and armed conflict.

ACCORD seeks to address this challenge by building the conflict management capacity of selected representatives from political parties and civil society entities representing women, youth, traditional leaders, religious leaders, the media, trade unions and business associations, as well as government officials. Forums are created for them to dialogue, seek consensus where required and resolve differences through peaceful means.

The Context in Which ACCORD's Legal Aid Clinic Project Operates

It is important to discuss why the project was established and, more importantly, which challenges the project aims to address. This discussion will begin by explaining the importance of repatriation, reintegration and reconciliation of returnees, given that returnees (former refugees) are the main beneficiaries of the project, and to explain the context in which ACCORD operates.

Repatriation, Reintegration and Reconciliation

Burundi, like other countries emerging from years of civil strife, faced enormous challenges. Some of these challenges were related to the repatriation, reintegration and reconciliation of thousands of refugees, some of whom left the country as far back as 1993 and even 1972. The crisis of 1972 led to between 200,000 and 300,000 people fleeing the country,[4] mainly to Tanzania. In 1993, the assassination

[4]This number varies depending on the source that one consults; according to UNHCR the figure is 200,000, but according to the African Report No. 70 (from ICG) the number is 300,000.

of the first democratically-elected president, Melchoir Ndadaye, and the crisis that followed resulted in approximately 400,000 people fleeing Burundi. Following the 1993 crisis some 880,000 people were displaced internally, while 300,000 lost their lives (UNHCR-WFP 2007) (ICG 2003).

The signing of the Arusha Agreement in 2000, followed by the establishment of a transitional government, resulted in peace, though fragile, and an improvement in the security situation in Burundi.[5] This created the expectation that refugees would now return to their country of origin. Taking into consideration historical happenings in Burundi with regard to refugees returning to the country, preparations for the repatriation and reintegration process were of extreme importance. Historically, in 1993, following the establishment of a newly democratically elected government with the election of President Ndadaye, some 50,000 refugees who fled Burundi in 1972 returned to the country. Many of these returnees expected that upon their return they would be able to reclaim their lands. These lands were distributed to soldiers, influential administrative authorities, including their relatives and friends, by the government following the 1972 killings and the fleeing of thousands (Ould-Abdallah 2000).

In 1993, the return of refugees was not handled effectively by the new government, who on the one hand was trapped between the importance of returning to the refugees what the former regime stole from them, and, on the other hand, the occupants' fear that they would be the 'losers.' The demonstrations by the expropriated occupants' families resulted in a deterioration of the political situation in Burundi which is considered by many as one of the important causes of the crisis in 1993 (ICG 2003).

This clearly shows the importance of the repatriation and reintegration process in a post-conflict country and the effects on political stability. This was recognized during the Arusha negotiations; included in the Arusha Agreement is a protocol focusing on reconstruction and development, including provisions for the rehabilitation and resettlement of refugees and *sinistrés*.[6] These provisions pay attention to physical and political reconstruction, as well as economic and social development (Arusha Peace and Reconciliation Agreement 2000b).

Repatriation

On 15 January 2002, the Governments of Burundi and Tanzania as well as the United Nations High Commissioner for Refugees (UNHCR) signed a Tripartite Agreement focusing on the repatriation of Burundian refugees. Following this, the

[5]Note that an increase in security was especially brought about at a later stage through the signing of various ceasefire agreements, especially the *Global Ceasefire Agreement between the Transitional Government of Burundi and the National Council for the Defence for the Democracy-Forces for the Defence of Democracy*, which was signed in 2003.

[6]In the Arusha Agreement the term '*sinistrés*' refers to all displaced, regrouped and dispersed persons and returnees (Arusha Agreement, Protocol IV, Chapter I, Article 1.1).

UNHCR began facilitating the repatriation from refugee camps in western Tanzania of those refugees who expressed a willingness to return. In June 2006, UNHCR began promoting repatriation (UNHCR–WFP 2007). From 2002 until the end of 2009, the UNHCR, in collaboration with partner organizations, repatriated a total of 488,478 refugees from Tanzania back to Burundi (UNHCR Burundi 2009). This process is still ongoing.

The repatriation of refugees cannot, however, be viewed in isolation, since without reintegration and reconciliation this process is often not sustainable. Once refugees have been repatriated, there is a need to provide them with assistance in terms of reintegration and reconciliation.

Reintegration

One of the major challenges faced by returnees to Burundi is the issue of land. Burundi is a densely populated country. Access to land means access to 0.7 ha, down to 0.4 ha for more or less 40 % of the population of the central plateau. These are important figures since 90 % of the population is dependent on land, including agriculture and livestock. Land-based activities constitute less than half of the total gross domestic product (GDP) of Burundi and opportunities for non-land-based work are limited overall and almost non-existent in rural areas. In addition, the population growth rate is 3.4 %. These factors result in the over-exploitation of land, soil degradation and crop disease. Land, therefore, becomes a valuable and limited commodity resulting in frequent land disputes (UNHCR–WFP 2007; Gahama et al. 1999; Oketch and Polzer 2002).

The issue of land is crucial not only for the reintegration of returnees, but also for the stability of Burundi. If a large number of returnees are unable to recover their property, their frustrations may be expressed violently and/or this could become an issue for upcoming elections. The Arusha Agreement tried to recognise the importance of this issue through stating that: "All refugees and/or *sinistrés* must be able to recover their property, especially land" (Arusha Peace and Reconciliation Agreement 2000). The reintegration of returnees, therefore, includes the recovery and ownership of properties left behind by them when they fled the country. Without this, returnees might be physically back in their country of origin, but are unable to participate in the country's economic and political life. This could result in the repatriation process being merely a relocation process in which refugees return home only to become internally displaced persons (El Abdellaoui 2005).

Reconciliation

The successful reintegration of returnees depends on reconciliation between returnees and hosting communities. As stated in the Arusha Agreement when referring to the establishment of a Sub-Commission on Land: "It [the Sub-Commission on Land] must always remain aware of the fact that the objective is not only restoration of their property to returnees, but also reconciliation between the groups as well as peace in the country." (Arusha Peace and Reconciliation Agreement 2000). Furthermore, the Arusha Agreement called for the establishment of a National Truth and Reconciliation Commission, and an International Judicial Commission of Inquiry. The latter was envisaged as a means to investigate genocide, crimes against humanity and war crimes, while the former was to handle other crimes related to conflicts since Burundi's independence in 1962. The agreement also included a provision for an International Criminal Tribunal in the case where evidence of genocide, crimes against humanity or war crimes were found by the International Judicial Commission of Inquiry. According to the Arusha Agreement, both institutions were to be established within 6 months after the inauguration of a transitional government. However, in 2010, the Government of Burundi and the United Nations (UN) were still in the process of negotiating modalities regarding the establishment of transitional justice mechanisms in Burundi. These initial mechanisms, envisaged to assist with the reconciliation of the Burundian population, had yet to be established, indicating the need for initiatives at all levels (such as at the community and national levels) to promote reconciliation within Burundi.

Connections Among Repatriation, Reintegration and Reconciliation

Reconciliation is closely linked to the issue of land in Burundi. In line with the approach of the Arusha Agreement is the fact that in addition to restoring people's rights to land and other properties, it is also of importance to restore the bond of trust between citizens. Refugees who left the country during the crises in Burundi and community members who stayed behind have had different experiences and went through different kinds of sufferings. "Experiences" can further differ based on: ethnicity, gender, social status, the time of return of the refugee and the place of asylum. It is therefore important for such groups to understand the experience and suffering of other groups, allowing for reconciliation to take place (El Abdellaoui 2005).

There is also the challenge of the damaged relationship between the state and its citizens. The history of Burundi saw both the state and rebel movements violate people's rights with impunity. When examining land issues, for example, local authorities sometimes incorrectly allocated land for public purposes. This resulted in a large number of land disputes involving returnees and local authorities (El Abdellaoui 2005), which naturally does not create a conducive environment for the restoration of relationships and the promotion of reconciliation in Burundi. It is, therefore, important when dealing with land disputes as part of the reintegration of returnees, that reconciliation is promoted throughout this process.

Repatriation, reintegration and reconciliation in post-conflict countries, including Burundi, are of extreme importance. It is important that these processes not be viewed in isolation from one another. In the case of Burundi, in addition to the assistance provided by UNHCR, the governments of Tanzania and Burundi, and other partner organizations for the repatriation of refugees, assistance also is provided in terms of the reintegration and reconciliation of returnees. In order to assist with the reintegration of returnees in communities and reconciliation between Burundians, ACCORD (in partnership with UNHCR) established its Legal Aid Clinic Project.

Capacity Building on a Community Level: ACCORD's Legal Aid Clinic Project

Establishment of the ACCORD Legal Aid Clinic Project

By 2004, UNHCR was already funding legal aid clinics. These clinics were being implemented by partner organizations and focused mainly on providing legal assistance.[7] UNHCR recognized the need for mediation skills to be provided in addition to legal assistance. The UNHCR therefore approached ACCORD as a conflict management organization with experience in mediation and requested that ACCORD undertake a Legal Aid Clinic Project that would include a mediation component. ACCORD began to implement its Legal Aid Clinic Project (hereafter referred to as the project) in November 2004, with support from UNHCR. As part of this project, legal aid clinics were established to act as local conflict mitigation mechanisms in Burundi in the provinces of Bururi, Makamba, Rutana, Ruyigi, Gitega and Cankuzo[8] (Fig. 12.1).

Objectives

At the time of its establishment, the principal objective of the project was to assist with the reintegration of returnees and the reconciliation between Burundians through activities that would provide legal assistance to beneficiaries, inculcate

[7]Information provided about the ACCORD Legal Aid Clinic Project is based on the experience of Jenny Theron as the former Coordinator of ACCORD's Burundi Operations, as well as on interviews with Pamphile Nyandwi, the current Legal Aid Clinic Project Manager (6–8 May 2008); Adelin Hatungimana, the current ACCORD Burundi Intervention Senior Programme Officer (former Legal Aid Clinic Project Manager) (9 & 12 May 2008); and Jamila El Abdellaoui, former ACCORD Senior Interventions Department Officer (13 & 14 May 2008).

[8]These provinces were selected as they received the highest number of returnees and, accordingly, faced the highest number of conflicts, especially land conflicts.

Fig. 12.1 Burundi provinces with ACCORD legal aid offices

a culture of non-violent transformation of conflict, and promote dialogue and reconciliation (El Abdellaoui 2005). These aims were further expanded at a later stage to include the protection of returnees.[9] The principle objective of the project, therefore, is to contribute to reconciliation and non-violent conflict resolution at a community level.

[9]In terms of the protection of returnees, ACCORD firstly provides legal assistance for beneficiaries as well as capacity-building workshops in legal matters. However, in addition, in 2006, ACCORD established a partnership with an organization, *Advocates Sans Frontières (ASF),* which provides legal representation for beneficiaries. These initiatives assist returnees by providing them with protection of their rights.

By providing training in conflict management, reconciliation and legal matters for community leaders and local administrative authorities; by conducting sensitization, listening and mediation missions into selected *collines*[10]; and by providing legal assistance, the immediate objectives of the legal clinics are met. The objectives are to:

- Inform returnees and local communities about their social, economic and political rights;
- Provide returnees and local communities with support networks to help them overcome challenges;
- Provide mediation and facilitation services to returnees and local communities to address any potential conflicts appropriate for mediation;
- Reinforce the capacity of the population in terms of conflict management so that they can themselves prevent and peacefully transform conflicts that may arise;
- Promote a culture of reconciliation and peaceful cohabitation among returnees and local communities;
- Promote dialogue between returnees and local communities;
- Strengthen the relationships between various groups in communities through confidence building and developing skills in communication, mediation and negotiation; and
- Contribute to the protection of returnees and other vulnerable groups through legal and/or judicial assistance.

Recruitment

In line with ACCORD's principle to build local capacity, Burundian nationals were recruited to staff the legal aid clinics. Staff members are expected to be neutral and impartial and so they will not work in their province of origin. This aims to prevent staff having to deal with cases in which they have a personal interest or with communities in which they have personal ties. Gender equality and ethnicity were considered throughout the recruitment process in addition to the professional backgrounds of applicants. The recruitment process was conducted in accordance with Burundian legislation.

Based on the focus of the project, ACCORD identified the need to first recruit lawyers and then to recruit organizers with a social science background. The nature of the challenges faced by returnees and hosting communities during the repatriation and reintegration processes meant that lawyers were selected based on their knowledge and experience with Burundian legal procedures and legislation regarding issues of human rights, family law and land law. This knowledge is useful

---

[10]In Burundi, the provinces are divided into communes. The communes contain zones which are divided into *collines*.

not only when conducting capacity-building workshops in legal matters, but also when conducting mediation sessions as a lawyer. A lawyer who also is a mediator can motivate parties to come to the mediation table since he or she can inform the parties to the conflict about their legal rights. For example, if a party to a conflict does not have the right to property under Burundian legislation and is informed about this situation, the party might be more motivated to come to the mediation table and to reach an agreement. In addition, lawyers were required since agreements reached through mediation need to be drafted in such a way that they are respectful of and legally binding according to Burundian legislation.

To assist the lawyers, organizers with social science backgrounds were recruited. Even though ACCORD is not a trauma specialist organization, the nature of some of the cases that were expected to be presented to the organization showed there was still a need for the organization to have the professional capacity to deal with sensitive and emotionally severe cases.

Finally, to ensure the project would function effectively on an administrative and financial level, a finance and administration agent was recruited. Secretaries and drivers also were hired.

Launching of Activities

In 2004, UNHCR and ACCORD established the project in two cities in the provinces of Bururi and Ruyigi. The Bururi Province was facing a large number of complex land disputes largely due to the return of people who left during the crisis of 1972. The Ruyigi Province received the highest number of returnees, most of whom had left the country in 1993 (El Abdellaoui 2005).[11]

The project originally commenced with sessions that introduced ACCORD to the communities and local authorities, but in addition served as information gathering exercises about the types of conflicts that were occurring at the time in the respective communities. These sessions also provided ACCORD with valuable insight on how community members and returnees were responding to those conflicts. Based on the information gathered, it was concluded that local capacity to deal with these disputes was limited and that there was indeed a need for the mediation services that ACCORD could offer. That said, there was a need to work alongside local administrative authorities, as well as traditional mechanisms to recognize the importance of such institutions (Dexter and Ntahombaye 2005).

One such traditional mechanism in Burundi is the *Bashingantahe* institution. Traditionally this institution consisted of an organized group of men (Hutu and Tutsi) considered to be 'wise men' with a sense of truth, justice and responsibility for the overall good (Nindorera 1998). The most important role of the *Bashingantahe* was the peaceful resolution of disputes as well as reconciliation

[11] This is still the situation today in these two provinces.

within communities. However, as a result of colonialism and the political, social and economic crises, the credibility of this institution was weakened. This resulted in communities doubting the *Bashingantahe* as not always being an effective conflict mitigation mechanism (El Abdellaoui 2005). There was therefore a need to build the capacity and credibility of this institution and ACCORD included the *Bashingantahe* in its capacity-building workshops in conflict management and legal matters.

In addition to confirming the need for the mediation services that ACCORD could offer, the original information gathering sessions also highlighted the need for building the capacity of community leaders and local administrative authorities to manage conflict and deal with legal matters such as human rights, family law and land law. Most cases of conflict recorded during the original information gathering sessions were in relation to one of those three laws. Moreover, communities also needed more capacity in conflict management to prevent disputes from escalating into violent conflict and to provide them with the necessary skills to mediate conflicts themselves should the need arise. This would ensure local ownership and sustainability.

A lack of reconciliation between some returnees, especially those who found their properties occupied, and receiving communities were also noted. With this in mind the mediation services provided by ACCORD were expected to promote reconciliation within communities. It was also decided to use the capacity-building workshops as opportunities for the different groups to speak to each other in order to develop an understanding of the experiences and sufferings of other groups. Once again, the aim was to promote reconciliation. Since not all cases would have been appropriate for mediation, there was a need to provide potential beneficiaries with legal advice regarding, for example, individual's rights or legal procedures. With this in mind, the project started with sensitization, listening and mediation missions, and by providing community members and returnees with legal assistance. Thereafter the project expanded its activities to include capacity-building workshops for community leaders and local administrative authorities. Conducting missions first, before commencing with capacity-building workshops, provided ACCORD with the opportunity to further gather information regarding the challenges faced by returnees and receiving communities. This information assisted in focusing the capacity-building workshops to meet the specific needs of communities.

The Protection of Returnees Through Legal Assistance and Representation

In order not to undermine traditional and governmental structures in communities, ACCORD's policy is to first consult with the local administrative authorities of the relevant province, communes and collines before entering into a new community. Once a common understanding has been established between ACCORD and the relevant local administrative authorities, ACCORD will then commence with sensitization, listening and mediation missions in the relevant collines.

Sensitization and Listening Missions

These missions are undertaken almost daily in collines and returnee transit camps. During the original information gathering sessions and following consultations with UNHCR and other stakeholders, it was determined that the greatest challenges experienced by returnees and hosting communities lie at this level. Consequently, in order to ensure maximum impact, these missions are conducted at a community-based level, rather than a provincial or national level.

More specifically, the Ruyigi office conducts missions in the collines of seven communes in three provinces and in the transit camp of Nyabitare. The Rutana office conducts missions in the collines of three communes, all in Rutana Province. The Makamba office conducts missions in the collines of two communes in one province and the transit camp of Mabanda. Finally, the Rumonge office conducts missions in the collines of a commune in one province.

Sensitization missions are used to familiarize the population with ACCORD as an organization, its objectives and the services offered by the project. Once sensitization missions are successfully concluded, listening missions follow. During listening missions, cases are registered. The project then determines which cases should be oriented to judicial institutions, administrative authorities or our partner organization, *Advocates Sans Frontières* (ASF, Attorneys Without Borders),[12] and which cases are appropriate for mediation.

Legal Assistance and Sounding Boards

In cases that are not appropriate for mediation, ACCORD's experience has proven that it remains useful in the case of emotionally-loaded cases to allow individuals to share their challenges with the project staff rather than expressing themselves through other possibly more violent means at a later stage. Consequently, the listening missions also serve as *sounding boards* for beneficiaries. Cases not considered to be appropriate for mediation include the following, but are not limited to those cases:

- Already submitted to or already tried by judicial institutions;
- About murder and other serious crimes;
- Regarding human rights violations, including physical abuse and sexual violence; and
- Involving local administration or public companies.

[12] ASF is a Belgium non-governmental organization that works in the field of justice.

Depending on the nature of the case, the location of the case,[13] and the willingness of the beneficiary, ACCORD will either refer the case to judicial institutions, administrative authorities, or to our partnership organization, ASF.

If cases are oriented to judicial institutions or administrative authorities, the beneficiary will first receive legal advice from ACCORD to ensure s/he is aware of his/her rights under Burundian legislation and understands the legal procedures in place. The project staff also can provide legal assistance by assisting beneficiaries in the preparation of documents to be submitted to judicial authorities. Alternatively, if considered appropriate and with the consent of the beneficiary, ACCORD will refer cases to *Advocates Sans Frontières* (ASF) as ASF can provide legal representation in courts.[14]

In 2006, ACCORD and ASF signed a partnership agreement. During the first five years of the partnership, the ACCORD Rumonge Legal Aid Clinic submitted 461 cases to the ASF office of which a total of 382 received legal assistance in the form of legal advice, while 64 cases received legal representation. This partnership ensures the protection of returnees, as well as a continuation of the services provided by the project.

Resolving Conflicts Through Mediation on a Community Level (Intervention)

Benefits of Mediation

The project works alongside the Burundi legal system, rather than against it. As a result of the numerous crises in Burundi, the legal system has been severely weakened which tends to result in legal institutions being overwhelmed with cases. Consequently, cases may only appear in court months after being filed, intensifying the frustrations of the conflicting parties. The period between the submission of the case and the time when the case appears in court is of extreme importance since this is when tensions are likely to escalate. The mediation services offered by the project tend to be less time consuming and more easily accessible to beneficiaries. The ACCORD legal aid clinics are mobile whereas the courts are centered around developed areas which are not always accessible for vulnerable groups in rural areas, including returnees, who are often unable to afford the travel. In addition, the mediation services offered by the project are free of charge whereas judicial institutions do not have the capacity to provide services for free (Dexter and Ntahombaye 2005).

[13]At the time of writing the ACCORD – ASF partnership covered the provinces of Bururi and Makamba only. Discussions to expand this partnership to the other provinces have been initiated.

[14]ACCORD can only provide beneficiaries with mediation services and legal assistance (legal advice).

The project aims to offer an alternative conflict mitigation mechanism for vulnerable groups. This ensures that justice is done, but also promotes the peaceful cohabitation of parties to the conflict, since parties reach their own agreement avoiding a win-lose situation. If the mediation is successful, it tends to result in the promotion of reconciliation between the parties and assists in building relationships.

That said, when a case is considered to be appropriate for mediation, the party who submitted the case is firstly informed regarding the different processes available to him or her for resolving the case. These processes are: judicial, administrative authority, negotiation and mediation. Beneficiaries are presented with a summary of each process. In terms of mediation, it is explained to the beneficiary that the project would aim to bring the various parties to the conflict together to dialogue with each other and to find their own solution. Very importantly, this solution will not be imposed on them. It is also made clear to beneficiaries that the selection of a process to resolve their conflict is their own decision. In most cases, however, beneficiaries tend to select mediation based on the advantages discussed above. The relevant case will then be assigned to a team.

Methodology of Mediation

Once a case has been assigned to an ACCORD team, the team will consult with the claimant and then will draft an invitation for the other party, inviting him or her to take part in the mediation. If the other party agrees, the mediation will commence.[15] The majority of mediations take place in towns in the various collines that the project works in which means the project staff travels to the towns to meet with beneficiaries. The specific location depends on what is made available by community leaders, but, in general, can include schools, community centers, empty buildings or even under trees. The mediation process has four stages:

Stage 1: Preparation

Preparing for the mediation includes gathering as much information as possible about the parties, learning about the dynamics and substance of the conflict and then conducting an analysis of the conflict. In addition, logistical arrangements need to be made in terms of the location and physical set-up of the first meeting (ACCORD 2002).

Stage 2: Opening the Negotiation

At the first meeting, with all parties to the conflict in attendance, the mediator will make an opening statement explaining the basic principles underlying his/her role in the process, outlining the process to be followed and covering the basic ground rules and behavioral guidelines. Other issues to be clarified will include, for example, the principle of confidentiality. The parties will then have an opportunity to make opening statements explaining their perspectives on the

[15]This points to the importance of the willingness of the parties to come to the mediation table.

history of the conflict and the need to find a resolution, as well as to define and explain other issues they consider important for the conflict to be resolved. The mediator can assist the parties in defining topic areas and issues for discussion (ACCORD 2002).

Stage 3: The Negotiation Proper

The mediator will develop a general strategy and problem-solving approach that will encourage parties to see the problem as one that they share in common. The mediator also will help the parties see that it is important that they contribute to the problem's solution. The parties will then work together to develop an agenda to systematically deal with the issues to be addressed. For each issue a specific strategy should be designed. It is important to note that the mediator should assist parties to focus more on their interests rather than their positions. The problem-solving process then includes the following steps:

- Joint acknowledgement of the problem;
- Defining and analyzing the problem;
- Jointly generating possible solutions and options; and
- Evaluating the options and selecting the most satisfactory one (ACCORD 2002).

Stage 4: Agreement and Closure

At this stage an agreement will be reached between the parties. Once an agreement has been reached, the final stage of the mediation should generate an implementation plan, including procedural steps (and a monitoring plan if they so wish). Also, parties will write down their agreements and sign them to make them legally binding. The formal written agreement contains the substantive settlement and a sense of procedural and psychological closure (ACCORD 2002).

The Nature of Mediated Cases in Burundi

More than 80 % of cases dealt with by the ACCORD legal aid clinics concern land. Depending on the parties to the dispute, the following vulnerable groups generally experience challenges in reclaiming their land:

- Female heads of returnee households often experience challenges recovering land previously owned by their family due to traditional social views regarding women and administrative difficulties (UNHCR–WFP 2007) since there is a lack of inheritance rights for women;
- Those who left Burundi in 1972 given that their land was often expropriated and redistributed. Even though the Arusha Agreement states that all refugees must be able to recover their property, especially land, the Burundi Land Code of 1986 states that if land is owned by someone for longer than 30 years, then that person becomes the legal owner of the land (République du Burundi 1986). Since many people who left in 1972 only returned to Burundi after 30 years, they have lost the right to reclaim their land; and

- Refugees (now returnees) of 1993 whose land also was expropriated and re-distributed or occupied during their absence. These cases tend to be less complicated than those involving returnees from 1972 (Kamungi et al. 2004). However, they are still numerous and of importance.

ACCORD's experience on the ground has indicated that in the provinces of Bururi, Makamba, and Rutana, most conflicts relate to land, but, more specifically, relate to land and other properties of refugees who left the country in 1972. Recorded cases in these provinces mostly include the following parties to the conflict:

- Refugees who left Burundi in 1972 and local administration; and
- Returnees and the new occupants of their land or property, which normally tends to be former neighbours or family members.

Concerning the first category, without following the legal procedures in terms of the expropriation of land for public use, local administration often took land and redistributed it to other persons, or utilized the land for public projects. Examples include the Rumonge Palm Oil Company, and the construction of military camps in Nyanza-Lac and Rumonge Communes. In these instances, land that was previously privately-owned was used for public projects without following the legal procedures. This is often the result of unclear policies and/or government officials not being informed properly on the relevant policies in place. These and similar cases are referred to either judicial institutions or administrative authorities with legal assistance from ACCORD or ASF.

Mediation of Land Conflict Mr. Juma Gahungu* left Burundi during the 1993 crisis and settled down in a refugee camp in Tanzania, called Mutabira. In the camp he met his wife, Immaculate, and soon they had two sons. In 2008, the family moved to Mr. Gahungu's hometown in Burundi, Kinyinya in the Ruyigi Province. When Mr. Gahungu fled Burundi in 1993, he left behind his land. Upon his return, he found his land occupied by his neighbour, Mr. Pamphile Kanyange. Mr. Kanyange refused to return the land to Mr. Gahungu, but Mr. Gahungu felt that he needed to get his land back in order to secure a future for his two sons and, accordingly, started asking others in his community for options as to how he could claim his land. During an ACCORD sensitization mission he heard about mediation as an option and decided to try it. Mr. Kanyange agreed to participate. During the mediation Mr. Kanyange explained that when Mr. Gahungu left Burundi he still owed Mr. Kanyange 30,000 Fbu and accordingly he took his land. The mediation was successfully concluded with an agreement that Mr. Gahungu will reimburse Mr. Kanyange the 30,000Fbu and pay an additional 5000 Fbu as interest. Following the mediation, Mr. Gahungu and Mr. Kanyange became friends again. Mr. Kanyange helped Mr. Gahungu to build a house on his reclaimed land, and they even testified to their new relationship during an ACCORD training.
*Please note all the names presented in this example are pseudonyms.

Concerning the second category, land or properties of refugees were often sold or occupied during their absence by either neighbors or family members. In order to resolve these cases, mediation is attempted and most of the time does indeed succeed.

In the provinces of Ruyigi and Gitega most land conflicts stem from the more recent 1993 refugee flow, rendering them significantly easier to resolve. Cases in these provinces most frequently include the refugees and new occupants of their land or property, which normally tends to be former neighbors or family members.

In the majority of cases, neighbors of the refugees' properties changed the boundaries of the relevant properties. These cases are mostly submitted to mediation and tend to succeed. However, Ruyigi and Gitega Provinces also experience cases concerning the violation of family law. Examples include situations where refugees return with a new spouse or family after being separated from their original spouse and family. In these cases, there tends to be conflict between the original family and the new family, with regard to inheritance rights and the issue of divorce.[16]

Number of Successful Mediations

Cases submitted to mediation are, in most cases, resolved. Since the establishment of the project, the staff has successfully concluded 1,220 mediations. In summary, allowing returnees and members of the various communities to use mediation as a mechanism for conflict transformation, as well as to reach their own agreement versus a judgment being passed, tends to assist not only in the reintegration of returnees in communities, but also result in the promotion of reconciliation within communities.

Building Local Capacity for Constructively Managing Conflict: Analyzing What Has Been Accomplished

In addition to the mediation services offered by the project, the project also conducts capacity building workshops in conflict management, reconciliation and legal matters for the benefit of community leaders who represent the following groups: women, youth, media, religious, returnees, Internally Displaced Persons (IDPs), demobilized combatants, *Bashintangtahe*, local administrative authorities, and others.

[16] According to Burundian family law, a man can only have one wife, meaning unless he is divorced from his original wife, he cannot marry a second.

The aim of the capacity-building workshops in conflict management and reconciliation is twofold. First, to improve the ability of community leaders and local administrative authorities to identify disputes, assess the situations and design appropriate responses before disputes develop into violent conflict. Second, as a result of the civil war, issues regarding land conflict, violations of human rights and the separation of family members have became very prominent concerns in local communities. This situation poses extreme challenges when communities and local administrative authorities are not informed about how to deal with such issues, especially within the legal system. Accordingly, the project also conducts workshops in legal matters such as land law, family law and human rights law to build the capacity of community leaders and local administrative authorities to function effectively within the legal system, when needed, and to promote appreciation of and respect for Burundian law. When local communities have capacity to deal with conflicts themselves, the result is the sustainable prevention and non-violent transformation of conflicts (El Abdellaoui 2005).

Methodology of Capacity Building Workshops

The capacity-building workshops in conflict management and reconciliation are each three days long and consist of various conflict management and reconciliation modules that are based on ACCORD's experience. The three-day workshops on legal matters basically contain legal modules based on Burundian law. The workshops are conducted in Kirundi, the general language spoken in communities. The training methodology used is participatory and consists of lecturers, case studies and role-play exercises. ACCORD's training experience indicates that applied participatory learning methods are the most effective.

Confidence Building in Communities

In addition to building the capacity of community leaders and local administrative authorities, the workshops serve as confidence-building initiatives within communities. There are often two groups in communities: (1) those who fled the country and (2) those who stayed behind. In order to reconcile these groups, dialogue is necessary to generate an understanding of each other's experiences, trauma and grievances. Through interaction with each other in a 'neutral environment,' participants often realize that they have more in common than they thought. ACCORD's experience shows that it is more effective to bring groups together under the banner of a workshop, than under the banner of a dialogue session, during which people may feel forced to discuss certain issues. During the workshops, participants are then given opportunities to interact with each other and to share their experiences with one another. This tends to promote understanding and reconciliation.

Number of Workshops

In the five years since the establishment of the project in November 2004, the project staff conducted 204 workshops in conflict management and/or legal matters for 4,958 community leaders and local administrative authorities. This figure also includes training sessions organized following requests for training for staff of other conflict management or related NGOs that work at a community level.

Measuring the Impact and Value of the ACCORD Legal Aid Clinic Project

In order to evaluate the impact of the project, ACCORD undertook a series of assessments in 2007 and 2009. The first aim of these initiatives was to determine whether trainees have actually used the skills and knowledge acquired during the workshops. The second aim was to determine the real impact of the mediation work ACCORD has done in communities. These assessments consisted of informal interviews conducted by project staff, followed by 160 formal interviews conducted by two ACCORD Burundi Intervention interns in 2007 and 80 formal interviews conducted by an ACCORD Burundi intern in 2009. Among others, the following stakeholders were interviewed: beneficiaries of capacity-building workshops, other community leaders and local administrative authorities, beneficiaries of mediation services, other community members and returnees, judicial authorities, and representatives of partner organizations. Whereas the first sets of interviews were done informally, the second sets of 160 and then 80 interviews were done formally with a structured questionnaire that allowed for quantitative analyses. The assessments indicate that the project is having an impact. The outcomes can be summarized as follows:

Capacity Building Workshops in Conflict Management

The assessments showed the following impacts:

- In more than 660 cases, trainees who attended conflict management capacity-building workshops successfully mediated cases without the assistance of ACCORD staff. This shows that the capacity-building work conducted by the project at the community level is indeed sustainable and promotes local ownership;

Mediation Successfully Conducted by Trainee Mr. Claude Minani* fled Burundi in 1972 with his two sons and one daughter. They settled in Mutabira refugee camp in Tanzania. Mr. Minani passed away in 1986. In 2008, his children returned to Burundi and found part of their family's land occupied by the government (for public use). The sons shared the remaining part, by themselves, leaving their sister, Sara, with nothing. Ms. Minani decided to request assistance from a local administrative authority, Mr. Joseph Niyongere, who had been trained by ACCORD. Mr. Niyongere proposed mediation as a process to resolve the dispute. Ms. Minani and her brothers agreed, and the mediation process started. During the mediation process, Mr. Niyongere informed the brothers that according to Burundian law, their sister also has a right to the land inherited from their father as long as she did not get married. In the end, they agreed to share the land with their sister. During discussions with Mr. Niyongere, he indicated that before attending the ACCORD training sessions, he was not familiar with mediation as a means to resolving conflict. In addition, he also was not aware of women's inheritance rights. Accordingly, if he mediated the case before attending the training sessions he would not have been able to inform the parties to the conflict about Ms. Minani's rights.
*Please note all the names presented in this example are pseudonyms.

- These cases also show that capacity-building workshops have contributed to a culture of dialogue and reconciliation, since trainees applied the conflict management skills acquired.

Capacity-Building Workshops in Legal Matters

The assessments showed the following impacts:

- There is a decrease in cases being submitted to judicial institutions involving local administrative authorities. According to judicial authorities, the capacity-building workshops being conducted by the project provide local administrative authorities with required knowledge regarding Burundian legislation to ensure they respect the laws and act accordingly[17];
- By providing community leaders with knowledge about Burundian legislation, they are able to advise returnees and vulnerable groups, which, in turn, assists in the protection of the rights of these groups.

[17]Note that according to Burundian legal procedures, these cases should, in fact, have been submitted to administrative courts, but, due to various reasons including a lack of information, the population tends to submit cases to communal tribunals. This explains why the information was gathered from judicial authorities.

Mediation Sessions

Successful mediation initiatives showed the following:

- Returnees and community members are being reconciled as a result of reaching a mutually-acceptable agreement based on their own terms. These agreements are easier to implement than judgments passed by the courts; in addition, the participants build sustainable relationships;
- There is a successful reintegration of returnees into communities, since many returnees managed to reclaim their properties that were occupied during their absence, or at least come to an acceptable agreement regarding the relevant property;
- Fewer cases are submitted to judicial institutions. This is a positive development, especially because the legal system in Burundi has been weakened by the civil war. Assisting the government in dealing with cases reduces the strain on the limited resources; and
- The caseload of the National Commission for Land and Other Properties (CNTB) decreased due to the number of cases successfully resolved by the project, especially in relation to land and other properties. Considering the limited resources available to this administrative commission as well as the vast number of cases it is expected to face, this is a significant impact.

Partnership Between ACCORD and ASF

This partnership has contributed to the protection of returnees and other vulnerable groups as they are provided legal representation that they otherwise would not have been able to afford. Moreover, the ASF's advice to beneficiaries informs them of their rights, once again assisting in the protection of the returnees and other vulnerable groups.

Based on the 2007 and 2009 impact assessments, the project is having an impact on the community level in Burundi, not only by providing mediation services to vulnerable groups, but also by building sustainable capacity in conflict management and legal matters. The project will continue to monitor the impact of its activities and, should the need arise, adjust its focus.

Limitations and Challenges Facing ACCORD's Legal Aid Clinic Project

The Legal Aid Clinic Project dealt with various challenges and limitations in implementing its activities. In terms of logistical challenges, it is necessary to keep in mind that Burundi is a post-conflict country and certain areas of the country are still developing. There is limited access, for example, to internet facilities, phone services, tarred roads and other infrastructure. Consequently, a substantial amount of time is taken up by logistical aspects such as traveling to communities and/or finding internet access to relay reports.

In addition, like other NGOs, funding constraints limit the number of activities that can be undertaken, which limits the overall impact of the project. In Burundi, for example, we have found that due to the complexity and the number of land conflicts aggravated by high population density, the demand for services offered by the project is far greater than what the project can offer. The project, therefore, in collaboration with its partner organisation, UNHCR, uses information gathering missions to determine which areas have the greatest demand and, accordingly, should receive assistance first.

When looking at the environment in which the project operates, one notes a variety of factors that could be considered challenges. These are largely the result of the civil war and include, for example, the issue of illiteracy. Community leaders and local administrative authorities who take part in the project's training sessions are sometimes not literate. This makes it challenging for them to access training notes and to consult Burundian legislation. Moreover, even though the general language spoken in Burundi is Kirundi, in provinces like Bururi and Makamba, the first language of some of the returnees who were born in exile in Tanzania is Swahili. Cases involving Swahili-speaking returnees have to wait until an ACCORD lawyer and an organizer who are fluent in Swahili are available.

Also, the cycle of violence that has plagued the country since independence keeps on repeating itself. The current situation in Burundi, therefore, requires a renewed commitment to the people of Burundi to assist them in breaking this cycle and to build a culture of dialogue and reconciliation. Breaking a cycle of violence and promoting a culture of dialogue and reconciliation is a time-consuming process that could take generations.

Finally, for ACCORD to operate as an impartial, neutral organization, it is important to limit its activities to those that follow these principles. For example, even though there might be great demand for legal representation for vulnerable groups in Burundi, it is important to ACCORD to limit its activities to those of mediation, legal assistance and capacity-building workshops. Providing legal representation means choosing a side and that could compromise ACCORD's principles of impartiality and neutrality. As a result, the trust of local communities may erode. ACCORD does not want to do anything that would adversely affect its work to help local communities resolve disputes peacefully through mediation. This remains a challenge, however, as various requests are received from communities and funding institutions to provide legal representation to vulnerable groups.

Conclusion: Lessons Learned

There are four main lessons learned by ACCORD in terms of capacity-building in conflict management at a community level in Burundi, a developing, post-conflict country. These lessons are:

The Importance of Including All Stakeholders

It is important to provide assistance to both returnees and their welcoming communities. This is crucial in order to prevent a situation where returnees are perceived to be more privileged than the receiving communities. Aggrieved receiving communities do not create a conducive environment for successful community reintegration or reconciliation. It is, therefore, crucial to recognize the challenges welcoming communities face and to provide them with required assistance, especially since the reintegration of returnees is likely to affect them.

The concept of including all stakeholders stretches further than this example. As per the discussion regarding the Arusha negotiations, one of the requirements for a negotiation or mediation to be successful and have a sustainable outcome is the inclusion of all stakeholders. On a community level, it is of the utmost importance to ensure that all possible stakeholders are included when mediation is undertaken. This greatly assists in ensuring that the agreement reached is implementable and sustainable. Since all parties are included, the risk of the original dispute arising again is reduced because the interests of all parties have been taken into consideration during the mediation process.

The Importance of Local Ownership and Respect for Traditional and Government Institutions

Throughout its involvement in Burundi, ACCORD has been working closely with local Burundian structures, both at a governmental and non-governmental level. This ensures that the process of contributing to peace in Burundi becomes a joint initiative between ACCORD and local organizations in the country and thus promotes greater local ownership. On the community level, ACCORD respects local administrative authorities and traditional institutions such as the *Bashingantahe.* It is necessary to formally recognize the importance of such institutions, provide them with capacity-building opportunities and assist them to play their roles in society, rather than working in a parallel and isolated way. By building the capacity of local institutions, the local entities are able to function more effectively and are encouraged to take greater ownership of community problems.

The Importance of Building Sustainable Local Capacity

The composition of the ACCORD Burundi staff reflects the organization's focus on local ownership and building sustainable local capacity. In 2010, for instance, ACCORD employed 48 staff members in Burundi of which one is a Sierra Leonean and 47 are Burundian nationals. The staff members are provided with capacity-building opportunities on an annual basis. ACCORD prioritizes capacity-building for staff and other stakeholders with the aim that stakeholders will internalize the skills and contribute towards sustainable peace in the country. One way of ensuring this is to also provide stakeholders with follow-up capacity-building workshops to enhance their skills and discuss potential challenges they might have faced in applying the skills previously provided.

The Applicability of Lessons Learned from the Case of Burundi to Other Settings

The case of Burundi and the environment in which the project operates may be unique in many ways. Consequently, lessons learned from this case study might not necessarily be applicable to all settings. Unique elements include:

- The size of the country, if relatively small, will accelerate the process of building a culture of dialogue. This allows for a unique social fabric. In Burundi, communities in general are small and the environment is one in which "everybody knows everyone." This assists in the interaction with communities, as well as in conducting mediation sessions when searching for testimonies, for example. Word also travels fast. This helps to build a culture of dialogue since the successes of using mediation as a tool for resolving conflicts are discussed and confidence builds that way. Therefore, in other countries, such as the Democratic Republic of the Congo (DRC) which occupies a much larger geographical space, the resulting social dynamics will be very different (UN Statistics Division 2010).
- The majority of land-conflict cases in Burundi involve returnees and members of welcoming communities. In applying lessons learned from this case study in dealing with land conflict, it would be important to ensure the nature of the land conflict is appropriate for mediation. In some parts of North Sudan, South Sudan and Nigeria, for example, differences between pastoralists and agriculturalist continue to fuel land conflict (Kok et al. 2009; Ploughshares 2009). Mediation may or may not be an appropriate means for resolving these conflicts, but the dynamics of such land conflicts need to be considered before attempting mediation;
- Land in Burundi is mainly used for agriculture and livestock and, therefore, directly relates to people's ability to make a living. In the DRC and Nigeria, for example, the situation is more complex, as land, in addition to agriculture and

raising of livestock, is also used to satisfy economic interests (making a profit) through mining and oil production respectively (Kok et al. 2009; ICG 2008). This brings new elements to the land conflicts that should be taken into consideration when deciding whether mediation should be attempted;

- The strength and effectiveness of the legal system and legislation in the relevant country are critical. This together with the economic, social and political history could determine, for example, whether there is a need for training in legal matters. The history of the country also will determine whether issues such as human rights violations, family law and so on are relevant to the current situation;
- Burundi is in a post-conflict stage following decades of repetitive cycles of violence, whereas other countries could still be experiencing elements of violent conflict. Again, North Sudan, South Sudan and Nigeria are good cases in point.

References

Africa Centre for the Constructive Resolution of Disputes (ACCORD). (2002). *Transforming conflict: Seeking Africa solutions to Africa challenges through a participatory learning process – reference manual* (pp. 91–109). Durban: ACCORD.

African Centre for the Constructive Resolution of Disputes (ACCORD). (2010). *ACCORD homepage*. www.accord.org.za. Retrieved 30 Jan 2010.

All, P., Miltenberger, Lt. Col. D., & Weiss, T. G. (2003). *Guide to IGOs, NGOs and the military in peace and relief operations* (pp. 85–167). Washington, DC: United States Institute of Peace Press.

Arusha Peace and Reconciliation Agreement. (2000a). *Protocol I: Nature of the Burundi conflict, problems of genocide and exclusion and their solutions* (pp. 17–23), Chapter II, Article 6 and 8.

Arusha Peace and Reconciliation Agreement. (2000b). *Protocol IV: Reconstruction and development* (pp. 77–86), Chapter I, Article 1.1 and 8.k.

Bentley, K. A., & Southall, R. (2005). *An African peace process: Mandela, South Africa and Burundi*. Cape Town: Human Science Research Council.

Department of Foreign Affairs (DFA), South Africa. (2006). *President Thabo Mbeki appoints minister Charles Nqakula as facilitator for Burundi peace process*. Media statement.

Dexter, T., & Ntahombaye, P. (2005). *The role of informal justice systems in fostering the rule of law in post-conflict situations: The case of Burundi* (pp. 6–21). Geneva: Centre for Humanitarian Dialogue. http://www.hdcentre.org/publications/role-informal-justice-systems-fostering-rule-law-post-conflict-situations-case-burundi. Retrieved 30 Jan 2008.

Eggers, E. (1997). *Historical dictionary of Burundi*. London: The Scarecrow Press, Inc.

El Abdellaoui, J. (2005). Repatriation, reintegration and reconciliation: The case of Burundi. *Conflict Trends Magazine, 2002*(3), 45–47. Washington, DC: United States Institute of Peace Library.

Gahama, J., et al. (1999). Burundi. In A. Adedeji (Ed.), *Comprehending and mastering African conflict. The search for sustainable peace and good governance* (pp. 80–103). London/New York: Zed Books.

Hatungimana, A., Theron, J., & Popic, A. (2007). Peace agreements in Burundi: Assessing the impact. *Conflict Trends Magazine, 2007*(3), 19–20.

Institute for Security Studies (ISS) Resource Centre. (2009). *Bujumbura declaration.* http://www.iss.co.za/dynamic/administration/file_manager/file_links/BUJUMBURADECJAN09.PDF?link_id=29&slink_id=7186&link_type=12&slink_type=13&tmpl_id=3. Retrieved 23 Mar 2009.
International Crisis Group (ICG). (2003). Refugees and displaced person in Burundi – defusing the land time-bomb. Africa report no. 70.
International Crisis Group (ICG). (2008). Nigeria: Ogoni land after shell. Africa briefing no. 54.
Kamungi, P. M., Oketch, J. S., & Huggins, C. (2004). Land access and refugee repatriation: The case of Burundi. *Eco-Conflicts, 3*(2).
Kok, A., Lotze, W., & Van Jaarsveld, S. (2009). *Natural resources, the environment and conflict.* South Africa: Fishwicks. p. 27, 37.
Montville, J. (1982). In J. Hottinger (Ed.) (2005), *The relationship between track one and track two diplomacy.* http://www.c-r.org/our-work/accord/engaging-groups/trackone-tracktwo.php. Retrieved 5 May 2010.
Ndikumana, L. (2005). Distributional conflict, the state, and peacebuilding in Burundi, research paper no. 2005/45, United Nations University World Institute for Development Economic Research (UNU-WIDER), p. 5.
Nindorera, L. M. (1998). Keepers of peace: Reviving the tradition of *bashingantahe* in Burundi. *Online Journal of Peace and Conflict Resolution 1.4.* http://www.trinstitute.org/ojpcr/tracktwo3.htm. Retrieved 30 Jan 2008.
Oketch, J. S., & Polzer, T. (2002). Conflict and coffee in Burundi. In J. Lind & K. Sturman (Eds.), *Scarcity and surfeit: The ecology of Africa's conflicts* (pp. 85–156). Pretoria: Institute for Security Studies.
Ould-Abdallah, A. (2000). *Burundi on the brink: 1993–1995* (p. 35). Washington, DC: United States Institute of Peace.
Ploughshares. (2009). *Armed conflicts report: Nigeria.* http://www.ploughshares.ca/libraries/ACRText/ACR-Nigeria.html. Retrieved 27 Jan 2010.
Rẻpublique du Burundi. (1986). *Loi Portant Code Froncier du Burundi,* Chapter I, Section I, Article 29.
UNHCR–WFP. (2007). Report of the joint assessment mission of Burundian returnees: 7–11 May 2007, pp. 9–16.
United Nations (UN) Statistics Division. (2010). *UN data – A world of information.* http://data.un.org/. Retrieved 27 Jan 2010.
United Nations Department of Public Information. (1996). *The United Nations system-wide special initiative on Africa document.* p. 22.
United Nations High Commission for Refugees (UNHCR) Burundi. (2009). *UNHCR Burundi fact sheet.* Bujumbura: UNHCR.
United Nations Security Council (UNSC). (2009). Fifth report of the secretary-general on the United Nations Integrated Office in Burundi, S/2009/.270. http://www.un.org/Docs/sc/sgrep09.htm. Retrieved 21 Jan 2010.

Chapter 13
UN Security Council Resolution 1325, Inclusive Peacebuilding and Countries in Transition

Jan Marie Fritz

When countries experience a wave of dramatic social-economic-political change, particularly after long periods of authoritarian rule,[1] few in those nations have as much reason to be optimistic and fearful as the women and girls who endured years of difficult times, have taken part in movements for change (e.g., Wright 2011; Woodrow Wilson Center Middle East 2012; Barnard 2011) and have real chances to see dramatic improvement in their lives in terms of safety, health, education, and inclusion. In countries emerging from authoritarian regimes, the new policymakers, their advisers, citizens, and interested civil society organizations (local, national, regional and international) can learn from countries that have succeeded in having women and girls centrally included, at least in some ways, in their societies.

This chapter focuses on the mandates of United Nations Security Council Resolution (UNSCR) 1325 (Women and Peace and Security) to include women in peacebuilding efforts – with particular interest here in women who are in decision-making, peacekeeping and peacemaking roles – in countries that have gone through or are going through big transitions. The UN Resolution (UNSCR 1325 2000, p. 2) "urges Member States to ensure increased representation of women (in) all... mechanisms for the prevention, management, and resolution of conflict" and at all decision-making levels (national, regional and international).

[1]Authoritarian regimes (Economist Intelligence Unit 2011, p. 30) are in countries in which "state political pluralism is absent of heavily circumscribed. Many countries in this category are outright dictatorships." In these circumstances, usually media is controlled, criticism of the government is repressed, the judiciary is not independent and civil liberties are not respected.

J.M. Fritz (✉)
Professor, University of Cincinnati, USA and Senior Research Fellow, Centre for Sociological Research, University of Johannesburg, South Africa
e-mail: jan.fritz@uc.edu

J.M. Fritz (ed.), *Moving Toward a Just Peace: The Mediation Continuum*,
Clinical Sociology: Research and Practice, DOI 10.1007/978-94-007-2885-1_13,

After inclusive peacebuilding is defined, there is an explanation of UNSCR 1325 and its mandates regarding peacebuilding. This is followed by a discussion of some of the barriers women face in their societies, information about peacebuilding efforts in selected countries and a list of ideas to foster gender justice.

Inclusive Peacebuilding

The term *peacebuilding* first appeared in Johan Galtung's 1976 essay "Three Approaches to Peace: Peacekeeping, Peacemaking and Peacebuilding." According to Tschirgi (2011), the concept "was embraced by peace studies and practitioners of conflict transformation, (but) it only gained widespread usage at the end of the Cold War with the release of the UN Secretary-General Boutros Boutros-Ghali's landmark report *An Agenda for Peace* (1992)."

As with many of the concepts discussed in this book (e.g., cultural competency, creativity), peacebuilding has a number of definitions (see International Association for Humanitarian Policy and Conflict Research 2007–2008; Etchart and Baksh 2005, pp. 29–32). For instance, Fisher et al. (2000, pp. 13–14), based on UN approaches, noted there are different kinds of intervention that can result in peace. In addition to humanitarian aid/emergency assistance (providing immediate means for survival), Fisher and his colleagues indicated there are three main categories:

> *Peace-making*: interventions designed to end hostilities and bring about an agreement using diplomatic, political and military means.
>
> *Peace-keeping:* monitoring and enforcing an agreement, using force as necessary. This includes verifying whether agreements are being kept and supervising agreed confidence-building activities.
>
> *Peace-building*: undertaking programmes designed to address the causes of conflict and the grievances of the past and to promote long-term stability and justice . . . Peace-building is not primarily concerned with conflict behaviour but addresses the underlying context and attitudes that give rise to violence, such as unequal access to employment, discrimination, unacknowledged and unforgiven responsibility for past crimes, prejudice, mistrust, fear, hostility between groups. It is therefore low-profile work that can, at least in theory, continue through all stages of a conflict . . . . It is likely to be strongest either in later stages after a settlement and a reduction in violent behaviour or in earlier stages before any open violence has occurred.

Michella Maiese (2003) noted that there are two ways to define "peacebuilding." The first is tied to the United Nations definition (Boutros-Ghali 1992), as mentioned above, and links peacebuilding to a wide range of activities such as capacity building, reconciliation and societal transformation. This definition of peacebuilding, according to Maiese, refers to a "long-term process that occurs after violent conflict has slowed down or come to a halt" and peacebuilding takes place after peacemaking and peacekeeping.

But Maiese (2003) also mentioned a second definition. Both Maiese (2003) and Ouellet (2003) noted that some non-governmental organizations (NGOs) prefer peacebuilding to be defined in a broader, all-encompassing way. Maiese's (2003) broad definition is as follows:

> Peacebuilding (is) an umbrella concept that encompasses not only long-term transformative efforts, but also peacemaking and peacekeeping. In this view, peacebuilding includes early warning and response efforts, violence prevention, advocacy work, civilian and military peacekeeping, military intervention, humanitarian assistance, ceasefire agreements, and the establishment of peace zones.

This definition of peacebuilding includes the prevention of disputes and conflicts as well as intervention efforts such as mediation.

It should be noted that not only NGOs favor a broad definition. John Paul Lederach (1997, p. 20), for instance, writing in the late 1990s, offered a broad definition of peacebuilding. He indicated that peacebuilding is "more than post-accord reconstruction;" the term "encompasses, generates, and sustains the full array of processes, approaches and stages needed to transform conflict toward more sustainable, peaceful relationships."

A broad definition of peacebuilding is used in this chapter.[2] It is an umbrella concept that emphasizes *inclusiveness* and involves the low-profile work mentioned by Fisher and his colleagues (2000), the post-conflict work emphasized by the UN (Boutros-Ghali 1992), and work at all stages of a country's development[3] in support of a just peace, including the high and low-profile efforts involved, for example, in peacekeeping and peacemaking. *Inclusive peacebuilding* takes into account the underlying structural, relational and cultural roots of conflict in an all-encompassing way (e.g., including women, different ages, different ethnicities) in order to achieve sustainable continuity and/or transformation of people's lives in a particular setting (e.g., community, city, nation, region). Inclusive peacebuilding is "context specific as the issues that concern people in one country or sub-region will be similar to but distinct from those of people in other countries or regions" (Etchart and Baksh 2005, p. 31). It includes approaches such as prevention; promotion of stability and justice; capacity-building; humanitarian assistance; establishment of peace zones; reconciliation; peacekeeping; and informal as well as official peacemaking.

Peacebuilding can occur before, during and after conflict. The word "inclusive" is emphasized here because it sometimes is not seen as an essential part of peacebuilding. For example, certain groups of people (e.g., women, feminist researchers, those focusing on human security) are more likely than others to talk about the importance of gender (the roles of women and men) when discussing peacebuilding. Others may mention it at times as a consideration or not give it any attention at all. One way to make sure that gender is part of any peacebuilding effort is to have the definition of peacebuilding – and its component processes such as peacekeeping and peacemaking – stress inclusivity. By explicitly referring to inclusivity in the name of the term as well as in the definition, it becomes difficult not to remember that for peacebuilding to be effective, it *has* to be inclusive.

---

[2]Sometimes the term "peace operations" is used broadly and "entails the activities of conflict prevention and peacemaking, peacekeeping and peace-building" (Kondoch 2007, p. xiv).

[3]As Lederach (1999, p. 9) noted, "peace is never made; it is always in the making."

While peacebuilding can go on in all societies, the real concern in this chapter is the relation between UNSCR 1325 and inclusive peacebuilding efforts in those countries that are making or have made a transition from authoritarian rule. Gurr et al. (1990, pp. 74–5) noted that several "broad processes have reshaped the global landscape of state structures during the last two centuries." Two of these processes – "the extraordinary expansion in the absolute and relative power of the state" and "the transformation of the structures of political participation and legitimation" are particularly important here.

Recent literature (e.g., Rost and Booth 2008; Donno and Russett 2004; Okeke-Ihejirika and Franceschet 2002; Aoláin 2009) has indicated the following about countries making a transition from authoritarian rule: uncertainty is an important circumstance; the problems of a new government might be overwhelming even if there are good intentions and assistance from international bodies; different groups might have strong and conflicting stands (leading to violence); and cultural differences might hinder the development of national, democratic structures. If one looks specifically at what the literature says about women, one notes that there are different opinions about whether autocratic governments particularly repress women's rights systematically; "accountability and restructuring mechanisms (need to be examined) for biases and exclusions" (Aoláin 2009, p. 2009) in relation to the situation of women and girls; and timing[4] and the ability to have one's message heard are particularly important in meeting the needs of women and girls. Given all this, it is important for policymakers and civil society representatives in the many states undergoing transitions – and those who are assisting them – to learn from the successful experiences in countries that are going through or have experienced these kinds of dramatic transitions.

UN Security Council Resolution 1325 (Women and Peace and Security)

Due, in part, to the lobbying of dozens of women's organizations and UNIFEM (1325 Forum Norge 2008), the concerted efforts of the NGO Working Group on Women, Peace, and Security as well as the work of Ambassador Anwarul Chowdhury,[5] UNSCR 1325 was adopted unanimously on October 31, 2000. The

[4] Aoláin (2009, p. 1058) refers to this as "the transitional moment."

[5] Ambassador Anwarul K. Chowdhury (2010a), the former Under-Secretary-General and High Representative of the United Nations (2001–2007), was President of the Security Council (March 2000) when he issued a presidential statement on behalf of the UN Security Council. The statement "formally brought to global attention the unrecognized, under-utilized and under-valued contribution women have been making to preventing war, to building peace and to engaging individuals and societies (to) live in harmony." With his statement, "the seed for the Security Council resolution 1325 was sown." Chowdhury (2010b) also prepared what he described as a "doable, realistic (and) practical... set of indicators to monitor and measure progress in the implementation of 1325."

resolution, which highlights the terrible consequences of violent conflict on women and girls as well as the important role of women in the peacebuilding processes, is one of the most important UN resolutions within the field of peace and security policy.

A number of important international and regional documents have a bearing on the full participation and advancement of women (e.g., the Beijing Platform passed by the World Conference on Women in Beijing in 1995, States Parties to the Convention on the Elimination of All Forms of Discrimination against Women, Convention on the Rights of the Child, UN Declaration of Human Rights and the UN Charter). UN Security Council Resolution 1325 is particularly important because it **mandates** Member States of the UN to take actions to address the situation of women and girls (Fritz et al. 2011).

There has been a pressing need for Security Council resolutions about women, peace and security. In contemporary conflicts, soldiers are not the most numerous of casualties; instead, according to the UN Secretary-General (2008, p. 2), "millions of women and children continue to account for the majority of casualties in hostilities, often in flagrant violation of human rights and humanitarian laws." Mass displacement, use of children in combat, and violence against ethnic and religious groups, as well as gender-based and sexual violence, are common in certain areas of the world.

Women and girls have been particularly vulnerable to violence. They are often seen as "bearers of cultural identity" and, therefore, become major targets subjected to "rape, forced immigration, forced abortion, trafficking, sexual slavery and the intentional spread of sexually transmitted infections (STIs), including... HIV/AIDS" (UN Secretary-General 2002, p. 2). The Secretary-General's (2009, pp. 2–3) report continues to note that "sexual and gender-based violence remained one of the most pernicious consequences of armed conflict [as a]... weapon of war." The report particularly mentioned the Democratic Republic of Congo (1,100 rapes reported each month with more than 10 % of the child victims being 10 years or younger), Somalia, Burundi, Myanmar, Timor-Leste, Côte d'Ivoire and Chad. The Secretary-General's 2012 report (2012b) on conflict-related sexual violence (covering the period December 2010 to November 2011) focused on Columbia ("sexual violence... was a habitual, extensive, systemic and invisible practice"), Côte d'Ivoire ("increase in rape and gang rape targeting civilians during the recent post-elections crisis"), Democratic Republic of Congo ("mass rapes"), Libya ("women and men were subjected to rape"), Myanmar ("widespread perpetration of rape by Government armed forces in militarized ethnic border areas"), Somalia ("sexual violence including forcing women into marriages and acts of sexual slavery") and eight other countries.

Women and girls are both *victims* of, and *participants* in, armed conflict. O'Neill and Vary (2011, p. 84) wrote the following about women as participants:

> Women fight in virtually every conflict. They engage in combat, operate weapons, spy on enemies, and direct men and women within their command. Their presence is often sparsely acknowledged, however, and their roles are poorly documented. Rates vary, but

> women are thought to account for between 10 and 33 percent of most fighting forces.... Women accounted for between a third and a half of Viet Cong troops. Women also assumed leadership positions...

Wenche Hauge (2011) wrote about women in Guatemala who were former child soldiers with the guerilla movement, the Unidad Revolucionaria Nacional Guatemalteca (URNG). Hauge found that those interviewed had deliberately joined the armed movement.[6] Because the war in Guatemala lasted for such a long period of time (36 years), some of the girls had grown up as soldiers.

In addition to being participants, women can be – and are – *agents of peaceful change*. The participation of women in peacebuilding (including prevention of disputes, peacemaking and peacekeeping) assures that their experiences, priorities, and solutions contribute to stability and inclusive governance. When women are included in national peace negotiations, they can bring the views of women and girls to the discussions, for example "by ensuring that peace accords address demands for gender equality in new constitutional, judicial and electoral structures" (UN Secretary-General 2002, p. 3).

UNSCR 1325 covers a lot of ground in outlining what must be done. It is also confusing as it (1) is written in a polite, diplomatic way (e.g., invites, encourages) when the points are mandates about what *must* be done; (2) has little order in the way the mandates are presented and (3) combines what Member States must do with requirements that must be met by the United Nations. Because of the second and third points, Fritz et al. (2011, pp. 13–19) made a separate list of the UNSCR 1325 requirements[7] for nation states and grouped these requirements by topic. This, hopefully, will make it easier for countries that wish to follow the mandates.

Here are the mandates in UNSCR 1325 that can be connected with a broad definition of peacebuilding (UNSC 2000; Fritz et al. 2011, pp. 13–19):

- **Urges Member States to ensure increased representation of women at all decision-making levels in national, regional, and international institutions;**
- **Invites Member States to incorporate . . . training guidelines and materials on (1) the protection, rights and the particular needs of women, as well as on (2) the importance of involving women in all peacekeeping and peacebuilding measures;**
- Calls on all actors involved, when negotiating and implementing peace agreements, to adopt a gender perspective, including . . . the special needs of women and girls during repatriation and resettlement and for rehabilitation, reintegration and post-conflict reconstruction;
- **Urges Member States to ensure increased representation of women (in) all . . . mechanisms for the prevention, management, and resolution of conflict;**
- **Calls on all actors involved, when negotiating and implementing peace agreements, to adopt a gender perspective, including measures that support local women's peace initiatives and indigenous processes for conflict resolution and, that involve women in all of the implementation mechanisms of the peace agreements;**

---

[6]This was mainly because they wanted to escape from "atrocities and massacres by the army" and join family members who were already part of the movement (Hauge 2011, p. 101).

[7]At the time the list was compiled, there were three other important Security Council resolutions that supported and extended UNSCR 1325. Those mandates also are included in the list.

- Calls on all actors involved, when negotiating and implementing peace agreements, to adopt a gender perspective, including measures that ensure the protection of and respect for human rights of women and girls, particularly as they relate to the constitution, the electoral system, the police and the judiciary;
- Calls on all parties to armed conflict to take special measures to protect women and girls from gender-based violence, particularly rape and other forms of sexual abuse, and all other forms of violence in situations of armed conflict;
- Emphasizes the responsibility of all States to put an end to impunity and to prosecute those responsible for genocide, crimes against humanity, and war crimes including those relating to sexual and other violence against women and girls, and in this regard stresses the need to exclude these crimes, where feasible from amnesty provisions;
- Calls upon all parties to armed conflict to respect the civilian and humanitarian character of refugee camps and settlements, and to take into account the particular needs of women and girls, including in their design (of refugee camps and settlements);
- Encourages all those involved in the planning for disarmament, demobilization and reintegration to consider the different needs of female and male ex-combatants and to take into account the needs of their dependants.

Some of the mandates listed above are presented in boldface. Three topics connected to these mandates – the representation of women in elected government positions, peacekeeping forces and peacemaking positions – will be examined here after a brief discussion of some of the barriers that face women.

Barriers Facing Women Engaged in Peacebuilding Activities

The inclusion of women and girls in societies and their safety are among the world's most important issues. The United Nations, researchers and representatives of women's organizations (e.g., UN Secretary-General 2010; Fritz 2009; Kvinna till Kvinna 2009; Kuehnast et al. 2011; IDRC 2010; Hentschel 2005) frequently have reported that women and girls in many countries are not safe, their basic needs are not being met and they are not centrally included in peacekeeping and peacemaking. Responding to these problems, the UN Security Council (2000, 2008, 2009a, 2009b, 2010) and the UN Secretary-General (e.g., 2010, 2011, 2012a, 2012b) have insisted that the situation be improved, but progress has been limited and slow in many instances.

There has been considerable research on the difficult situations. Some of the information is just mentioned in passing while discussing other topics. Theodore Trefon (2011, pp. 65, 109, 126), for instance, writing about inefficient aid and the failure of reforms in the Democratic Republic of the Congo (DRC), had this to say about the situation of women in the DRC:

> (The) armed forces continue to perpetrate violence, rape and other forms of abusive behaviour towards civilians. They are corrupt... Margot Wallstrom, the UN's special representative on sexual violence in conflict, called the Congo 'the rape capital of the world'...
>
> The gender gap is... a social reality. Although women are largely responsible for family survival and cohesion and have become important protagonists in the dominant informal

> economy, they tend to be sidelined in decision-making processes, whether it is within the family or at the national political level. There were forty-three ministers and vice-ministers in the second Muzito government in 2010: only five were women . . .
>
> Women, who could be drivers of positive change, are marginalized and under-represented in civil society forums.

Other research focuses directly on the difficult situation for women and the barriers they face in particular countries. For instance, Mwenda Mbatiah (2011), the chair of the Department of Linguistics and Languages at the University of Nairobi, discussed the status of women in Kenya. He surveyed traditional Swahili literature (because of the long tradition of written literature) and indicated that women are portrayed in a negative way. Mbatiah (2011, pp. 26–28) concluded:

> The traditional Swahili society perpetuated numerous stereotypes that eroded the dignity of women . . . Apart from portraying women negatively . . . stereotypes that characterize women as liars, adulterous, schemers, hypocrites and greedy people are often used by men to justify their mistreatment of women . . . . It is important to point out that these stereotypes still exist and are widespread. Moreover, they are not confined to the Swahili traditional community but are common in many other Kenyan communities. For example it is widely acknowledged that wife-beating takes place in many parts of the country and this is generally acceptable . . . Traditional gender roles have been used to oppress, marginalize and deny women their rights.

Women in Serbia also face challenges. Serbia's national action plan for women, peace and security (Belgrade Fund for Political Excellence and the Republic of Serbia Ministry of Defense 2010, p. 11) includes a section with some very specific information about women's situation in the political sector:

> The right to equal representation of women and men in the process of decision-making in the public sphere is guaranteed by the Constitution of the Republic of Serbia, adopted in 2006 . . . Of the total population, of the Republic of Serbia, 51.4 % are women.
>
> The electoral legislation stipulates 30 % as a minimal level of women's representation in election lists (which is no longer in effect as regards local elections). However, following the May 2008 parliamentary election, the women's representation is below the legally defined minimum: they account for 22.4 % of all the deputies in the National Assembly of the Republic of Serbia. In the executive branch of power, the situation is even worse. Five out of twenty-five ministerial positions, i.e., 18.5 % are held by women of whom none is involved in the security sector; 22.7 % are in positions of state secretaries, and 42.6 % assistants to ministers.

And speaking out for equality or women's rights can be dangerous in some parts of the world. For instance, Kenya's general election for parliament in 2007 had a record number of women candidates – 269 (out of 2,548) compared to only 44 in the 2002 election. There also were "unprecedented levels of violence" (UNIFEM 2008, p. 17) One woman candidate was shot and killed and another was tortured by a gang of men. The violence experienced by these Kenyan women reminds us that there can be strong "obstacles to women's political participation that limit their effectiveness in making political accountability systems work for gender equality in many parts of the world" (UNIFEM 2008, p. 17).

In addition to looking at experiences in single countries, it is useful to review the literature that compares the situation in many countries. According to the World Bank's 2012 report (pp. xx–xxi) on gender equality and development, over the last 25 years gains have been made for females in educational enrollment, life expectancy, and labor force participation. The report (p. 13) also indicates "change has come slowly or not at all for many women and girls in many... dimensions of gender equality." Persistent gender gaps are noted in four particular areas: *excess deaths* (in comparison to males) of girls and women; *disparities in girls' schooling* (particularly in Sub-Saharan countries and some parts of South Asia); *unequal access to economic opportunities* (e.g., "women everywhere tend to earn less than men"); *and less say in making decisions and control of resources in households and society* ("in most countries, women participate less in formal politics... and are underrepresented in its upper echelons") (World Bank 2012, p. 76). Regarding political representation, the report (pp. 84–5), indicates that the number of women holding seats in parliament is "very low" and "progress... has been slow". According to the report (p. 13), persistent problems remain for three main reasons:

> First, there may only be a single institutional or policy "fix," which can be difficult and easily blocked... Second, disparities persist when multiple reinforcing constraints combine to block progress. We use disparities in the economic sphere (the persistence of gender earnings gaps and gender segregation in employment) and in agency (differences in societal voice and household decision making) to illustrate this problem. Third, gender differences are particularly persistent when rooted in deeply entrenched gender roles and social norms – such as those about who is responsible for care and housework in the home, and what is 'acceptable' for women and men to study, do and aspire to. And these gaps tend to be reproduced across generations.

At least some of the barriers have been identified here. These include long-standing traditions regarding limited roles for males and females that are passed down to generations of children and the lack of imagination and political will of those in power for instituting new policies and facilitating effective implementation of existing policies.

Inclusive Peacebuilding Efforts

The focus of this chapter is on selected mandates of UNSCR 1325 in relation to inclusive peacebuilding. This section examines women's involvement in peace-building activities in three ways that are identified in UNSCR 1325: through elected political offices, in peacekeeping operations and through peacemaking efforts.

Women in Elected Government Positions

Both women's and men's views are needed in making decisions for a society and in setting the priorities. Yet, according to the Inter-Parliamentary Union (2012a), in 2012, 20.2 % of parliamentarians around the world were women. And it may be unsettling for some to learn that this low figure is as high as it is in good part because of quota mechanisms. The World Bank's 2012 report (p. 85) indicates that:

> Ninety countries have some quota mechanism for parliamentary representation, whether in seat reservation, candidate quota legislation, or voluntary political party quotas.[8] Sixteen countries, all in Africa and Asia, explicitly reserve parliamentary seats for women. In (countries without quotas or reserved seats), such as Finland, there has been little change. For instance, 38.5 percent of newly elected members of parliament in Finland in 1991 were women, and by 2011, this share had increased marginally to 42.5 percent.

While Finland's percentage may be viewed by some as acceptable, it has become increasing clear that countries that do not have some type of quota mechanism in place will not see substantial gains for a very long time.

Of the 90 countries with quota mechanisms, two will be discussed here: Afghanistan and the Republic of Rwanda. *Afghanistan* is a country that in 2000 was described by Rubin Barnett (p. 1790) as "devastated" by over 20 years of war. In 2009, Barnett indicated that "decades, indeed centuries, of strife had marked the society; but so, just as irreversibly, had 7 years of revival." This revival is uneven and has not reached some of the women. Valentine Moghadam (2011, pp. 75–76) has noted that "only 9 % of girls attending primary school continue to high school,... married women are barred from attending high school (in a country where 57 % of girls are married before the age of 16),... women experience considerable violence... and self immolations (tied to forced marriage) appear to be on the rise." A 2012 report by Sean Carberry noted that Afghan women "are still being beaten, raped and forced into early marriage at alarming rates" and, as an example of the threats faced by advocates, indicated that the only female prosecutor general in the country has had her house set on fire, always must be escorted by security personnel, received bullets in an envelope sent to her house, and had her house bombed.

A survey of the Afghan people by The Asia Foundation (Rene 2010, pp. 3–7, 135–146) found 47 % of the respondents thought the country was moving in the right direction, but 60 % expressed fear about voting in a national election and 76 % said corruption is a major problem. Support for equal opportunities for women in education continued to be high (86 %), but support for women to work outside the home continued to fall to 64 %. Almost twice as many women (61 %) as men (38 %) thought there should be equal representation in political leadership at different levels

[8]Mona Lena Krook (2007, p. 367), also discussed three types of quota mechanisms: "*Reserved seats*, which set aside a certain number of positions for women among elected representatives through constitutional reforms; *party quotas*, which aim to increase the proportion of women among a particular party's candidates through party reforms; and *legislative quotas*, which require parties to nominate a certain proportion of women among their candidates through constitutional or legal reforms" [italics added].

while 49 % (with little difference between men and women) said they would object to being represented by a woman in the national parliament.

Afghanistan put a quota system in place in its new constitution, adopted in 2004. According to DCAF (2011, p. 61):

> Afghanistan's new constitution... guaranteed women equal rights and their formal inclusion in political decision-making processes. According to Article 83, at least two female candidates from each province should be elected to parliament. In 2007, and following results from the 2005 elections, sixty-eight women, representing about 27 per cent of the 249 members of the Wolesi Jirga, were elected... Examples also exist of efforts to include women in decision-making at the community level – such as the creation of Community Development Councils as part of the National Solidarity Programme.

Being elected through quota systems does not mean that parliamentarians who are women will be easily accepted. As Borchgrevink et al. (2008, p. 7) have noted about Afghanistan:

> There are numerous obstacles to women's political mobilization, participation and influence... It is difficult for women to place issues on the political agenda. It is even more difficult to get access to those forums where the actual decision-making takes place. The leadership role of women within the parliament is insignificant, and female MPs receive little support from their male colleagues, who show few signs of interest in their activities. While female MPs are often invited to meetings to talk about the situation of women in Afghanistan, they are rarely asked about public finance, counter-narcotics, security or terrorism. Both the government of Afghanistan and the international community are part of defining women's political participation and reducing their domains to 'women's issues'...
>
> (Including) women in decisionmaking (of the) Community Development Councils (CDCs) (is) a positive step, (but) the women's CDCs established as part of this process are often locked in to small, low-budget projects, while the big decisions that affect communities are taken by the main CDCs. In mixed-gender CDCs, women still have little say.

Another country with a quota system is the *Republic of Rwanda*. Rwanda's war and genocide in the early to mid-1990s resulted in the "slaughter of more than a half million individuals and unprecedented population movements... Rwanda's agriculture-based economy was completely destroyed... forcing most of its population to live in a state of extreme precariousness... It is estimated that 250,000 women were raped." (Gervais 2004, pp. 303–4).

Before the civil war, Rwandan women had never held more than 18 % of the parliament seats. After a "gender-sensitive" constitution (DCAF 2011, p. 62) was put in place in 2003, 30 % of the seats in parliament were designated for women. In 2012, Rwanda had the highest percentage – 56.3 % – of women parliamentarians (Inter-Parliamentary Union 2012b; Waring 2010, p. 29) in the world[9] and was the

[9]Devlin and Elgie (2008, pp. 250–251) were interested in whether the large number of women representatives in Rwanda made a difference. They concluded that after 2003 "women's issues certainly... (were) raised more easily and more often" than before, and that a "gender agenda is now perceived to be 'guaranteed.' The deputies "insistence that the Rwandan situation of gender equity should be campaigned for and replicated in other parliaments seems new." Though the authors noted the new 'Law on the Prevention, Protection and Punishment of Any Gender-Based Violence' is a "notable policy achievement," they stated that "in the area of policy, a significant impact from the greater numbers of women is not to be seen."

first country that had more women than men in its parliament. DCAF (2011, p. 62) discussed the gains:

> In the lower house (the Chamber of Deputies), there are eighty members in total, each serving five-year terms. Fifty-three of these members are directly elected to represent political parties in a proportional representation system. The additional seats are contested in the following manner: twenty-four members are elected by women from each province and the capital city of Kigali, two are elected by the National Youth Council, and one is elected by the Federation of the Associations of the Disabled. In addition to the twenty-four seats set aside in the Chamber of Deputies, the 2003 elections saw an additional fifteen women elected in openly competed seats for a total of thirty-nine out of eighty, or 48.8 per cent of seats – the world's highest rate of women in parliament... In 1996, women in Rwanda's parliament formed a cross-party caucus, the Forum of Women Parliamentarians (FFRP), which included all female members of Parliament... They work together across party lines on issues of common importance to women...

Quota mechanisms of various kinds, particularly in combination with some kind of networking (e.g., among women parliamentarians, with male political leaders) and/or national leadership by women (as in Liberia and Mozambique), can change the participation rate as well as increase the possibility of inclusive and effective peacebuilding efforts.[10]

Inclusive Peacekeeping

Peacekeeping refers to the period when a ceasefire has been negotiated, but conflict still remains or could easily erupt. Peacekeeping forces are expected to reduce tensions between parties to a conflict after a ceasefire has been negotiated in order for peaceful relations to be more-fully established or resume. Although peacekeeping is not specifically authorized or even mentioned in the UN Charter,[11] the UN has been providing peacekeeping since 1948, when the UN Security Council authorized the deployment of UN military observers "to monitor the Armistice Agreement between Israel and its Arab neighbors" (UN Department of Peacekeeping Operations, n.d.). The UN, "the main actor" (Kondoch 2007, p. xiv) in peacekeeping, does not have its own military and relies on the assistance of Member States to put peacekeeping

[10]However, Sheila Meintjes (2010, p. 4) has concluded, "From a review of a wide range of literature, both general and country-specific, it seems clear that women politicians, who are members of an elite political class, are no more likely than men to champion women's rights, needs and interests."

[11]The Charter of the United Nations was signed in 1945 and "is the foundation document for all the United Nations work" (United Nations Department of Peacekeeping Operations 2008, p. 13). A former UN Secretary-General, Dag Hammarskjöld, referred to peacekeeping as "'chapter six and a half' because it fell between the UN Charter's chapter six (peaceful methods for resolving conflicts) and chapter seven (peace enforcement)" (Adebajo 2011, p. 19; Kondoch 2007, p. xvi).

operations in place.[12] UN peacekeeping, involving "military, civilian and police personnel, has been the most frequent military operation conducted by the UN" (Kondoch 2007, p. xiv). UN peacekeeping has three basic principles: "consent of the parties; impartiality; (and) non-use of force except in self-defence and defence of the mandate" (UN Department of Peacekeeping Operations, n.d.).

UN peacekeeping forces now not only are expected to maintain peace and provide security, they "facilitate the political process, protect civilians, assist in the disarmament, demobilization and reintegration of former combatants; support the organization of elections, protect and promote human rights and assist in restoring the rule of law" (UN Department of Peacekeeping Operations, n.d.). Peacekeeping forces have taken on daunting tasks[13] and, as Angela Mackay has noted (2003, p. 218), "often with little or no specific preparation or training" particularly "in the gender implications of an unknown society." In 2011, the UN had 16 peace operations ("15 peacekeeping operations and one special political mission") on four continents (UN Department of Peacekeeping Operations, n.d.).

The number of women in uniform in peacekeeping roles is very small – only 2 or 3 % of military personnel and 9 % of police officers.[14] The UN Department of Peacekeeping Operations (n.d.) has said the "need for women peacekeepers is more pressing than ever" particularly to assist with "interviewing victims of sexual and gender-based violence, working in women's prisons, assisting female ex-combatants during the process of demobilizing and reintegration into civilian life and mentoring female cadets at police academies." When women are not included in peacekeeping operations, negative consequences have been noted (Etchart 2005, pp. 72–77) including an increase in "sex work, prostitution (and rape),[15] fatherless children . . . , human rights violations and human trafficking."

---

[12]Regional organizations/groups of states (e.g., European Union, NATO, African Union) can conduct their own peacekeeping operations and also can contribute (e.g., mediation before peacekeeping, logistical support, joint efforts) to UN efforts (e.g., Kondoch 2007, p. xiv). Victor (2010, p. 217) emphasized that Western governments have "come to depend on African peacekeepers to manage and resolve" conflicts in Africa. He also noted that the peacekeepers frequently come from the less-economically developed states (e.g., Ethiopia, Ghana, Nigeria, Rwanda and Uganda).

[13]Bove and Elia (2011, p. 700) and Victor (2010, p. 217) noted that some recent interventions (e.g., in Bosnia and Somalia) have seen peacekeeping forces engage in active defense to accomplish their mandates.

[14]This may reflect, in part, the small group of women in the police and military. This can be due to a number of factors such as tradition, lack of acceptance and/or lack of qualifications such as level of education. The Liberian National Police (LNP), for example, established a Female Recruitment Programme but found the lack of educational qualifications was a barrier. The LNP Programme "selected 150 women to attend classes to receive their high school diplomas . . . (and) the women, in return, promised to join and serve the LNP for a minimum number of years" (DCAF 2011, p. 9).

[15]A 1995 study found significantly fewer incidents of prostitution and rape when there was just a token female presence (De Groot 2002).

An incentive for some women to join peacekeeping forces, particularly if they are from countries with low salaries, is the amount of money to be made for this work. A barrier is the length of the tour may be too long for those mothers who do not want to be away from their children or their families for a long period of time.

There are some positive points that should be mentioned about women in peacekeeping forces. The 9 % of police peacekeepers includes the all-women police units. The first all-woman police unit was from India in 2007 (stationed in Liberia)[16] and, since then, there have been all-women police units from Bangladesh, Samoa and Rwanda assigned to other countries. According to a news account (Raza 2010), "the Liberian National Police received 3 times the usual number of female applicants in the month following the deployment of the Indian all-female police contingent. Female police officers now comprise 15 % of the Liberian National Police..." While the 10 % of all Canada's police deployed for peacekeeping are women (UN Department of Peacekeeping Operations, n.d.)[17] may seem low, "the Canadian Government has been at the forefront of gender mainstreaming in peacekeeping operations" (Etchart 2005, p. 69). Women also have contributed to the success of peacekeeping missions in Guatemala and Namibia (Etchart 2005, p. 69). And, in 2011, women were 21 % of the global 18,362 non-uniformed/civilian peacekeeping staff (UN Department of Public Information 2012, p. 73).

While there has been some increase in the number of women in peacekeeping forces, much more needs to be done. According to Etchart (2005, p. 81):

> A gender perspective must be brought to bear in the elaboration of ceasefire agreements and peace accords; militaries must endeavour to recruit equal numbers of women and men in peace support operations at all levels; sex-disaggregated statistics should be collected for all aspects of peacekeeping operations; efforts must be made to maintain family life for personnel in peacekeeping operations: this may include 'accompanied' tours with husbands, wives and children being kept together, where possible; gender and human rights training must be supplied to military personnel in peace support operations; gender sensitization modules should be introduced in the initial stages of police and military training; and disciplinary action and effective accountability mechanisms need to be established to prevent impunity for violations of human rights by peacekeeping personnel.

---

[16]The all-woman Indian police unit of 103 women in Liberia also brought "22 men, who are the cooks, mechanics and drivers" (Carvajal 2010) for the unit. In 2010, women accounted for 14 % of the 1,354 police peacekeepers in Liberia (Carvajal 2010).

[17]According to Baksh et al. (2005, p. 69), "Canada and the USA have the highest percentage of women (12 %) in their armed forces compared with the rest of the world, but the percentages of women assigned to peacekeeping operations in 2002 were low...." Mackay (2003, p. 217) noted that around 2000 a former Canadian minister of foreign affairs and a former US Secretary of State "agreed to support the development of a training programme on 'gender' for civilian and military personnel working on peacekeeping missions." (Training materials constantly need to be reviewed to make sure that they are clear and effective and there needs to be continuing follow-up.)

Inclusive Peacemaking

Peacemaking has been defined (Fisher et al. 2000, p. 14) as "interventions designed to end hostilities and bring about an agreement using diplomatic, political and military means." The inclusion of the word "military" seems to point to violent conflicts and the use of the word "diplomatic" most likely refers to intra-state or interstate conflicts that would require national and/or international diplomatic approaches. The term peacemaking usually seems to be used in relation to conflicts that are large, violent and systemic often involving factions and affecting a community, nation or region, but the term also has been used for disputes involving individuals and/or small groups. The definition, then, needs to cover activities as varied as Navajo peacemaking (e.g., Zion 1998; Wall 2001; Bluehouse 2003), John Winslade's (2009, p. 560) discussion of his mother as a peacemaker with his father, and the peacemaking activities of young children and chimpanzees (see Verbeek 2008).

Peacemaking is defined here as interventions that are based on principles (such as equality, harmony, inclusion and restorative justice) and aim to end difficulties between parties and bring about agreement. This definition covers violent intra-state conflicts as well as disputes involving individuals. *Inclusive peacemaking* means that the peacemakers will, in different ways, see that any peacemaking process is all-encompassing (so that all viewpoints are represented) and that the peacemakers and teams of peacemakers will represent a variety of backgrounds. In regard to the roles of men and women, for example, women would be included as peacemakers as well as members of any peacemaking team.

Peacemaking in relation to intra-state, violent conflicts is discussed in this section. These undertakings are usually complicated and difficult. Some of the approaches used in "official" peacemaking are well known – third-party mediation; official and unofficial diplomacy; negotiation or bargaining – while others – problem-solving workshops, citizen diplomacy, economic incentives, mediation training, conflict transformation education, attention-getting activities – are less well known. Three topics will be covered in this section about women and peacemaking: women's activities leading up to and around peace negotiations (informal peacemaking); participation in peace negotiations; and mediating or negotiating peace agreements.

Informal Peacemaking

The Centre for Humanitarian Dialogue (2010a) held a meeting of women from Asia and the Pacific in which participants underlined the importance of informal peacemaking (outside of formal/official peacemaking). The participants felt that women's organizations "need to be constantly organizing and considering ways to link informal processes to formal talks." It was also suggested that mediators and other third parties need to value informal peacemaking and that international agencies need to support these women, "including with resources."

There are numerous examples of the ways in which individual women, demonstrations of women and women's organizations have worked to diminish conflict and encourage participation in peace processes. O'Neill and Vary (2011, pp. 85–86) presented many examples including these:

> In 2002, the Columbia government broke off formal negotiations with the FARC and initiated a major armed offensive. Women's groups, united across the ideological spectrum, responded with a protest march 40,000 strong against the war and the growing militarization of society. The organizers roused the desire for peace in the female population and built the women's coalition into leaders of the movement in Columbia.
>
> In 1999, women from Sierra Leone, Liberia and Guinea banded together to fight for an end to the brutal conflict in their countries. Facing intransigence from three Presidents who had vowed to never talk to one another, the Mano River Women's Peace Network used unorthodox tactics including threatening to lock the President of Guinea in a room until he agreed to attend negotiations. Thousands of women came together again in Liberia in 2004 to nonviolently force a resolution to stalled peace talks.
>
> Naga women used innovative approaches to mediate among armed actors and mobilize for peace and reconciliation in northeastern India in 1997. As the ceasefire faltered, they began to negotiate successfully with Indian security forces, underground armed opposition forces, and a variety of tribal factions and groups to sustain it. Women also led intercommunity and intertribal events and ceremonies considered key to promoting long-term peace and reconciliation.

Anderlini (2004) also presented many examples including ones from South Africa, Northern Ireland, Burundi, Somalia, Columbia, Guatemala, Georgia-Abkhazia conflict, Sri Lanka, Argentina, and the Middle East. And mediator Günther Baechler (2010, p. 5) has many examples from Nepal including this one about mobilization:

> The issue of human rights violations, impunity, and human security helped to create a nation-wide women's movement across sectors, professional groups, parties, and identity groups. The movement gave women greater space to raise their voices in the streets of Kathmandu and district headquarters (provincial towns), as well as in the political sphere of the state institutions.

Participation in Peace Negotiations

The documents developed during peace negotiations include *ceasefire and pre-negotiation agreements*; *framework agreements or accords* – "a formal commitment between hostile parties to end a war" (Anderlini 2004, p. 16) that specifies arrangements for substantively settling the conflict; and *implementation agreements* (documents that address enactment). According to Bell and O'Rourke (2011, p. 4), framework agreements (or comprehensive agreements):

> typically set out complex arrangements for new democratic institutions, human rights and minority protections, and reform or overhaul of security and justice sector institutions. They therefore operate as 'power-maps'[18] ...

[18] A "power map" might be a gendered peace agreement, "one which has taken into account the perspectives, rights and needs of all people affected by it from the particular standpoint of their sex" (Potter 2011, p. 3).

Women need to be included in the development of all the documents in peace negotiations and women and girls need to be specifically mentioned in the documents because these documents will easily lead – or serve as a block – to full participation in a changing society. A study of 585 peace agreements in 102 peace processes, signed between January 1, 1990 and May 1, 2010, found that only 16 % even have references to women and that they are "qualitatively often poor, constituting scattered references to women, sometimes contravening CEDAW provisions, and on rare occasions illustrating good practice" (Bell and O'Rourke 2011, p. 7)[19] The inclusion of women and girls in the texts of peace agreements "is the starting point in achieving other political, legal and social gains for women" (Bell and O'Rourke 2011, p. 3). What is contained in a peace agreement can become part of a constitution (Bell and O'Rourke 2011, p. 4), as was the case with the Dayton Peace Accords for ending the conflict in Bosnia Herzegovina (Mazurana 2010, p. 17).

It should be noted that equality provisions in agreements that are gender-neutral may actually be open to misinterpretation. There are times when being gender-neutral is useful, but other times there needs to be specificity regarding women and girls. For instance, the Dayton Accords did not "express positive measures for the inclusion of women in the highest levels of the new government with the result being that from the beginning women were underrepresented within government and administrative and economic positions" (Mazurana 2010, p. 17).

According to UNIFEM (2010, p. 1) in an analysis of a sample of 24 major peace processes, "women's participation in negotiating delegations averaged less than 8 % in the 14 cases for which such information was available." And it was noted that "fewer than 3 % of signatories were women." UNIFEM (2010, p. 2) also indicated that only "marginal progress" has been made either quantitatively (numbers involved) or qualitatively (provisions that address the rights of women) since the UN Security Council unanimously adopted Resolution 1325 on October 31, 2000.

Irene Khan (Centre for Humanitarian Dialogue 2010b), a former Secretary-General of Amnesty International, has said "to date, there has not been a peace process where gender parity, or anything approximating it, has been observed." According to Onubogu and Etchart (2005, pp. 38–9), the obstacles to women taking part in peace talks include (1) fewer women have been armed and the power might be seen as in the hands of the fighters, (2) men fighters may be seen as having the same views as women fighters, (3) negotiating teams often come from existing power structures where women may be absent, (4) women may be excluded from public life by local traditions, (5) women's activities may not be seen as political,

[19]The study did note that since UNSCR 1325 was adopted in 2000, the references to women increased from 11 % to 27 %. Potter (2011) gave numerous examples of how language in actual agreements could have been improved.

(6) security discussions may not be seen as needing to hear from women,[20] and (7) a lack of access to resources that will allow them to attend.

Gitti Hentschel (2005, p. 3) provides specific examples of the problems:

> Not a single woman was involved in the peace talks about ending the Bosnian conflict in Dayton 1995, even though the massive violence against and marginalization of women and girls in this conflict was internationally known. Only one woman – from the (Kosovo) side – took part in the negotiations of Rambouillet, that proceeded the bombing of (Kosovo). Women's organizations in Serbia, that advocated a non-violent solution, were not included.

There are examples of participation, however. Kumudini Samuel (2010, pp. 2–3), for instance, discussed her participation in a Sub Committee for Gender Issues (SGI) in Sri Lanka:

> While none of the previous attempts at formal peacemaking in Sri Lanka allowed women any role in the negotiating process, the peace talks which commenced in 2002 established a formal space for their engagement by creating . . . (the) SGI to report directly to the plenary of the peace talks. (The SGI) was mandated to 'explore the effective inclusion of gender concerns in the peace process' . . . The SGI was appointed at the third round of plenary talks . . . It was possibly the first of its kind set-up within a formal peace process at a pre-substantive stage of negotiations . . . The (five) Government delegates . . . comprised mainly of feminist activists engaged in women's rights and peace work from the non-governmental sector, while those (five) of the LTTE (Liberation Tigers of Tamil Eelam) included senior women cadre from the organisation's political, research, media and district administrative units.

And UNIFEM (2010) indicated:

> In the *Republic of El Salvador* in the 1990s, women were present at nearly all the post-accord negotiating tables. One technical table, the Reinsertion Commission, was formed by six women and one man. In the end, women made up one third of the beneficiaries of land redistribution and reintegration packages . . .[21]
>
> In the *Republic of South Africa*, the Women's National Commission demanded that 50 per cent of participants in the Multi-Party Negotiating Process be women and succeeded in establishing that one out of every two representatives per party had to be a woman, or the seat would remain vacant. Approximately 3 million women across the country participated in focus groups and discussions, and a 30 per cent female quota was adopted for the upcoming elections.
>
> In Northern Ireland, women secured a seat at the peace table by forming the first women-dominated political party and winning some seats in the election. The Northern Ireland Women's Coalition successfully built bridges between Catholics and Protestants and promoted reconciliation and reintegration of political prisoners.

---

[20]A practical guide by The Institute for Inclusive Security and the Geneva Centre for the Democratic Control of Armed Forces (DCAF) (Bastick and Whitman 2013) is designed to assist women in changing the security sector in their own countries. It contains advice and sample documents (e.g., invitation to join a coalition, meeting agenda, action plan, recommendations, letter to ask for a meeting).

[21]Others (e.g., Naslund 1999; Mazurana 2010) have noted that even though some 30 % of the FMLN negotiators were women, gender equality issues were not included in the peace agreements and the final agreements even kept women, and their dependents (to different degrees) from benefitting from reconstruction programs.

Another example is provided by Dyan Mazurana (2010, p. 15):

> (In) Guatemala, the presence of a lone woman in one of the official parties to the peace negotiations, and support by hundreds of local women activists, ensured that the final agreements incorporated a number of important mandates regarding women.... The participation of women in the Guatemalan peace process, for example, resulted in peace agreements which include specific commitments to women, including access to housing, credit, land and other productive resources; the obligation of the government to implement a national program on integral health for women, adolescent girls, and girl children; government commitments to review the national legislation with the purpose of eradicating all forms of discrimination against women; the penalization of sexual harassment; a guarantee of the participation of women at all decision and power levels of the local, regional and national bodies, on equal terms with men; and the creation of the National Women's Forum and the Office for the Defense of Indigenous Women...

During the last 30 years, feminists, women's rights organizations and some international statespersons, donors and agencies have been outspoken about women having seats at peace tables. As Dyan Mazurana (2010, p. 16) has noted, in a number of countries where peace negotiations were undertaken, some women were at the peace tables, but the results were disappointing. In part this was because the women representatives may have been "the wives, lovers and daughters of government or armed group leaders" or women who were chosen by the government or opposition groups because they supported or were expected to support their party's line. These women did not come to the table as women's rights advocates.

Cynthia Enloe (2004) has written about the strong influences in peace talks. She concluded that for effective participation a party needs to have some or all of the following resources – a base of organized political support, ready access to soldiers and arms, economic resources and credibility (for instance as a "threat, a rival, an ally, a technocrat") – and that women do not usually have these resources.

Mediating Peace Agreements

Katia Papagianni (2011), head of the Centre for Humanitarian Dialogue's Mediation Support Programme, relays a lot of good advice[22] for mediators in societies that are trying to end violent internal conflicts. Mediators, she wrote, can help by preparing parties for the "long-terms challenges of implementing peace deals" and to understand that they have to "build robust political processes and not simply 'strike deals'." On the other hand, in some cases the long-term challenges can't be addressed immediately and the mediator should resist drawing up "hastily-drafted, and unrealistic, agreements." Mediators need to "be aware of the dangers of detailed, over-ambitious agreements which face significant implementation challenges." Mediators also must "understand that power-sharing agreements tend to obstruct the development of inclusive political processes, even if they are useful tools for ending conflicts" and know they "can advocate for diplomatic activity and political

[22]The advice comes from those taking part in the 2010 Oslo Forum, a meeting of mediation professionals.

engagements to continue after the agreement is signed." At this point so few women are mediating peace agreements, would-be mediators will only be able to use this advice in an indirect way.

It is a well-documented fact that women are absent from "formally convened international meetings, including those for conflict resolution" (Onubogu and Etchart 2005, p. 34). The 2009 UN Secretary-General's report noted (p. 4) "a persistent cause of concern is that women continue to be virtually absent from the peace table and to be severely underrepresented as third-party mediators or even as representatives of the United Nations in most conflict-affected countries." In 2012, the Secretary-General (2012a, pp. 22, 24) "remain(ed) concerned" and noted that "considerable obstacles persist to women's participation and representation in public decision-making in relation to peace and transition processes."

According to the Centre for Humanitarian Dialogue (2011, pp. 10–11), track-one mediation (between official diplomats) is "almost exclusively male-dominated" and the European Union (EU) "is even worse in this regard. Of 11 EU Special Representatives in conflict areas, (in 2011) only one is a woman... and she is the first ever female appointment." The Organization of American States (OAS) also "appears not" to have selected any women to be mediators "though women do feature in other relevant leadership positions."

And another example, if one is even needed, comes from Nepal. In 2006, after "a 10-year-long armed internal conflict" (Falch 2010a), where "peaceful mass protests" by women and women's organizations "pushed persistently to get access to political leaders and institutions" (Falch 2010b), women "were not included as mediators, participants, observers or signatories in the peace negotiations" (Falch 2010a).

UNIFEM's (2010, p. 3) review of a sample of 24 major peace processes since 1992 found "women were absent from chief mediating roles in UN-brokered talks." While the UN has never officially appointed a woman as chief mediator, in recent years a number of women did have mediation roles. According to UNIFEM (2010, pp. 5–6) Dame Margaret Anstee was the Special Representative of the Secretary-General in the Republic of Angola in the early 1990s and, for part of the UN-led process, was the lead mediator. Dame Ann Hercus, when she was the Special Adviser of the Secretary-General, conducted "shuttle talks" in Cyprus.

There are other examples of mediation – some sponsored and some not. Aili Mari Tripp et al. (2011, p. 357) discussed the women activists from Guinea, Sierra Leone and Liberia who formed the Mano River Union Women Peace Network (MARWOPNET):

> The network mediated an intense conflict between Guinea and Liberia in 2001 in spite of minimal resources and being excluded from the formal peace process. MARWOPNET was able to get the feuding heads of state to a regional peace Summit. At one point, President Lansana Conte of Guinea had been adamant about not meeting with Charles Taylor of Liberia. Mary Brownell, a Liberian peace activist of the MARWOPNET delegation, told Mr. Conte: 'You and President Taylor have to meet as men and iron out your differences, and we the women want to be present. We will lock you in this room until you come to your senses, and I will sit on the key.' Conte relented and met with Taylor as a result of the sheer audacity of a woman telling him what to do, saying 'What man do you think would say that to me? Only a woman could do such a thing and get by with it. As a result of

their actions the women were given delegate status at the twenty-fourth ECOWAS summit in December 2001, where they were able to make an appeal for African leaders to support women's peacemaking initiatives. They were also given observer status in the 2003 Accra talks that led to a ceasefire agreement and the establishment of an interim government in Liberia.

Visaka Dharmadasa (Berkley Center for Religion, Peace and World Affairs 2010), from Sri Lanka, was a founder of the country's Association of Parents of Service Men Missing in Action and the Association of War Affected Women. The war in Sri Lanka (from 1976 to 2009) was "Asia's longest civil war" (Hunt Alternatives Fund 2010). Anderlini (2004, pp. 19–20) has described Dharmadasa as an "inside neutral" as well as a facilitator and mediator. According to O'Neill and Vary (2011, pp. 85–86):

> (Dharmadasa) designed and facilitated track two dialogues, bringing together influential civil society leaders from both sides of the conflict. In 2002, as peace talks were faltering, the LTTE (Liberation Tigers of Tamil Eelam) refused direct contact with the government, accusing it of noncompliance. LTTE leaders conveyed their concerns to the government through Ms. Dharmadasa, foreign diplomats, and Norwegian negotiators. She remained an impartial bridge between the parties for years.

And there are some examples of women who have been official mediators. For instance, there is Betty Bigombe from the Republic of Uganda. Her early work with the government of Uganda and the Lord's Resistance Army (LRA) paved the way for "the signing of a ceasefire in September 2006" (Tripp et al. 2011, p. 354). Her "inside" work was described in the following way by the Hunt Alternatives Fund (2006):

> Since March 2004 Bigombe has been the chief mediator between the LRA and the government of Uganda, in an effort to end 20 years of conflict. Under President Yoweri Museveni's government, Bigombe was appointed minister to the parliament in 1986. In 1988 she was selected Minister of State for Pacification of north and northeastern Uganda... and tasked with seeking a peaceful means to end the war... Bigombe initiated contact with rebel leader Joseph Kony in May 1992; this initiative gave birth to the "Bigombe talks."

While Bigombe's efforts in the 1990s were undertaken while she lived in Uganda, her work in 2004 began when she was living in the United States and working for the World Bank. She took a leave of absence from her job and, spending some "$8,300 of her own money on the peace front – on things like calls to rebels' satellite phones," she spent 18 months involved in a "one-woman peace effort with no official position or outside funding" (McLaughlin 2005). In 2004, "Bigombe engineered the first face-to-face talks between the government and the LRA in a decade. Hopes were high... but at the last minute, the deal collapsed" (McLaughlin 2005).

And there is Graça Machel (UNIFEM 2010, p. 3), one of three mediators for talks in Kenya that were led by the African Union[23] in 2008 following the violent

[23]Ghanian President John Kufuor, acting as Chairman of the African Union (AU), announced an AU "Panel of Eminent African Personalities to facilitate resolution of the crisis. Under the chairmanship of Kofi Annan, the panel would include former President Benjamin Mkapa of Tanzania and former First Lady Graça Machel of Mozambique" (McGhie and Wamai 2011, p. 15).

dispute over the results of the presidential elections of December 2007. As part of her work, Graça Machel brought women together. McGhie and Wamai (2011, p. 19) described her approach to a meeting where she found "party affiliations and ethnic tensions... prevented any meaningful engagement among the women:"

> Mrs. Machel... advised women to sit together to find common ground. This resulted in, what became known as, the 'spitting session' by the women involved. This was a session in which they raised all of the issues that were dividing them, allowed themselves to get angry (to 'spit' at one another) in order to allow themselves to move forward and find commonality in their position on the crisis. The airing of differences, and building of confidence, subsequently enabled this group of women to constructively draft a Women's Memorandum, which was presented to the mediation team...

At the end of 42 days of negotiations, a power-sharing agreement ended "the violence and political stalemate" (McGhie and Wamai 2011, p. 3).

Making Progress

If a country wants to make progress in achieving gender justice for women and girls, and do so in a timely way, it needs to plan (including women representatives from government and civil society), fund, implement, monitor, evaluate and revise (as necessary) the change initiative. Luckily, there are many excellent ideas that can be considered regarding effective change. For instance, assess the political will in the country to do what needs to be done and establish a supportive culture. Establish quotas and reservations to assure a minimum of participation for both males and females in most areas of employment, political decisionmaking and peacemaking roles. Institute self-assessment mechanisms for the police and military (e.g., DCAF 2011, pp. 92–94) to help increase recruitment of women in those areas. Look for numerous ways to work with young people to reduce generational continuity in problematic areas. Find ways to support women to continue to mobilize groups that initiate, support and monitor developments. Help women and women's groups develop easy access to political leadership to provide information, discuss and move forward on important issues. Find resources that are sufficient for the line items in action plans that support identified initiatives. Work with international donors to make sure that they are not just relying only on information from established political elites in supporting changes and target certain resources for smaller, less established change initiatives.

Other important ideas include integrating gender into post-conflict needs assessments (e.g., DCAF 2011, pp.86–90) and conducting gender audits (e.g., DCAF 2011, pp. 95–99). Karama (2012a),[24] an organization that aims to end violence

[24]Karama (2012b) brings together local women's groups and other civil society organizations. It's main office is in Cairo, Egypt and it has organizational partners in Egypt, Jordan, Lebanon, Syria, Algeria, Morocco, Sudan, Tunisia and Palestine.

against women in the Middle East and North Africa and increase women's involvement in civil society, has three recommendations that emerged from its analysis of the state of women's rights after Arab revolutions: (1) strengthen coalitions and build new ones to develop civil society; (2) build capacity to take part in discussions regarding new constitutions and increase women's political representation; and (3) increase the number of women in reconciliation and peacebuilding efforts.

Peace agreements can be a particular challenge. O'Neill and Vary (2011, pp. 101–2) have put forward a number of suggestions concerning these agreements:

> As an incentive, offer negotiating teams extra seats at the table, but only if they are filled by women;
>
> Having a critical mass of women (at least 30 percent) involved in peace negotiations could fundamentally alter traditional approaches to DDR and SSR and increase the likelihood that these programs will more meaningfully serve all members of conflict-affected communities;
>
> Enable women to participate in negotiations as civil society observers, particularly when they do not make up at least 25 percent of negotiating delegations. Fund their participation and ensure they have access to the same resources as negotiators. Ensure they stay in the same hotels as other delegates as negotiations often happen between formal sessions;
>
> Establish an advisory group or appoint a dedicated gender adviser in the office of the facilitator or mediator;
>
> Hire senior-level gender experts to work hand in hand with planners from the beginning;
>
> Encourage male champions to be spokespersons on issues of women's inclusion.

Conclusion

UN Security Council Resolution 1325 clearly states that women are to be centrally involved in the political life of their countries, peacekeeping forces and peacemaking activities. States going through a transition, particularly from authoritarian regimes, have a big opportunity to make dramatic changes in the lives of their people in a rather short period of time. One of these changes needs to be the central inclusion of girls and women in their societies. Countries going through transitions as well as the countries and non-governmental organizations that offer assistance to the countries in transition, need to make the most of this unparalleled opportunity.

This chapter has shown that while there has been progress in the number of women in elected office, this gain has been made when quota mechanisms have been instituted. We also have seen that the number of women in peacekeeping forces is extremely low. Most countries need to change the police and military culture to make it acceptable and interesting for women to be part of those forces. If those numbers can't be increased substantially, it is difficult to see how the number of women in peacekeeping forces will dramatically increase.

We know that the numbers of women in negotiations is very important. However, it has been easy to see that women who are negotiating on behalf of a central party in a conflict often are under pressure to make the party's interests the first (and perhaps only) order of business and they also may have been selected for participation for that same reason. Because of this, women, particularly those representing women's organizations, need to be brought in to the negotiations in a variety of ways and women need to head and be members of mediating teams.

There are so many excellent ideas about how the lives of women and girls can be dramatically improved. Of all the suggestions, we know that political will is of utmost importance. Countries also need to remember that a sufficient number of women and girls in a country's core activities is only a starting point in centrally including women and girls in the life of the country.

References

1325 Forum Norge. (2008). Norway's implementation of Resolution 1325. http://www.peacewomen.org/pages/about-1325/national-action-plans-naps

Adebajo, A. (2011). *UN peacekeeping in Africa: From the Suez crisis to the Sudan conflicts*. London/Boulder: Lynne Rienner.

Anderlini, S. N. (2004). Peace negotiations and agreements. In International Alert & Women Waging Peace (Eds.), *Inclusive security, sustainable peace: A toolkit for advocacy and action*. http://huntalternatives.org/pages/87_inclusive_security_toolkit.cfm

Aoláin, F. N. (2009). Women, security, and the patriarchy of internationalized transitional justice. *Human Rights Quarterly, 31*, 1055–1085.

Baechler, G. (2010). *A mediator's perspective: Women and the Nepali peace process*. Centre for Humanitarian Dialogue. www.peacewomen.org/portal_resources_resource.php?id=797

Baksh, R., Etchart, L., Onubogu, E., & Johnson, T. (2005). *Gender mainstreaming in conflict transformation: Building sustainable peace*. London: Commonwealth Secretariat.

Barnard, A. (2011, September 11). Libya's war-tested women hope to keep new power. *The New York Times*.

Barnett, R. R. (2000). The political economy of war and peace in Afghanistan. *World Development, 28*(10), 1789–1803.

Barnett, R. R. (2009, January/February). A tribe apart. *Boston Review*. http://bostonreview.net/BR34.1/rubin.php

Bastick, M., & Whitman, T. (2013). *A women's guide to security sector reform*. Washington, DC: The Institute for Inclusive Security and DCAF.

Belgrade Fund for Political Excellence and the Republic of Serbia Ministry of Defense. (2010). *United Nations Security Council Resolution 1325 in Serbia – on women, peace and security*. Belgrade: Belgrade Fund for Political Excellence and the Republic of Serbia Ministry of Defense.

Bell, C., & O'Rourke, C. (2011, March). UN Security Council 1325 and peace negotiations and agreements. *Opinion*. Centre for Humanitarian Dialogue.

Berkley Center For Religion, Peace and World Affairs. (2010, November 26). *A discussion with Visaka Dhamadasa, chairperson of the association of war affected women*. Georgetown University. http://berkleycenter.georgetown.edu/interviews/a-discussion-with-visaka-dharmadasa-chairperson-of-the-association-of-war-affected-women

Bluehouse, P. (2003). Is it "peacemakers teaching?" or is it "teaching peacemakers?". *Conflict Resolution Quarterly, 20*(4), 495–500.

Borchgrevink, K., Hernes, H., & Haavardsson, I. (2008, February 16). Peacebuilding in Afghanistan: How to reach the women. In PRIO conference report.

Boutros-Ghali, B. (1992). *An agenda for peace*. New York: United Nations.

Bove, V., & Elia, L. (2011). Supplying peace: Participation in and troop contribution to peacekeeping missions. *Journal of Peace Research, 48*(6), 699–714.

Carberry, S. (2012). Afghan women fear backsliding on key gains. http://www.npr.org/2012/08/27/158522519/afghan-women-fear-backsliding-on-key-gains

Carvajal, D. (2010, March 5). A female approach to peacekeeping. *The New York Times*.

Centre for Humanitarian Dialogue. (2010a, September 27–30). Experts meeting: Women at the peace table – Asia Pacific summary report. Kathmandu, Nepal: Centre for Humanitarian Dialogue. http://www.hdcentre.org

Centre for Humanitarian Dialogue. (2010b, November). Women at the Indonesian peace table: Enhancing the contributions of women to conflict resolution. Geneva: Centre for Humanitarian Dialogue. www.hdcentre.org/women-indonesian-peace-table-enhancing-contributions-women-conflict-resolution

Centre for Humanitarian Dialogue. (2011). Peacemaking in Asia and the Pacific: Women's participation, perspectives and priorities. Geneva: Centre for Humanitarian Dialogue. www.hdcentre.org/peacemaking-asia-and-pacificwomens-participation-perspectives-priorities

Chowdhury, A. K. (2010a, July 27). *Genesis of 1325 – What next after ten years?* Keynote address at the working meeting on UNSCR 1325: Strategies for Implementation at the United States Institute of Peace. Washington, DC. http://www.gc-council.org/en/download/Keynote_address_on_27_July-Genesis_of_1325.pdf

Chowdhury, A. K. (2010b, July 27). *Double fast-track indicators for turning the 1325 promise into reality.* Paper distributed at the U.S. Institute of Peace. Washington, DC.

DCAF. (2011). *Gender and security sector reform: Examples from the ground.* Geneva: DCAF.

De Groot, G. J. (2002, May 26–31). *Wanted: A few good women: Gender stereotypes and their implications for peacebuilding.* Presentation at the annual meeting of Women in NATO Forces, Brussels.

Devlin, C., & Elgie, R. (2008). The effect of increased women's representation in parliament: The case of Rwanda. *Parliamentary Affairs, 61*(2), 237–254.

Donno, D., & Russett, B. (2004). Islam, authoritarianism, and female empowerment: What are the linkages? *World Politics, 56*(July), 582–607.

Economist Intelligence Unit. (2011). *Democracy Index 2011: Democracy under stress.* Report. http://www.eiu.com

Enloe, C. (2004). Updating the Gendered Empire. In *The curious feminist, searching for women in the new age of empire*. Berkeley: University of California Press.

Etchart, L. (2005). Progress in gender mainstreaming in peace support operations. In R. Baksh, L. Etchart, E. Onubogu, & T. Johnson (Eds.), *Gender mainstreaming in conflict transformation: Building sustainable peace* (pp. 56–81). London: The Commonwealth Secretariat.

Etchart, L., & Baksh, R. (2005). Applying a gender lens to armed conflict, violence and conflict transformation. In R. Baksh, L. Etchart, E. Onubogu, & T. Johnson (Eds.), *Gender mainstreaming in conflict transformation: Building sustainable peace* (pp. 14–33). London: The Commonwealth Secretariat.

Falch, Å. (2010a). *Women's political participation and influence in post-conflict Burundi and Nepal*. Oslo: Peace Research Institute Oslo.

Falch, Å. (2010b). *Women's organizations: A driving force behind women's participation and rights* (PRIO peace policy brief, Vol. 3). Oslo: Peace Research Institute Oslo.

Fisher, S., Abdi, D. I., Ludin, J., Smith, R., Williams, S., & Williams, S. (2000). *Working with conflict: Skills and strategies for action*. London/New York: Zed Books.

Fritz, J. M. (2009). Women, peace and security: National plans, international interests, sociological possibilities. *Bulletin of the Kharkiv University Herald, Ukraine, 881*, 25–31.

Fritz, J. M., Doering, S., & Gumru, F. G. (2011). Women, peace, security and the national action plans. *Journal of Applied Social Science, 5*(1), 1–23.

Galtung, J. (1976). Three approaches to peace: Peacekeeping, peacemaking, and peacebuilding. In *Peace, war and defense: Essays in peace research*. Copenhagen: Ejlers. II (297–298).

Gervais, M. (2004). Human security and reconstruction efforts in Rwanda: Impact on the lives of women. In H. Afshar & D. Eade (Eds.), *Development, women and war: Feminist perspectives* (pp. 301–314). Oxford: Oxfam.

Gurr, T. R., Jaggers, K., & Moore, W. H. (1990). The transformation of the western state: The growth of democracy, autocracy, and state power since 1800. *Studies in Comparative International Development, 25*(Spring), 73–108.
Hauge, W. (2011). Girl soldiers in Guatemala. In A. Özerdem & S. Podder (Eds.), *Child soldiers: From recruitment to reintegration* (pp. 91–103). Basingstoke, Hampshire: Palgrave Macmillan.
Hentschel, G. (2005). Gender justice in peace and security politics: Feminist approaches and perspectives in the 21st century. English translation of a chapter that appeared in German. http://www.glow-boell.de/media/de/txt_rubrik_3/gender_justice.pdf In J. Davy, K. Hagemann, & U. Kätzel (Eds.), *Frieden – Gewalt – Geschlecht*: *Friedens- und Geschlechterforschung als Konfliktforschung*. Essen: Klartext Verlag.
Hunt Alternatives Fund. (2006, November). Betty Begombe. http://www.huntalternatives.org/pages/489_betty_bigombe.cfm
Hunt Alternatives Fund. (2010, April). Vikasa Dharmadasa. http://www.huntalternatives.org/pages8335_visaka_dharmadasa.cfm
International Association for Humanitarian Policy and Conflict Research. (2007–2008). www.peacebuildinginitiative.org
International Development Research Centre. (2010). *Democratic governance, women's rights and gender equality*: *Synthesis report*. http://idl-bnc.idrc.ca
Inter-Parliamentary Union. (2012a, September 30). Women in national parliaments: World average. http://www.ipu.org/wmn-e/world.htm
Inter-Parliamentary Union. (2012b, September 30). Women in national parliaments: World classification. http://www.ipu.org/wmn-e/classif.htm
Karama. (2012a). Women's rights following the Arab revolutions. http://www.wunrn.com/news/2012/10_12/10.../102912_women' s.htm
Karama. (2012b). About Karama. http://www.el-karama.org/content/about-karama
Kondoch, B. (2007). *International peacekeeping*. Surrey/Burlington: Ashgate.
Krook, M. L. (2007). Candidate gender quotas: A framework for analysis. *European Journal of Political Research, 46*, 367–394.
Kuehnast, K., de Jonge Oudraat, C., & Hernes, H. (Eds.). (2011). *Women & war: Power and protection in the 21st century*. Washington, DC: US Institute of Peace.
Kvinna Till Kvinna Foundation. (2009). *How to include women and sexual and gender-based violence in peace negotiations and agreements*. http://www.iktk.se
Lederach, J. P. (1997). *Building peace: Sustainable reconciliation in divided societies*. Washington, DC: United States Institute for Peace.
Lederach, J. P. (1999). *The journey toward reconciliation*. Scottdale: Herald Press.
Mackay, A. (2003). Training the uniforms: Gender and peacekeeping operations. *Development in practice, 13*(2&3), 217–22. Reprinted (pp. 100–132) In H. Afshar, & D. Eade (Eds.) (2004). *Development, women and war: Feminist perspectives*. Oxford: Oxfam.
Maiese, M. (2003). *What it means to build a lasting peace*. Beyond Intractability. http://www.beyondintractabiity.org/action/essay.jsp?id=28721&nid=5154
Mazurana, D. (2010). *Understanding the gendered legacies of armed conflict: Women's rights and lives during armed conflict and transition periods and governance*. Report sponsored by UK's Department for International Development and the International Development Research Centre in Canada. idl-bnc.idrc.ca/dspace/bitstream/10625/43897/1/130394.pdf
Mbatiah, M. (2011). The status of women in the traditional Swahili society. In P. I. Iribemwangi (Ed.), *Human rights, African values and traditions: An inter-disciplinary approach* (pp. 25–32). Nairobi: Haki-Africa.
McGhie, M. P., & Wamai, E. N. (2011). *Women's participation in the Kenya national dialogue and reconciliation*. Geneva: Centre for Humanitarian Dialogue.
McLaughlin, A. (2005, September 13). Africa's peace seekers: Betty Bigombe. *The Christian Science Monitor*. http://www.csmonitor.com/2005/0913/p01s04-woaf.html
Meintjes, S. (2010). Gender Governance and Democracy: Southern and Eastern Africa. Report. Canada: Department for International Development (IDRC in the UK) and the International Development Research Centre (IDRC in Canada).

Moghadam, V. M. (2011). Peace-building and reconstruction with women: Reflections on Afghanistan, Iraq and Palestine. In N. Visvanathan, L. Duggan, N. Wiegersma, & L. Nisonoff (Eds.), *The women, gender and development reader* (2nd ed., pp. 74–82). Halifax/London: Fernwood Publishing and Zed Books.

Naslund, E. (1999). Looking at peace through women's eyes: Gender-based discrimination in the Salvadoran peace process. *Journal of Public and International Affairs, 10*, 30.

Okeke-Ihejirika, P. E., & Franceschet, S. (2002). Democratization and state feminism: Gender politics in Africa and Latin America. *Development and Change, 33*(3), 439–466.

O'Neill, J., & Vary, J. (2011). Allies and assets: Strengthening DDR and SSR through women's inclusion. In M. Civic & M. Miklaucic (Eds.), *Monopoly of force: The Nexus of DDR and SSR* (pp. 77–107). Washington, DC: National Defense University Press.

Onubogu, E., & Etchart, L. (2005). Achieving gender equality and equity in peace processes. In R. Baksh, L. Etchart, E. Onubogu, & T. Johnson (Eds.), *Gender mainstreaming in conflict transformation: Building sustainable peace* (pp. 34–55). London: The Commonwealth Secretariat.

Ouellet, J. (2003, September). *Peacekeeping.* Beyond Intractability. http://www.beyondinractability.org/action/essay.jsp?id=18722&nid=1336

Papagianni, K. (2011). *Can mediation transform societies?* Issues emerging from the Oslo forum. www.hdcentre.org/publications/can-mediation-transform-societies-0

Potter, A. (2011). *G is for gendered: Taking the mystery out of gendering peace agreements.* Opinion. April, Geneva: Centre for Humanitarian Dialogue. February.

Raza, R. (2010, May 26). Bangladesh police in Haiti. *Blitz.* http://www.weeklyblitz.net/755/bangladesh-police-in-haiti

Rene, R. (Ed.). (2010). *Afghanistan in 2010: A survey of the Afghan people.* San Francisco: The Asia Foundation.

Rost, N., & Booth, J. A. (2008). Determinants of regime type in newly independent states. *European Journal of Political Research, 47*, 635–664.

Samuel, K. (2010, November). *The importance of autonomy: Women and the Sri Lankan peace negotiations*. Geneva: Centre for Humanitarian Dialogue. www.peacewomen.org/portal_resources_resource.php?id=1123

Trefon, T. (2011). *Congo masquerade: The political culture of aid inefficiency and reform failure*. London: Zed.

Tripp, A. M., Casimiro, I., Kwesiga, J., & Mungwa, A. (2011). African women's movements negotiating peace. In N. Visvanathan, L. Duggan, N. Wiegersma, & L. Nisonoff (Eds.), *The women, gender and development reader* (2nd ed., pp. 349–359). Halifax/London: Fernwood Publishing and Zed Books.

Tschirgi, N. (2011). *Conflict, education and peacebuilding: Converging perspectives.* http://conflictandeducation.org/?p=61

UNIFEM. (2008). *Who answers to women? gender & accountability*. New York: UNIFEM.

UNIFEM. (2010). *Women's participation in peace negotiations: Connections between presence and influence*. UNIFEM: New York.

United Nations Department of Peacekeeping Operations. (n.d.). http://www.un.org.peacekeeping

United Nations Department of Peacekeeping Operations. (2008). *United Nations peacekeeping operations; Principles and guidelines*. New York: UNDPO.

United Nations Department of Public Information, Peace and Security Section. (2012). *United Nations peace operations 2011: Year in review*. New York: United Nations.

United Nations Secretary-General. (2002). *Women, peace and security: Study submitted by the secretary-general pursuant to security council resolution 1325 (2000)*. New York: United Nations.

United Nations Secretary-General. (2008, September 25). *Report of the secretary-general on women and peace and security*. http://www.securitycouncilreport.org/atf/cf/%7B65BFCF9B-6D27-4E9C-8CD3-CF6E4FF96FF9%7D/WPS%20S2008622.pdf

United Nations Secretary-General. (2009, September 16). *Report of the secretary-general on women and peace and security.* http://www.securitycouncilreport.org/atf/cf/%7B65BFCF9B-6D27-4E9C-8CD3-CF6E4FF96FF9%7D/WPS%20S%202009%20465.pdf

United Nations Secretary-General. (2010, April 6). *Report of the secretary-general on women and peace and security.* S/2010/173. http://www.securitycouncilreport.org/atf/cf/%7B65BFCF9B-6D27-4E9C-8CD3-CF6E4FF96FF9%7D/WPS%20S2010%20173.pdf

United Nations Secretary-General. (2011, September 29). *Report of the secretary-general on women and peace and security.* http://www.securitycouncilreport.org/atf/cf/%7B65BFCF9B-6D27-4E9C-8CD3-CF6E4FF96FF9%7D/WPS%20S%202011%20598.pdf

United Nations Secretary-General. (2012a, October 2) *Report of the secretary-general on women and peace and security.* S/2012/732. http://www.securitycouncilreport.org/atf/cf/%7B65BFCF9B-6D27-4E9C-8CD3-CF6E4FF96FF9%7D/s_2012_732.pdf

United Nations Secretary-General. (2012b, January 13). *Conflict-related sexual violence: Report of the secretary general.* http://www.securitycouncilreport.org/atf/cf/%7B65BFCF9B-6D27-4E9C-8CD3-CF6E4FF96FF9%7D/WPS%20S%202012%2033.pdf

United Nations Security Council. (2000). *Resolution 1325 on women and peace and security.* http://www.un.org/events/res_1325e.pdf

United Nations Security Council. (2008). *Resolution 1820 on women and peace and security.* October 31. http://daccess-ods.un.org/TMP/7856949.html

United Nations Security Council. (2009a). *Resolution 1889 on women and peace and security.* http://daccess-ods.un.org/TMP/3886898.html

United Nations Security Council. (2009b). *Resolution 1888 on women and peace and security.* http://daccess-ods.un.org/TMP/1230558.html

United Nations Security Council. (2010). *Resolution 1960 on women and peace and Security.* http://un.org/documents/sres.htm

Verbeek, P. (2008). Peace ethology. *Behaviour, 145*, 1497–1524.

Victor, J. (2010). African peacekeeping in Africa: Warlord politics, defense economics, and state legitimacy. *Journal of Peace Research, 47*(2), 217–229.

Wall, B. E. (2001). Navajo conceptions of justice in the peacemaker court. *Journal of Social Philosophy, 32*(4), 532–546.

Waring, M. (2010). Women's political participation. Report. Idl-bnc.idrc.ca/dspace/bitstream/10625/43896/1/130393.pdf

Winslade, J. (2009). The secret knowledge of peacemaking. *Negotiation Journal, 25*, 559–568.

Woodrow Wilson Center Middle East Program. (2012). *Is the Arab awakening marginalizing women?* Occasional Paper Series. Summer. http://www.wilsoncenter.org/sites/default/files/Arab%20Awakening%20Marginalizing%20Women_0.pdf

World Bank. (2012). *Gender equality and development: World development report 2012.* Washington, DC: The International Bank for Reconstruction and Development/The World Bank.

Wright, R. B. (2011). *Rock the casbah: Rage and rebellion across the Islamic world.* New York: Simon and Schuster.

Zion, J. (1998). The dynamics of Navajo peacemaking. *Journal of Contemporary Criminal Justice, 14*(1), 58–74.

Chapter 14
The Role and Effectiveness of Non-governmental Third Parties in Peacebuilding

Diana Chigas

Beginning with the 1992 Agenda for Peace,[1] the conceptions of peacebuilding, as well as of mediation, have expanded dramatically. Peace work is no longer seen only in terms of peacemaking – mediation, good offices, conciliation – among leaders, or of peacekeeping undertaken by governmental actors. A broad consensus has emerged that "the end of civil war does not end societal suffering, division, and conflict" and that "alongside the top-down implementation of [a] peace agreement, concurrent bottom-up processes aimed at constructing a new social contract and healing societal divisions" are needed (Prendergast and Plumb 2002, p. 327). Peacebuilding has thus come to comprise all efforts that are "aimed at preventing the outbreak, the recurrence or continuation of armed conflict and therefore encompass a wide range of political, developmental, humanitarian and human rights programmes and mechanisms" (United Nations Security Council 2001). These include activities undertaken at different levels of society to promote socio-economic development, good governance, justice and security sector reform, reconciliation, and truth and justice activities (OECD-DAC 2007).

As a result, the number and variety of non-governmental actors engaged directly or indirectly in peace work has increased tremendously, ranging from conflict resolution non-governmental organizations (NGOs) to human rights organizations,

---

[1]The Agenda for Peace, officially known as the "Agenda for Peace: Preventive diplomacy, peacemaking and peacekeeping: Report of the Secretary General," was prepared by then Secretary-General Boutros Boutros Ghali. It identified "four areas for action, taken together, and carried out with the backing of all Members, offer a coherent contribution towards securing peace in the spirit of the Charter" in the post-Cold War environment: preventive diplomacy, peacemaking, peacekeeping and peacebuilding (Agenda for Peace, para. 22). It was one of the first documents to introduce and define the notion of post-conflict peacebuilding.

D. Chigas (✉)
Professor, Fletcher School of Law and Diplomacy, Tufts University (US)
e-mail: dchigas@cdacollaborative.org; diana.chigas@tufts.edu

J.M. Fritz (ed.), *Moving Toward a Just Peace: The Mediation Continuum*,
Clinical Sociology: Research and Practice, DOI 10.1007/978-94-007-2885-1_14,

to organizations supporting democratic development and governance, development organizations, the media, advocacy organizations, and protection and non-violent peacekeeping. Acceptance that both international and local civil society actors have a role to play in achieving sustainable peace is also now widespread (Paffenholz 2010; Pouligny 2005).

This expansion of the meaning of "peacebuilding" and the recognition that it entails a multiplicity of roles and activities, conducted at multiple levels in a broad range of sectors, reflects a useful evolution in our understanding of the realities of building and consolidating peace. However, it also has created confusion in practice, making it challenging to assess the roles non-governmental initiatives play in building peace. The lack of definitional specificity and intellectual rigor about peacebuilding has allowed an attitude of "anything goes" – that is, anything that anyone chooses to call peacebuilding is embraced as relevant, without further examination. Evaluations often assess "micro-level" results – whether they have achieved the specific goals set for the program, with the specific beneficiaries targeted – but rarely assess whether they have contributed to the broader peace. Moreover, because the idea of civil society's role in peacebuilding is, as one analyst has noted, "a concept strongly permeated by normative values," empirical evidence about the roles and contributions of these initiatives is limited (Paffenholz 2010, p. 43).

This chapter focuses on a subset of the large range of activities non-governmental actors have come to play in peacemaking and peacebuilding: *mediatory* roles of non-governmental third parties, in other words, roles undertaken both by internal and external civil society actors to promote joint decision making in conflicts.[2] This chapter presents a typology for understanding the varying mediatory roles non-governmental third parties play in peacebuilding. Drawing on recent research on the broader roles of civil society actors in peacebuilding and on the effectiveness of peace practice more generally,[3] it also will provide a framework for understanding the contributions, as well as the limitations, of non-governmental third party peace initiatives.

---

[2]External third parties, ranging from simple "go-betweens" to arbitrators or enforcers, have been a common resource for parties who are unable to resolve differences by themselves. Many of the functions external third parties fill can be, and often are, performed by insiders to the conflict, or members of the communities themselves (Ury 2000).

[3]*See*, e.g., Paffenholz (2010), Fischer (2006), Fisher (2005), Pouligny (2005), Fitzduff and Church (2004). The work of Future Generations on "Engaging Citizens and Communities to Create Peace and Security," conducted between 2008 and 2012 (see www.future.org/publications/peacebuilding) of the "People Building Peace" program of the European Centre for Conflict Prevention (collecting stories of civil society peace initiatives) on the contributions of civil society to peacebuilding and of CDA Collaborative Learning Projects' Reflecting on Peace Practice Program on the effectiveness and impacts of peace initiatives, especially NGO peace work, is also relevant here (www.cdacollaborative.org).

Non-governmental Roles in Peacebuilding

There are many ways to classify non-governmental roles and activities in peacebuilding. Historically, non-governmental approaches have been defined in relation and contrast to "track one" peacemaking and peacebuilding. "Track one" efforts are carried out at the official level; the intervenors are almost always official – a government, such as Norway in Sri Lanka, or an international organization, such as the Intergovernmental Authority on Development in East Africa (IGAD) in Sudan, the North Atlantic Treaty Organization (NATO) in Afghanistan or the United Nations Mission in Liberia – and the participants are mainly officials or key representatives of the conflicting parties.[4] "Track two," a term coined initially by former diplomat Joseph Montville, comprises "unofficial, informal interactions between members of adversarial groups or nations with the goals of developing strategies, influencing public opinions, and organizing human and material resources in ways that might help resolve the conflict" (Montville 1991, p. 262). Diamond and McDonald later refined the concept of "track two" to describe nine "tracks" of diplomacy needed for sustainable peacebuilding – of which only one involves decision makers (Diamond and McDonald 1996). This is the domain of non-official intervention.

John Paul Lederach's "pyramid," now widely used as a lens for analyzing and designing peace programs, similarly identifies three "levels" of actors – top leadership, middle-range leadership and grassroots – that need to be engaged for sustainable peace, along with an articulation of the different ways each contributes to peacebuilding (Lederach 1997). This conceptualization of peacebuilding as requiring many "tracks" of activity and work with populations at different levels of society was meant to underline the inadequacy of official, "top-down" processes, as well as the (often power-based) methods of conflict resolution used in them for resolving deep-rooted, societal conflicts.

In recent years, as the value of non-governmental involvement in peace processes has been accepted widely, the roles of non-governmental actors in peacebuilding have increasingly been framed in terms of *civil society* engagement. And, increasingly, analysis has focused on understanding the functions civil society performs in support of sustainable peace (Paffenholz 2010; World Bank 2010).[5] The advantage

---

[4]Peace operations mounted by international organizations or coalitions of governments, such as the United Nations in Liberia or NATO in Afghanistan, have greatly expanded the scope of interventions undertaken by "track one" (official) actors, bringing them into day-to-day governance and statebuilding in post-war societies, both at the central and regional levels.

[5]The World Bank has shifted its language from "non-governmental organizations and other civil society organizations" (World Bank 1998) to "civil society organizations," noting that the scope of organizations with which it consults has expanded beyond non-governmental organizations to include social movements, faith-based organizations, labor unions, community-based organizations and foundations (World Bank 2010).

Fig. 14.1 Tracks of non-governmental peacebuilding

of this shift in emphasis is that the notion of civil society has an even broader scope than non-governmental organizations, and therefore captures a number of activities of actors, especially local actors such as labor unions, professional associations, the media, and others that traditionally have not been analyzed in the context of "non-governmental" roles (Fischer 2006). It has also paved the way for a more robust analysis of the functions civil society actors play in peacebuilding.

The typology presented in this chapter (see Fig. 14.1) categorizes non-governmental interventions according to "tracks" or levels of intervention as a simple way of understanding the range of roles played by civil society actors. Drawing heavily on Lederach's pyramid, it divides non-governmental third-party roles into three "tracks," or levels, based on the level of society at which the intervention occurs, the kinds of activities undertaken and the broad expected results of the activities. At each level, the third party works with different participants (from decision makers in track one-and-a-half to grassroots in track three), and engages in different types of conflict transformation activities (from pre-mediation dialogue with negotiators in track one-and-a-half to training, peace education, trauma healing, empowerment and other activities to promote broad engagement in the peace process in track three).

This typology is designed to highlight a fundamental characteristic of third party assistance to peacebuilding: that it can and does occur at many levels of society and includes a wide range of roles. The remainder of this chapter elaborates on these various roles non-governmental third parties play and the activities they undertake. The chapter then analyzes their effectiveness: in particular, it asks what functions these efforts serve in building peace and what contributions they have made in practice to peacebuilding.

Unofficial Interventions with Decision Makers: Track One-and-a-Half Interventions

In track one-and-a-half interventions, unofficial (non-governmental or civil society) actors, such as former government officials, NGOs or religious or social organizations (such as the Catholic Church or Quaker organizations) intervene with official representatives or decision makers from the parties to promote peaceful resolution of conflict. As Susan Allen Nan notes, it is a role that "defies categorization" (Nan 2004, p. 57), as it "brings a strength of track-one diplomacy, the direct engagement of senior official representatives of the conflict parties, together with a strength of track-two diplomacy, informal off-the-record workshops on conflict resolution" (Nan 2005, p. 161).[6]

Unofficial actors have acted as direct mediators or conciliators between conflicting parties by hosting or facilitating official negotiation processes. At times this role has been played by local civil society organizations. In South Africa, for example, the South African Council of Churches (SACC) and the Consultative Business Movement (CBM) worked together to initiate and facilitate negotiations between political parties that led to the 1991 National Peace Accord, an unprecedented structure of national, regional and local structures aimed at ending the violence that prevailed at the time (Spies 2002). When negotiations began in South Africa in 1990, political violence had escalated dramatically and posed a threat to them. CBM and senior church leaders stepped in when a 1991 announcement by then President F.W. De Klerk calling a peace summit of political, church and community leaders had been rejected by the African National Congress (ANC) as a propaganda ploy. Through back-channel talks with political leaders, they developed a formula that allowed the summit to go forward as a part of an ongoing process, and a facilitating committee drawn from the church and business community organized and led consultative process that prepared and developed consensus on the text of the National Peace Accord (Spies 2002).[7]

---

[6]"Track Two" diplomacy is discussed later in this chapter.

[7]The facilitation committee had assessed that direct negotiations between the political parties would likely be unproductive, as they would become mired in positional bargaining. They decided that they would consult with and shuttle between the main parties to develop an acceptable negotiated solution. They launched the process with a low-key preparatory meeting, which attracted 120 participants from nearly all political persuasions, and was the first time the parties had met to discuss the violence. The facilitators established ground rules, and led the participants through a non-evaluative brainstorming session to identify the causes of violence and ways to

Frequently, mediators are outside third parties, acting alone or in collaboration with local civil society structures attempting to facilitate negotiations. The Community of Sant'Egidio, for example, a private voluntary Catholic organization based in Rome with contacts in the Vatican, played a key role in hosting and mediating peace talks in Mozambique. Building on 14 years of providing humanitarian aid in Mozambique, of relationship building with the two sides, and of pre-negotiation facilitation of contacts between them by the Mozambican churches, the Community of Sant'Egidio assumed the role of primary mediator in 1990 (Murdock and Zunguza 2010; Bartoli 2005). Convening the negotiators at its home in Rome, Sant'Egidio facilitators, with significant support from official diplomats from the international community, mediated the peace agreement that ended the civil war in that country. The HD Centre (formerly the Henri Dunant Centre) similarly mediated talks between the Government of Indonesia and the Free Aceh Movement (GAM) that led to the signing of a ceasefire agreement in 2002 (Schiller 2008; HD Centre 2010; Sebenius and Green 2010), and former Finnish President Martti Ahtisaari, under the auspices of another NGO, the Helsinki-based Conflict Management Initiative (CMI) mediated the talks that led to the peace agreement concluded between the parties in 2005 (Schiller 2008; HD Centre 2010). In that case, the establishment of the mediation process itself was facilitated by a private Finnish businessman (Schiller 2008).

Such direct mediation by unofficial third parties, however, is rare. There are few people or organizations with the sufficient stature, moral authority or connections with key decision makers to play such a role. Moreover, unofficial intermediaries can be seen as interfering with domestic politics, and even when they are accepted, as the breakdown of the cessation of hostilities mediated by the HD Centre reminds us, they often do not have the resources or stature to facilitate sustainable commitments.

More often non-governmental third parties play what Ronald Fisher has called a "consultant" role (Fisher 1972). In a consultant role, the unofficial third party brings key people (decision makers or their advisors) together in their *personal* capacities, rather than in their roles as representatives of their side, for direct dialogue and problem-solving. The meetings are low-key, closed to the public and non-binding. In a structured process, participants share their perceptions and concerns about the conflict, focusing on interests and basic needs underlying the positions their sides have taken, jointly analyze the issues and their relationship and develop ideas for moving the process forward. They are not asked to "agree" to any idea or to commit their side to any action, except insofar as they *personally* commit to take steps to

---

address them. The factors were grouped into themes and five working groups established to draft proposals. The facilitation committee, expanded and transformed into a preparatory committee with nine additional members from the main political parties, drafted proposals in consultation with the parties. The five working group texts were combined into a single text that formed the National Peace Accord, signed by 27 political parties, trade unions and government leaders at the National Peace Convention convened by the preparatory committee in September 1991 (Spies 2002).

follow-up on their discussions. The setting, the ground-rules of the process, the agenda and the facilitation permit a different kind of discussion than is normally possible in official interactions.

Negotiation and conflict resolution training have also been used in track one-and-a-half intervention. The training brings key participants from the conflict parties together for a common learning experienced focused on the development of skills and knowledge, which they use during the workshop to analyze and discuss the conflict (Fisher and Diamond 1995). These trainings often are joint – bringing the parties together – but have also been conducted separately (in parallel) with the parties to develop analytic and operational skills and a common vocabulary that can help them engage productively in negotiation when they come together (Chigas 1997). In El Salvador and South Africa, for example, a team from the Conflict Management Group (CMG), of which I was a part,[8] provided negotiation training to members of the negotiation teams on both sides. In the trainings, which were conducted separately for each of the negotiating teams and their advisors, participants were introduced to interest-based, joint gains models of negotiation using interactive exercises and applied them to analyze and develop options for managing the negotiation processes that were beginning in both situations. In addition to providing an opportunity for the parties to reflect on the process of their negotiations, the trainings helped build a common vocabulary and approach that facilitated more productive negotiations (Chigas 1997).

The Georgia-South Ossetia Dialogue Project, implemented between 1995 and 2000 also by CMG, in cooperation with the Norwegian Refugee Council (NRC), is an example of a track one-and-a-half intervention that combined both consultation and training approaches.[9] This initiative comprised a series of "facilitated joint brainstorming" meetings between members of the negotiating teams, their advisors and other influential officials (e.g., parliamentarians) aimed ultimately at developing productive processes and options for the negotiations. The project was initiated at a time when official negotiations were stalled, but the ceasefire that had been agreed was still holding. This, in many ways, was a propitious time for a track one-and-a-half intervention, in that it could not detract from an official process, yet had the potential to pave the way for negotiations to recommence productively (Nan 2005, p. 167).

The agendas of the first meetings included exercises and skill-building in negotiation, designed to stimulate reflection on participants' assumptions about

[8]CMG is a United States-based NGO founded by Roger Fisher, author of the well-known book on interest-based negotiation, *Getting to YES*, with expertise in negotiation training, advice and facilitated dialogue. It is currently part of the US-based international humanitarian and development NGO, Mercy Corps.

[9]The author participated in this initiative as part of the CMG team. The experience of the facilitation team, as well as of the participants in the project, are well-documented in the research of Susan Allen Nan (2002, 2004, 2005) and Lara Olson (2001), both scholar-practitioners with extensive experience in the region. Olson served as coordinator for the project in Georgia with NRC.

the negotiation process and how a mutual gains process might be developed. In structured communication processes facilitated by the CMG-NRC team, participants shared their own experiences, interests, needs and fears and listened to and explored those of the other side. Participants also brainstormed ideas for dealing with significant issues in the conflict, especially those of common concern such as refugees, cultural and economic ties and development.

During the first meetings, participants began to develop relationships, understand each other's interests and perspectives and enhance their skill in mutual gains approaches to negotiation. The later meetings focused more directly on the substantive issues in negotiation in a process of joint learning about governance arrangements in Catalonia and the Basque regions of Spain. Participants traveled to those regions, met with officials involved in government (both at the center and in the regions) and discussed how the learnings might be relevant to the Georgia-South Ossetia context (Nan 2005, p. 168). Following the last overseas meetings, a core group of Georgians and South Ossetians formed a steering committee that met on a regular basis closer to home, especially before official sessions mediated by Russia and the Organization for Security and Cooperation in Europe (OSCE), to share perspectives, correct any misunderstandings, and explore ideas for negotiation (Chigas 2007). These meetings, conducted with less intensive CMG/NRC facilitation and support, provided a forum for the negotiators to meet unofficially to reflect on the negotiation process (Nan 2005).

The Woodrow Wilson Center for International Scholars' Burundi Leadership Training Program (BLTP) is another example of a track one-and-a-half intervention using training to stimulate dialogue and build skills and relationships to support implementation of peace agreements. Begun in 2002 to aid the transition to peace following the Arusha and later the Pretoria Accords, BLTP conducted a series of intensive 6-day training workshops in interest-based negotiation, communication, mediation, conflict analysis, strategic planning and organizational change for close to 100 political, military and civil society leaders. The leadership of the program by former Ambassador to Burundi, Howard Wolpe, provided legitimacy to the program and, significantly, access to high level leaders and policy makers across the political spectrum. The workshops were designed to "build a cohesive, sustainable network of leaders who could work together across all ethnic and political divides in order to advance Burundi's reconstruction" (Wolpe and McDonald 2006). These workshops catalyzed profound transformations in the way participants saw and related to one another (Uvin and Campbell forthcoming). Follow-up workshops specifically for key security sector actors led to significant breakthroughs in negotiations related to the integration of the Burundian army (ibid.).[10]

---

[10]The non-targeted follow-up workshops for participants in the initial trainings were found by evaluators to be less effective than the targeted trainings. While participants did interact more outside the workshops following the initial trainings, the contact was primarily social, not widespread, and resulted in little professional or political change (Uvin and Campbell forthcoming).

Unofficial Interventions with Unofficial Actors: Track Two

Track two interventions engage influential unofficial actors from civil society, business or religious communities, and local leaders and politicians who are considered to be experts in the area or issue being discussed (Search for Common Ground 2010). They usually seek to supplement track one diplomacy by working with middle levels of society to improve communication, understanding and relationships across conflict lines and to develop ideas for resolving the conflict. The participants have no official status, and, as in track one-and-a-half, do not negotiate or commit to ideas.

A number of methodologies for track two interventions have been developed and have been well-documented since the 1970s. Perhaps the best known is the interactive problem-solving workshop originated by John Burton, Herbert Kelman, Ron Fisher and others (Burton 1969; Kelman 1972; Fisher 1972; Kelman 2000). The workshops bring together "politically involved and often politically influential" members of conflicting societies who are not officials for direct, private interaction, joint analysis of the conflict and joint problem solving (Kelman 2000). They may be parliamentarians, political activists or leaders, civil society leaders, journalists, members of think tanks, or academics – people who are within the mainstream of their societies and close (but not necessarily in) the political center. The third parties are non-governmental actors, often scholar/practitioners, who are impartial and whose training and expertise enable them to facilitate productive dialogue and problem-solving between the participants (Fisher and Keashly 1988, 1991). The unofficial stature of the participants and the quasi-academic setting of the workshops permit a greater degree of freedom to explore alternative perspectives on the conflict and to formulate new ideas (Kelman 2000).

Although practitioners vary in how actively they facilitate the meetings, their role is "strictly facilitative" in the sense that they do not engage in or offer suggestions on the substantive issues in discussion (Kelman 2005a). The facilitators' goal is to facilitate communication between participants and joint analysis of the conflict, as well as development of shared approaches for dealing with them.

Kelman and his colleagues have applied this approach to workshops between Israelis and Palestinians since the early 1970s. These workshops have been credited with contributing to the breakthrough achieved in the Oslo Accords in 1993 (Kelman 2005b) by preparing cadres (many of whom eventually moved into official leadership positions) to negotiate productively, by preparing the political atmosphere for negotiations, and by providing substantive inputs (both in terms of ideas and understanding of the perspective of the other) to the negotiations (Kelman 2005b, 2000).

Many participants in these problem-solving workshops were part of the Geneva Initiative, a track two process that produced an unofficial Draft Status Permanent Status agreement (the Geneva Accord) launched in 2003 (Klein 2007; Kelman 2005b). The Geneva process was initiated after the failure of the Camp David process in 2000 and the start of the second *Intifada*, and was spearheaded by Israelis and Palestinians. It was conducted with Swiss support but no heavy third-party facilitation. Unlike many track two processes, the Geneva initiative was both widely publicized and produced a detailed blueprint for Israeli-Palestinian peace, agreed and signed by the participants in the process (Klein 2007; Kelman 2005b). The Accords, however, remain unofficial; the detailed nature of the Accord and its continuing wide publicity are designed to "bring that moment of peace closer, by showing the way and preparing public opinion and leadership to be accepting of the real compromises required to solve the conflict" (Geneva Initiative 2010).

Another model for track two diplomacy was developed by former US diplomat Harold Saunders initially to "engage representative citizens from the conflicting parties in designing steps to be taken in the political arena to change perceptions and stereotypes, to create a sense that peace may be possible, and to involve more and more of their compatriots" (Chufrin and Saunders 1993). This "public peace process," as Saunders calls it, proceeds through five phases. The first phase comprises defining the problem and deciding to engage with the other side. In the Inter-Tajik Dialogue begun in 1993, the organizers (Saunders and colleagues at the Dartmouth Conference Regional Conflicts Task Force) contacted more than 100 people in Tajikistan, seeking broad representation of the different factions in the conflict, at a second or third tier of authority, in order to ensure they could explore ideas freely (Saunders 2005; Slim and Saunders 2001).

The second phase, mapping issues and relationships and identifying possibilities for working together, began with the first meeting in 1993. That meeting, in which the participants "were absorbed with unloading their feelings about the origins and conduct of the civil war" (Slim and Saunders 2001), ushered in the third phase, analyzing the problem through dialogue and designing ways of changing the relationship. Participants explored approaches to key issues and came to broad conclusions about how to address them. The fourth phase, building scenarios of interacting steps that can be taken in the political arena to change the relationships, and the fifth phase, acting together, resulted in at least 18 joint memoranda.

Until the beginning of the UN–sponsored official negotiations, the Inter-Tajik Dialogue was one of the few existing channels of communication between the opposition and the government (Jean and Mujollanov 2010). The participants shared their ideas with the negotiators and international actors, as well as with the population at large in a number of public events inside and outside Tajikistan. Some participants became involved in the official negotiations and thus were able to transmit the ideas developed in the dialogue to their teams directly. The conclusion of a peace agreement in 1997 did not obviate the need for dialogue; rather, the track two process began to focus on implementation of the accords, which was fraught with many divisive issues. As a representative of the ruling political party in Tajikistan today, and a former Inter-Tajik Dialogue member, noted, "meetings held after 1997 were as important as the ones before and during the peace talks" (Jean and Mujollanov 2010). The Inter-Tajik Dialogue made recommendations for implementing the details of the agreement and introducing the necessary changes to the constitution and legislative processes, among others. They also began to broaden the scope of the dialogues to include regional dialogues amongst local government, traditional leadership and local political party leaders, in order to engage citizens in the peace process (Jean and Mujollanov 2010).

Non-governmental Roles at the Grassroots: Track Three Interventions

This level of non-governmental activity has seen the greatest growth since the beginning of the 1990s. Track three

> is essentially 'people to people' diplomacy undertaken by both individuals and private groups from non-government international organizations that are dedicated to promoting specific causes, universal ideals and norms, and enacting systematic social change. This type of diplomacy often involves organizing meetings and conferences, generating media exposure, and political and legal advocacy for people and communities who are largely marginalized from political power centers and are unable to achieve positive change without outside assistance (Search for Common Ground 2010).

Many track three efforts operate at the local, or community, level. Many involve long-term relationship building across conflict lines and capacity-building endeavors among ordinary citizens, promotion of a culture of peace, peace education and establishment of structures and mechanisms for local conflict resolution. The underlying theory is that conflict is experienced most intensely by people at the grassroots, and that sustainable peace requires *transformation* of relationships and structures throughout society, not merely resolution of the issues in conflict (Lederach 1997).[11] Transformation involves "a process of engaging with and transforming the relationships, interests, discourses and, if necessary, the very constitution of society that supports the continuation of violent conflict," in which "people within the conflict parties, within the society or region affected and outsiders with relevant human and material resources all have complementary roles to play" (Miall 2004).

The range of activities at this level is broad. In addition to more traditional "people-to-people" activities such as dialogue, training and other mediatory activities that bring people together across conflict lines in order to promote mutual understanding, relationship-building and breaking down of stereotypes, track three interventions include: psychosocial work to help communities deal with the trauma that violent conflict has produced; joint social, sports and arts events; joint business and economic activity to promote cooperation; economic and social development projects designed to promote interdependence of the conflict parties and provide concrete incentives for support of peace; and work with media, religious organizations and other shapers of public opinion. They also include support for community-based development and conflict resolution mechanisms, as well as protection of civilians and human rights promotion.

In Liberia, for example, the Locally Initiated Networks for Community Strengthening (LINCS) program, funded by the US Agency for International Development and implemented by CHF International beginning in 2004, worked with citizens in a number of communities in Lofa County to form Community Peace Councils (CPCs)

---

[11] While this transformation approach is quite popular, it is not universal; many practitioners adopt more limited views of what is necessary and possible, including more utilitarian and interest-based approaches to institutional and structural change that do not aspire to fundamental transformation.

that would mediate disputes in the community that could escalate to violence, especially conflicts associated with returns of internally displaced people (IDPs) and refugees and reintegration of ex-combatants (CHF 2007; CDA 2006). Efforts were made to ensure that all key groups in the community were represented in the CPCs, and they received training in conflict management and mediation skills, leadership, human rights and trauma healing. Other elements of the program included inter-ethnic dialogue forums in "flash point" communities where tensions were high as a result of intense violence during the war and community and livelihood projects (CDA 2006). In many communities, these CPCs were able to facilitate smooth returns of refugees and internally displaced people, and handle most community-level disputes (CDA 2006). According to CHF, they also were able in some instances to mediate community-level peace agreements that prevented violence (CHF 2007). In addition, they may have, through their very existence, promoted an atmosphere of conflict resolution and problem solving without resort to violence (CDA 2006).

In the Philippines, a significant amount of training in the "Culture of Peace"[12] has been done with a wide variety of groups. The Mindanaoan Association for Natives (IMAN), for example, a local Islamic-based organization, uses Culture of Peace workshops and emphasizes holistic Islamic practices to promote peace and as a basis for confidence in initiating inter-religious dialogue (Leguro and Rudy 2010). Non-governmental actors there also have become involved in protection and monitoring at the grassroots level. Nonviolent Peaceforce, for example, "deploys internationals to work with local peacekeepers, contribute to their safety, help maintain ceasefires and advance the peace process" (Nonviolent Peaceforce 2010). It has supported such local civil society agencies as Bantay Ceasefire, which has investigated specific instances of breach of the ceasefire in Mindanao since 2002 and maintained contact with field commanders on both sides to defuse potentially lethal firefights (Leguro and Rudy 2010).

Much work is done with youth and increasingly with the media. Seeds of Peace (SOP), a US-based nongovernmental organization is one example. SOP works with teenage youth from the Middle East (Israel, Palestine, Jordan, Egypt) and other conflict areas at its 150-acre International Camp for Conflict Resolution in Otisfield, Maine. The goal of the program is to create a safe place where teenagers who have grown up perceiving the "other" as a permanent enemy can begin to see the human face of their adversaries and form lasting friendships. Follow-up activities, from continuing dialogues to community service projects and seminars, are designed to support and sustain the changes in attitude and relationships achieved during the camp experience (Seeds of Peace 2010). With the Ministries of Education of the various parties managing the selection process for the camps, SOP believes that the governments help send the signal that the involvement of ordinary people in the peace process is as vital as that of governments (Wallach 2000).

[12]The "Culture of Peace" trainings are a program aimed at changing the way people think about their own history, culture and patterns of interacting with others. They are designed to promote personal transformation, as negative biases are challenged through modules that include historical analysis from various perspectives, trauma healing, and forums for talking about conflict (Leguro and Rudy 2010).

In Burundi, Studio Ijambo, one of Search for Common Ground's many media programs, is representative of the increasing use of media as a form of track three intervention. Established in 1995 as an independent radio station, Studio Ijambo produces programs dedicated to peace, national reconciliation and dialogue among polarized groups in Burundi. In a country where radio reaches an estimated 85 % of the population and has been used in the past to promote hatred and fear and incite the population to commit unspeakable acts of violence, Studio Ijambo undertook to provide balanced, anti-inflammatory programming.

Finally, humanitarian and development organizations have become involved in track three peacebuilding by adjusting many traditional development or humanitarian activities – such as health, education, agriculture, income generation, reconstruction of homes and facilitation of returns of displaced people – to include conflict transformation elements. For example, the Medical Network for Social Reconstruction in the former Yugoslavia brings together health professionals from the entire region. They have received intensive training in conflict resolution and reconciliation concepts, and with those skills, convene conferences to promote professional exchange and cooperation across conflict lines, as well as train other health professionals in psychosocial assistance and trauma recovery (Gutlove and Thompson 2003). Community-driven reconstruction processes, now implemented in many post-war countries, support the creation of broad-based local councils that decide the community's reconstruction priorities, for which they then receive a block grant. The aim is not only to deliver reconstruction assistance more quickly and efficiently, but to create forums and processes that foster cooperation and reconciliation (Strand et al. 2003).

The premise of these track three activities is that peace must be built from the bottom up as well as from the top down. As Louise Diamond, one of the originators of the concept of multi-track diplomacy, notes:

> The forces of war have an existing infrastructure that enables them to mobilize and actualize their aims—they have armies and arms suppliers; transportation, commerce and communications systems; banking, taxing and other funding mechanisms; media, education and propaganda systems; and government ministries, clans, villages, political parties and other entities capable of taking action. The forces of peace have little of this... Much more needs to be done to create both a human and institutional infrastructure for peace-building, in order to concretize these methods in social, political and economic systems that can both stand on their own and work together towards a shared goal. (Diamond 1999)

Track three interventions work to rebuild "social capital" (Varshney 2001) and the economic, social and governance structures in society at large in order to ensure that peace is sustained.[13]

---

[13]Robert Putnam introduced the notion of social capital in his work, *Making Democracy Work* (1993), to refer to civic networks. He subsequently distinguished between "bridging" and nonbridging civic networks. Varshney (2001, 2002) uses the term "networks of engagement" to emphasize the fact that not all civic networks are important for prevention of violence, but specifically *inter-ethnic* ones, and that the more institutionalized these networks are, the more effective they are.

Contributions of Non-governmental Third Party Interventions to Peace

Identifying and assessing the contributions of non-governmental, or civil society, activities to the promotion of peace is challenging for a number of reasons. First, there is no consensus on what "peace" is; it varies from context to context, in different stages of conflict, and from person to person. There is general agreement that "peace" is more than just "stopping war and destructive conflict" (Anderson and Olson 2003) or absence of direct violence– or "negative peace," in Johan Galtung's terms (Galtung 1969). But what a "just and sustainable peace" (Anderson and Olson 2003), or positive peace (in Galtung's terms), entails is elusive and varied, making assessments of "effectiveness" difficult. Second, since the 1990s especially, the dominant model of peacebuilding has been the liberal democratic peace. All activities seen to further democracy, human rights, and economic and political liberalism are seen *ipso facto* to promote peace, but the assumptions about their contributions to peace are not tested. Third, as Paffenholz and her co-authors (2010, p. 43) note, "civil society is often seen as the 'good society,' inevitably contributing to peacebuilding in a positive way" – in other words, it is often viewed in normative, rather than analytic, terms (Fischer 2006). As a result, empirical evidence about the contributions of civil society initiatives to peacebuilding is weak.

Fourth, non-governmental efforts are generally not designed to achieve agreements or to effect major policy shifts in the short term. Rather, they often seek to influence more intangible – and harder to measure – factors driving conflict, such as attitudes and relationships, in longer time frames. And even where the impacts of interventions on attitudes and relationships can be measured, the significance of these "micro" level achievements for the larger peace is often not clear.

Finally, attribution of impact to civil society initiatives among the myriad interdependent influences on peace is difficult. Civil society initiatives are often not at the center of, or the most significant contributors to, positive turning points in the conflict, but are often involved in preparing the ground for them or contributing to them in other ways. Assessing this indirect contribution is difficult.

Despite these challenges, some real, substantiated contributions of non-governmental third parties can be identified by looking at the functions and roles they fulfill, and the importance of those functions for addressing the drivers of conflict. Paffenholz (2010) provides a useful framework for categorizing the functions civil society plays in peacebuilding. Building on the literature on the roles of civil society in democracies and on the policies and practices in development cooperation, she proposes seven civil society "peacebuilding functions," summarized in Table 14.1, and assesses the relevance and effectiveness of these functions in various phases of conflict. Her framework is taken as a point of departure for categorizing and assessing the functions of non-governmental third parties in peacebuilding, along with Bill Ury's work (2000) on the general roles

Table 14.1 Comparison of Paffenholz civil society functions and Ury roles of the third side (Descriptions of the functions and roles, including quotes, are taken from Paffenholz (ed.) 2010 and from Ury 2000)

Paffenholz: civil society peacebuilding functions	Ury: "third side" roles
Protection	***Peacekeeper***
Protection of citizens "not only vis-à-vis a despotic state but also against any armed actor, ranging from the national army to local groups" (p. 67), e.g. accompaniment, humanitarian aid, human security activities	Providing protection when the rules are broken and the limits on fighting exceeded
Monitoring	***Witness***
Early warning and reporting on human rights abuses	Paying attention to escalation of conflict and providing early warning signals
Advocacy and public communication	***Equalizer***
"Promoting relevant social and political themes on the public agenda" (p. 69)	"Democratizing power" by empowering the weak and unrepresented to negotiate a fair and mutually satisfactory solution with the more powerful, e.g., through bringing the powerful to the table, supporting nonviolent action, supporting inclusive processes
In-group socialization	***Teacher***
Promoting attitude change by developing peaceful conflict resolution and reconciliation and inculcating a culture of peace within societal groups	Giving people skills, values, perspectives to handle conflict productively
Social cohesion	***Bridge-builder***
Building community, relationships, attitude change between groups: building relationships, bringing people together to produce outcomes for peacebuilding, bringing people together to cooperate for non-peace objectives	Forging relationships across conflict lines, e.g., through dialogue, joint projects, and other cross-cutting ties
	Healer
	Repairing injured relationships
Intermediation and facilitation	***Mediator***
Mediation, facilitation and other intermediatory processes between the citizens and the state and between conflicting groups	Facilitating communication, dispute resolution, problem solving amongst parties
	Arbiter
	Determining disputed rights
Service delivery	***Provider***
Provision of aid and services	Enabling people to meet their needs, helping people satisfy basic human needs (food, safety, identity, freedom)
	Referee
	Setting limits to fighting, e.g., rules for fair fighting, removing destructive arms, etc.

(irrespective of actor – insider or outsider – or of conflict setting or nature) that "third siders" take on to help communities prevent, resolve and contain destructive conflict (see Table 14.1).[14]

Drawing on both frameworks of useful functions, the areas in which non-governmental third party mediatory activities have the most significant impacts (potential and actual) are grouped into five categories: (1) Improved communication and dialogue; (2) Skills and attitudes for more productive interaction with the "other"; (3) Bridge-building and improved relationships and trust; (4) Strengthening of local advocacy and empowerment for peace; and (5) Engagement of the "hard to reach" in the peace process (Anderson and Olson 2003). The protection/peacekeeping and advocacy/equalizer roles have become increasingly important and effective civil society roles in peacebuilding. Because they are not mediatory roles,[15] these are not addressed here, except insofar as intermediary-type activities have strengthened local capacities for such advocacy for peace.

I have also not included monitoring and service delivery as important non-governmental third party mediatory functions. Non-governmental third parties, both insiders and outsiders, engage in a significant amount of monitoring and service delivery. Indeed, service delivery constitutes a large proportion of international NGO activity in conflict and post-war settings. Like Paffenholz (2010), I have found that monitoring is generally not a stand-alone function, but a pre-condition or part of a strategy for protection, advocacy or intermediation. Similarly, while service delivery may quantitatively be the most performed function in all phases of conflict (Paffenholz 2010), it is again not in itself a peacebuilding function, but a precursor to or entry point for the other peacebuilding functions. I have thus not included monitoring and service delivery as separate peacebuilding functions, even while they both are often critical parts of a strategy leading to positive peacebuilding impacts.

These functions can, and should be, carried out at all levels – from track one-and-a-half to track three – albeit with different foci and activities. Indeed, their impacts

---

[14] Adopting a framework based in the dominant liberal democratic model for peacebuilding, as Paffenholz and her co-authors do, carries a potential limitation of restricting inquiry into potentially useful roles that do not conform to the conception of civil society in democratic theory. For this reason, I draw also on Ury's work on "third sider" roles in conflict, both because of its anthropological perspective and because of its focus on "a systemic approach to handling conflict" and on "transforming conflict from destructive conflict into constructive change" (Ury and Weiss 2010). Their categories of functions are similar, but Ury's emphasis on roles that contribute to effective conflict handling at different stages of escalation, rather than on specific actors, emphasizes some different dimensions and helps to avoid potential biases that could result from reliance on democracy-theory based conceptions of civil society roles.

[15] Indeed, some would juxtapose the advocacy and public communication role with the mediatory roles of non-governmental third parties. *See,* e.g., Fisher and Zimina 2009.

occur not in isolation – from a single function or set of activities at one level of society – but, as will be discussed later, from linkages and transfers across levels, to track one, and amongst the different functions themselves.

1. Facilitation of communication and dialogue

Negative perceptions, mutual distrust, deadlock and hostility are reinforced and perpetuated by lack of communication between the conflict parties at all levels of society. In some cases, the barrier is physical. In Cyprus, for example, until 2003, the UN-patrolled Green Line dividing the two communities was difficult to cross, and telecommunications were limited to three lines. Ceasefire lines and restrictions on travel between Georgia and South Ossetia and Abkhazia, or between India and Pakistan similarly impede communication. Even when no physical barrier exists, political, legal, social or psychological barriers – ranging from legal restrictions and requirements, such as the legal prohibition in Israel on contact with Palestine Liberation Organization members that existed prior to the Oslo process, to social pressure and self-censorship, restrict possibilities for communication. The communication vacuum "provides a greenhouse in which rumours flourish. Facts are embellished or distorted" (Pruitt and Kim 2004, p. 108).

Non-governmental third parties have made significant contributions in opening channels of communication between parties who are not negotiating and who would otherwise find it difficult to meet or to acknowledge any contact with the "other." They have also helped improve the quality of communication and mutual understanding between parties at all levels of society. At a time when there was no official communication between the United States and the Palestine Liberation Organization (PLO), for example, Landrum Bolling, former President of Earlham College in Richmond, Indiana and a Quaker peacemaker, served as an unofficial liaison between Yasir Arafat and President Jimmy Carter. Track one-and-a-half and track two dialogues have offered a similar opportunity for Israeli-Syrian dialogue in an environment in which political constraints limited official contacts (Kaye 2001). In Mozambique and Aceh, when it was difficult for the Government to initiate contacts with rebel groups, non-governmental organizations – the Catholic Church in the case of Mozambique and the Swiss-based HD Centre and CMI in Aceh – were asked to make a connection with rebel leaders and facilitate contact between the parties (Murdock and Zunzuga 2010; Schiller 2008). Government concerns about legitimizing the status of rebel groups, and both parties concerns about looking weak or prejudicing their positions, can be lessened by the unofficial identity of the third party and the facilitative, informal nature of the process.

At the grassroots level, non-governmental third parties have convened youth camps, sport and cultural events, community development committees and joint technical training, as well as joint economic cooperation projects that in some cases provide the only forum for safe cross-conflict contact and communication. In Ambon, Indonesia, for example, Mercy Corps' humanitarian program, established 15 months after Christian-Muslim conflict began, had a mixed (Christian-Muslim) staff worked out of a single office in a neutral area of the divided city. Mercy Corps enlarged the neutral space by establishing a resource center in which Christians and Muslims could gather (Mercy Corps 2002). It was one of the only places members of both communities could come together.[16] In Kosovo, NGO-sponsored programs provided a safe and legitimate place for Serb-Albanian interaction, as security concerns and intra-group intimidation prevented inter-group contact for anything other than necessary business. As one participant in a youth dialogue in Eastern Kosovo noted, "If there were no NGOs, things would be very different in Gjilan town. There would be no communication, and people would not be as close as they are now" (Chigas et al. 2007).

The ground rules, structure, venue and agenda for unofficial discussions also make possible a quality of communication that is often not possible in more official (track one) processes or in nonfacilitated interactions between members of the conflicting parties. Polarization of communication, characterized by blaming, accusations and use of language that is provocative or threatening to the other side, occurs at all levels of society (Fisher and Keashly 1991). This perpetuates confrontation, mistrust and hopelessness about the possibilities for change. Negotiation and problem-solving, at any level, become impossible under these conditions.

Unofficial processes can change this dynamic. Participants exchange personal stories about their experiences in the conflict, and listen to the stories of the other. In more systematic track two and three processes, participants begin to analyze the conflict in a structured way, delving under positions and arguments to understand underlying needs, fears, concerns, interests, and values motivating the parties, and to understand the deeper causes that have led to conflict. They become aware of the ways in which their language reinforces mutual mistrust because it is experienced as disrespectful, unjust, or threatening by the other side and begin to develop de-escalatory language that can create an environment in which they discuss the heart of the problem for them in a more productive way. Interacting with the "enemy" in a different way in the meetings and casually during meals and free time rehumanizes the other and helps parties realize that they have many similar fears, concerns and needs. This becomes the basis for developing a mode of communication and working trust between the participants that allows them jointly to analyze and develop solutions to the issues driving the conflict (Meyer 2002; Kelman 2000).

These facilitated processes have led to the transformation of the mode of communication and of attitudes, relationships and analysis of the conflict. A number of significant contributions to peacebuilding, that is, effects beyond the participants themselves, have resulted, both directly on peacemaking/negotiation (track one) processes and indirectly through building capacities to manage conflict.

[16]Mercy Corps also selected a Muslim and a Christian partner for emergency warehousing for food distribution. These partners agreed to work with each other, even though they had had no contact since the war had begun. Over two years of working together on procurement and in mixed communities, they developed a relationship that led them to form a consortium of Christian and Muslim organizations to advocate for the rights of conflict-affected people (Mercy Corps 2002).

(a) New options for constructive negotiations

A number of track one-and-a-half and track two initiatives have produced new ideas for de-escalation and settlement of the conflict that otherwise could not have been raised or developed in an official negotiation. Typically, these ideas represent a consensus among all (or most) participants. In most instances, the recommendations are presented, either jointly or separately through participants' own channels of influence, to key decision makers and negotiators, as well as international actors. The Dartmouth Conference's Inter-Tajik Dialogue, for example, produced 18 joint memoranda with recommendations on the organization of the official negotiation process. The Commission on National Reconciliation (CNR), the central implementation mechanism of the 1997 peace agreement in Tajikistan, later organized its program through four subcommissions that echoed the recommendations of the first memorandum (Slim and Saunders 2001). Similarly, CMG's Georgia-South Ossetia Dialogue Project resulted in a number of concrete ideas for confidence-building measures, cooperation in law enforcement and steps for normalization of life in the conflict zone. Many of these ideas were adopted in the formal negotiation process, and for a period of time before the change of government (and renewed attempts to force a resolution), tensions between the parties de-escalated significantly (Olson 2001).[17]

Ideas developed and explored in track one-and-a-half and track two discussions have also influenced the platforms and positions of particular parties. High-level members of the pro-settlement Republican Turkish Party (CTP) in northern Cyprus, for example, reported that the discussions held and the ideas produced in track two dialogues enriched their own party's platform. The ideas developed were integrated into the party's thinking about possible solutions to the conflict, including on constitutional provisions, and led to a change in its position on important issues, such as the right of return (Chigas forthcoming). In South Africa, the Mont Fleur Scenario process brought together a diverse team of South Africans from the establishment and the opposition, a variety of political perspectives, trade unions, community workers, business and academia to use the Shell scenario methodology to explore how to effect a successful transition to democracy. The process had a profound effect on the ANC's thinking about economic policy (Kahane 2002).[18]

[17]For example, partly as a result of the meetings, Georgia lifted its policy of withholding reconstruction assistance to South Ossetia. In addition, protocols signed in the negotiations regarding refugee return, mutually acceptable identity documents, installation of telephone lines, reduction of peacekeeping posts and assistance to joint business ventures had their origins in the Dialogue Project discussion (Olson 2001).

[18]The "Mont Fleur" scenario exercise, undertaken in South Africa during 1991–92, as negotiations began, brought people together from across organizations to think creatively about the future of their country. The scenario team met three times in a series of 3-day workshops at the Mont Fleur conference center outside Cape Town. After considering many possible stories, the participants agreed on four scenarios that they believed to be plausible and relevant for the evolution of the country's economy. The Mont Fleur project produced several different types of results: substantive messages about the future of South Africa and the consequences of choices on how to manage the conflict, politics and the economy; informal networks and understandings amongst a broad spectrum of key people, and changed ways of thinking about policies and decisions (Kahane 2002).

In these examples, the unofficial and informal nature of the discussions and the intermediaries made it possible to develop and explore ideas that might have been too bold or sensitive to raise in official negotiations or too challenging of conventional wisdom to discuss openly. The connections of the participants to the negotiations – direct, in the case of track one-and-a-half processes and more indirect in the case of track two – enabled transfer to track one.

(b) Enhanced capacity to negotiate

In addition to generating new ideas for negotiation, unofficial intermediation processes can be a way of nurturing cadres able to negotiate productively with the other side and resolve difficult issues when a window of opportunity opens. In many instances, participants in track two initiatives end up in official positions and are able to take advantage of their previous experience interacting with the "other." In South Africa, for example, key African National Congress (ANC) and National Party negotiators in the constitutional talks that ended apartheid were veterans of previous informal discussions (Lieberfeld 2002). The Oslo Process that led to the 1993 Declaration of Principles between Israelis and Palestinians also involved negotiators who had long experience with track two processes. In Cyprus, experience in track one-and-a-half and track two processes was valued by the Republican Turkish Party (CTP)-led leadership. They appointed veterans of bicommunal dialogue and activities to working groups, as well as to coordinating positions for the negotiations. Equipped with working relationships with counterparts on the other side, with a deep understanding of the perspectives, interests, fears and needs of the other, and of the dynamics of a mutual gains process, these people have been able to work together effectively to find solutions to overcome barriers in negotiation (Angelica 1999).

At the track three level, local-level dialogues, development committees and peace committees also build institutional structures and the capacity of community members to work together and deal with local-level disputes that could escalate into violence. The Lofa County, Liberia Community Peace Councils (CPCs) supported by CHF International (see above) institutionalized a capacity within communities to handle disputes. CPCs were capable, in many cases, of addressing most of the conflicts that arose at the community level; they promoted communications among parties, and performed a referral function for cases they could not handle (CDA 2006). Similarly, inter-group relationships, communication and understanding developed in a broad-based dialogue program in another "flash point" county in Liberia were observed to have led to the resolution of some important community-level land disputes and more peaceful management of those that could not be resolved (Taylor 2008). While many of these mechanisms, such as community dispute resolution committees, are not often able to handle broader social tensions (Barron et al. 2007), they represent important prevention capacities, particularly for dealing with the "microfoundations" of civil war – the local conflicts and personal disputes that are given space to escalate (or be prosecuted) in the context of a larger, "macro" conflict (Kalyvas 2006).

2. Building skills and attitudes for more productive interaction with the "other"

Attitude change about the "other" and the conflict, skill building and the forging of relationships of cooperation and friendship across conflict lines are amongst the most commonly observed goals and results of non-governmental third party activities. Enemy images and stereotypes serve both as tools for mobilizing public opinion and resources in support of continued confrontation and as psychological constructs that enable leaders and followers to justify violence against another group (Ayres 1997). And, as Halpern and Weinstein (2004, p. 565) note, the perceptual shifts "that occur when one becomes interested in another's distinct subjective perspective are central to rehumanization" and to the rebuilding of social fabric after war.

Some programs, such as nationwide media programs, have broad impact on public attitudes about the "other" and the possibilities of coexistence. A widely viewed children's television series created by Search for Common Ground in Macedonia, for example, was found to have had significant impact on children's knowledge about the other ethnic groups in the country as well as attitudes and skills in managing conflict (and those of their parents, with whom 45 % of the child viewers discussed the show) (Brusset and Otto 2004). Although the program was considered by many to be "unrealistic as an inspiration for personal orientation", that is, the program's values could not be applied in daily life, the vision of cooperative interethnic relations explored in the series was influential as an ideal that children and their parents wished for Macedonia (Brusset and Otto 2004, p. 61).

Dialogue and training-based programs can deepen this kind of attitude change at the small-group level by helping participants develop in an experiential way mutual understanding of the other's experience, perspectives, intentions and underlying needs and concerns. Evaluations of Seeds of Peace youth camps, for example, have found evidence of change of attitudes – particularly changes in stereotype attributions and perceptions of the other side's willingness to work for peace (Schleien 2007).[19]

In many cases, participants note that workshops clarify misinformation about the other and help them understand that the other community, like their own, has suffered in the conflict (Angelica 1999). In CMG and NRC's Georgia-South Ossetia Dialogue Project, for example, a South Ossetian participant reported that he realized in a way he had not before that the Georgians genuinely were interested in the conflict resolution process. This realization made it possible for him truly to listen to the Georgian perspective for the first time since the (1992) war had begun (Nan 2002). Kaye reports similar changes among elite participants in track two dialogues in the Middle East and South Asia. One Israeli general, for example, became aware of Arab perceptions of their own weakness vis-à-vis Israel, contrary to his own belief

[19]Other studies in the Israeli-Palestinian context have found that these kinds of programs do not have significant positive effects on hatred and mistrust, at least in deep-rooted, intractable active conflicts (e.g., Giton and Salomon 2006; Salomon 2004), but may nonetheless have a prevention effect of forestalling a worsening of negative feelings.

that "Arabs should be more confident because they have more numbers" (Kaye 2001, p. 57). This realization led him to be more sensitive to misperceptions and, the participant reported, led to concrete Israeli actions, such as notifications of large-scale military exercises and greater openness to certain arms control agreements (Kaye 2007). Similar stories of profound personal transformation emerge from other processes, both at the elite and grassroots levels, such as the nationalist who became an activist for inter-group rapprochement and the journalist who changed the language he used in reporting on the conflict because of his experience with the other side in the workshop (see, e.g., Kaye 2007; Chigas and Ganson 2003; Kenyon 1999).

Non-governmental dialogue and capacity-building initiatives can also help transform participants' conceptions of conflict in general, and their conflict specifically, transforming win-lose, survive or perish framings of conflict to ones that hold open the possibilities of mutual gains. They often are based on and provide analytic frameworks for conflict that are based on basic human needs (Burton 1969) or mutual gains approaches to problem solving (e.g., Fisher et al. 2011), and engage the social-psychological dimensions of conflict directly. Identifying underlying interests, needs, fears and values that they discover to be compatible can form the basis for a re-definition of the conflict as a common problem that the sides share an interest in resolving. Participants often become more open to abandoning previously non-negotiable positions (Kaye 2007; Meyer 2002; Saunders 1985). They also report greater hope and confidence that joint solutions can be found and a greater willingness to engage with the other side (Slim and Saunders 2001; CMG 1994, 1996). As one participant in Georgian-Abkhaz dialogues facilitated by London-based Conciliation Resources noted, "I believed that Georgia was right in all matters and saw Abkhazia only as enemies. Then we put ourselves in their shoes and came to the conclusion, 'they can be right too'" (Ganson 2010).

3. Bridge-building, improved relationships and trust

The transformation of attitudes and improvement of communication and problem-solving are generally linked inextricably to the establishment of relationships of understanding and trust amongst participants in unofficial processes. Initially, these relationships are personal relationships that may not necessarily extend beyond the boundaries of the workshop or cooperative project to greater trust and confidence in the other side as a whole. A group of Georgians displaced from Abkhazia proudly recount how they rallied to bring an Abkhazian woman from Sukhumi to Georgia proper for medical treatment that likely saved her life (Ganson 2010). Over a decade earlier, in the late 1990s, a member of the Georgian negotiating team with South Ossetia made similar arrangements for the son of a South Ossetian counterpart with whom he had developed a friendship through the Georgia-South Ossetia Dialogue Project. The personal connections and working relationships developed during these sessions "'greased the wheels' of Georgian-Ossetian relations," leading to increased communication, meetings and joint work on declarations and agreements once participants returned to the region (Nan 2004; Olson 2001). A Kosovo Albanian farmer recounted that "I got to know Vesco better" at one of Mercy Corps' Dialogue and Development conferences in Kosovo, "and our cooperation has grown" (Preuss 2003, p. 45). Similar stories of relationship and trust-building emerging from dialogues, joint trainings, work or non-peace related cooperative projects and people-to-people social and sports activities. These friendships increase the likelihood that participants legitimize the perspective of the other side (Schleien 2007).

These personal relationships can be key to progress in negotiations and the establishment of cooperation across conflict lines. In the Georgian-South Ossetian negotiations in 2002, for example, participants reported that their improved relationships facilitated the official negotiations; they were able to talk informally on breaks from intense official negotiating sessions and to call each other when hot issues erupted (Nan 2002). OSCE mediators also noted these shifts in relationship and attributed the improved tone of negotiations to the relationship building achieved during the workshops (Nan 2005). Similarly, inter-personal relationships developed during a track two "facilitated joint brainstorming" series of meetings between influentials from Peru and Ecuador during the 1995 war between the two countries facilitated the establishment of back channels to discuss difficult issues when several members of the group were integrated into the official negotiating teams (Kaufman and Sosnowski 2005; Raiffa et al. 2002).

More broadly, the relationships and trust built in these small-group activities aim to and can contribute to the establishment of bridging social capital – social networks and formal and informal civic ties across ethnic or other groups that help communities avoid, resist or mitigate violence (Varshney 2002).[20] Many track two and track three initiatives result in concrete joint activities intended to build relationships, trust and cooperation across conflict lines. Others use joint activities, ranging from inter-ethnic women's cooperatives to produce baked goods or handicrafts to youth internet cafes and multi-ethnic radio stations and other organizations, as a springboard for relationship- and trust-building (Colleton and Afzali 2003; Chigas et al. 2007).

In Cyprus, for example, numerous joint projects provided practical experience and a model of cross-conflict cooperation as Greek and Turkish Cypriots worked together in a bicommunal choir, joint academic research, an EU study group, joint environmental projects and a lawyers' group identifying areas of divergence of the two communities' laws since division. The Inter-Tajik Dialogue established the Public Committee for the Promotion of Democratic Processes, which has organized regional economic development committees in areas that suffered the most destruction during the war. It has developed academic curricula on conflict resolution in cooperation with the Ministry of Education and launched an Issues

[20]Robert Putnam defines social capital as "features of social organization such as networks, norms and social trust that facilitate coordination and cooperation for mutual benefit" (Putnam 1995). He goes on to distinguish "bridging" from "non-bridging," or "bonding" social capital, which refers civic ties that keep homogenous groups cohesive (Putnam 2000). Varshney (2002) builds on this and notes that it is inter-ethnic civic ties, not civic ties per se, that matter for inter-ethnic violence, and that formal, associational forms of inter-group engagement are more effective than everyday forms, especially in larger settings.

Forums Network to promote deliberative public discussion of policy issues in the country (Jean and Mujollanov 2010). Mercy Corps' Eastern Kosovo Stabilization Program, implemented shortly after the 1999 war, developed and reinforced inter-ethnic agricultural linkages that provided new business opportunities to Serbs and Albanians who worked together (Chigas and Ganson 2003), led to increased economic cooperation, and, significantly, improvement in participants' economic fortunes as a result (Preuss 2003).

The idea is that these cross-ethnic ties will create or reinforce peace constituencies "and a capacity to support and sustain peacemaking efforts at the top levels, and to resist repolarization of the conflict when the inevitable setbacks occur" (Saunders 1995; Varshney 2002). They create "coalitions that cut across conflict lines" – common agendas, linkages and common action across among people across fault lines that could be the basis for a societal capacity to resist extremist images and rhetoric and to promote and support a peace process (Kelman 2001).

At this level, bridge-building and social cohesion activities have not had the hoped-for impacts, despite their obvious relevance and proliferation in numbers.[21] These "coalitions" are necessarily "uneasy" because of "the powerful bonds of the coalition members to the very groups that the coalition tries to transcend" (Kelman 2001, p. 242). As will be discussed in greater depth below, these efforts face tremendous obstacles to achieving impacts beyond the small groups with which they work. They have difficulty engaging strong socialization institutions that promote division – such as families, schools, military groups, political parties, professional associations and others – or achieving sufficient scale to overcome their influence. "[T]he scattered, short-term, and fragmented nature of most initiatives" also undermines their effectiveness, as many initiatives are too isolated and lack sufficient follow-up to deepen the ties and changes of attitudes, move beyond individual-level relationships, or deal sufficiently with intra-community resistance to rapprochement (Paffenholz 2010; Chigas et al. 2007).

Despite these very real limitations on the broader impacts of bridge-building activities,[22] there are examples of success that highlight the potential of these bridge-building activities to create real cross-ethnic engagement that mitigates or resists violence. The experience of "community relations" work in Northern Ireland provides an example of the potential importance and impact of these bridge-building activities. Cross-community bridge-building work, which long preceded the negotiations that led to the 1997 Good Friday Agreement, established dense social networks across conflict lines and institutionalized a number of practices, including common history texts and curricula, that effectively restrained a return to violence, even while divisions persisted and difficulties continued in the political

---

[21] *See* Paffenholz (2010). Indeed, a 2007 study in Kosovo found that inter-ethnic ties did not play a significant role in areas that resisted or avoided violence in 2004, and areas with the greatest density of ties were overcome by violence, despite often heroic efforts by individuals to protect members of the other ethnic group from attack (Chigas et al. 2007).

[22] These and other limitations on the effectiveness of these and other non-governmental third party activities are discussed more fully below.

process on intractable issues such as decommissioning of weapons and police reform (Fitzduff 2002). Similarly, in Cyprus, the bicommunal networks formed through the dialogues and joint projects in the 1990s were able to organize counteraction to a belligerent nationalist demonstration following violent incidents in the buffer zone in 1996. The bicommunal UN Day celebration organized by the United Nations Mission with the encouragement of these bicommunal groups attracted thousands of people and helped prevent a potentially explosive border clash from escalating further (Wolleh 2001).

4. Strengthening local advocacy for peace

Intermediation and facilitation processes, as well as other bridge-building and cross-conflict communication, can strengthen advocacy for peace in a number of ways. By building coalitions across conflict lines, they can strengthen the "negotiating middle" and give voice to previously silenced voices for moderation. For example, a workshop organized at American University in Washington, D.C. for East Timorese who fell into the "negotiating middle" helped reinforce the position of political moderates and the formulation of joint options (Salla 1998). Similarly, in South Africa, a successful 1987 conference that brought together 61 predominately Afrikaans-speaking intellectuals with 17 ANC representatives in Dakar, Senegal reinforced the influence of the "diplomats," such as Thabo Mbeki, over those who supported insurrection and mass mobilization (Lieberfeld 2002).

These facilitation and bridge-building processes can strengthen more public advocacy for negotiation and peacebuilding. The Dakar Conference, for example, not only strengthened the position of the moderates *within* the ANC, but also contributed to wider shifts in white public opinion in South Africa. As white participants engaged in "debriefings and house meetings," or informal advocacy, based on their experience in these meetings, even creating an alternative Afrikaans newspaper, they were able to increase public discussion of the possibility of negotiation. Daniel Lieberfeld concludes that Dakar and the activities conducted by participants after Dakar "desensitized" whites to the idea of talks with the ANC, as evidenced by the relative lack of controversy and media coverage over the follow-up meeting a year later (Lieberfeld 2002).

Similarly, several pro-settlement Turkish Cypriot members of the "Harvard Study Group," a 2-year track two problem-solving initiative which the author helped to facilitated under the auspices of The World Peace Foundation, commented that the deeper understanding of their counterparts and the very specific and concrete nature of the options they discussed in the group helped them become better advocates for negotiation and settlement. "When we were asked a specific question," one participant noted, "for example, how will the customs work, how the tax system will work, we need [to have] answers." And when they found themselves being criticized or questioned, they noted, they could respond, "If this happens, this is what the Greeks would say," because they had discussed these issues in the group. Their ability to offer specific answers to specific questions people posed about how a re-united Cyprus state would operate allowed them to paint a more precise picture of what a non-status quo solution would look like and to deal more substantially with people's concerns (Chigas forthcoming).

5. Engagement of the "hard to reach"

Engagement of the "hard to reach" has not traditionally been considered a separate peacebuilding function, as it often occurs through a number of the functional activities, such as service provision, skills development or intermediation. It is included here as a separate role and function of non-governmental parties because of its importance to effective peace practice (Anderson and Olson 2003) and the importance of civil society actors in it. The "hard to reach" are people or groups who hold some decision-making power in regard to the conflict. In other words, they can have a significant effect on whether and how conflict continues or systems for sustaining peace are maintained – but are not easily engaged in the peace process (Anderson and Olson 2003). They may be "spoilers" of the peace process, in that they may have an interest in the continuation of conflict or may not benefit from the achievement of peace (Stedman 1997), or may be hard to influence or hard to access, either because of physical location or because of political or other obstacles.

As Anderson and Olson (2003) have found, engaging these "hard to reach" is important to effective peace work:

> Unless it is possible to find ways either to include [the hard to reach] in peace, or to ensure that their actions to undo peace are ineffective (in terms of public response), they will always be able to undermine the effectiveness of peace practice.
>
> Much experience shows the necessity of working with these forces for a variety of reasons—to stop the fighting, to sustain agreements, to reach (through government institutions) large numbers of people. (Anderson and Olson 2003, p. 59)

Peace programs often do not reach these groups; they often preach to the converted or work with the "easy to reach," those who are more moderate, more apolitical, or more likely to be willing to engage with the "other" (Paffenholz 2010; Anderson and Olson 2003). As a result, peace processes often remain fragile and vulnerable to disruption.

Non-governmental third parties have been key actors in engaging the "hard to reach" in peace processes, especially those who have interests, needs or demands that are not being met by the peace process.[23] In Northern Ireland, for example, political prisoners have been identified by many as one of the most important constituencies contributing to change in the situation there. The status of prisoners and attitudes towards them were highly contested, with some supporting their questioning of the legitimacy of the government in Northern Ireland and others viewing them as mere criminals (Williams and Fitzduff 2007). Many were convicted only for belonging to an illegal organization. Work with these political prisoners, begun in 1971 after a series of raids had led to internment without trial of 342 Catholics/Republicans, was led largely by civil society and aimed at reforming the treatment of prisoners – a source of additional tension in Northern Ireland – and including their views in the political process (Williams and Fitzduff 2007). Civil society organizations, working initially to provide services to the prisoners and their

[23]Stedman refers to these groups as "limited" spoilers, in contrast to "total" spoilers, who "pursue total power and exclusive recognition of authority and hold immutable preferences" (Stedman 1997, p. 10).

families, built relationships of trust with the prisoners and facilitated dialogue with members of opposing (armed) groups. Once released, the prisoners expanded the cross-community relationships they had built in prison, making it acceptable for their own wider communities to engage with the "other." These former prisoners attribute the development of their distinctive role to these relationships of trust with civil society and leadership by figures within the prisons themselves.

Similarly, in Burundi, the Political Dialogue Project initiated by South African parliamentarian and human rights activist Jan van Eck helped to facilitate dialogue and build trust between all the major political and military stakeholders in the conflict there. This included work with the key rebel groups that had remained outside the Arusha peace talks that led to the 2000 Accords to establish lines of communication to the peace process, and convincing them to make contact with and interact with the mediators (Wohlgemuth 2000). Van Eck organized an internal consultation in 2002 within the main rebel group not party to the peace accords to debate its prospective participation in the negotiations. These informal efforts helped to set the stage for the decisive turning points in the Burundian peace process (Sebudandi, Icoyitungye, et al. 2008).

Limitations of Non-governmental Roles

For every example of a positive or effective non-governmental third party role in peacebuilding, there is an example of a program or activity that is less effective. Indeed, may programs and activities exhibit elements both of effectiveness and ineffectiveness. Many non-governmental initiatives are small, and in the case of track three activities, very localized. They often can lead to profound changes in the individuals or in the communities involved. As a result, many people assume that they are contributing building blocks of peace and that their efforts will "add up" some day. Yet as Mary Anderson and Lara Olson, in a multiyear, multiagency collaborative learning effort, Reflecting on Peace Practice, found, "the evidence is that ... this does not automatically or inevitably occur" (Anderson and Olson 2003, p. 64).[24]

[24]The Reflecting on Peace Practice Program (RPP) is an experience-based learning process that involves agencies whose programs attempt to prevent or mitigate violent conflict. Its purpose is to analyze experience at the individual program level across a broad range of agencies and contexts. Its goal is to improve the effectiveness of international peacebuilding efforts. During its first phase, from 1999 through early 2003, RPP engaged over 200 agencies and many individuals who work on conflict around the world in the development of 26 case studies and joint analysis of peacebuilding experience. The findings from this 3-year effort were published in *Confronting War: Critical Lessons for Peace Practitioners*, by Mary Anderson and Lara Olson (2003). Since 2003, RPP has focused on testing, revising and expanding the findings in the field, with a particular focus on monitoring and evaluation and on cumulative impacts of peacebuilding.

Two types of constraints limit the impacts non-governmental third parties can have on the macro level peace and conflict situation: the conflict environment itself, which is hostile to the kinds of initiatives non-governmental third parties undertake, and limitations on effectiveness created by the way non-governmental organizations (and their donors) plan and carry out their roles.

1. Hostile Political Environment

Non-governmental third parties often operate in environments in which the political space for peacebuilding is very limited. In hot conflicts, repressive situations, and post-conflict situations, this environment is invariably hostile, as the efforts tend to run against the current of local and national politics. "Spoilers," who themselves frequently are political, religious or opinion leaders, actively try to undermine and marginalize efforts to build bridges across conflict lines. Rejectionists and hardliners harass, intimidate, ostracize and sometimes employ violence against participants in these efforts to deter, discredit or marginalize them. Attacks in the media are also not uncommon. Other less overtly hostile actions by political authorities create equally difficult barriers to effective bridge-building, facilitation and any activity that reaches across conflict lines. These can include failure to grant visas or permissions or enforcement of laws forbidding contact with the "other."

In Bosnia, for example, in one community, a Croat school principal refused to authorize the use of a school for "bi-ethnic" programs, while in another, the Serb-controlled local government denied a construction permit to a Bosniak-led coexistence project (Chigas and Ganson 2003). In Cyprus, the Greek Cypriot government refused to protect people crossing into the UN-patrolled buffer zone to participate in peacebuilding activities from harassment by demonstrating nationalists, while the Turkish Cypriot government prosecuted participants in bicommunal events under a law prohibiting such contact (Chigas and Ganson 2003). The Israeli prohibition on contact with the PLO prior to the process that led to the 1994 Oslo Accords is well-known. As two veteran leaders of non-governmental peacebuilding activities in that conflict have remarked:

> [I]n the not remote past, and for a long period of time, the Palestinian leadership first and then the Israeli leadership later forbade any contacts amongst our peoples - although there has been direct contact since 1967. Palestinian dialogue pioneers have been killed by extremist groups and -no doubt a more moderate level of limitation- Israeli peaceniks have been jailed, or politically ostracized, for talking to PLO representatives. (Kaufman and Hassassian 1999)

These constant and relenting attacks on the political space for dialogue can have a harsh effect on morale and deter all but the most intrepid and committed participants. As Dalia Kaye remarks about security dialogues in the Middle East, "It is an ironic aspect of track two that when such dialogue is most needed, it is often most difficult to bring about" or to sustain (Kaye 2001). As a result, although these efforts can be and often are instrumental in opening space for a different interaction between the parties to overcome stalemate and confrontation, their scale, scope and effectiveness are limited in scale by the very political forces they are trying to change.

Civil society actors have tried to prevent these attacks by depoliticizing the space they create for interaction – by focusing, for example, on non-political issues and issues of common interest such as the environment, social interaction and sports, or by focusing on less political constituencies, such as women. Economic development and reconstruction projects have also sought to overcome this challenge by offering an incentive – economic rewards – for engaging in cooperation across conflict lines. Yet while such depoliticization is often necessary and effective for initiating and protecting to initiate and to protect space for inter-group interaction, politics again intrude to limit the effectiveness of these initiatives. Participants cannot completely insulate themselves from the political environment in which they live and act. Economic development-focused programs have not led automatically to sustained changes in attitudes, stereotypes or reduction of enemy images (Chigas et al. 2007; Lund and Wanchek 2004; Chigas and Ganson 2003). And bridge-building, training and education programs have little impact on peace because they often remain apolitical (Paffenholz 2010). Indeed, some critics suggest that they can mask or avoid the real underlying issues in conflict. In the Israeli-Palestinian conflict, for example, Palestinians have often complained that the agendas and structure of dialogues and joint projects have reinforced the asymmetry of power between the two groups and inadvertently privileged the Israeli agenda (Jean and Mendelsohn 2008; Abu-Nimer 1999).[25] Civil society-led mediatory efforts thus face a dilemma that limits their effectiveness: the very qualities that make it possible for them to bring people together and engage them in the peacebuilding process – their independence, informality, lack of official status and the apolitical nature of their work – also constrain the capacity of the initiatives to have an impact on the larger conflict situation, if they do not eventually find a way to reconnect their activities to the political process.

The same political forces that hinder participation in inter-group activities also make it difficult to achieve and maintain the attitude changes, relationships and even communication channels that non-governmental third parties help establish. A new and meaningful experience of who "we" and "they" are may be activated in these initiatives, but many other social contexts and institutions reinforce participants' identity as a member of their "side" – with all the attendant stereotypes, prejudices,

---

[25] Abu Nimer (1999) notes that Palestinians come to groups with the express purpose of changing Israeli political views, while Jewish participants tend to be more concerned with establishing lines of communication and social connections. To the extent the interventions remain apolitical, they reinforce the Israeli agenda. Similarly, Paffenholz (2010, p. 397) notes in a study that Greek Cypriots complained that the bicommunal activities in Cyprus gave the impression that the conflict there was only a problem of inter-ethnic relations, while many believed it was a fundamentally political problem with international dimensions.

fears and myths that come with it (Paffenholz 2010; Chigas and Ganson 2003). As Laitin (1998, 23) has noted:

> Multiple identities . . . can coexist within a person only insofar as choice is not necessary. . . . [W]hen the actions or behaviors consistent with one identity conflict with those of another identity held by the same person, as they do when the two groups represent antagonistic groups on the political stage, people are compelled to give priority to one identity over another.

Thus, even when profound personal transformations experienced by participants in civil society-facilitated processes are sustained, they often remain just that: *personal*. Participants are subject to the pressure to conform to the norms, values and attitudes of their own communities and may do so to retain standing in their own groups. And they often are able to work together effectively in groups or on projects whose norms are to be hospitable, or where there is a financial or other incentive to cooperate, without any change in their original attitudes. If not reinforced by substantial follow-up, and in some cases intra-group work to create a more hospitable climate for inter-group cooperation, attitude change and relationships can quickly dissipate as people fall back into old habits.

2. Planning and Implementation of Non-governmental Programs

A second set of limitations on the effectiveness and impacts of non-governmental roles in peacebuilding stems from the planning and implementation of the programs themselves. CDA Collaborative Learning Projects has identified three aspects of program planning and implementation processes that have undermined non-governmental organizations' ability to carry out their roles effectively.[26]

(a) Failure to address the driving factors of conflict

"Analysis is not optional; it is essential and obligatory for peace work," a participant in the Reflecting on Peace Practice (RPP) learning effort emphasized. Practitioners uniformly assert that good analysis is needed in order to avoid costly mistakes, to find the correct program focus (in terms of issues and people), to identify priorities

---

[26]Two multi-year, multi-agency, global collaborative learning efforts at CDA Collaborative Learning Projects have explored the impacts of non-governmental programming for peacebuilding. In addition to the Reflecting on Peace Practice Program (RPP), described above (note) the Listening Program (LP) has explored the ideas and insights of people who live in societies that have been recipients of international assistance of all types about what has worked and what has not worked, in order to identify lessons for aid effectiveness. Begun in 2005, 21 listening exercises were conducted in collaboration with local and international agencies working in these societies and have included a wide range of people – from grassroots community members to government officials, religious leaders, youth, women and local NGOs. While LP has not focused solely on peacebuilding-related assistance programming, several of the exercises were conducted in conflict-affected countries and significant evidence gathered on local people's perceptions and experiences of peacebuilding programming was gathered. The findings are contained in Anderson, Brown and Jean, *Time to Listen: Hearing People on the Receiving End of International Aid,* published in 2013 and available on CDA's website, http://www.cdacollaborative.org

and strategic points of intervention, and to match agency skills and resources to the situation (Anderson and Olson 2003; CDA 2009a). Yet many agencies, especially international ones, often fail to do such analysis. They typically focus on areas that immediately relate to their own activities – on how their own particular approach or methodology might be implemented in the context – and often do not conduct a broad conflict analysis that identifies the driving factors and dynamics of the conflict (Anderson and Olson 2003). And even when they do conflict analysis, the analysis is often *too* comprehensive, with long lists of factors with no priorities.

As a result, programs fail to identify what would be priority areas for intervention and whether their particular approach (whether it be trauma healing, dialogue, bridge-building through sports or culture or any other approach) would address those factors that make a difference to peace. Consequently, they often have important effects on the individual participants in or beneficiaries of the program, but they do not make a broader contribution to conflict transformation. A Lebanese NGO director commented on the proliferation of bridge-building conflict resolution activities in his country, "Conflict resolution concepts don't work in Lebanon – it's not about two people not liking each other, you need a political solution. Aid money for preventing violence is promoting a false reality" (CDA 2009b, p. 24). A compatriot agreed about the consequences of basing programs on inadequate or biased analysis: "All the conflict work had the same mind frame of doing dialogue. This was out of touch with what was needed on the ground. It has given conflict resolution and peace building a bad name.... Conflict resolution paradigms may work for the cultures that produced them, but they don't fit here" (CDA 2009b, p. 24).

In addition, even when agencies produce good analysis, it is often not integrated into program strategies. CDA's Listening Project found a widely shared perception among people in countries that have received significant amounts of international assistance that donors and aid agency staff "sit in their offices" and devise strategies and projects based on their own assumptions and agendas, rather than spending significant time in communities to ask what people really think (Anderson, Brown, and Jean 2013). As one observer in Kenya put it, "The weakness of donors is to sit somewhere and read reports. Quite often, donors assume they know every problem and can therefore prescribe solutions" (CDA 2010a, p. 6).

Many people perceive international aid programs, including peacebuilding programming, to be "pre-packaged," with pre-determined needs, set in categories that they feel are inappropriate in their societies, and biased in their assumptions about what works (Anderson, Brown, and Jean 2013, CDA 2008a). People talk frequently about how outside agencies often assume that a strategy or project implemented in one location can easily be replicated in another area without taking into account differences in the context and without spending time to understand the unique resources or challenges of that location. An international consultant in Lebanon described this practice, saying, "They white out Somalia and insert Lebanon in the conflict resolution proposal" (CDA 2010a, p. 6). While the experience that outsiders bring to a context from other countries is often valued by local people, the failure to devise and monitor program strategies to address the particular driving forces in the context undermines effectiveness.

(b) Donor Agendas and Time Lines

Donor engagement, mostly from Western OECD governments, faith-based organizations and foundations, has played a key role in enabling and strengthening non-governmental roles in peacebuilding, both local and international. Many non-governmental activities would not take place without donor money. Donor engagement has also contributed significantly to the professionalization of peace work since the 1990s.

At the same time, donor agendas, policies and procedures have (unwittingly) undermined the impacts of the very work they are supporting. Donor agendas and policies often result in economic or political conditionalities for the disbursement of aid, or in the prioritization of certain populations, areas or issues (and concomitant exclusion of other populations, areas or issues) in the peace process. Such conditionalities often result in programming that favor the priorities and political preferences of the donors rather than the needs of the local communities or national political processes (Anderson, Brown, and Jean 2013).

Donor priorities also make it difficult for non-governmental third parties who focus on different, but equally urgent, issues to secure funding for their activities. For example, in Bosnia, many donors (especially European donors, which hosted many Bosnian refugees during the war) wanted to encourage the return of refugees and recovery efforts partly to reduce the burden of the refugee populations in their own countries. Donors also were pursuing a multi-ethnic "reconciliation" strategy as an international priority. As a result, they funded many efforts, often implemented by international and local NGOs, to support the return of refugees, even though this was not what many of the people on the ground wanted at the time (CDA 2008b).

Similarly, in Kosovo, donor prioritization of returns of refugees and internally displaced people, as well as the promotion of multi-ethnicity, led to a concentration of resources in the area of returns and in multi-ethnic communities and projects. Because, as Larry Minear and his co-authors found in their study on the perceptions of local communities, of assistance agencies and peace operations, "[t]he reestablishment of a multi-ethnic society runs at odds with the desires of large sections of the population ... efforts to establish it can, and do, lead to a rise in tensions" (Donini et al. 2005). The availability of funds for multi-ethnic programs was perceived in communities not as a "carrot" or reward for cooperation, but as "conditionality" that was resented, and, ultimately, circumvented by recipients of funds. As a result, the bridge-building and other programs bringing Kosovo Albanians and Kosovo Serbs together did not result in real improvements in relationships, but rather increased cynicism and resentment. In addition, key hard to reach constituencies for peace – in particular, veterans and war-affected – were excluded from assistance, a factor that contributed to exacerbating, rather than mitigating, tensions between Serbs and Albanians (Chigas et al. 2007).[27]

Finally, shifting donor priorities and trends and short time frames limit the impacts of non-governmental third party efforts by making it difficult for them to invest adequately (in terms of resources, time and effort) in planning and follow-up processes that allow participants in their efforts to sustain, deepen and expand their the attitudes, skills and relationships they develop. The Eastern Kosovo Stabilization Program, a program implemented shortly after the 1999 war to promote inter-ethnic cooperation and interdependence among agricultural producers, intermediary suppliers and processes, is a typical example.[28] Although this program achieved promising results in terms of cross-ethnic cooperation, relationships and communication, the NGO leading the program was unable to deepen what it had started, as it was forced to move on to other geographic areas after the 1-year grant ended. As a result, its impact was limited (Schlemmer 2005).

Other inter-ethnic engagements in Kosovo and elsewhere – from sports competitions and youth camps to dialogue about refugee returns and joint activities – have suffered the same fate; they are not built upon or expanded, either because the projects are deemed to have "succeeded" or achieved results (and therefore ended), or because donor priorities change (Chigas et al. 2007). A university lecturer and development consultant in Kenya captured the problem experienced by many non-governmental programs:

> International development partners (International Organizations, Bilaterals, and NGOs) have a tendency to have agendas which change. For instance, one year the emphasis will be on the water sector, then HIV/AIDS, gender, etc. They are enthusiastic over about 5 years and then their priorities change. Projects are time-specific, but you can't talk about 5 years to change people's lives—you leave communities with ruins, not development. (CDA 2007b, 10)

In this context, non-governmental activities – especially skill-building, dialogue and bridge-building – become too isolated, fragmented and short-lived to have significant macro level impact in a conflict.

(c) Failure to Create Linkages

Inherent in practitioners' and donors' decisions about what to do or support in a particular situation are assumptions about how their role or intervention will contribute to peace. These underlying assumptions are often implicit, embedded

---

[27] As one person interviewed in a Listening exercise in 2007 commented, "To get aid, not only does your community have to have many ethnic groups, but they have to have problems with each other too!" In another community, people explained that they had gotten a school, a health clinic and an electrical grid in their village "because the village was 'multi-ethnic.' The NGOs were fulfilling their own conditions. We heard this on TV" (CDA 2007a, p. 20).

[28] The Eastern Kosovo Stabilization Program, implemented by Mercy Corps, was designed to "make it bad business to harm your neighbor" (Chigas and Ganson 2003). In addition to providing support for inter-ethnic market linkages, the program brought participants in the program together for dialogue to strengthen relationships, address difficult issues and expand the cooperation.

in the skills and approaches that non-governmental third parties bring to the various roles they play, their perspectives on conflict and their methodologies. The Reflecting on Peace Practice Program (RPP) found that two kinds of assumptions are particularly important – and problematic – for non-governmental organizations' effectiveness. First, NGOs typically assume that the impacts of their activities will automatically spill over into other domains of participants lives – in other words that the individual-personal and relationship changes experienced by participants in NGO activities will lead to changes in political attitudes, and, more importantly, in behavior and actions in the socio-political realm. Thus, for example, facilitators of dialogue, cross-community training or bridge-building activities often "assume that personal impacts on participants will affect the dynamics of a conflict" (Anderson and Olson 2003, p. 67). Second, a common implicit assumption in non-governmental work at track two and three levels is that "all of our good efforts must be adding up" because "peace requires that many people work at many levels in different ways" (Anderson and Olson 2003, p. 9).

RPP found that neither happens – at least not automatically. It found that programming that focuses on or achieves change at the individual/personal level – in attitudes, relationships, feelings, perceptions or more broadly in the "hearts and minds" of people, but is never connected to or translated into action or results at the socio-political level, has no discernible effect on peace. As Anderson and Olson (2003, p. 68) note in relation to dialogue programs:

> Some of these impacts are felt to be significant by individuals. But by themselves, these impacts on individuals do not affect the factors driving conflict. Experience shows that individuals may continue to talk across conflicts lines, in times of calm or crisis, without any discernable impact on a conflict.

The profound transformations in attitudes, perceptions, relationships, skills and trust of participating individuals are significant for the broader peace only if they are translated into action at the sociopolitical level – the public, political or institutional sphere of activity. Many NGO programs do not make these linkages; in other words, the changes they catalyze remain at the individual/personal level (see Fig. 14.2). Such linkages would entail additional follow-up work and accompaniment of participants (or collaboration with others) to build on these changes in order to take action in the public or political domain demonstrating responsiveness to the concerns of the opposing group(s), to mobilize people to demand actions for peace or to resist provocations to violence, to develop options for resolving key issues in conflict, to create institutions or processes for dealing with violence or addressing issues that are at the root of the conflict (Anderson and Olson 2003).

Similarly, RPP found that activities that focus on "more people" – working with grassroots or middle-level elites to create a peace constituency – fall short of their potential and may even risk becoming marginalized if they do nothing to link to or affect "key people," decision makers and other groups whose decisions and behavior significantly affect the course of conflict (Anderson and Olson 2003).

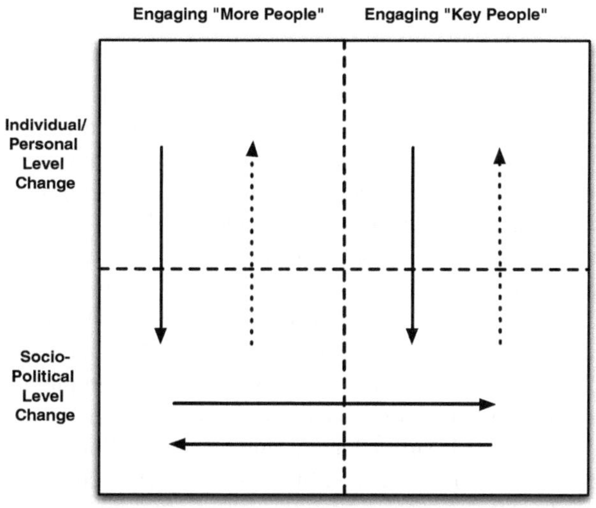

Fig. 14.2 RPP matrix of approaches to and effectiveness in programming

The inverse was also found to be true; strategies that focus on key people, often at the track one, one-and-a-half or two levels, without including or reaching out to "more people" can quickly become stuck or unsustainable. Indeed, in the CMG-NRC Georgia-South Ossetia Dialogue Program described earlier, although the participants in the effort had made significant progress on a number of important issues, including convergence of thinking on a political resolution, the process reached an impasse, as leaders on both sides claimed that public opinion was "not ready" for the steps they were prepared to take. In other words, the effort became stuck because it had focused on "key people" without affecting "more people."

Here again, non-governmental third parties, as well as official third parties working with key decision makers in peace processes, have frequently not made sufficient connections between levels and constituencies, leaving peace processes vulnerable. Such linkages may be as simple as simultaneous work at different levels on similar issues, or outreach to "more people" by negotiators or participants in track two dialogues through the media, as Turkish Cypriot members of the Harvard Study Group (described earlier in this chapter) did in Cyprus, to more complex structures linking activity at the track one level to grassroots and community-based activity. The 1992 National Peace Accord (NPA) in South Africa is an example of the latter; in establishing national, regional and local structures that were linked with each other, the NPA created an overarching policy framework linking and promoting interaction between local-level and political level (track one) activity, and created opportunities for key actors to engage with each other at the local as well as the national level (Mulcahy et al. 2009).

Conclusion

In this chapter, I have suggested that mediatory or facilitative roles by non-governmental third parties can make a valuable contribution to peacemaking and peacebuilding processes. Non-governmental third parties have played important roles in bringing parties to the negotiating table and in assisting them to overcome stalemate by helping them generate new understandings and new options for resolving their differences. They have been instrumental in engaging those who have been excluded (or who have excluded themselves) from peace processes. And by building skills and attitudes to support non-violent conflict resolution, as well as relationships of trust across conflict lines at all levels of society, they build "peace constituencies" and capacity at multiple levels of society to implement reforms that are instituted and manage the inevitable difficulties that occur.

Non-governmental third parties have a number of qualities that allow them to fulfill these roles. First, they are flexible. As non-state actors with little or no coercive power, they have greater flexibility than official third parties to initiate conversations with the parties in a conflict, including "illegitimate" actors or actors who have rejected participation in a peace process. Non-governmental third parties' unofficial status also creates lower barriers to participation in dialogue, cooperative activities or other contact across conflict lines – in part because the voluntary nature of participation allows them to leave these processes at any time.

Second, they are often on the ground and committed to local environments for long periods of time. They are able to work directly with grassroots populations and help link them to elite peace processes. Non-governmental third parties have been key to engaging local civil society actors in peace processes and in building peace constituencies.

Third, non-governmental third parties are able to deal with social-psychological dimensions of conflict that official processes do not. Track one peacemaking and peacebuilding processes tend to be well-suited to resolving resource-based issues (e.g., land, property, distribution of economic opportunities, power-sharing) and to support institutions and structures that could indeed deal with identity and human needs-based concerns. But they often are not as capable of addressing directly the identity, survival, trust and demonization of the "other" that are important for sustaining the power-sharing and structural reforms that are agreed and for promoting reconciliation. Finally, non-governmental third parties are often independent and non-partisan, in that they do not have a particular political or substantive agenda to advance, even if they are committed to the promotion of social justice and inclusive politics. This allows NGOs to talk to several parties simultaneously without losing credibility and to gain access to "hard to reach" actors (Van Tongeren 1998).

Critics have questioned the effectiveness of the contributions of non-governmental third parties in bridge-building and facilitative roles and called for a "fundamental rethinking" about design, context and timing of these initiatives, noting also that advocacy, rather than mediation or facilitation, has been the most effective civil society function (Paffenholz 2010).

These critiques about the effectiveness of non-governmental facilitative, bridge-building and socialization roles have raised valid questions. This challenge to non-governmental third parties to scale up and improve their impacts does not call into question the value of the roles and functions they play in peacebuilding, but is pushing them to think more systematically about how they can fulfill the potential these functions imply. The functions performed by non-governmental third parties can and should be carried out more effectively. Non-governmental actors can engage more effectively with the "hard to reach" (Anderson and Olson 2003), ranging from communication with and encouragement of extremists or rejectionists to participate in peace processes, to addressing more effectively the mainstream institutions in society that sustain the hostile socio-political climate that these efforts are trying to change. These have been valuable functions civil society actors have played, yet many efforts tend to work only with the "easy to reach" such as women, youth and political moderates (Paffenholz 2010; Anderson and Olson 2003).

The "adding up" of non-governmental activities and the establishment of linkages – even if not explicit ones – to track one is another area in which non-governmental third parties have potential to improve their own effectiveness. This does not entail a "fundamental rethinking" requiring non-governmental third parties to have programming or activity in all "quadrants" of the matrix depicted in Fig. 14.2, even when that falls outside their expertise. But it does challenge NGOs to improve planning and implementation processes to develop follow-up activities that support participants in translating individual/personal change into socio-political action, as well as promote linkages (either within their efforts or in cooperation with others) between "more people," grassroots and civil society-based initiatives and processes involving key people.

As non-governmental third parties are urged, however, to strengthen and enhance their impacts, their contributions should not be overestimated. Non-governmental roles cannot substitute for coherent political action at the track one level. Their impact depends as much on the "receptivity" of contending parties to conflict transformation and peacebuilding as to the quality of the interventions themselves, even if non-governmental actors, especially local ones, working far before a conflict is "ripe," can affect public opinion over time (Fisher 2005). Non-governmental organizations' lack of coercive power – their lack of resources to offer as "carrots" or "sticks" to encourage parties to come to the table or encourage change – allows them to work with people who might otherwise have remained outside peacebuilding processes, but also gives them little leverage with those unwilling to participate (often those who could benefit most from such interaction with the other side). Non-governmental peacebuilding roles and functions are most effective when linked, even if not formally, with official (track one) efforts. Unofficial and official methods must take place alongside each other, in a complementary manner, in order to achieve real impacts in de-escalation, peacemaking and peacebuilding processes.

References

Abu-Nimer, M. (1999). *Dialogue, conflict resolution, and change: Arab-Jewish encounters in Israel*. New York: State University of New York Press.

Anderson, M., & Olson, L. (2003). *Confronting war: Critical lessons for peace practitioners*. Cambridge, MA: CDA Collaborative Learning Projects.

Anderson, M., Brown, D., & Jean, J. (2013). *Time to listen: Hearing people on the receiving end of international aid*. Cambridge, MA: CDA Collaborative Learning Projects.

Angelica, M. (1999). *Evaluation of conflict resolution training efforts sponsored by the Cyprus Fulbright Commission, 1993–1998*. Nicosia: Cyprus Fulbright Commission.

Ayres, R. W. (1997). Mediating international conflicts: Is image change necessary? *Journal of Peace Research, 34*(4), 431–447.

Barron, P., Diprose, R., & Woolcock, M. (2007). *Local conflict and development projects in Indonesia: Part of the problem or part of a solution?* (World bank policy research paper, Vol. 4212). Washington, DC: World Bank.

Bartoli, A. (2005). Learning from the Mozambique process: The role of the community of Sant'Egidio. In R. Fisher (Ed.), *Paving the way: Contributions of interactive conflict resolution to peacemaking*. Lanham: Lexington.

Brusset, E., & Otto, R. (2004). Evaluation of Nashe Maalo: Design, implementation, outcomes, and social transformation through the media (On behalf of search for common ground). Ohain, Belgium: Channel Research. http://www.sfcg.org/sfcg/evaluations/nash2004.pdf

Burton, J. (1969). *Conflict and communication: The use of controlled communication in international relations*. London: Macmillan.

CDA Collaborative Learning Projects. (2006). *Creating a river between two fires: Impact assessment of the locally initiated networks for community strengthening program (LINCS), a program of CHF international – Liberia, with financial support from USAID*. Cambridge: CDA Collaborative Learning Projects.

CDA Collaborative Learning Projects. (2007a). Listening project field visit report: Kosovo. Cambridge: CDA Collaborative Learning Projects. Retrieved on 24 Sep 2013 at http://www.cdacollaborative.org/media/5382/Kosovo-Listening-Exercise-English.pdf

CDA Collaborative Learning Projects. (2007b). *Listening project field visit report: Kenya*. Cambridge: CDA Collaborative Learning Projects. Retrieved on 24 Sep 2013 at http://www.cdacollaborative.org/media/53373/Kenya-Listening-Exercise.pdf

CDA Collaborative Learning Projects. (2008a). *International assistance as a delivery system. Listening project issue paper*. Cambridge: CDA Collaborative Learning Projects. Retrieved on 24 Sep 2013 at http://www.cdacollaborative.org/media/53445/International-Assistance-as-a-Delivery-System.pdf

CDA Collaborative Learning Projects. (2008b). *The cascading effects of international agendas and priorities. Listening project issue paper*. Cambridge: CDA Collaborative Learning Projects. Retrieved on 24 Sep 2013 at http://www.cdacollaborative.org/media/53463/The-Cascading-Effects-of-International-Agendas-and-Priorities.pdf

CDA Collaborative Learning Projects. (2009a). *Reflecting on peace practice participant training manual*. Cambridge: CDA Collaborative Learning Projects. Retrieved on 24 Sep 2013 at http://www.cdacollaborative.org

CDA Collaborative Learning Projects. (2009b). *Listening project field visit report: Lebanon*. Cambridge: CDA Collaborative Learning Projects. Retrieved on 24 Sep 2013 at http://www.cdacollaborative.org/media/53391/Lebanon-Listening-Exercise-English.pdf

CDA Collaborative Learning Projects. (2010a). *The importance of listening. Listening project issue paper*. Cambridge: CDA Collaborative Learning Projects. Retrieved on 24 Sep 2013 at http://www.cdacollaborative.org/media/48012/The-Listening-ProjectIssue-Paper-The-Importance-of-Listening.pdf

CHF International. (2007). LINCS program final and phase-out report. Cooperative agreement # 669-A-00-04-00009-00. http://pdf.usaid.gov/pdf_docs/PDACJ304.pdf

Chigas, D. (forthcoming). The Harvard study group on Cyprus: Contributions to an in successful peace process? In Lund, M., & Wolpe, H. (Eds.), *Preventing and rebuilding failed states*. Washington, DC: Woodrow Wilson Center for International Scholars.
Chigas, D. (1997). Unofficial interventions with official actors: Parallel negotiation training in violent intrastate conflicts. *International Negotiation, 2*, 409–436.
Chigas, D. (2007). Capacities and limits of NGOs as conflict managers. In C. Crocker, F. Hampson, & P. Aall (Eds.), *Leashing the dogs of war: Conflict management in a divided world*. Washington, DC: USIP Press.
Chigas, D., & Ganson, B. (2003). Grand visions and small projects: Coexistence efforts in Southeastern Europe. In A. H. Chayes & M. Minow (Eds.), *Imagine coexistence: Restoring humanity after violent ethnic conflict*. San Francisco: Jossey Bass.
Chigas, D., Church, C., De La Haye, J., Llamazares, M., Markovic, O., & Venhari, A. (2007). *Has peacebuilding made a difference in Kosovo? A study of the effectiveness of peacebuilding in preventing violence: Lessons learned from the March 2004 Riots in Kosovo*. Cambridge and Prishtine/Pristina, Kosovo: CDA Collaborative Learning Projects and CARE Kosovo.
Chufrin, G., & Saunders, H. (1993). A public peace process. *Negotiation Journal, 9*, 155–177.
Colleton, L., & Afzali, A. (2003). Constructing coexistence: A survey of coexistence projects in areas of ethnic conflict. In A. H. Chayes & M. Minow (Eds.), *Imagine coexistence: Restoring humanity after violent ethnic conflict*. San Francisco: Jossey Bass.
Conflict Management Group. (1994 and 1997). Final report to AMIDEAST: Cyprus conflict management program. Cambridge: Conflict Management Group.
Diamond, L. (1999). *The courage for peace: Daring to create harmony in ourselves and the world*. York Beach: Conari Press.
Diamond, L., & McDonald, J. (1996). *Multitrack diplomacy: A systems approach to peace* (3rd ed.). West Hartford: Kumarian Press.
Donini, A., Minear, L., Smillie, I., van Baarda, T., & Welch, A. (2005). *Mapping the security environment: Understanding the perceptions of local communities, peace operations, and assistance agencies*. Medford: Feinstein International Famine Center.
Fischer, M. (2006). Civil society in conflict transformation: Ambivalence, potentials and challenges. In M. Fischer & N. Ropers (Eds.), *Berghof handbook for conflict transformation. Section One (Concepts and cross-cutting challenges)*. Berlin: Berghof Research Centre for Constructive Conflict Management.
Fisher, R. (1972). Third party consultation: A method for the study and resolution of conflict. *Journal of Conflict Resolution, 16*, 67–94.
Fisher, R. (2005). Conclusion: Evidence for the essential contributions of interactive conflict resolution. In R. Fisher (Ed.), *Paving the way: Contributions of interactive conflict resolution to peacemaking*. Lanham: Lexington Books.
Fisher, R., & Diamond, L. (1995). Integrating conflict resolution training and consultation: A Cyprus example. *Negotiation Journal, 11*(3), 287–301.
Fisher, R., & Keashly, L. (1988). Distinguishing third party interventions in intergroup conflict: Consultation is *not* mediation. *Negotiation Journal, 4*, 383.
Fisher, R., & Keashly, L. (1991). The potential complementarity of mediation and consultation within a contingency model of third party intervention. *Journal of Peace Research, 28*(1), 29–42.
Fisher, R., Ury, W., & Patton, B. (2011). *Getting to YES: Negotiating agreement without giving in* (3rd ed.). New York: Penguin.
Fisher, S., & Zimina, L. (2009). Just wasting our time? Provocative thoughts for peacebuilders. In B. Schmelzle & M. Fischer (Eds.), *Peacebuilding at a crossroads? Berghof handbook for conflict transformation* (Dialogue series, Vol. 7). Berlin: Berghof Conflict Research.
Fitzduff, M. (2002). *Beyond violence: Conflict resolution processes in Northern Ireland*. Washington, DC: Brookings Institution.
Galtung, J. (1969). Violence, Peace and Peace Research. *Journal of Peace Research, 6*(3), 167–191.

Ganson, B. (2010). Shifting the focus from politics to people: Peacebuilding in Georgia/Abkhazia. Unpublished Case Study.

Geneva Initiative. (2010). Mission statement. Retrieved on 22 Aug 2010 from http://www.geneva-accord.org/mainmenu/mission-statement

Giton, Y., & Salomon, G. (2006). Peace in the eyes of Israeli and Palestinian youths: Effects of collective narratives and peace education program. *Journal of Peace Research, 43*(2), 167–180.

Gutlove, P., & Thompson, G. (2003). Human security: Expanding the scope of public health. *Medicine Conflict and Survival, 19*(1), 17–34.

Halpern, J., & Weinstein, H. (2004). Rehumanizing the other: Empathy and reconciliation. *Human Rights Quarterly, 26*, 561–583.

HD Centre. (2010). *Past projects: Aceh, Indonesia*. Retrieved on 22 Aug 2010 from http://www.hdcentre.org/projects/aceh-indonesia

Jean, I., & Mendelsohn, E. (2008). *Much process and no peace: Israel-Palestine, 1993–2008*. Cumulative impacts case study, Reflecting on Peace Practice Program. Cambridge: CDA Collaborative Learning Projects.

Jean, I., & Mujollanov, P. (2010). *Conflict and peacebuilding in Tajikistan*. Cumulative impacts case study, Reflecting on Peace Practice Program. Cambridge: CDA Collaborative Learning Projects.

Kahane, A. (2002). The Mont fleur scenarios: What will South Africa be like in 2002? *Deeper News, 7*(1). Retrieved on 22 Aug 2010 from http://www.google.com/#hl=en&q=deeper+news+mont+fleur&aq=f&aqi=&aql=&oq=&gs_rfai=&pbx=1&fp=ad526d12389e3c08

Kalyvas, S. (2006). *The logic of violence in civil war*. New York: Cambridge University Press.

Kaufman, E., & Hassassian, M. (1999). Israeli-Palestinian peace-building: Lessons learnt. In European Centre for Conflict Prevention (Ed.), *People building peace: 35 inspiring stories from around the world*. Utrecht: European Centre for Conflict Prevention.

Kaufman, E., & Sosnowski, S. (2005). The Peru-Ecuador peace process: The contribution of track two diplomacy. In R. Fisher (Ed.), *Paving the way: Contributions of interactive conflict resolution to peacemaking*. Lanham: Lexington Books.

Kaye, D. (2001). Track two diplomacy and regional security in the middle East. *International Negotiation, 6*, 49–77.

Kaye, D. (2007). *Talking to the enemy: Track two diplomacy in the middle East and South Asia*. Santa Monica: RAND Corporation.

Kelman, H. C. (1972). The problem-solving workshop in conflict resolution. In R. Merritt (Ed.), *Communication in international politics*. Urbana: University of Illinois Press.

Kelman, H. C. (1993). Coalitions across conflict lines: The interplay of conflicts within and between the Israeli and Palestinian communities. In J. Simpson & S. Worchel (Eds.), *Conflict between people and groups*. Chicago: Nelson-Hall.

Kelman, H. C. (2000). The role of the scholar-practitioner in international conflict resolution. *International Studies Quarterly, 1*(3), 273–288.

Kelman, H. C. (2005a). Building trust among enemies: The central challenge for international conflict resolution. *International Journal of Intercultural Relations, 29*(6), 639–650.

Kelman, H. C. (2005b). Interactive problem solving in the Israeli-Palestinian case: Past contributions and present challenges. In R. Fisher (Ed.), *Paving the way: Contributions of interactive conflict resolution to peacemaking*. Lanham: Lexington Books.

Kenyon, K. (1999). The development of a comprehensive interdisciplinary learning model for international peacebuilding: The case of Cyprus. Ph.D. Dissertation, University of Idaho.

Klein, M. (2007). *A possible peace between Israel and Palestine: An insider's account of the Geneva initiative*. New York: Columbia University Press.

Laitin, D. (1998). *Identity in formation: The Russian speaking populations in the near abroad*. Ithaca: Cornell University Press.

Lederach, J. P. (1997). *Building peace: Sustainable reconciliation in divided societies*. Washington, DC: USIP Press.

Leguro, M., & Rudy, J. (2010). *The diverse terrain of peacebuilding in Mindanao: Gains and challenges in the government of the republic of the Philippines/Moro Islamic liberation front peace process*. Cumulative impacts case study, Reflecting on Peace Practice Program. Cambridge: CDA Collaborative Learning Projects.

Lieberfeld, D. (2002). Evaluating the contributions of track-two diplomacy to conflict termination in South Africa, 1984–1990. *Journal of Peace Research, 39*(3), 355–375.

Lund, M., & Wanchek, N. (2004). Effectiveness of participatory community development in managing conflicts: Local democracy, social capital, and peace. Report to USAID. Washington, DC: Management Systems International.

Mercy Corps. (2002). *Maluku case study. Mercy corps Indonesia: Integrating relief, recovery, and civil society in a conflict-affected environment*. Portland: Mercy Corps.

Meyer, R. (2002). Paradigm shift – the essence of social change? INCORE occasional paper. Derry/Londonderry: INCORE. Retrieved on 22 Aug 2010 from http://www.incore.ulst.ac.uk/publicationsoccasional/R_M_Paradigm_Shift.pdf

Miall, H. (2004). Conflict transformation: A multi-dimensional task. In M. Fischer & N. Ropers (Eds.), *Berghof handbook for conflict transformation. Section one (Concepts and cross-cutting challenges)*. Berlin: Berghof Research Centre for Constructive Conflict Management.

Montville, J. (1991). Transnationalism and the role of track-two diplomacy. In W. S. Thompson, K. Jensen, R. N. Smith, & K. M. Schraum (Eds.), *Approaches to peace: An intellectual map*. Washington, DC: USIP Press.

Mulcahy, J., Mulcahy, M., & Christie, P. (2009). *Reflecting on peace practice: A South African case study. Cumulative impacts case study, Reflecting on Peace Practice Program*. Cambridge: CDA Collaborative Learning Projects.

Murdock, J., & Zunzuga, A. (2010). *The cumulative impacts of peacebuilding in Mozambique. Cumulative impacts case study, Reflecting on Peace Practice Program*. Cambridge: CDA Collaborative Learning Projects.

Nan, Susan Allen. (2002). Unofficial conflict resolution as a complement to diplomacy: A case study of Georgian-South Ossetian peace process highlighting track one and a half diplomacy." Paper presented at the international studies association conference, New Orleans.

Nan, S. A. (2004). Track one and a half diplomacy: Searching for political agreement in the Caucasus. In M. Fitzduff & C. Church (Eds.), *NGOs at the table: Strategies for influencing policies in areas of conflict*. New York: Rowman and Littlefield.

Nan, S. A. (2005). Track one-and-a-half diplomacy: Contributions to Georgian-South Ossetian peacemaking. In R. Fisher (Ed.), *Paving the way: Contributions of interactive conflict resolution to peacemaking*. Lanham: Lexington.

Nonviolent Peaceforce. (2010). *Philippines project*. http://www.nonviolentpeaceforce.org/fieldwork/all-projects/philippines-project. Accessed 22 Aug 2010.

Olson, L. (2001). *The Georgia-South Ossetia dialogue: A view from the inside. Case study, Reflecting on Peace Practice Program*. Cambridge: CDA Collaborative Learning Projects.

Organization for Economic Development and Cooperation, Development Assistance Committee. (2007). *Guidance on evaluating conflict prevention and peacebuilding activities: Working draft for application period*. Paris: OECD-DAC.

Paffenholz, T. (Ed.). (2010). *Civil society and peacebuilding: A critical assessment*. Boulder: Lynne Rienner.

Pouligny, B. (2005). Civil society and post-conflict peacebuilding: Ambiguities of international programmes aimed at building 'New' societies. *Security Dialogue, 36*(4), 495–510.

Prendergast, J., & Plumb, E. (2002). Building local capacity: From implementation to peacebuilding. In S. Stedman, D. Rothchild, & E. Cousens (Eds.), *Ending civil wars*. Boulder: Lynne Rienner.

Preuss, G. (2003). Dialogical development: A Kosovo case study. *Journal of Peacebuilding and Development, 1*(2), 36–48.

Pruitt, D., & Kim, S. (2004). *Social conflict: Escalation, stalemate, and settlement*. New York: McGraw-Hill.

Putnam, R. (1995). Bowling alone: America's declining social capital. *Journal of Democracy, 1*, 65–78.
Putnam, R. (2000). *Bowling alone: The collapse and revival of American community*. New York: Simon with Shuster.
Putnam, R., Leonardi, R., & Nanetti, R. (1993). *Making democracy work: civil traditions in modern Italy*. Princeton: Princeton University Press.
Raiffa, H., Richardson, J., & Metcalfe, D. (2002). *Negotiation analysis: The science and art of collaborative decision making*. Cambridge: Harvard University Press.
Salla, M. (1998). East Timor. In D. Smock (Ed.), *Private peacemaking: USIP-assisted peacemaking projects of nonprofit organizations*. Washington, DC: USIP.
Salomon, G. (2004). Does peace education make a difference? *Peace and Conflict: Journal of Peace Psychology, 10*, 257–274.
Saunders, H. (1985). We need a larger theory of negotiation: The importance of prenegotiation phases. *Negotiation Journal, 1*(3), 249–262.
Saunders, H. (1995). Possibilities and challenges: Another way to consider unofficial third party intervention. *Negotiation Journal, 11*(3), 271–275.
Saunders, H. (2005). Sustained dialogue in Tajikistan: Transferring learning from the public to the official peace process. In R. Fisher (Ed.), *Paving the way: Contributions of interactive conflict resolution to peacemaking*. Lanham: Lexington.
Schiller, R., with Hanafi, D. (2008). *The impacts of peacebuilding work on the Aceh conflict*. Cumulative impacts case study, Reflecting on Peace Practice Program. Cambridge: CDA Collaborative Learning Projects.
Schleien, S. (2007). Confronting the intractable: An evaluation of the seeds of peace experience. Ph.D. Dissertation. University of Waterloo.
Schlemmer, D. (2005). *Building peace in Kosovo: An assessment of Mercy Corps' PRM refugee assistance programs*. Policy Analysis Exercise. Cambridge: Kennedy School of Government, Harvard University.
Search for Common Ground. (2010). *Commonly used terms*. Retrieved 22 Aug 2010 from http://www.sfcg.org/resources/resources_terms.html
Sebudandi, C., Icoyitungye, J., et al. (2008). *The cumulative impacts of peacebuilding in Burundi: Strengths and weaknesses of a process*. Cumulative impacts case study, Reflecting on Peace Practice Program. Cambridge: CDA Collaborative Learning Projects.
Seeds of Peace. (2010.). *Programs*. Retrieved 22 Aug 2010 from http://www.seedsofpeace.org/programs
Slim, R., & Saunders, H. (2001). The inter-Tajik dialogue: From civil war towards civil society. In K. Abdullaev & C. Barnes (Eds.), *Politics of compromise: The Tajikistan peace process* (ACCORD series). London: Conciliation Resources.
Spies, C. (2002). South Africa's National peace accord: Its structures and functions. In C. Barnes (Ed.), *Owning the process: Public participation in peacemaking* (ACCORD, issue 13, pp. 20–25). London: Conciliation Resources.
Stedman, S. (1997). Spoiler problems in peace processes. *International Security, 22*(2), 5–53.
Strand, A., Toje, H., Jerve, A., & Samset, I. (2003). *Community-driven development in contexts of conflict. Concept paper commissioned by ESSD, World Bank*. Oslo: Chr. Michelsen Institute.
Taylor, G. (2008). *Interpeace project in Nimba County: External evaluation*. Geneva: Interpeace.
United Nations Security Council. (2001). Prevention of armed conflict: Report of the secretary-general. New York: United Nations Security Council. S/2001/574.
Ury, W. (2000). *The third side: Why we fight and how we can stop*. New York: Penguin.
Ury, W., & Weiss, J. (2010). *What is the third side?* Retrieved on 22 Aug 2010 from http://www.thirdside.org/thirdside.cfm
Uvin, P., & Campbell, S. (forthcoming). The Burundi Leadership training program. In Lund, M., & Wolpe, H. (Eds.), *Preventing and rebuilding failed states*. Washington, DC: Woodrow Wilson Center for International Scholars.

van Tongeren, P. (1998). Exploring the local capacity for peace – the role of NGOs. In P. van Tongeren (Ed.), *Prevention and management of violent conflicts. An international directory* (pp. 21–26). Utrecht: European Platform for Conflict Transformation.
Varshney, A. (2001). Ethnic conflict and civil society: India and beyond. *World Politics, 53*(3), 362–398.
Varshney, A. (2002). *Ethnic conflict and civic life: Hindus and Muslims in India* (2nd ed.). New Haven: Yale University Press.
Wallach, J. (2000). *The enemy has a face: The seeds of peace experience*. Washington, DC: USIP Press.
Williams, S., & Fitzduff, N. (2007). *How did Northern Ireland move toward peace*? Cumulative impacts case study, Reflecting on Peace Practice Program. Cambridge: CDA Collaborative Learning Projects.
Wohlgemuth, L. (2000). *NGO participation in conflict prevention in Burundi*. Case study, Reflecting on Peace Practice Program. Cambridge: CDA Collaborative Learning Projects.
Wolleh, O. (2001). *Local peace constituencies in Cyprus: Citizens' rapprochement by the bicommunal conflict resolution trainer group* (Berghof report, Vol. 8). Berlin: Berghof Conflict Research.
Wolpe, H., & McDonald, S. (2006). Training leaders for peace. *Journal of Democracy, 17*(1), 132–138.
World Bank. (1998). Involving nongovernmental organizations in Bank-supported activities. Operational policy note GP 14.70. Available at http://web.worldbank.org/WBSITE/EXTERNAL/TOPICS/CSO/0,,contentMDK:22511723~pagePK:220503~piPK:220476~theSitePK:228717,00.html. Accessed 22 Aug 2010.
World Bank. (2010). The World Bank and civil society. http://web.worldbank.org/WBSITE/EXTERNAL/TOPICS/CSO/0,,contentMDK:20092185~menuPK:220422~pagePK:220503~piPK:220476~theSitePK:228717,00.html. Accessed 22 Aug 2010.

Appendices

Appendix 1: Map of Africa Highlighting Three Countries

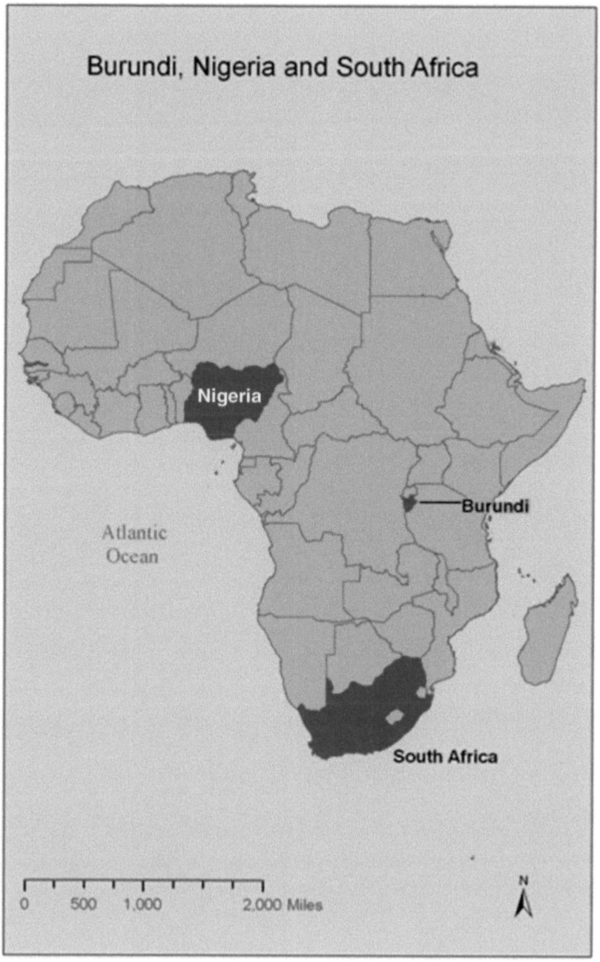

Fig. A1 Burundi, Nigeria and South Africa

J.M. Fritz (ed.), *Moving Toward a Just Peace: The Mediation Continuum*, Clinical Sociology: Research and Practice, DOI 10.1007/978-94-007-2885-1,

Appendix 2: Convention on the Rights of Persons with Disabilities

Preamble

The States Parties to the present Convention,

(a) Recalling the principles proclaimed in the Charter of the United Nations which recognize the inherent dignity and worth and the equal and inalienable rights of all members of the human family as the foundation of freedom, justice and peace in the world,

(b) Recognizing that the United Nations, in the Universal Declaration of Human Rights and in the International Covenants on Human Rights, has proclaimed and agreed that everyone is entitled to all the rights and freedoms set forth therein, without distinction of any kind,

(c) Reaffirming the universality, indivisibility, interdependence and interrelatedness of all human rights and fundamental freedoms and the need for persons with disabilities to be guaranteed their full enjoyment without discrimination,

(d) Recalling the International Covenant on Economic, Social and Cultural Rights, the International Covenant on Civil and Political Rights, the International Convention on the Elimination of All Forms of Racial Discrimination, the Convention on the Elimination of All Forms of Discrimination against Women, the Convention against Torture and Other Cruel, Inhuman or Degrading Treatment or Punishment, the Convention on the Rights of the Child, and the International Convention on the Protection of the Rights of All Migrant Workers and Members of Their Families,

(e) Recognizing that disability is an evolving concept and that disability results from the interaction between persons with impairments and attitudinal and environmental barriers that hinders their full and effective participation in society on an equal basis with others,

(f) Recognizing the importance of the principles and policy guidelines contained in the World Programme of Action concerning Disabled Persons and in the Standard Rules on the Equalization of Opportunities for Persons with Disabilities in influencing the promotion, formulation and evaluation of the policies, plans, programmes and actions at the national, regional and international levels to further equalize opportunities for persons with disabilities,

(g) Emphasizing the importance of mainstreaming disability issues as an integral part of relevant strategies of sustainable development,

J.M. Fritz (ed.), *Moving Toward a Just Peace: The Mediation Continuum*,
Clinical Sociology: Research and Practice, DOI 10.1007/978-94-007-2885-1,

(h) Recognizing also that discrimination against any person on the basis of disability is a violation of the inherent dignity and worth of the human person,
(i) Recognizing further the diversity of persons with disabilities,
(j) Recognizing the need to promote and protect the human rights of all persons with disabilities, including those who require more intensive support,
(k) Concerned that, despite these various instruments and undertakings, persons with disabilities continue to face barriers in their participation as equal members of society and violations of their human rights in all parts of the world,
(l) Recognizing the importance of international cooperation for improving the living conditions of persons with disabilities in every country, particularly in developing countries,
(m) Recognizing the valued existing and potential contributions made by persons with disabilities to the overall well-being and diversity of their communities, and that the promotion of the full enjoyment by persons with disabilities of their human rights and fundamental freedoms and of full participation by persons with disabilities will result in their enhanced sense of belonging and in significant advances in the human, social and economic development of society and the eradication of poverty,
(n) Recognizing the importance for persons with disabilities of their individual autonomy and independence, including the freedom to make their own choices,
(o) Considering that persons with disabilities should have the opportunity to be actively involved in decision-making processes about policies and programmes, including those directly concerning them,
(p) Concerned about the difficult conditions faced by persons with disabilities who are subject to multiple or aggravated forms of discrimination on the basis of race, colour, sex, language, religion, political or other opinion, national, ethnic, indigenous or social origin, property, birth, age or other status,
(q) Recognizing that women and girls with disabilities are often at greater risk, both within and outside the home of violence, injury or abuse, neglect or negligent treatment, maltreatment or exploitation,
(r) Recognizing that children with disabilities should have full enjoyment of all human rights and fundamental freedoms on an equal basis with other children, and recalling obligations to that end undertaken by States Parties to the Convention on the Rights of the Child,
(s) Emphasizing the need to incorporate a gender perspective in all efforts to promote the full enjoyment of human rights and fundamental freedoms by persons with disabilities,
(t) Highlighting the fact that the majority of persons with disabilities live in conditions of poverty, and in this regard recognizing the critical need to address the negative impact of poverty on persons with disabilities,
(u) Bearing in mind that conditions of peace and security based on full respect for the purposes and principles contained in the Charter of the United Nations and observance of applicable human rights instruments are indispensable for the full protection of persons with disabilities, in particular during armed conflicts and foreign occupation,

(v) Recognizing the importance of accessibility to the physical, social, economic and cultural environment, to health and education and to information and communication, in enabling persons with disabilities to fully enjoy all human rights and fundamental freedoms,
(w) Realizing that the individual, having duties to other individuals and to the community to which he or she belongs, is under a responsibility to strive for the promotion and observance of the rights recognized in the International Bill of Human Rights,
(x) Convinced that the family is the natural and fundamental group unit of society and is entitled to protection by society and the State, and that persons with disabilities and their family members should receive the necessary protection and assistance to enable families to contribute towards the full and equal enjoyment of the rights of persons with disabilities,
(y) Convinced that a comprehensive and integral international convention to promote and protect the rights and dignity of persons with disabilities will make a significant contribution to redressing the profound social disadvantage of persons with disabilities and promote their participation in the civil, political, economic, social and cultural spheres with equal opportunities, in both developing and developed countries,

Have agreed as follows:

Article 1: Purpose

The purpose of the present Convention is to promote, protect and ensure the full and equal enjoyment of all human rights and fundamental freedoms by all persons with disabilities, and to promote respect for their inherent dignity.

Persons with disabilities include those who have long-term physical, mental, intellectual or sensory impairments which in interaction with various barriers may hinder their full and effective participation in society on an equal basis with others.

Article 2: Definitions

For the purposes of the present Convention:

- "Communication" includes languages, display of text, Braille, tactile communication, large print, accessible multimedia as well as written, audio, plain-language, human-reader and augmentative and alternative modes, means and formats of communication, including accessible information and communication technology;
- "Language" includes spoken and signed languages and other forms of non spoken languages;

- "Discrimination on the basis of disability" means any distinction, exclusion or restriction on the basis of disability which has the purpose or effect of impairing or nullifying the recognition, enjoyment or exercise, on an equal basis with others, of all human rights and fundamental freedoms in the political, economic, social, cultural, civil or any other field. It includes all forms of discrimination, including denial of reasonable accommodation;
- "Reasonable accommodation" means necessary and appropriate modification and adjustments not imposing a disproportionate or undue burden, where needed in a particular case, to ensure to persons with disabilities the enjoyment or exercise on an equal basis with others of all human rights and fundamental freedoms;
- "Universal design" means the design of products, environments, programmes and services to be usable by all people, to the greatest extent possible, without the need for adaptation or specialized design. "Universal design" shall not exclude assistive devices for particular groups of persons with disabilities where this is needed.

Article 3: General Principles

The principles of the present Convention shall be:

(a) Respect for inherent dignity, individual autonomy including the freedom to make one's own choices, and independence of persons;
(b) Non-discrimination;
(c) Full and effective participation and inclusion in society;
(d) Respect for difference and acceptance of persons with disabilities as part of human diversity and humanity;
(e) Equality of opportunity;
(f) Accessibility;
(g) Equality between men and women;
(h) Respect for the evolving capacities of children with disabilities and respect for the right of children with disabilities to preserve their identities.

Article 4: General Obligations

1. States Parties undertake to ensure and promote the full realization of all human rights and fundamental freedoms for all persons with disabilities without discrimination of any kind on the basis of disability. To this end, States Parties undertake:

   (a) To adopt all appropriate legislative, administrative and other measures for the implementation of the rights recognized in the present Convention;

(b) To take all appropriate measures, including legislation, to modify or abolish existing laws, regulations, customs and practices that constitute discrimination against persons with disabilities;
(c) To take into account the protection and promotion of the human rights of persons with disabilities in all policies and programmes;
(d) To refrain from engaging in any act or practice that is inconsistent with the present Convention and to ensure that public authorities and institutions act in conformity with the present Convention;
(e) To take all appropriate measures to eliminate discrimination on the basis of disability by any person, organization or private enterprise;
(f) To undertake or promote research and development of universally designed goods, services, equipment and facilities, as defined in article 2 of the present Convention, which should require the minimum possible adaptation and the least cost to meet the specific needs of a person with disabilities, to promote their availability and use, and to promote universal design in the development of standards and guidelines;
(g) To undertake or promote research and development of, and to promote the availability and use of new technologies, including information and communications technologies, mobility aids, devices and assistive technologies, suitable for persons with disabilities, giving priority to technologies at an affordable cost;
(h) To provide accessible information to persons with disabilities about mobility aids, devices and assistive technologies, including new technologies, as well as other forms of assistance, support services and facilities;
(i) To promote the training of professionals and staff working with persons with disabilities in the rights recognized in this Convention so as to better provide the assistance and services guaranteed by those rights.

2. With regard to economic, social and cultural rights, each State Party undertakes to take measures to the maximum of its available resources and, where needed, within the framework of international cooperation, with a view to achieving progressively the full realization of these rights, without prejudice to those obligations contained in the present Convention that are immediately applicable according to international law.
3. In the development and implementation of legislation and policies to implement the present Convention, and in other decision-making processes concerning issues relating to persons with disabilities, States Parties shall closely consult with and actively involve persons with disabilities, including children with disabilities, through their representative organizations.
4. Nothing in the present Convention shall affect any provisions which are more conducive to the realization of the rights of persons with disabilities and which may be contained in the law of a State Party or international law in force for that State. There shall be no restriction upon or derogation from any of the human rights and fundamental freedoms recognized or existing in any State Party to the present Convention pursuant to law, conventions, regulation or custom on the

pretext that the present Convention does not recognize such rights or freedoms or that it recognizes them to a lesser extent.

5. The provisions of the present Convention shall extend to all parts of federal states without any limitations or exceptions.

Article 5: Equality and Non-discrimination

1. States Parties recognize that all persons are equal before and under the law and are entitled without any discrimination to the equal protection and equal benefit of the law.
2. States Parties shall prohibit all discrimination on the basis of disability and guarantee to persons with disabilities equal and effective legal protection against discrimination on all grounds.
3. In order to promote equality and eliminate discrimination, States Parties shall take all appropriate steps to ensure that reasonable accommodation is provided.
4. Specific measures which are necessary to accelerate or achieve de facto equality of persons with disabilities shall not be considered discrimination under the terms of the present Convention.

Article 6: Women with Disabilities

1. States Parties recognize that women and girls with disabilities are subject to multiple discrimination, and in this regard shall take measures to ensure the full and equal enjoyment by them of all human rights and fundamental freedoms.
2. States Parties shall take all appropriate measures to ensure the full development, advancement and empowerment of women, for the purpose of guaranteeing them the exercise and enjoyment of the human rights and fundamental freedoms set out in the present Convention.

Article 7: Children with Disabilities

1. States Parties shall take all necessary measures to ensure the full enjoyment by children with disabilities of all human rights and fundamental freedoms on an equal basis with other children.
2. In all actions concerning children with disabilities, the best interests of the child shall be a primary consideration.
3. States Parties shall ensure that children with disabilities have the right to express their views freely on all matters affecting them, their views being given due weight in accordance with their age and maturity, on an equal basis with other children, and to be provided with disability and age-appropriate assistance to realize that right.

Article 8: Awareness-Raising

1. States Parties undertake to adopt immediate, effective and appropriate measures:
   (a) To raise awareness throughout society, including at the family level, regarding persons with disabilities, and to foster respect for the rights and dignity of persons with disabilities;
   (b) To combat stereotypes, prejudices and harmful practices relating to persons with disabilities, including those based on sex and age, in all areas of life;
   (c) To promote awareness of the capabilities and contributions of persons with disabilities.

   Measures to this end include:

(a) Initiating and maintaining effective public awareness campaigns designed:
   (i) To nurture receptiveness to the rights of persons with disabilities;
   (ii) To promote positive perceptions and greater social awareness towards persons with disabilities;
   (iii) To promote recognition of the skills, merits and abilities of persons with disabilities, and of their contributions to the workplace and the labour market;

(b) Fostering at all levels of the education system, including in all children from an early age, an attitude of respect for the rights of persons with disabilities;
(c) Encouraging all organs of the media to portray persons with disabilities in a manner consistent with the purpose of the present Convention;
(d) Promoting awareness-training programmes regarding persons with disabilities and the rights of persons with disabilities.

Article 9: Accessibility

1. To enable persons with disabilities to live independently and participate fully in all aspects of life, States Parties shall take appropriate measures to ensure to persons with disabilities access, on an equal basis with others, to the physical environment, to transportation, to information and communications, including information and communications technologies and systems, and to other facilities and services open or provided to the public, both in urban and in rural areas. These measures, which shall include the identification and elimination of obstacles and barriers to accessibility, shall apply to, inter alia:
   (a) Buildings, roads, transportation and other indoor and outdoor facilities, including schools, housing, medical facilities and workplaces;
   (b) Information, communications and other services, including electronic services and emergency services.

2. States Parties shall also take appropriate measures to:
   (a) Develop, promulgate and monitor the implementation of minimum standards and guidelines for the accessibility of facilities and services open or provided to the public;
   (b) Ensure that private entities that offer facilities and services which are open or provided to the public take into account all aspects of accessibility for persons with disabilities;
   (c) Provide training for stakeholders on accessibility issues facing persons with disabilities;
   (d) Provide in buildings and other facilities open to the public signage in Braille and in easy to read and understand forms;
   (e) Provide forms of live assistance and intermediaries, including guides, readers and professional sign language interpreters, to facilitate accessibility to buildings and other facilities open to the public;
   (f) Promote other appropriate forms of assistance and support to persons with disabilities to ensure their access to information;
   (g) Promote access for persons with disabilities to new information and communications technologies and systems, including the Internet;
   (h) Promote the design, development, production and distribution of accessible information and communications technologies and systems at an early stage, so that these technologies and systems become accessible at minimum cost.

Article 10: Right to Life

States Parties reaffirm that every human being has the inherent right to life and shall take all necessary measures to ensure its effective enjoyment by persons with disabilities on an equal basis with others.

Article 11: Situations of Risk and Humanitarian Emergencies

States Parties shall take, in accordance with their obligations under international law, including international humanitarian law and international human rights law, all necessary measures to ensure the protection and safety of persons with disabilities in situations of risk, including situations of armed conflict, humanitarian emergencies and the occurrence of natural disasters.

Article 12: Equal Recognition Before the Law

1. States Parties reaffirm that persons with disabilities have the right to recognition everywhere as persons before the law.

2. States Parties shall recognize that persons with disabilities enjoy legal capacity on an equal basis with others in all aspects of life.
3. States Parties shall take appropriate measures to provide access by persons with disabilities to the support they may require in exercising their legal capacity.
4. States Parties shall ensure that all measures that relate to the exercise of legal capacity provide for appropriate and effective safeguards to prevent abuse in accordance with international human rights law. Such safeguards shall ensure that measures relating to the exercise of legal capacity respect the rights, will and preferences of the person, are free of conflict of interest and undue influence, are proportional and tailored to the person's circumstances, apply for the shortest time possible and are subject to regular review by a competent, independent and impartial authority or judicial body. The safeguards shall be proportional to the degree to which such measures affect the person's rights and interests.
5. Subject to the provisions of this article, States Parties shall take all appropriate and effective measures to ensure the equal right of persons with disabilities to own or inherit property, to control their own financial affairs and to have equal access to bank loans, mortgages and other forms of financial credit, and shall ensure that persons with disabilities are not arbitrarily deprived of their property.

Article 13: Access to Justice

1. States Parties shall ensure effective access to justice for persons with disabilities on an equal basis with others, including through the provision of procedural and age-appropriate accommodations, in order to facilitate their effective role as direct and indirect participants, including as witnesses, in all legal proceedings, including at investigative and other preliminary stages.
2. In order to help to ensure effective access to justice for persons with disabilities, States Parties shall promote appropriate training for those working in the field of administration of justice, including police and prison staff.

Article 14: Liberty and Security of the Person

1. States Parties shall ensure that persons with disabilities, on an equal basis with others:

   (a) Enjoy the right to liberty and security of person;
   (b) Are not deprived of their liberty unlawfully or arbitrarily, and that any deprivation of liberty is in conformity with the law, and that the existence of a disability shall in no case justify a deprivation of liberty.

2. States Parties shall ensure that if persons with disabilities are deprived of their liberty through any process, they are, on an equal basis with others, entitled to guarantees in accordance with international human rights law and shall be treated in compliance with the objectives and principles of this Convention, including by provision of reasonable accommodation.

Article 15: Freedom from Torture or Cruel, Inhuman or Degrading Treatment or Punishment

1. No one shall be subjected to torture or to cruel, inhuman or degrading treatment or punishment. In particular, no one shall be subjected without his or her free consent to medical or scientific experimentation.
2. States Parties shall take all effective legislative, administrative, judicial or other measures to prevent persons with disabilities, on an equal basis with others, from being subjected to torture or cruel, inhuman or degrading treatment or punishment.

Article 16: Freedom from Exploitation, Violence and Abuse

1. States Parties shall take all appropriate legislative, administrative, social, educational and other measures to protect persons with disabilities, both within and outside the home, from all forms of exploitation, violence and abuse, including their gender-based aspects.
2. States Parties shall also take all appropriate measures to prevent all forms of exploitation, violence and abuse by ensuring, inter alia, appropriate forms of gender- and age-sensitive assistance and support for persons with disabilities and their families and caregivers, including through the provision of information and education on how to avoid, recognize and report instances of exploitation, violence and abuse. States Parties shall ensure that protection services are age-, gender- and disability-sensitive.
3. In order to prevent the occurrence of all forms of exploitation, violence and abuse, States Parties shall ensure that all facilities and programmes designed to serve persons with disabilities are effectively monitored by independent authorities.
4. States Parties shall take all appropriate measures to promote the physical, cognitive and psychological recovery, rehabilitation and social reintegration of persons with disabilities who become victims of any form of exploitation, violence or abuse, including through the provision of protection services. Such recovery and reintegration shall take place in an environment that fosters the

health, welfare, self-respect, dignity and autonomy of the person and takes into account gender- and age-specific needs.

5. States Parties shall put in place effective legislation and policies, including women- and child-focused legislation and policies, to ensure that instances of exploitation, violence and abuse against persons with disabilities are identified, investigated and, where appropriate, prosecuted.

Article 17: Protecting the Integrity of the Person

Every person with disabilities has a right to respect for his or her physical and mental integrity on an equal basis with others.

Article 18: Liberty of Movement and Nationality

1. States Parties shall recognize the rights of persons with disabilities to liberty of movement, to freedom to choose their residence and to a nationality, on an equal basis with others, including by ensuring that persons with disabilities:
   (a) Have the right to acquire and change a nationality and are not deprived of their nationality arbitrarily or on the basis of disability;
   (b) Are not deprived, on the basis of disability, of their ability to obtain, possess and utilize documentation of their nationality or other documentation of identification, or to utilize relevant processes such as immigration proceedings, that may be needed to facilitate exercise of the right to liberty of movement;
   (c) Are free to leave any country, including their own;
   (d) Are not deprived, arbitrarily or on the basis of disability, of the right to enter their own country.
2. Children with disabilities shall be registered immediately after birth and shall have the right from birth to a name, the right to acquire a nationality and, as far as possible, the right to know and be cared for by their parents.

Article 19: Living Independently and Being Included in the Community

States Parties to this Convention recognize the equal right of all persons with disabilities to live in the community, with choices equal to others, and shall take effective and appropriate measures to facilitate full enjoyment by persons with disabilities of this right and their full inclusion and participation in the community, including by ensuring that:

(a) Persons with disabilities have the opportunity to choose their place of residence and where and with whom they live on an equal basis with others and are not obliged to live in a particular living arrangement;
(b) Persons with disabilities have access to a range of in-home, residential and other community support services, including personal assistance necessary to support living and inclusion in the community, and to prevent isolation or segregation from the community;
(c) Community services and facilities for the general population are available on an equal basis to persons with disabilities and are responsive to their needs.

Article 20: Personal Mobility

States Parties shall take effective measures to ensure personal mobility with the greatest possible independence for persons with disabilities, including by:

(a) Facilitating the personal mobility of persons with disabilities in the manner and at the time of their choice, and at affordable cost;
(b) Facilitating access by persons with disabilities to quality mobility aids, devices, assistive technologies and forms of live assistance and intermediaries, including by making them available at affordable cost;
(c) Providing training in mobility skills to persons with disabilities and to specialist staff working with persons with disabilities;
(d) Encouraging entities that produce mobility aids, devices and assistive technologies to take into account all aspects of mobility for persons with disabilities.

Article 21: Freedom of Expression and Opinion, and Access to Information

States Parties shall take all appropriate measures to ensure that persons with disabilities can exercise the right to freedom of expression and opinion, including the freedom to seek, receive and impart information and ideas on an equal basis with others and through all forms of communication of their choice, as defined in article 2 of the present Convention, including by:

(a) Providing information intended for the general public to persons with disabilities in accessible formats and technologies appropriate to different kinds of disabilities in a timely manner and without additional cost;
(b) Accepting and facilitating the use of sign languages, Braille, augmentative and alternative communication, and all other accessible means, modes and

formats of communication of their choice by persons with disabilities in official interactions;

(c) Urging private entities that provide services to the general public, including through the Internet, to provide information and services in accessible and usable formats for persons with disabilities;
(d) Encouraging the mass media, including providers of information through the Internet, to make their services accessible to persons with disabilities;
(e) Recognizing and promoting the use of sign languages.

Article 22: Respect for Privacy

1. No person with disabilities, regardless of place of residence or living arrangements, shall be subjected to arbitrary or unlawful interference with his or her privacy, family, home or correspondence or other types of communication or to unlawful attacks on his or her honour and reputation. Persons with disabilities have the right to the protection of the law against such interference or attacks.
2. States Parties shall protect the privacy of personal, health and rehabilitation information of persons with disabilities on an equal basis with others.

Article 23: Respect for Home and the Family

1. States Parties shall take effective and appropriate measures to eliminate discrimination against persons with disabilities in all matters relating to marriage, family, parenthood and relationships, on an equal basis with others, so as to ensure that:

   (a) The right of all persons with disabilities who are of marriageable age to marry and to found a family on the basis of free and full consent of the intending spouses is recognized;
   (b) The rights of persons with disabilities to decide freely and responsibly on the number and spacing of their children and to have access to age-appropriate information, reproductive and family planning education are recognized, and the means necessary to enable them to exercise these rights are provided;
   (c) Persons with disabilities, including children, retain their fertility on an equal basis with others.

2. States Parties shall ensure the rights and responsibilities of persons with disabilities, with regard to guardianship, wardship, trusteeship, adoption of children or similar institutions, where these concepts exist in national legislation; in all cases the best interests of the child shall be paramount. States Parties shall render appropriate assistance to persons with disabilities in the performance of their child-rearing responsibilities.

3. States Parties shall ensure that children with disabilities have equal rights with respect to family life. With a view to realizing these rights, and to prevent concealment, abandonment, neglect and segregation of children with disabilities, States Parties shall undertake to provide early and comprehensive information, services and support to children with disabilities and their families.
4. States Parties shall ensure that a child shall not be separated from his or her parents against their will, except when competent authorities subject to judicial review determine, in accordance with applicable law and procedures, that such separation is necessary for the best interests of the child. In no case shall a child be separated from parents on the basis of a disability of either the child or one or both of the parents.
5. States Parties shall, where the immediate family is unable to care for a child with disabilities, undertake every effort to provide alternative care within the wider family, and failing that, within the community in a family setting.

Article 24: Education

1. States Parties recognize the right of persons with disabilities to education. With a view to realizing this right without discrimination and on the basis of equal opportunity, States Parties shall ensure an inclusive education system at all levels and life long learning directed to:

   (a) The full development of human potential and sense of dignity and self-worth, and the strengthening of respect for human rights, fundamental freedoms and human diversity;
   (b) The development by persons with disabilities of their personality, talents and creativity, as well as their mental and physical abilities, to their fullest potential;
   (c) Enabling persons with disabilities to participate effectively in a free society.

2. In realizing this right, States Parties shall ensure that:

   (a) Persons with disabilities are not excluded from the general education system on the basis of disability, and that children with disabilities are not excluded from free and compulsory primary education, or from secondary education, on the basis of disability;
   (b) Persons with disabilities can access an inclusive, quality and free primary education and secondary education on an equal basis with others in the communities in which they live;
   (c) Reasonable accommodation of the individual's requirements is provided;
   (d) Persons with disabilities receive the support required, within the general education system, to facilitate their effective education;
   (e) Effective individualized support measures are provided in environments that maximize academic and social development, consistent with the goal of full inclusion.

3. States Parties shall enable persons with disabilities to learn life and social development skills to facilitate their full and equal participation in education and as members of the community. To this end, States Parties shall take appropriate measures, including:

    (a) Facilitating the learning of Braille, alternative script, augmentative and alternative modes, means and formats of communication and orientation and mobility skills, and facilitating peer support and mentoring;
    (b) Facilitating the learning of sign language and the promotion of the linguistic identity of the deaf community;
    (c) Ensuring that the education of persons, and in particular children, who are blind, deaf or deafblind, is delivered in the most appropriate languages and modes and means of communication for the individual, and in environments which maximize academic and social development.

4. In order to help ensure the realization of this right, States Parties shall take appropriate measures to employ teachers, including teachers with disabilities, who are qualified in sign language and/or Braille, and to train professionals and staff who work at all levels of education. Such training shall incorporate disability awareness and the use of appropriate augmentative and alternative modes, means and formats of communication, educational techniques and materials to support persons with disabilities.
5. States Parties shall ensure that persons with disabilities are able to access general tertiary education, vocational training, adult education and lifelong learning without discrimination and on an equal basis with others. To this end, States Parties shall ensure that reasonable accommodation is provided to persons with disabilities.

Article 25: Health

States Parties recognize that persons with disabilities have the right to the enjoyment of the highest attainable standard of health without discrimination on the basis of disability. States Parties shall take all appropriate measures to ensure access for persons with disabilities to health services that are gender-sensitive, including health-related rehabilitation. In particular, States Parties shall:

(a) Provide persons with disabilities with the same range, quality and standard of free or affordable health care and programmes as provided to other persons, including in the area of sexual and reproductive health and population-based public health programmes;
(b) Provide those health services needed by persons with disabilities specifically because of their disabilities, including early identification and intervention as appropriate, and services designed to minimize and prevent further disabilities, including among children and older persons;

(c) Provide these health services as close as possible to people's own communities, including in rural areas;
(d) Require health professionals to provide care of the same quality to persons with disabilities as to others, including on the basis of free and informed consent by, inter alia, raising awareness of the human rights, dignity, autonomy and needs of persons with disabilities through training and the promulgation of ethical standards for public and private health care;
(e) Prohibit discrimination against persons with disabilities in the provision of health insurance, and life insurance where such insurance is permitted by national law, which shall be provided in a fair and reasonable manner;
(f) Prevent discriminatory denial of health care or health services or food and fluids on the basis of disability.

Article 26: Habilitation and Rehabilitation

1. States Parties shall take effective and appropriate measures, including through peer support, to enable persons with disabilities to attain and maintain maximum independence, full physical, mental, social and vocational ability, and full inclusion and participation in all aspects of life. To that end, States Parties shall organize, strengthen and extend comprehensive habilitation and rehabilitation services and programmes, particularly in the areas of health, employment, education and social services, in such a way that these services and programmes:

   (a) Begin at the earliest possible stage, and are based on the multidisciplinary assessment of individual needs and strengths;
   (b) Support participation and inclusion in the community and all aspects of society, are voluntary, and are available to persons with disabilities as close as possible to their own communities, including in rural areas.

2. States Parties shall promote the development of initial and continuing training for professionals and staff working in habilitation and rehabilitation services.
3. States Parties shall promote the availability, knowledge and use of assistive devices and technologies, designed for persons with disabilities, as they relate to habilitation and rehabilitation.

Article 27: Work and Employment

1. States Parties recognize the right of persons with disabilities to work, on an equal basis with others; this includes the right to the opportunity to gain a living by work freely chosen or accepted in a labour market and work environment that is open, inclusive and accessible to persons with disabilities. States Parties shall safeguard and promote the realization of the right to work, including for those

who acquire a disability during the course of employment, by taking appropriate steps, including through legislation, to, inter alia:

(a) Prohibit discrimination on the basis of disability with regard to all matters concerning all forms of employment, including conditions of recruitment, hiring and employment, continuance of employment, career advancement and safe and healthy working conditions;
(b) Protect the rights of persons with disabilities, on an equal basis with others, to just and favourable conditions of work, including equal opportunities and equal remuneration for work of equal value, safe and healthy working conditions, including protection from harassment, and the redress of grievances;
(c) Ensure that persons with disabilities are able to exercise their labour and trade union rights on an equal basis with others;
(d) Enable persons with disabilities to have effective access to general technical and vocational guidance programmes, placement services and vocational and continuing training;
(e) Promote employment opportunities and career advancement for persons with disabilities in the labour market, as well as assistance in finding, obtaining, maintaining and returning to employment;
(f) Promote opportunities for self-employment, entrepreneurship, the development of cooperatives and starting one's own business;
(g) Employ persons with disabilities in the public sector;
(h) Promote the employment of persons with disabilities in the private sector through appropriate policies and measures, which may include affirmative action programmes, incentives and other measures;
(i) Ensure that reasonable accommodation is provided to persons with disabilities in the workplace;
(j) Promote the acquisition by persons with disabilities of work experience in the open labour market;
(k) Promote vocational and professional rehabilitation, job retention and return-to-work programmes for persons with disabilities.

2. States Parties shall ensure that persons with disabilities are not held in slavery or in servitude, and are protected, on an equal basis with others, from forced or compulsory labour.

Article 28: Adequate Standard of Living and Social Protection

1. States Parties recognize the right of persons with disabilities to an adequate standard of living for themselves and their families, including adequate food, clothing and housing, and to the continuous improvement of living conditions,

and shall take appropriate steps to safeguard and promote the realization of this right without discrimination on the basis of disability.

2. States Parties recognize the right of persons with disabilities to social protection and to the enjoyment of that right without discrimination on the basis of disability, and shall take appropriate steps to safeguard and promote the realization of this right, including measures:
   (a) To ensure equal access by persons with disabilities to clean water services, and to ensure access to appropriate and affordable services, devices and other assistance for disability-related needs;
   (b) To ensure access by persons with disabilities, in particular women and girls with disabilities and older persons with disabilities, to social protection programmes and poverty reduction programmes;
   (c) To ensure access by persons with disabilities and their families living in situations of poverty to assistance from the State with disability-related expenses, including adequate training, counselling, financial assistance and respite care;
   (d) To ensure access by persons with disabilities to public housing programmes;
   (e) To ensure equal access by persons with disabilities to retirement benefits and programmes.

Article 29: Participation in Political and Public Life

States Parties shall guarantee to persons with disabilities political rights and the opportunity to enjoy them on an equal basis with others, and shall undertake to:

(a) Ensure that persons with disabilities can effectively and fully participate in political and public life on an equal basis with others, directly or through freely chosen representatives, including the right and opportunity for persons with disabilities to vote and be elected, inter alia, by:
   (i) Ensuring that voting procedures, facilities and materials are appropriate, accessible and easy to understand and use;
   (ii) Protecting the right of persons with disabilities to vote by secret ballot in elections and public referendums without intimidation, and to stand for elections, to effectively hold office and perform all public functions at all levels of government, facilitating the use of assistive and new technologies where appropriate;
   (iii) Guaranteeing the free expression of the will of persons with disabilities as electors and to this end, where necessary, at their request, allowing assistance in voting by a person of their own choice;

(b) Promote actively an environment in which persons with disabilities can effectively and fully participate in the conduct of public affairs, without discrimination and on an equal basis with others, and encourage their participation in public affairs, including:

(i) Participation in non-governmental organizations and associations concerned with the public and political life of the country, and in the activities and administration of political parties;
(ii) Forming and joining organizations of persons with disabilities to represent persons with disabilities at international, national, regional and local levels.

Article 30: Participation in Cultural Life, Recreation, Leisure and Sport

1. States Parties recognize the right of persons with disabilities to take part on an equal basis with others in cultural life, and shall take all appropriate measures to ensure that persons with disabilities:

   (a) Enjoy access to cultural materials in accessible formats;
   (b) Enjoy access to television programmes, films, theatre and other cultural activities, in accessible formats;
   (c) Enjoy access to places for cultural performances or services, such as theatres, museums, cinemas, libraries and tourism services, and, as far as possible, enjoy access to monuments and sites of national cultural importance.

2. States Parties shall take appropriate measures to enable persons with disabilities to have the opportunity to develop and utilize their creative, artistic and intellectual potential, not only for their own benefit, but also for the enrichment of society.
3. States Parties shall take all appropriate steps, in accordance with international law, to ensure that laws protecting intellectual property rights do not constitute an unreasonable or discriminatory barrier to access by persons with disabilities to cultural materials.
4. Persons with disabilities shall be entitled, on an equal basis with others, to recognition and support of their specific cultural and linguistic identity, including sign languages and deaf culture.
5. With a view to enabling persons with disabilities to participate on an equal basis with others in recreational, leisure and sporting activities, States Parties shall take appropriate measures:

   (a) To encourage and promote the participation, to the fullest extent possible, of persons with disabilities in mainstream sporting activities at all levels;
   (b) To ensure that persons with disabilities have an opportunity to organize, develop and participate in disability-specific sporting and recreational activities and, to this end, encourage the provision, on an equal basis with others, of appropriate instruction, training and resources;

(c) To ensure that persons with disabilities have access to sporting, recreational and tourism venues;
(d) To ensure that children with disabilities have equal access with other children to participation in play, recreation and leisure and sporting activities, including those activities in the school system;
(e) To ensure that persons with disabilities have access to services from those involved in the organization of recreational, tourism, leisure and sporting activities.

Article 31: Statistics and Data Collection

1. States Parties undertake to collect appropriate information, including statistical and research data, to enable them to formulate and implement policies to give effect to the present Convention. The process of collecting and maintaining this information shall:

   (a) Comply with legally established safeguards, including legislation on data protection, to ensure confidentiality and respect for the privacy of persons with disabilities;
   (b) Comply with internationally accepted norms to protect human rights and fundamental freedoms and ethical principles in the collection and use of statistics.

2. The information collected in accordance with this article shall be disaggregated, as appropriate, and used to help assess the implementation of States Parties' obligations under the present Convention and to identify and address the barriers faced by persons with disabilities in exercising their rights.
3. States Parties shall assume responsibility for the dissemination of these statistics and ensure their accessibility to persons with disabilities and others.

Article 32: International Cooperation

1. States Parties recognize the importance of international cooperation and its promotion, in support of national efforts for the realization of the purpose and objectives of the present Convention, and will undertake appropriate and effective measures in this regard, between and among States and, as appropriate, in partnership with relevant international and regional organizations and civil society, in particular organizations of persons with disabilities. Such measures could include, inter alia:

   (a) Ensuring that international cooperation, including international development programmes, is inclusive of and accessible to persons with disabilities;

(b) Facilitating and supporting capacity-building, including through the exchange and sharing of information, experiences, training programmes and best practices;
(c) Facilitating cooperation in research and access to scientific and technical knowledge;
(d) Providing, as appropriate, technical and economic assistance, including by facilitating access to and sharing of accessible and assistive technologies, and through the transfer of technologies.

2. The provisions of this article are without prejudice to the obligations of each State Party to fulfil its obligations under the present Convention.

Article 33: National Implementation and Monitoring

1. States Parties, in accordance with their system of organization, shall designate one or more focal points within government for matters relating to the implementation of the present Convention, and shall give due consideration to the establishment or designation of a coordination mechanism within government to facilitate related action in different sectors and at different levels.
2. States Parties shall, in accordance with their legal and administrative systems, maintain, strengthen, designate or establish within the State Party, a framework, including one or more independent mechanisms, as appropriate, to promote, protect and monitor implementation of the present Convention. When designating or establishing such a mechanism, States Parties shall take into account the principles relating to the status and functioning of national institutions for protection and promotion of human rights.
3. Civil society, in particular persons with disabilities and their representative organizations, shall be involved and participate fully in the monitoring process.

Article 34: Committee on the Rights of Persons with Disabilities

1. There shall be established a Committee on the Rights of Persons with Disabilities (hereafter referred to as "the Committee"), which shall carry out the functions hereinafter provided.
2. The Committee shall consist, at the time of entry into force of the present Convention, of 12 experts. After an additional 60 ratifications or accessions to the Convention, the membership of the Committee shall increase by six members, attaining a maximum number of eighteen members.
3. The members of the Committee shall serve in their personal capacity and shall be of high moral standing and recognized competence and experience in the field covered by the present Convention. When nominating their candidates,

States Parties are invited to give due consideration to the provision set out in article 4.3 of the present Convention.

4. The members of the Committee shall be elected by States Parties, consideration being given to equitable geographical distribution, representation of the different forms of civilization and of the principal legal systems, balanced gender representation and participation of experts with disabilities.
5. The members of the Committee shall be elected by secret ballot from a list of persons nominated by the States Parties from among their nationals at meetings of the Conference of States Parties. At those meetings, for which two thirds of States Parties shall constitute a quorum, the persons elected to the Committee shall be those who obtain the largest number of votes and an absolute majority of the votes of the representatives of States Parties present and voting.
6. The initial election shall be held no later than six months after the date of entry into force of the present Convention. At least four months before the date of each election, the Secretary-General of the United Nations shall address a letter to the States Parties inviting them to submit the nominations within two months. The Secretary-General shall subsequently prepare a list in alphabetical order of all persons thus nominated, indicating the State Parties which have nominated them, and shall submit it to the States Parties to the present Convention.
7. The members of the Committee shall be elected for a term of four years. They shall be eligible for re-election once. However, the term of six of the members elected at the first election shall expire at the end of two years; immediately after the first election, the names of these six members shall be chosen by lot by the chairperson of the meeting referred to in paragraph 5 of this article.
8. The election of the six additional members of the Committee shall be held on the occasion of regular elections, in accordance with the relevant provisions of this article.
9. If a member of the Committee dies or resigns or declares that for any other cause she or he can no longer perform her or his duties, the State Party which nominated the member shall appoint another expert possessing the qualifications and meeting the requirements set out in the relevant provisions of this article, to serve for the remainder of the term.
10. The Committee shall establish its own rules of procedure.
11. The Secretary-General of the United Nations shall provide the necessary staff and facilities for the effective performance of the functions of the Committee under the present Convention, and shall convene its initial meeting.
12. With the approval of the General Assembly, the members of the Committee established under the present Convention shall receive emoluments from United Nations resources on such terms and conditions as the Assembly may decide, having regard to the importance of the Committee's responsibilities.
13. The members of the Committee shall be entitled to the facilities, privileges and immunities of experts on mission for the United Nations as laid down in the relevant sections of the Convention on the Privileges and Immunities of the United Nations.

Article 35: Reports by States Parties

1. Each State Party shall submit to the Committee, through the Secretary-General of the United Nations, a comprehensive report on measures taken to give effect to its obligations under the present Convention and on the progress made in that regard, within two years after the entry into force of the present Convention for the State Party concerned.
2. Thereafter, States Parties shall submit subsequent reports at least every four years and further whenever the Committee so requests.
3. The Committee shall decide any guidelines applicable to the content of the reports.
4. A State Party which has submitted a comprehensive initial report to the Committee need not, in its subsequent reports, repeat information previously provided. When preparing reports to the Committee, States Parties are invited to consider doing so in an open and transparent process and to give due consideration to the provision set out in article 4.3 of the present Convention.
5. Reports may indicate factors and difficulties affecting the degree of fulfilment of obligations under the present Convention.

Article 36: Consideration of Reports

1. Each report shall be considered by the Committee, which shall make such suggestions and general recommendations on the report as it may consider appropriate and shall forward these to the State Party concerned. The State Party may respond with any information it chooses to the Committee. The Committee may request further information from States Parties relevant to the implementation of the present Convention.
2. If a State Party is significantly overdue in the submission of a report, the Committee may notify the State Party concerned of the need to examine the implementation of the present Convention in that State Party, on the basis of reliable information available to the Committee, if the relevant report is not submitted within three months following the notification. The Committee shall invite the State Party concerned to participate in such examination. Should the State Party respond by submitting the relevant report, the provisions of paragraph 1 of this article will apply.
3. The Secretary-General of the United Nations shall make available the reports to all States Parties.
4. States Parties shall make their reports widely available to the public in their own countries and facilitate access to the suggestions and general recommendations relating to these reports.
5. The Committee shall transmit, as it may consider appropriate, to the specialized agencies, funds and programmes of the United Nations, and other competent

bodies, reports from States Parties in order to address a request or indication of a need for technical advice or assistance contained therein, along with the Committee's observations and recommendations, if any, on these requests or indications.

Article 37: Cooperation Between States Parties and the Committee

1. Each State Party shall cooperate with the Committee and assist its members in the fulfilment of their mandate.
2. In its relationship with States Parties, the Committee shall give due consideration to ways and means of enhancing national capacities for the implementation of the present Convention, including through international cooperation.

Article 38: Relationship of the Committee with Other Bodies

In order to foster the effective implementation of the present Convention and to encourage international cooperation in the field covered by the present Convention:

(a) The specialized agencies and other United Nations organs shall be entitled to be represented at the consideration of the implementation of such provisions of the present Convention as fall within the scope of their mandate. The Committee may invite the specialized agencies and other competent bodies as it may consider appropriate to provide expert advice on the implementation of the Convention in areas falling within the scope of their respective mandates. The Committee may invite specialized agencies and other United Nations organs to submit reports on the implementation of the Convention in areas falling within the scope of their activities;

(b) The Committee, as it discharges its mandate, shall consult, as appropriate, other relevant bodies instituted by international human rights treaties, with a view to ensuring the consistency of their respective reporting guidelines, suggestions and general recommendations, and avoiding duplication and overlap in the performance of their functions.

Article 39: Report of the Committee

The Committee shall report every two years to the General Assembly and to the Economic and Social Council on its activities, and may make suggestions and general recommendations based on the examination of reports and information received from the States Parties. Such suggestions and general recommendations shall be included in the report of the Committee together with comments, if any, from States Parties.

Article 40: Conference of States Parties

1. The States Parties shall meet regularly in a Conference of States Parties in order to consider any matter with regard to the implementation of the present Convention.
2. No later than six months after the entry into force of the present Convention, the Conference of the States Parties shall be convened by the Secretary-General of the United Nations. The subsequent meetings shall be convened by the Secretary-General of the United Nations biennially or upon the decision of the Conference of States Parties.

Article 41: Depositary

The Secretary-General of the United Nations shall be the depositary of the present Convention.

Article 42: Signature

The present Convention shall be open for signature by all States and by regional integration organizations at United Nations Headquarters in New York as of 30 March 2007.

Article 43: Consent to be Bound

The present Convention shall be subject to ratification by signatory States and to formal confirmation by signatory regional integration organizations. It shall be open for accession by any State or regional integration organization which has not signed the Convention.

Article 44: Regional Integration Organizations

1. "Regional integration organization" shall mean an organization constituted by sovereign States of a given region, to which its member States have transferred competence in respect of matters governed by this Convention. Such organizations shall declare, in their instruments of formal confirmation or accession, the extent of their competence with respect to matters governed by this Convention. Subsequently, they shall inform the depositary of any substantial modification in the extent of their competence.
2. References to "States Parties" in the present Convention shall apply to such organizations within the limits of their competence.
3. For the purposes of article 45, paragraph 1, and article 47, paragraphs 2 and 3, any instrument deposited by a regional integration organization shall not be counted.
4. Regional integration organizations, in matters within their competence, may exercise their right to vote in the Conference of States Parties, with a number of votes equal to the number of their member States that are Parties to this Convention. Such an organization shall not exercise its right to vote if any of its member States exercises its right, and vice versa.

Article 45: Entry Into Force

1. The present Convention shall enter into force on the thirtieth day after the deposit of the twentieth instrument of ratification or accession.
2. For each State or regional integration organization ratifying, formally confirming or acceding to the Convention after the deposit of the twentieth such instrument, the Convention shall enter into force on the thirtieth day after the deposit of its own such instrument.

Article 46: Reservations

1. Reservations incompatible with the object and purpose of the present Convention shall not be permitted.
2. Reservations may be withdrawn at any time.

Article 47: Amendments

1. Any State Party may propose an amendment to the present Convention and submit it to the Secretary-General of the United Nations. The Secretary-General shall communicate any proposed amendments to States Parties, with a request to be notified whether they favour a conference of States Parties for the purpose

of considering and deciding upon the proposals. In the event that, within four months from the date of such communication, at least one third of the States Parties favour such a conference, the Secretary-General shall convene the conference under the auspices of the United Nations. Any amendment adopted by a majority of two thirds of the States Parties present and voting shall be submitted by the Secretary-General to the General Assembly for approval and thereafter to all States Parties for acceptance.

2. An amendment adopted and approved in accordance with paragraph 1 of this article shall enter into force on the thirtieth day after the number of instruments of acceptance deposited reaches two thirds of the number of States Parties at the date of adoption of the amendment. Thereafter, the amendment shall enter into force for any State Party on the thirtieth day following the deposit of its own instrument of acceptance. An amendment shall be binding only on those States Parties which have accepted it.
3. If so decided by the Conference of States Parties by consensus, an amendment adopted and approved in accordance with paragraph 1 of this article which relates exclusively to articles 34, 38, 39 and 40 shall enter into force for all States Parties on the thirtieth day after the number of instruments of acceptance deposited reaches two thirds of the number of States Parties at the date of adoption of the amendment.

Article 48: Denunciation

A State Party may denounce the present Convention by written notification to the Secretary-General of the United Nations. The denunciation shall become effective one year after the date of receipt of the notification by the Secretary-General.

Article 49: Accessible Format

The text of the present Convention shall be made available in accessible formats.

Article 50: Authentic Texts

The Arabic, Chinese, English, French, Russian and Spanish texts of the present Convention shall be equally authentic.

In witness thereof the undersigned plenipotentiaries, being duly authorized thereto by their respective Governments, have signed the present Convention.

Source: Annex 1, Final report of the Ad Hoc Committee on a Comprehensive and Integral International Convention on the Protection and Promotion of the Rights and Dignity of Persons with Disabilities (A/61/611 – PDF, 117KB)

Appendix 3: Radio Script

This is an example of one of the 2-minute radio scripts used by WiDO (see Chapter 10, Conflict Intervention on Behalf of Widows: Notes from Enugu State in Nigeria) in Enugu, Nigeria. The message opened with 50 seconds of a well-known song about grief that had been modified slightly and was sung by widows. The song was in Igbo (the local language) while the voice over is sometimes in English and sometimes in Igbo. The voice over was provided by one of the trustees of WiDO. There were different sponsors and Mama Cash (indicated below) was one of them. The taped announcements ran three times a week just before the 7 am news.

Wido Radio Announcement in Enugu, Nigeria

***Opens with a song about widowhood*:**

Ewoo ewoo Okokoko chim oo (*line repeated twice*)
Ewoo ewoo *(no translation of crying)* **Okokoko My God**
Okoko okoko, ewa – ooo (*line repeated twice,*
there is no translation as this is the sound of crying in grief)
Afufu uwa ejugo m onu (*line repeated twice*)
The suffering of the world has filled my mouth
Ewo Chimo O ka msi jee
My God is this how things have gone?
Mmiri elurelu a mago nu muo (line repeated twice)
I have been beaten by unexpected rain
Ikwu na ibe gbakwunu moo
All and sundry please come around me
Mmiri elurelu a mago nu mou
I have been beaten by unexpected rain
Nne na nna gbakwu nu moo
Mother and father please come around me
Mmiri elurelu a mago nu moo
I have been beaten by unexpected rain
Na ugwu m ana a
My support is gone
Ugebge tiwala na o tiwala o
The mirror is broken
Ezigbo Ugebebe tiwalala na o tiwalala
The priceless mirror is broken
Na o tiwalala na ike
It has broken irreparably

J.M. Fritz (ed.), *Moving Toward a Just Peace: The Mediation Continuum*, Clinical Sociology: Research and Practice, DOI 10.1007/978-94-007-2885-1,

The voice over *(with continuing song as soft background music)*:

Enugu State has made a law to protect widows and widowers.

No person shall force a widow or widower–

(a) To have the hairs on the head or any other part of the body shaved ;
(b) To remain in confinement for any given period;
(c) To vacate one's matrimonial home because there is no male child or no child at all;
(d) To give up property belonging to them.

PENALTY: Anyone who contravenes or assists another person to contravene this law shall be guilty of an offence and liable, on conviction, to a fine of 5,000 naira[1] or two-years imprisonment or both.

This law protects the rights of Widows and Widowers.

Don't break the Law!

Victims please report to the Widow Support Centre, 84 Nza Street, Independence layout, Enugu, Enugu State.
(in closing):
Message from: Widows Development Organisation, Enugu
Sponsor: Mama Cash, Netherlands, E.U

[1] Approximately 20 euros.

Appendix 4: UNSCR 1325

S/RES/1325 (2000)
Distr.: General
31 October 2000

United Nations Security Council Resolution 1325 (2000): Women and Peace and Security

Adopted by the Security Council at Its 4213th Meeting, on 31 October 2000

The Security Council,

Recalling its resolutions 1261 (1999) of 25 August 1999, 1265 (1999) of 17 September 1999, 1296 (2000) of 19 April 2000 and 1314 (2000) of 11 August 2000, as well as relevant statements of its President, and *recalling also* the statement of its President to the press on the occasion of the United Nations Day for Women's Rights and International Peace (International Women's Day) of 8 March 2000 (SC/6816),

Recalling also the commitments of the Beijing Declaration and Platform for Action (A/52/231) as well as those contained in the outcome document of the twenty-third Special Session of the United Nations General Assembly entitled "Women 2000: Gender Equality, Development and Peace for the Twenty-First Century" (A/S-23/10/Rev.1), in particular those concerning women and armed conflict,

Bearing in mind the purposes and principles of the Charter of the United Nations and the primary responsibility of the Security Council under the Charter for the maintenance of international peace and security,

Expressing concern that civilians, particularly women and children, account for the vast majority of those adversely affected by armed conflict, including as refugees and internally displaced persons, and increasingly are targeted by combatants and armed elements, and *recognizing* the consequent impact this has on durable peace and reconciliation,

Reaffirming the important role of women in the prevention and resolution of conflicts and in peace-building, and *stressing* the importance of their equal participation and full involvement in all efforts for the maintenance and promotion of peace and security, and the need to increase their role in decision-making with regard to conflict prevention and resolution,

Reaffirming also the need to implement fully international humanitarian and human rights law that protects the rights of women and girls during and after conflicts,

Emphasizing the need for all parties to ensure that mine clearance and mine awareness programmes take into account the special needs of women and girls,

J.M. Fritz (ed.), *Moving Toward a Just Peace: The Mediation Continuum*, Clinical Sociology: Research and Practice, DOI 10.1007/978-94-007-2885-1,

Recognizing the urgent need to mainstream a gender perspective into peacekeeping operations, and in this regard *noting* the Windhoek Declaration and the Namibia Plan of Action on Mainstreaming a Gender Perspective in Multidimensional Peace Support Operations (S/2000/693),

Recognizing also the importance of the recommendation contained in the statement of its President to the press of 8 March 2000 for specialized training for all peacekeeping personnel on the protection, special needs and human rights of women and children in conflict situations,

Recognizing that an understanding of the impact of armed conflict on women and girls, effective institutional arrangements to guarantee their protection and full participation in the peace process can significantly contribute to the maintenance and promotion of international peace and security,

Noting the need to consolidate data on the impact of armed conflict on women and girls,

1. *Urges* Member States to ensure increased representation of women at all decision-making levels in national, regional and international institutions and mechanisms for the prevention, management, and resolution of conflict;
2. *Encourages* the Secretary-General to implement his strategic plan of action (A/49/587) calling for an increase in the participation of women at decision-making levels in conflict resolution and peace processes;
3. *Urges* the Secretary-General to appoint more women as special representatives and envoys to pursue good offices on his behalf, and in this regard *calls on* Member States to provide candidates to the Secretary-General, for inclusion in a regularly updated centralized roster;
4. *Further urges* the Secretary-General to seek to expand the role and contribution of women in United Nations field-based operations, and especially among military observers, civilian police, human rights and humanitarian personnel;
5. *Expresses* its willingness to incorporate a gender perspective into peacekeeping operations, and *urges* the Secretary-General to ensure that, where appropriate, field operations include a gender component;
6. *Requests* the Secretary-General to provide to Member States training guidelines and materials on the protection, rights and the particular needs of women, as well as on the importance of involving women in all peacekeeping and peace- building measures, *invites* Member States to incorporate these elements as well as HIV/AIDS awareness training into their national training programmes for military and civilian police personnel in preparation for deployment, and *further requests* the Secretary-General to ensure that civilian personnel of peacekeeping operations receive similar training;
7. *Urges* Member States to increase their voluntary financial, technical and logistical support for gender-sensitive training efforts, including those undertaken by relevant funds and programmes, inter alia, the United Nations Fund for Women and United Nations Children's Fund, and by the Office of the United Nations High Commissioner for Refugees and other relevant bodies;
8. *Calls on* all actors involved, when negotiating and implementing peace agreements, to adopt a gender perspective, including, inter alia:

   (a) The special needs of women and girls during repatriation and resettlement and for rehabilitation, reintegration and post-conflict reconstruction;
   (b) Measures that support local women's peace initiatives and indigenous processes for conflict resolution, and that involve women in all of the implementation mechanisms of the peace agreements;
   (c) Measures that ensure the protection of and respect for human rights of women and girls, particularly as they relate to the constitution, the electoral system, the police and the judiciary;

9. *Calls upon* all parties to armed conflict to respect fully international law applicable to the rights and protection of women and girls, especially as civilians, in particular the obligations applicable to them under the Geneva Conventions of 1949 and the Additional Protocols thereto of 1977, the Refugee Convention of 1951 and the Protocol thereto of 1967, the Convention on the Elimination of All Forms of Discrimination against Women of 1979 and the Optional Protocol thereto of 1999 and the United Nations Convention on the Rights of the Child of 1989 and the two Optional Protocols thereto of 25 May 2000, and to bear in mind the relevant provisions of the Rome Statute of the International Criminal Court;
10. *Calls on* all parties to armed conflict to take special measures to protect women and girls from gender-based violence, particularly rape and other forms of sexual abuse, and all other forms of violence in situations of armed conflict;
11. *Emphasizes* the responsibility of all States to put an end to impunity and to prosecute those responsible for genocide, crimes against humanity, and war crimes including those relating to sexual and other violence against women and girls, and in this regard *stresses* the need to exclude these crimes, where feasible from amnesty provisions;
12. *Calls upon* all parties to armed conflict to respect the civilian and humanitarian character of refugee camps and settlements, and to take into account the particular needs of women and girls, including in their design, and recalls its resolutions 1208 (1998) of 19 November 1998 and 1296 (2000) of 19 April 2000;
13. *Encourages* all those involved in the planning for disarmament, demobilization and reintegration to consider the different needs of female and male ex-combatants and to take into account the needs of their dependants;
14. *Reaffirms* its readiness, whenever measures are adopted under Article 41 of the Charter of the United Nations, to give consideration to their potential impact on the civilian population, bearing in mind the special needs of women and girls, in order to consider appropriate humanitarian exemptions;
15. *Expresses* its willingness to ensure that Security Council missions take into account gender considerations and the rights of women, including through consultation with local and international women's groups;
16. *Invites* the Secretary-General to carry out a study on the impact of armed conflict on women and girls, the role of women in peace-building and the gender dimensions of peace processes and conflict resolution, and *further invites* him to submit a report to the Security Council on the results of this study and to make this available to all Member States of the United Nations;
17. *Requests* the Secretary-General, where appropriate, to include in his reporting to the Security Council progress on gender mainstreaming throughout peacekeeping missions and all other aspects relating to women and girls;
18. *Decides* to remain actively seized of the matter.

Index

J.M. Fritz (ed.), *Moving Toward a Just Peace: The Mediation Continuum*, Clinical Sociology: Research and Practice, DOI 10.1007/978-94-007-2885-1,

M

N

O

MIX
Papier aus verantwortungsvollen Quellen
Paper from responsible sources
FSC® C105338

If you have any concerns about our products,
you can contact us on
ProductSafety@springernature.com

In case Publisher is established outside the EU,
the EU authorized representative is:
Springer Nature Customer Service Center GmbH
Europaplatz 3, 69115 Heidelberg, Germany

Printed by Libri Plureos GmbH
in Hamburg, Germany